Imbibing Java™ Web Services

A Step by Step Approach for Learning Web Services™

Prepared by

Srinivas Mudunuri

Trademarks

Cover Design & Images By: Richard Castillo (http://www.digitizedchaos.com)

Printing History:

May 2012   First Print

ISBN-10: 1475237707

ISBN-13: 978-1475237702

Dedicated

To

My Mother
&
Son Abhishek

Table of Contents

Preface

This document provides a step-by-step approach for developing Java Web Services. It is specially designed to help the individuals who want to learn Java Web Services. This document can also be used as a reference book for any Java Web Services exam. This book avoids the fear and makes a favor for developing web services. This book can be used as a reference table guide for web service developers.

The Audience for this book is:

- Individuals who want to learn JAXP, SOAP, WSDL and Java Web Services technologies.
- Individuals who are looking for step-by-step approach for developing Java Web Services.
- Individuals who want to learn REST-based web services.
- Individuals who want to learn JAX-WS based web services.
- Individuals who want to learn web services development using Apache-CXF, Axis2 and Spring-WS frameworks.
- Individuals who want to design and implement Java web services in their projects.
- Architects who want to learn various web service client and endpoint design scenarios.
- Architects who want to compare the technical capabilities of various web services frameworks available in the web services landscape.
- Individuals who are preparing for Java Web Services certification exam. This book is a good reference for any Java Web Services exam.

A prior knowledge of Java programming and web application development is required. It is good to have some XML knowledge but an XML novice can understand without much difficulty. It is also good to have Spring framework knowledge but it is not mandatory. The chapters are arranged based on the increasing order of their complexity and its dependency. Inline code snippets are provided while explaining each topic and a complete working example is provided at the end of the each topic. A step-by-step approach is followed for developing web services, so it is easy for a beginner to understand the web service development.

The topics covered in this book are given below:

- Introduction
- JAXP
- Dom4j
- SOAP
- SAAJ
- WSDL
- JAX-RS
- JAX-WS
- Apache-CXF
- Apache-Axis2
- Spring-WS
- Tools, Ant Scripts and Deployment

This book does not cover for each and every objective, specific to any web services exam, but it will provide a good foundation. 60 objective type questions are provided to help the people who are preparing for web services certification exam. The book contains 60 diagrams and approximately 100 Java programs used for developing the web services tutorials. I ran these examples several times on my laptop before including them into this book.

Structure of the Book

This book contains 12 chapters. The structure of the book is given below.

Chapter 1 (Introduction) provides a brief introduction about Web Services, why do we need web services, web services advantages and its evolution.

Chapter 2 (JAXP) covers the complete JAXP specification. It provides the details of Java API for XML Processing (JAXP), the use of SAX, DOM, StAX-parsing techniques, comparison between SAX, DOM and StAX, how to read and write XML documents using JAXP technology. It also covers the complete JAXP API and its use with code examples.

Chapter 3 (Dom4j) covers the complete details of Document Object Model for Java (Dom4j) framework in application development. It explores the technical capabilities of Dom4j framework used for handling XML documents.

Chapter 4 (JAX-RS) provides the details about REST fundaments, REST principles, terminology, its advantages, using REST with Spring and CXF, REST URL design, client design and use of REST annotations for developing web services.

Chapter 5 (SOAP) covers the complete SOAP specification. It provide the details about SOAP message structure, SOAP binding, comparison between SOAP-1.1 and 1.2, basic profiles standards for soap messaging.

Chapter 6 (SAAJ) will help you to understand the SAAJ API used for SOAP message processing. It covers the SOAP message creation, getting the content from a SOAP message, SOAP with attachments, sending SOAP messages using SAAJ API.

Chapter 7 (WSDL) covers the complete WSDL specification. It provides the details about the structure of WSDL-1.1 and 2.0 documents, WSDL to Java mappings, message exchange patterns, messaging modes, comparison between WSDL-1.1 and 2.0.

Chapter 8 (JAX-WS) covers the complete JAX-WS specification. It provides the details about the JAX-WS fundamentals, JAX-WS architecture, JAX-WS annotations that include JSR-181, JSR-222, JSR-250 and JSR-224 annotations. The mapping between the JAX-WS annotations and the generated WSDL is covered for each annotation. It provides the XML generation using JAXB and use of JAXB annotations.

Chapter 9 (Apache-CXF) covers the web services development using Apache-CXF. It provides the details about web services development using CXF framework, using CXF with Spring, web services development methodologies, Web Service client and service endpoint design scenarios, details of SOAP message handlers using CXF, JAX-WS message handler framework and logging SOAP messages using CXF.

Chapter 10 (Apache-Axis2) covers the web services development using Apache-Axis2. It provides the details about web services development using Axis2 framework, developing Axis2 custom modules, web services development methodologies, Web Service client and service endpoint design scenarios, details of SOAP message handlers using Axis2 and logging SOAP messages using Axis2.

Chapter 11 (Spring-WS) covers the web services development using Spring-WS. It provides the details about web services development using Spring framework, web services development methodologies, Web Service client and service endpoint design scenarios, details of SOAP message handlers and its use with Spring-WS and logging SOAP messages using Spring-WS.

Chapter 12 (Tools, Ant Scripts and Deployment) provides the details of build and deployment instructions for web services. It provides the list of jar files required to compile and run the web services and it covers the debugging and testing tools used for monitoring the SOAP messages.

Code Examples – Code examples are provided for each topic. It will help you to develop the code; step-by-step instructions are provided for developing the code examples.

Test Yourself – Provides the objective type questions at the end of each chapter. It will assess your knowledge and understanding of the topic. It will guide you while preparing for any web services exam.

Answers to Test Yourself – Provides the answers to the test questions.

Acknowledgements

This book could not have been written without the encouragements, supports and contributions from many people.

The primary references to this book are Java Specification Requests (JSR's), various web services articles, white papers, tutorials available on the web, my own experience with web services development and web services certification exam. I would like to thank everyone who contributed to the Java community which I used to gain the knowledge of Java and Web Services technologies.

First of all, I would like to thank my friend Uday Thota who helped me to build my career in USA. We use to discuss Web Services almost every day while preparing for the Sun Java Web Services certification exam. The sad part is he is no more with us; may Almighty God grant him eternal rest and may his soul rest in peace.

I would like to thank my friend Purna Katrapati; who helped me while doing master's thesis using C programming language and Surfer package. I would say he was my first teacher helped me to start my programming career. I would like to thank another friend Kishori Sharan; who trained me in Oracle and Power Builder technologies. This book would not have completed without Kishori's help and guidance. He is there to help me all the time, time after time and every time.

I would like to thank Richard Castillo who designed the cover page for this book.

I would like to thank Weidong Zhang who was my lead Architect in my previous job; he gave me an opportunity to implement Restful Web Services for a student learning application. It helped me to gain in-depth practical knowledge in REST-based web services which I used later in several applications.

I would like to thank my colleagues Satyendra Singh, Vivek Sharma, Himanshu Mandalia, Li Du, Steve Charles, Venkata Srinivas Tripasuri, Rares Melaniuc, Wes Kelley, Brendon Gaul, Joseph Lee, Suk Fung and Alok Jena. At present I am working with them; thanks to everyone who helps me at work place every day and it is a great team.

I would like thank my friends Rama Raju Saripella, Prabhakar Kandikonda, Gopi Krishnam Raju Sangaraju, Vijay Polasani, Madhava Rao, Ramesh masa, Raghavendra Swamy, Ravi Nallakukkala, Suresh Pattipati, Neeraj Oberai, Rakesh Jaiswal, Tej Kalidindi, Ranga Anne, Rama Chitirala, Madhan Retnaswamy, Ramesh Kondru, Bala Talagadadeevi, Maruthi, Phani Narem and Phani Tangirala. I would say simple thanks are not enough for their help and support. A special thanks to Madhan who helped me during my initial days of stay in Phoenix, Arizona.

I would like to thank all my students who provided me an opportunity to teach Java and Web Services.

A special thanks to Sylburn Peterkin, Kishori Sharan, Narayan Sithemsetti, Gopinath Kakarla and Mallik Somepalli who helped me to review this book in spite of their busy schedules.

I would like to thank my childhood class mates Tulasi Narayana Rao, Venkata Appa Rao, Srinivas Baratam and Siva Kumar. I have spent so much time with them and I do carry lot of childhood memories. Once in a while, I go to my home town they are always there to give a helping hand and warm reception.

Finally I want to thank my wife Radha Mudunuri, my mother, father, brothers and in-laws who provide me great support and help all the time. I would like to thank my two year old son Aayush Mudunuri; he has just started speaking a few words and he always want to play with his cousin sister, Aakankhsa.

Source Code and Errata

Source code and errata for this volume may be downloaded from http://www.raju.jdojo.com.

Questions and Comments

Please direct all your questions and comments to *sraju@jdojo.com*

Chapter 1. Introduction

The phrase "Web Service" has been a box office hit for several years. Enterprise applications have been using it for more than a decade. It is an approach used for communication between two applications over the Internet. If an application exposes the business functionality as a Web service, other applications use that service. The application that exposes a service is called a *service publisher*, and applications that invoke the service are called *service consumers*. In general, a service provides a specific business function. A Web service is an approach used for sharing the business functions within and outside of an enterprise.

The history of distributed technology and Web service is shown in Figure 1-1. Java Remote Method Invocation (RMI) was first introduced in JDK-1.1 in 1997; later, many new features were added in each release. The latest release is Java-SE7, and RMI is part of it. The latest EJB release is EJB-3.1, and it is part of Java-EE6. The first Java Web services specification, JAX-RPC, which is part of J2EE-1.4, was introduced by Sun in 2003. The completely redesigned and re-architected Java Web services specification is called JAX-WS; it was introduced in 2005. JAX-WS is the latest Java Web services standard used for developing Web Services and is a replacement for the JAX-RPC specification. JAX-WS is used for developing Simple Object Access Protocol (SOAP)-based Web services.

Figure 1-1: History of distributed technology and web services

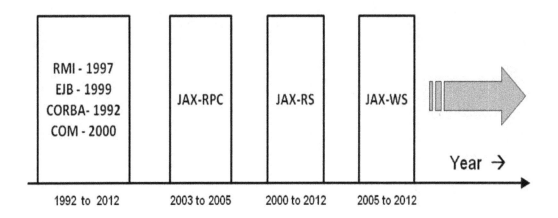

Java API for Restful web services (JAX-RS) is a Java specification used for implementing Restful Web services. The Representation State Transfer (REST) was first introduced and defined by *Roy Thomas Fielding* in 2000 in his PhD dissertation. Later, Sun adapted the REST specification; now it is part of Java EE. The JAX-RS is used for developing non-SOAP-based Web services.

To summarize, JAX-WS and JAX-RS are the Java specifications used for developing SOAP-based and non-SOAP-based Web services. Both are part of Java EE.

In this chapter will discuss the following topics:

- The history of Web Service technology
- The need for web services
- Advantages of Web Services

- The commonly used standards and technologies in Web services.

History of Web Services Evolution

The various types of architectures evolved over the period of time for enterprise integration are listed below.

- Point-to-point architectures
- Hub-and-spoke architectures using integration brokers
- Distributed architectures
- Service-oriented architectures

Point-to-Point Architectures

In case of point-to-point architecture style, each application requires one interface to connect to other application. This type of architecture is simple and easy to implement if there are only few applications and less number of interfaces. As the applications to be integrated are more in number, the total required interfaces increases exponentially, so the system becomes difficult to maintain and manage. The simple formula used to calculate the minimum number of interfaces needed in point-to-point communication is n(n-1)/2. Figure 1.2 shows three applications, so the number of interfaces needed in case of point to point communication is three. If the number of applications increases to 10, the number of interfaces needed is 45. Thus, although this approach works well for integrating two or three systems, due to its lightweight, simple approach, it becomes cumbersome for a corporation with a large number of applications. Point-to-point architecture is not a viable option in an enterprise with complex integrations. A diagram of point-to-point integration architecture is shown in Figure 1-2.

Figure 1-2: Point to Point Integration

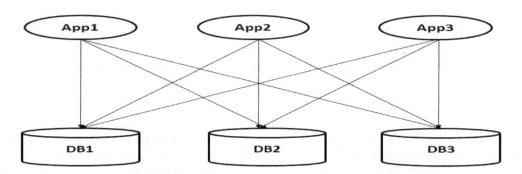

Point to Point Integration Architecture

The advantages and disadvantages of the point-to-point integration architectures are given below.

Advantages

- Simple and easy to implement.
- Fast and efficient solution.

- This approach is suitable for enterprises to integrate two or three systems.

Disadvantages

- There is a tight coupling between the integrated systems with their interfaces.
- There is a greater chance of a single point of failure. If one fails, all its dependents will fail.
- It requires too many interfaces if the number of applications increases over a period of time.
- This approach is not a viable option for corporations with complex integrations and many systems that need to be integrated.

Hub-and-Spoke Architectures using Integration Brokers

Hub-and-Spoke architecture is one of the most popular enterprise application integration (EAI) solutions used for application integration in an enterprise. It addresses the limitations of the point-to-point integrations but introduces other complexities. The big vendors play a significant contribution in hub-and-spoke integrations, and they have proprietary products available for enterprise application integration. The TIBCO, seeBeyond (also called as eGate, iCan, Java CAPS), Aqua Logic (Bea) and BizTalk (Microsoft) are some commonly available products in EAI used for application integration. In this type of architecture, the central component is called the "hub," and various applications connecting through this central hub are called "spokes". The applications communicate with each other through a central hub. This addresses the limitation of too many interfaces introduced in point-to-point architectures. The number of interfaces required in hub-and-spoke architecture is simply "n" instead of n(n-1)/2 interfaces required in point-to-point architectures.

Figure 1-3: Hub and Spoke integration

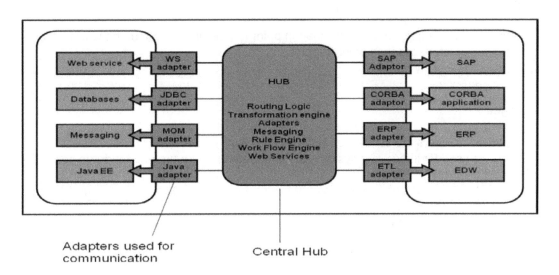

A central hub and its spokes are shown in Figure 1-3. The central hub is a piece of software component used for integrating applications. The integration broker (also called a hub) provides various types of adapters for integrating different applications. The integration hub also provides routing, transformation, messaging, business rules, and workflow related functionality. The various pluggable adapters are available to communicate with other external systems such as SAP, CRM, and ERP. These adapters are proprietary; in this context, proprietary means that the "TIBCO" SAP adapter cannot be replaced with the "eGate" SAP adapter.

The applications to be integrated will communicate through a central hub. These applications are loosed coupled and they are not dependent on each other. The data format and transformation logic is applied in the central hub instead of in the application. The hub-and-spoke integration architecture is shown in Figure 1-4

Figure 1-4: Hub and Spoke Integration Architecture

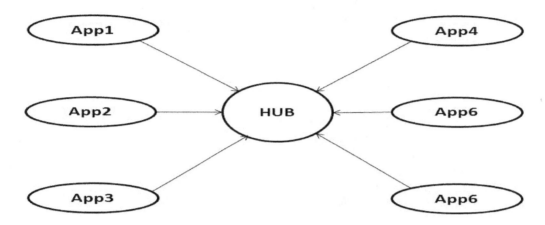

Hub and Spoke Integration Architecture

The advantages and disadvantages of the hub-and-spoke integration architectures are given below.

Advantages

- Integration is less complex and cleaner than in point-to-point integration architecture.
- It requires fewer interfaces than point-to-point architectures.
- Applications are loosely coupled.

Disadvantages

- The integration brokers are centralized but they are proprietary.
- The adapters used for integrating systems are proprietary. There are no standards specified for the adapter's implementation.
- There is a greater chance of a single point of failure. Integration hubs are centralized; if hub fails, all of its dependents will fail.
- The available integration products are very expensive.
- All traffic goes through a central hub, so it requires more processing power and capacity.
- This is a possible option only if both the sender and receiver agree to use the common hub for integration. There must be a common data format suitable for both parties.

Distributed Architectures

The popular Java based technologies used to enable the distributed architectures are RMI and EJB. The other available RPC-based technologies used for distributed computing are COM (now it is part of .NET) and CORBA. RMI uses JRMP as its underlying protocol, and it is used for communication between two Java applications. In the case of distributed architecture, the applications communicate through a common computer network. The applications must share a

History of Web Services Evolution

common computer network to share information. The distributed integration architecture is shown in Figure 1-5.

Figure 1-5: Distributed Architecture

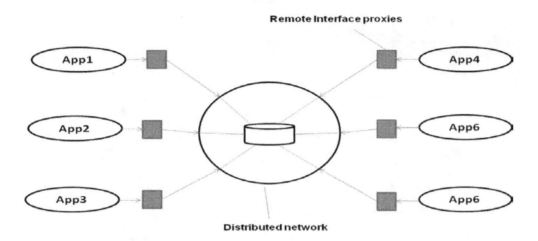

Distributed Integration Architecture

The applications communicate with each other through a remote proxy. Each of these applications uses a common communication network that connects several computers in an enterprise. The advantages and disadvantages of distributed architectures are given below.

Advantages

- It is a good solution if both the internal and external system uses the same distributed technology.
- It is easy to implement and maintain. High-level APIs are available for development.

Disadvantages

- The implementations using this approach are not truly interoperable and portable.
- There is no guarantee that all systems will use the same technology across the enterprise.

Service-Oriented Architectures

Service-oriented architecture is an approach used for sharing business functions in a systematic way between two applications. In service-oriented architecture, one set of applications exposes the functionality as a service, and other set of applications uses this functionality. The applications exchange information in a structured manner using an XML-based SOAP message protocol. These applications may exist within or outside of an enterprise. Service-oriented architecture is shown in Figure 1-6.

In this approach, the applications expose the business functionality as a service. Application publishes the description of the service to other applications so they can make use of this service. The applications to be communicated are independent of the service, and they are loosely coupled. In this approach, the application integration is much simpler and easier than in other types of integration approaches, and it does not require any special infrastructure.

Figure 1-6: Service Oriented Architecture

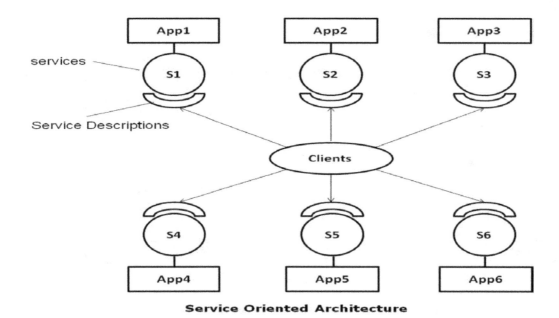

Service Oriented Architecture

The advantages and disadvantages of service-oriented architectures are given below.

Advantages

- The primary advantage of service-oriented architecture is reusability. The business functions can be reused within and outside the enterprise.
- The services developed are interoperable and portable across the platforms. It does not matter whether they are developed using Java or .Net or whether they are running on Windows or UNIX.
- The application to be integrated is loosely coupled, which improves the scalability of an application.
- No special hardware is required to deploy these services; the developed service can be part of your Web application.
- It addressed the problem of a single point of failure, which is a major concern for point-to-point and hub-and-spoke architectures.
- It is cheapest and most cost-effective.
- It makes the application integration much simpler and smoother than other types of architectures.

Disadvantages

- Too many standards and technologies are used; it requires a steep learning curve.
- It is not suitable for smaller, short-lived applications when reusability is not a prime criterion. It is a little overhead to use services within the application. It is a service, not a toy; use it only if it is necessary.

A classic implementation of service-oriented architecture is the Web Services and Enterprise Service Bus. Its primary objective is enterprise application integration of heterogeneous complex systems. It is an architecture model designed for application-to-application integration to share the business functions across the enterprise.

What Are the Advantages of Web Services?

Each technology has its own merits and demerits; Web services are not an exception. The advantages of using Web services in an enterprise are listed below.

- Web services provide a simple, flexible, standards-based integration approach for sharing business data with the outside world.
- Web services are platform independent and language independent. They are portable and interoperable across platforms and technologies, so a Java client can access a .Net service and vice versa.
- Another primary advantage is reusability of the business functions. For example, one address change service can be used for all applications within the group or organization instead of having one for each application. This avoids code duplication across the business units in an enterprise.
- It is easy to expose the existing legacy functionality as a Web service to the other applications in an enterprise. So it can be used to integrate with legacy applications.
- It provides support for various data formats and protocols used for communication.
- It can be deployed along with existing Web applications. No special packaging, tools, or deployment components are needed for deployment.
- It has a good return on investment. It provides a simple and flexible approach for application-to-application integration. It provides a longer life solution.
- Web services can be used as a replacement for RMI- and CORBA-based applications.
- It has many acronyms and keywords. You can add it to your resume; somebody will hire you.

Commonly Used Technologies in Web Services

The common criticism about Web services is that it contains too many technologies and standards. To some extent, that is true, but they are simple and easy to understand. Due to the addition of numerous standards, specifications, and product vendors, it has become more complex. There are 10 vendor-specific implementations and the same number of open-source frameworks available for developing Web services.

The technologies and standards commonly used during Web services development are listed below.

- XML
- JAXP
- SOAP
- SAAJ
- WSDL
- UDDI
- JAXR
- JAXB
- JAX-WS
- JAX-RS

Extensible Markup Language (XML) is the language used to represent the message structure in Web services. In general, Web service endpoint method parameter types and return values use XML-based messages.

The Java API for XML processing (also called JAXP) is a technique used for reading, creating, validating, and parsing XML documents.

Simple Object Access Protocol (SOAP) is an XML-based message structure used to exchange information between two applications within or outside of an enterprise. SOAP provides a standard XML-based message format in a structured manner for message exchange over the network. The SOAP message contains XML message used to communicate between client and service.

The API used for creating and reading SOAP messages is SAAJ. SAAJ stands for SOAP with Attachments API for Java. SAAJ can be used for sending SOAP-based XML messages over the Internet using the Java platform.

The specification used to document the details of the Web service endpoint structure is WSDL; it stands for Web Services Description Language.

The UDDI is a registry for Web services. It stands for Universal Description, Discovery, and Integration. It provides a mechanism to register and find Web services.

Java API for XML Registries (JAXR) provides a standard Java API for accessing different kinds of XML-based metadata registry. The JAXR API is used to find published Web services in the UDDI registry.

Java API for XML Binding (JAXB) provides the ability to convert the Java objects into XML and vice versa.

Java API for XML Web services (also called JAX-WS) is a Java specification for implementing Web services using Java and XML. The JAX-WS specification defines a set of Java API for the development of Web services using XML-based SOAP protocol. The JAX-WS specification is part of the Java EE platform.

Java API for Restful Web services (also called JAX-RS) is a Java specification for implementing Restful Web services. This specification defines a set of Java API for the development of Web services conforming to Representational State Transfer (REST) principles. The JAX-RS specification is part of the Java EE platform.

There are several Web services frameworks available for developing Java-based Web services. Almost all big vendors have their own implementations packaged with their IDEs. The open-source frameworks used for developing Java-based Web services are listed below.

- Apache-CXF
- Apache-Axis2
- Spring Web Services (Spring-WS)

Apache-CXF is the most popular open-source framework used to develop fully featured Web services conforming to JAX-WS standards. This project is derived from combining the two open-source projects "Celtix" and "XFire." The combined project is now available under Apache license.

Apache-Axis2 is another open-source framework used to develop fully featured Web services. It is the successor to its Axis1 Web services framework. This project is also available under Apache license.

Spring Web Services (also called Spring-WS) is another open-source Web services framework used for developing SOAP-based Web services. This project is developed and maintained by Spring community.

The book will cover the above-specified technologies and open-source frameworks. Chapter2 illustrates the use of various XML parsing techniques using JAXP.

Chapter 2. JAXP

The most commonly used technology for developing Java Web services is XML. It is necessary to learn how to create, read, validate, and manipulate an XML document before attempting to work in Web services development.

Let us review a simple XML document containing three elements: id, first name, and last name.

```
<?xml version="1.0" encoding="UTF-8"?>
<Students>
    <Student>
        <id>1</id>
        <firstName>John</firstName>
        <lastName>Smith</lastName>
    </Student>
</Students>
```

How do you read the element data from the above XML? The data specified in XML is "id" (value =1), "firstName" (value = John) and "lastName" (value = Smith).

The objective here is to read data from an XML document and populate it into a Java class. The equivalent Java object used to populate the above-specified XML data is given below. The input is an XML document, and the output will be a Java object with data.

```
public class Student {
    private String id;
    private String firstName;
    private String lastName;

    // Add getters and setters here
}
```

What are the possible ways to read the data from an XML document? The possible solutions are given below.

- Load the entire document, store it in your system memory, and then access the required element data using Java API.
- Read only the required portions of an XML document based on a generated event. Each generated event should map to a specific portion of the XML document. From a generated event you can pull the data from an XML document or you can ask the XML document to push the data for a generated event using Java API.

We have solutions available for reading the data from XML documents. Now the question is how to create (write) an XML document. The input in this scenario is a Java object containing data, and the output will be an XML document. The input Java object with hard-coded data is given below.

```
public class Student {
    private String id = "823147";
    private String firstName = "John";
    private String lastName = "Smith";
```

```
        // Add getters and setters
}
```

The output is an XML document.

```
<?xml version="1.0" encoding="UTF-8"?>
<Students>
    <Student>
        <id>823147</id>
        <firstName>John</firstName>
        <lastName>Smith</lastName>
    </Student>
</Students>
```

We have Java-based APIs available to create an XML document. The technique used for reading and writing XML documents is called Java API for XML processing; it is also called JAXP.

Java API for XML processing (JAXP) is a Java specification that introduces support for creating, manipulating, validating, and parsing XML documents using standardized Java APIs. XML is the most commonly used language in Web services, so it is necessary to understand XML processing, creation, validation, and manipulation techniques. This chapter does not address basic XML syntax and its rules; it focuses on XML processing techniques using JAXP. During Web services development, we often use these reading, writing, and manipulation techniques to read data from XML documents to populate the Java objects and vice versa. The three basic JAXP-provided interfaces used for this purpose are given below.

- Simple API for XML (called SAX)
- Document Object Model (called DOM)
- Streaming API for XML (called StAX)

SAX is used for reading XML documents; DOM and StAX are used for both reading and writing XML documents.

In this chapter will discuss the following topics:

- Simple API for XML (SAX)
- The use of the content handler interface in SAX
- What is the difference between SAX1 and SAX2?
- Reading XML documents using SAX API
- Document Object Model (DOM)
- What is the difference between DOM, DOM2, and DOM3?
- What is the difference between SAX and DOM?
- Reading and writing XML documents using DOM API
- Streaming API for XML (StAX)
- What is the difference between StAX1 and StAX2?
- Reading and writing XML documents using StAX AP
- What is the difference between SAX and StAX?

JAXP was first released in 2000. It is not a just a parser to read XML documents; it provides common interfaces to support various implementations of SAX, DOM, and StAX. DOM is Object based; SAX and StAX are event-based APIs. So we have a choice to parse the XML document data as a stream of events (SAX or StAX) or to use an object representation of it (DOM). The SAX and DOM APIs were defined by the XML-DEV and W3C, and StAX were initially developed by Bea with support from SUN. The primary packages of JAXP, SAX, DOM, and StAX are given below.

- javax.xml.parsers—JAXP APIs, which provide a common interface for different vendors for implementing SAX and DOM parsers
- org.w3c.dom—defines a "Document" class and many other components of the Document Object Model (DOM)
- org.xml.sax—defines the core SAX APIs
- javax.xml.stream—provides StAX-specific transformation APIs.

The three basic interfaces of JAXP are shown in Figure 2-1. Let us review each API to explore its capabilities.

Figure 2-1: JAXP parsing techniques

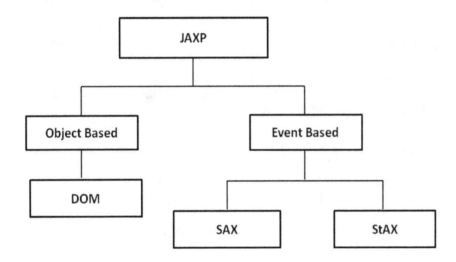

Simple API for XML (SAX)

Simple API for XML is used for reading (parsing) the XML documents. The points provided below explain the use and capabilities of a SAX parsing technique.

- Simple API for XML (SAX) is an event-based parser API used for processing XML documents serially, element by element, one after another.
- Each element of the XML document is parsed sequentially in forward direction from top to bottom.
- SAX parsing is unidirectional; the entire document must be reparsed to obtain the previously accessed data.
- It will access only a portion of the XML document based on the event generated by the client code.
- It uses the event-based, push model, streaming technique to read the XML documents.
- The main interface in all SAX parser implements is generally the *ContentHandler*; this interface has defined all methods to handle the parser generated events. For each generated client event, one interface method is executed to parse a certain portion of an XML document.

What is the difference between SAX and SAX2?

- The complete namespace support is included in SAX2.
- Many of the classes in SAX (sometimes also called SAX1) are deprecated.
- The newly introduced main parser interface in SAX2 is the org.xml.sax.XMLReader. It replaces the SAX1 org.xml.sax.Parser interface.
- There are adapters available to convert a SAX1 parser to a SAX2 XMLReader and vice-versa; thus, SAX1 and SAX2 codes can coexist in the same project.

The SAX2 XMLReader interface contains two important enhancements over the old SAX1 parser interface.

- It adds a standard way to query and set features and properties.
- The complete namespace support is added.

The SAX API is defined in the following three packages. These three packages hold the different classes of the SAX API.

- org.xml.sax—This package provides the core SAX APIs; it is used for document processing and error handling.
- org.xml.sax.ext—This package contains extensions to SAX API.
- org.xml.sax.helpers—This package contains helper classes; it has factory classes that support SAX2, and it contains adaptor classes converting from SAX1 to SAX2.

The primary classes and interfaces used for reading XML documents using SAX are given below.

- ContentHandler—This is the main interface used for handling SAX events.
- DefaultHandler—This is the adapter class used for the content handler interface.
- XMLReader—This SAX2 interface is used for reading an XML document using callbacks.
- XMLReaderFactory—This factory class is used for creating an XML reader.

Figure 2-2: SAX parsing terminology for event handling

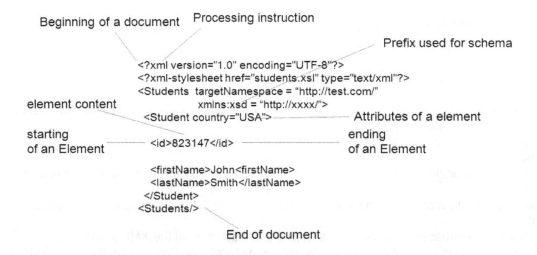

The terminology used while SAX parses an XML document is shown in Figure 2-2. There are methods defined to capture each generated event.

The SAX-generated events are mapped to the corresponding sections of an XML document. The main interface of any SAX parser implements is generally the "ContentHandler," and it defines eleven methods to handle the SAX parser-generated events. The developer may not use all eleven operations every time, so an adaptor class called the "DefaultHandler" is available for use. The "DefaultHandler" adapter class defines an empty implementation of eleven methods in the "ContentHandler" interface.

The definition of the "ContentHandler" interface is given below:

```
package org.xml.sax;

public interface ContentHandler {
    public void characters(char ch[], int start, int length)
                    throws SAXException;
    public void endDocument() throws SAXException;
    public void endElement(String uri, String localName, String
                    qName) throws SAXException;
    public void endPrefixMapping(String prefix) throws SAXException;
    public void ignorableWhitespace(char ch[], int start, int length)
                    throws SAXException;
    public void processingInstruction(String target, String data)
                    throws SAXException;
    public void setDocumentLocator(Locator locator);
    public void skippedEntity(String name) throws SAXException;
    public void startDocument() throws SAXException;
    public void startElement(String uri, String localName, String
                    qName, Attributes atts) throws SAXException;
    public void startPrefixMapping (String prefix, String uri)
                    throws SAXException;
}
```

Figure 2-3 explains the SAX parsing of an XML document.

Figure 2-3: SAX parsing events

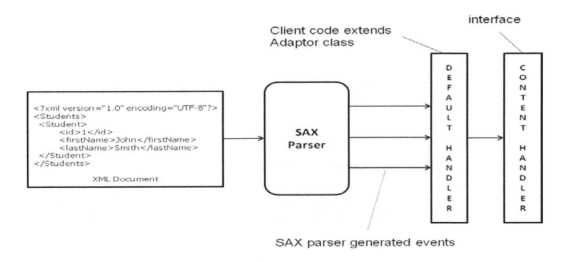

The SAX parser reads certain portions of an XML document based on the event generated. While parsing the XML documents, the application code extends the "DefaultHandler" class; it registers the instance with the SAX parser using the "setContentHandler()" method of the "XMLReader"

object. The methods of the "ContentHandler" interface read a particular section of an XML document, such as an element, document, processing instruction, and so forth, while parsing the XML document. The code provided below explains the purpose of each method of a ContentHandler interface.

```
public class SimpleSAXParser extends DefaultHandler {
    private StringBuilder currentTagContent = new StringBuilder();
    public static void main(String[] args) {
        try {
            DefaultHandler xmlHandler = new SimplaSAXParser();
            XMLReader xmlReader = XMLReaderFactory.createXMLReader();
            xmlReader.setContentHandler(xmlHandler);

            // use any valid xml file
            xmlReader.parse("students.xml");
        } catch (Exception ex) {
            ex.printStackTrace();
        }
    }
}
```

The XML provided below is used to demonstrate SAX event handling. Use this XML and view the output of each SAX generated event.

```
<?xml version="1.0" encoding="UTF-8"?>
<?xml-stylesheet href="students.xsl" type="text/xml"?>
<Students targetNamespace="http://jaxp.ws.learning.com/"
        xmlns:xsd="http://www.w3.org/2001/XMLSchema">
    <Student country="USA">
        <id>1</id>
        <firstName>John</firstName>
        <lastName>Smith</lastName>
    </Student>
    <Student>
        <id>2</id>
        <firstName>Steve</firstName>
        <lastName>Day</lastName>
    </Student>
    <Student>
        <id>3</id>
        <firstName>Joe</firstName>
        <lastName>Liner</lastName>
    </Student>
</Students>
```

1. startElement(String uri, String localName, String qName, Attributes atts)

It receives notification of the start of an element. The code implementation of this method is given below. Add the method provided below to the "SimpleSAXParser" class to obtain the element attributes.

```
public void startElement(String uri, String localName, String qName,
Attributes attr) {

    for(int i = 0; i<attr.getLength(); i++) {
        System.out.println("---- attribute value is ---" +
```

```
                              attr.getValue(i));
        }
}
```

Add the above method to the "SimpleSAXParser" class and view the output on the console. The above code prints the attributes of an element. An example is given below.

```
---- attribute value is ---- http://jaxp.ws.learning.com/
---- attribute value is ---- USA
```

Similarly, the method provided below is used to obtain the URI, localName, and qName.

```
public void startElement(String uri, String localName, String qName,
Attributes attr) {

    System.out.println("--- uri ---" + uri + "-- localName --" +
    localName + "--- qName ---" + qName);
}
```

The output of the above method is given below (for one student element).

```
--- uri --- localName --Students--- qName ---Students
--- uri --- localName --Student--- qName ---Student
--- uri --- localName --id--- qName ---id
--- uri --- localName --firstName--- qName ---firstName
--- uri --- localName --lastName--- qName ---lastName
```

Change the input XML to view different output. Rename the first name element to <xsd:firtName/>. Run the "SimpleSAXParser" class to see the output.

```
<xsd:firstName>John</xsd:firstName>
```

The output of the above method is given below (for one student element).

```
---- uri ----- localName --Students---- qName ----Students
---- uri ----- localName --Student---- qName ----Student
---- uri ----- localName --id---- qName ----id
---- uri ---http://www.w3.org/2001/XMLSchema-- localName --firstName----
qName ----xsd:firstName
---- uri ----- localName --lastName---- qName ----lastName
```

The details of the first name element are given below. In this scenario, the "qName" and "localName" are different. The qName includes the namespace prefix. The localName does not include the namespace prefix. The value of the "uri" specifies the complete namespace URL of an element.

The qName value is: xsd:firstName

The local name value is: firstName

The URI value is: http://www.w3.org/2001/XMLSchema

2. startDocument()

This method receives notification of the beginning of a document.

3. characters(char ch[], int start, int length)

This method receives notification of character data. This data is used for populating Java objects. Add the method provided below to the "SimpleSAXParser" class to obtain element data.

```
public void characters(char[] ch, int start, int length) throws
SAXException {
    System.out.println("--- element content ---" +
    currentTagContent.append(new String(ch, start, length)));
}
```

The output of the above method is given below.

```
1
John
Smith
2
Steve
Day
3
Joe
Liner
```

4. endDocument()

This method receives notification of the end of a document.

5. endElement()

This method receives notification of the end of an element. Add the method provided below to the "SimpleSAXParser" class to obtain the local name and qname.

```
public void endElement (String uri, String localName, String qName) {
    System.out.println("--- qName ---" + qName);
}
```

The output of the above method is given below (for one student element).

```
--- qName ---id
--- qName ---firstName
--- qName ---lastName
--- qName ---Student
```

6. startPrefixMapping()

This method receives notification of the beginning-scope of a prefix-URI namespace mapping. Add the method provided below to the "SimpleSAXParser" class to obtain the URI prefix and URI.

```
public void startPrefixMapping(String prefix, String uri) {
```

```
        System.out.println("-- prefix --" + prefix + "-- uri --" + uri);
}
```

The output of the above method is given below.

```
--- prefix ---xsd--- uri ---http://www.w3.org/2001/XMLSchema
```

7. endPrefixMapping()

This method receives notification of the end-scope of a prefix-URI namespace mapping. Add the method provided below to the "SimpleSAXParser" class to obtain the end URI prefix.

```
public void endPrefixMapping (String prefix) throws SAXException {
        System.out.println("--- end prefix ---" + prefix);
}
```

The output of the above method is given below.

```
--- end prefix ------xsd
```

8. ignorableWhitespace(char ch[], int start, int length)

This method receives notification of ignorable whitespace in the element content.

9. processingInstruction(String target, String data)

This receives notification of the processing instruction. XML documents starts with the XML declaration, which itself is a processing instruction. Add the method provided below to the "SimpleSAXParser" class to obtain the processing instruction-specific information.

```
public void processingInstruction (String target, String data) throws
SAXException {
        System.out.println("--- data ---" + data);
}
```

The output of the above method is given below.

```
--- data ---href="students.xsl" type="text/xml"
```

10. setDocumentLocator(Locator locator)

This method receives an object for locating the origin of SAX document events. It determines the current parsing location of the XML parser. The line number, column, and system id information are useful for debugging purposes. Add the method provided below to the "SimpleSAXParser" class to obtain the line number, column, and system id.

```
public void setDocumentLocator(Locator locator) {
        if (locator != null) {
                int col = locator.getColumnNumber();
                int line = locator.getLineNumber();
                String publicId = locator.getPublicId();
                String systemId = locator.getSystemId();
```

```
        System.out.println("-- col --" + col +  "-- line --" + line +
                        "-- publicId --" + publicId +
                        "-- systemId --" + systemId);
    }
}
```

The output of the above method is given below.

```
-- col --1-- line --1-- publicId --null-- systemId --
file:///C:/students.xml
```

11. skippedEntity(String name)

This method receives notification of a skipped entity. The parser will invoke this method once for each entity skipped. The skipped entities are related to DTDs; some parsers don't send any events to this method. Add the method provided below to the "SimpleSAXParser" class and view the output.

```
public void skippedEntity(String name) {
    System.out.println("Name: " + name);
}
```

The javax.xml.parsers Package

The classes of this package are used to process XML documents, and this package supports SAX and DOM parsers. This package has four classes; two are used for SAX parsing, and two are used for DOM parsing. The following classes support SAX and DOM parsing.

- SAXParser
- SAXParserFactory
- DocumentBuilder
- DocumentBuilderFactory

The "javax.xml.parsers.SAXParser" class is a wrapper that defines a number of convenience methods. It defines an API that wraps the "org.xml.sax.XMLReader" implementation class. The SAX1-provided "org.xml.sax.Parser" has been replaced with SAX2-provided "org.xml.sax.XMLReader" interface. An instance of the "org.xml.sax.XMLReader" class can be obtained using "javax.xml.parsers.SAXParserFactory". Once the instance of the "org.xml.sax.XMLReader" class is obtained, it can parse the XML with various input sources. The supported input sources are files, URLs, input streams, and SAX input sources.

Various parse methods of the "org.xml.sax.XMLReader" interface are used to parse XML documents. Thus, the SAX parser calls various methods of the "org.xml.sax.helpers.DeafultHandler" class to process the XML documents during runtime.

Obtaining the org.xml.sax.XMLReader Interface Handle

There are three possible methods to obtain the handle of the XMLReader interface. The parse() method of an XMLReader is used to parse any valid XML document.

CASE 1:

The getXMLReader() method of the "javax.xml.parsers.SAXParser" interface is used to get the instance of XMLReader. The parse() method of the XMLReader interface is used to parse the XML document. The SAX-parsing of an XML using this approach is given below.

```
// Create a JAXP SAXParser
SAXParserFactory parserFactory = SAXParserFactory.newInstance();
SAXParser saxParser = parserFactory.newSAXParser();

// Get the encapsulated SAX XMLReader using getXMLReader() method
XMLReader xmlReader = saxParser.getXMLReader();
xmlReader.setContentHandler(xmlHandler);
xmlReader.parse("students.xml");
```

CASE 2:

The createXMLReader() method of the "XMLReaderFactory" class is used to get the instance of XMLReader. The parse() method of the XMLReader interface is used to parse the XML document. The SAX-parsing of an XML using this approach is given below.

```
XMLReader xmlReader = XMLReaderFactory.createXMLReader();
xmlReader.setContentHandler(xmlHandler);
xmlReader.parse("students.xml");
```

CASE 3:

The code provided below will support backward compatibility, but this approach is not recommended for newer development. The SAX1-provided "org.sax.Parser" interface has been replaced with the SAX2-provided "org.xml.sax.XMLReader" interface. The parse() method of the SAXParser interface is used to parse the XML document.

```
SAXParserFactory parserFactory = SAXParserFactory.newInstance();
SAXParser saxParser = parserFactory.newSAXParser();
saxParser.parse(new ByteArrayInputStream(ouptData.getBytes()),
xmlHandler);
```

The supported method signatures of a "parse()" method are given below. All SAX interfaces are assumed to be synchronous; the parse methods must not return until parsing is complete.

```
// Parsing a file using "File" as input source
xmlReader.parse("students.xml");

// Parsing a file using "Source" input
xmlReader.parse(new InputSource("students.xml"));

// Parsing a file using "Stream" input
String myXML = ""; //Entire XML string to be parsed.
xmlReader.parse(new InputSource(new
ByteArrayInputStream(myXML.getBytes())));

// Parsing a file using "URL" as input source
xmlReader.parse(URL);
```

Example 1: How to Parse an XML Document Using SAX2 API

The steps required to parse any valid XML document using the SAX parser API are given below.

1. Identify the XML document to be parsed.
2. Create a Java data object to populate XML data.
3. Create a reusable utility class to handle SAX events while parsing an XML document.
4. Create an application-specific parser class.

The above-specified steps are described in the following sections:

Step 1: Identify the XML Document to Be Parsed.

The input is below provided XML document, and the output will be a Java data structure. The objective here is to parse the XML code provided below, obtain the element data, and populate the data into a Java data object. The complete XML is given below.

```xml
<?xml version="1.0" encoding="UTF-8"?>
<Students>
    <Student>
        <id>1</id>
        <firstName>John</firstName>
        <lastName>Smith</lastName>
    </Student>
    <Student>
        <id>2</id>
        <firstName>Steve</firstName>
        <lastName>Day</lastName>
    </Student>
    <Student>
        <id>3</id>
        <firstName>Joe</firstName>
        <lastName>Liner</lastName>
    </Student>
</Students>
```

The mapping between XML document and the Java data object is shown Figure 2-4. The SAX parser reads each sub-element of the <Student/> element and then populates it into a Java data object.

Figure 2-4: Mapping between XML and Java object

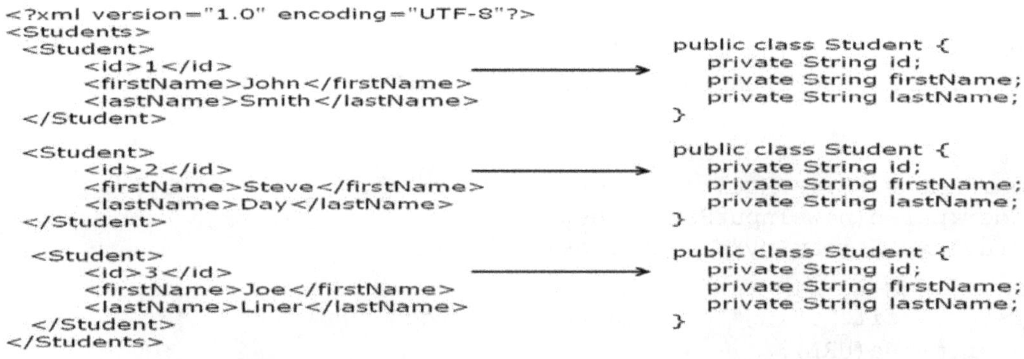

Mapping between XML document and java data object

Simple API for XML (SAX)

The resulting Java data structure contains three student objects, and each student object contains three attributes: id, firstName, and lastName.

Step 2: Create a Java Data Object to Populate XML Data.

Create a matching Java data object class to populate the extracted element data from the XML document. The structure of the Java object depends on the structure of the XML document. The Java object used to populate the above XML data is given below.

```
// Student.java
package com.learning.ws.jaxp;

public class Student {
    private String id;
    private String firstName;
    private String lastName;

    // Add getters and setters here
}
```

Step 3: Create a Reusable Utility Class to Handle SAX Events While Parsing an XML Document.

Create a re-usable parsing utility class to parse the XML document. So this class can be re-used to parse any valid XML document. This class contains five methods and it extends the "DefaultHandler" adapter class. The complete utility class code is provided in Listing 2-1.

Listing 2-1: Utility class used to handle SAX events.

```
// AbstractXmlSchemaParser.java
package com.learning.ws.jaxp;

import org.xml.sax.helpers.DefaultHandler;
import org.xml.sax.Attributes;
import org.xml.sax.SAXException;

public abstract class AbstractXmlSchemaParser extends DefaultHandler {
    private StringBuilder currentTagContent = new StringBuilder();
    private boolean nil;

    public void characters(char[] ch, int start, int length) throws
    SAXException {
        currentTagContent.append(new String(ch, start, length));
    }

    public void startElement(String uri, String localName, String qName,
    Attributes attr) {
        // To detect nil tags
        nil = Boolean.parseBoolean(attr.getValue("xsi:nil"));
        startTag(qName);
    }

    public void endElement(String uri, String localName, String qName) {
        String currentTag = currentTagContent.toString().trim();
        currentTagContent.setLength(0);
        if (nil) {
```

```
            nil = false;
        } else {
            endTag(qName, currentTag);
        }
    }

    // To be implemented in application code
    protected abstract void startTag(String name);

    // To be implemented in application code
    protected abstract void endTag(String name, String tagContent);
}
```

The method provided below is used to obtain the element content. It appends each character of an element content to form a string object.

```
public void characters(char[] ch, int start, int length) throws
SAXException {
    currentTagContent.append(new String(ch, start, length));
}
```

The method provided below is used to receive the start element event while parsing a document.

```
public void startElement(String uri, String localName, String qName,
Attributes attr) {
    // To detect nil tags
    nil = Boolean.parseBoolean(attr.getValue("xsi:nil"));
    startTag(qName);
}
```

The method provided below is used to receive the end element event while parsing a document.

```
public void endElement(String uri, String localName, String qName) {
    String currentTag = currentTagContent.toString().trim();
    currentTagContent.setLength(0);
    if (nil) {
        nil = false;
    } else {
        endTag(qName, currentTag);
    }
}
```

The methods provided below will be implemented in your parser to build the application-specific logic to populate the Java objects.

```
protected abstract void startTag(String name);
protected abstract void endTag(String name, String tagContent);
```

Step 4: Create an Application-Specific Parser Class.

This class will populate the data extracted from an XML document into Java objects. Listing 2-2 has a complete program that demonstrates how to parse an XML document using SAX API.

Listing 2-2: How to parse an XML document using SAX2 API

```java
// MySAXParser.java
package com.learning.ws.jaxp;

import org.xml.sax.helpers.DefaultHandler;
import org.xml.sax.helpers.XMLReaderFactory;
import org.xml.sax.XMLReader;
import java.util.*;

public class MySAXParser {
    public static void main(String[] args) {
        try {
            MySAXParser mySAXParser = new MySAXParser();
            // To print the data from java objects
            List<Student> studentsList = mySAXParser.getStudentData();
            for(Student student : studentsList) {
                System.out.println(" Id: " + student.getId());
                System.out.println(" firstName: " +
                        student.getFirstName());
                System.out.println(" lastName: " +
                        student.getLastName());
        } catch (Exception ex) {
            ex.printStackTrace();
        }
    }

    // Parse the output xml to get the result
    private List<Student> getStudentData() throws Exception {
        // Parse the output xml to get the result
        StudentInfoXmlSchemaParser studentOutputParser = new
        StudentInfoXmlSchemaParser();
        parseOutputXML(studentOutputParser);
        List<Student> studentsList = studentOutputParser.studentsList;
        return studentsList;
    }

    // Parse the xml file using XMLReader
    private void parseOutputXML(DefaultHandler xmlHandler) throws
    Exception {
        try {
            XMLReader xmlReader = XMLReaderFactory.createXMLReader();
            xmlReader.setContentHandler(xmlHandler);
            xmlReader.parse("C:/students.xml");
        } catch (Exception ex) {
            ex.printStackTrace();
            throw new Exception("Error occurred while parsing the
                            result", ex);
        }
    }

    /* Parse the xml file, extract the data from XML, populate into
    Java objects.*/
    private class StudentInfoXmlSchemaParser extends
        AbstractXmlSchemaParser {
        // List used to add each "Student" object.
        List<Student> studentsList = new ArrayList<Student>();
```

```
          //Student object used to populate the XML element content.
          Student student = null;

          // Create a Student object for each <Student/> element
          protected void startTag(String name) {
              if ("student".equalsIgnoreCase(name)) {
                  student = new Student();
                  studentsList.add(student);
              }
          }

          /* Get the content from each sub element of a <Student/>
          element */
          protected void endTag(String name, String tagContent) {
              if (tagContent != null) {
                  if ("id".equalsIgnoreCase(name)) {
                      student.setId(tagContent);
                  } else if ("firstName".equalsIgnoreCase(name)) {
                      student.setFirstName(tagContent);
                  } else if ("lastName".equalsIgnoreCase(name)) {
                      student.setLastName(tagContent);
                  }
              }
          }
      }
}
```

The inner class provided below is used to extract the data from an XML document and create a Java data structure. The resulting data structure is used in an application to address the application specific business need. It extends the previously created reusable utility class.

```
private class StudentInfoXmlSchemaParser extends AbstractXmlSchemaParser
{
      List<Student> studentsList = new ArrayList<Student>();
      Student student = null;

      protected void startTag(String name) {
          if ("student".equalsIgnoreCase(name)) {
              student = new Student();
              studentsList.add(student);
          }
      }

      protected void endTag(String name, String tagContent) {
          if (tagContent != null) {
              if ("id".equalsIgnoreCase(name)) {
                  student.setId(tagContent);
              } else if ("firstName".equalsIgnoreCase(name)) {
                  student.setFirstName(tagContent);
              } else if ("lastName".equalsIgnoreCase(name)) {
                  student.setLastName(tagContent);
              }
          }
      }
}
```

Run the `MySAXParser` class to view the output on the console. The output is shown below.

```
Id: 1
firstName: John
lastName: Smith
Id: 2
firstName: Steve
lastName: Day
Id: 3
firstName: Joe
lastName: Liner
```

Example 2: How to Implement the Error Handler

It is quite common to commit errors while dealing with XML documents. Let us review an invalid XML document. The XML provided below is invalid because the <firstName> element tag is not properly closed.

```xml
<?xml version="1.0" encoding="UTF-8"?>
<?xml-stylesheet href="students.xsl" type="text/xml"?>
<Students targetNamespace="http://jaxp.ws.learning.com/"
          xmlns:xsd="http://www.w3.org/2001/XMLSchema">
    <Student country="USA">
        <id>823147</id>
        <firstName>John<firstName>
        <lastName>Smith</lastName>
    </Student>
<Students/>
```

How do you determine the errors associated with any invalid XML document? The SAX API provides an error handling mechanism to report the errors associated with an invalid XML document.

The SAX API-provided "org.xml.sax.ErrorHandler" interface is used to report error and warning messages. The three methods defined for error handling are warning, error, and fatal Error. The warning level does not stop the processing of the parser. Listing 2-3 has a complete program that demonstrates the use of SAX provided error handler.

Listing 2-3: How to implement error handler

```java
// SAXErrorHandler.java
package com.learning.ws.jaxp;

import org.xml.sax.ErrorHandler;
import org.xml.sax.SAXException;
import org.xml.sax.SAXParseException;

public class SAXErrorHandler implements ErrorHandler {
    public void warning(SAXParseException e) throws SAXException {
        log("--Warning--", e);
        throw (e);
    }

    public void error(SAXParseException e) throws SAXException {
        log("---Error---", e);
```

```
        throw (e);
    }

    public void fatalError(SAXParseException e) throws SAXException {
        log("---Fatal Error---", e);
        throw (e);
    }

    private void log(String type, SAXParseException e) {
        System.out.println(type + ": " + e.getMessage());
        System.out.println("Line " + e.getLineNumber() +
            " Column " + e.getColumnNumber());
        System.out.println("System ID: " + e.getSystemId());
    }
}
```

Set the error handler to "XMLReader" before calling the "parse()" method. The code provided below explains the use of the error handler while parsing an XML document.

```
private void parseOutputXML(DefaultHandler xmlHandler) throws Exception {
    try {
        DefaultHandler xmlHandler = new SimpleSAXParser();
        XMLReader xmlReader = XMLReaderFactory.createXMLReader();
        xmlReader.setContentHandler(xmlHandler);

        // set the error handler
        xmlReader.setErrorHandler(new SAXErrorHandler());

        // use any valid XML document
        xmlReader.parse("C:/student.xml");
    } catch (Exception ex) {
        ex.printStackTrace();
        throw new Exception("ErrorParsing Result", ex);
    }
}
```

Provide an invalid XML document and view the output on the console. The error handler prints the error information on the console. The SAX parser-reported error is given below.

```
----Fatal Error----: The element type "firstName" must be terminated by
the matching end-tag "</firstName>".

org.xml.sax.SAXParseException: The element type "firstName" must be
terminated by the matching end-tag "</firstName>".

Line 9 Column 5

System ID: file:///C:/students.xml
```

Example 3: How to Handle Various ContentHandler Events

The Listing 2-4 has a complete Java program that demonstrates how to handle various events of the ContentHandler interface. The SimpleSAXParser code fires an appropriate event while parsing the XML document and displays the output on the console. The eleven methods of a

ContentHandler interface are implemented in this example. Run the code provided below to view the output on the console.

Listing 2-4: How to use ContentHandler methods for event handling

```java
// SimpleSAXParser.java
package com.learning.ws.jaxp;

import org.xml.sax.helpers.DefaultHandler;
import org.xml.sax.helpers.XMLReaderFactory;
import org.xml.sax.XMLReader;
import org.xml.sax.SAXException;
import org.xml.sax.Locator;
import org.xml.sax.Attributes;

public class SimpleSAXParser extends DefaultHandler {
    private StringBuilder currentTagContent = new StringBuilder();
    private Locator locator;

    public static void main(String[] args) {
        try {
            DefaultHandler xmlHandler = new SimpleSAXParser();
            XMLReader xmlReader = XMLReaderFactory.createXMLReader();
            xmlReader.setContentHandler(xmlHandler);

            // set the error handler
            xmlReader.setErrorHandler(new SAXErrorHandler());

            // use any valid XML document
            xmlReader.parse("C:/student.xml");
        } catch (Exception ex) {
            ex.printStackTrace();
        }
    }

    public void characters(char[] ch, int start, int length) throws
    SAXException {
        System.out.println("------ element content -----" +
        currentTagContent.append(new String(ch, start, length)));
    }

    public void startElement(String uri, String localName, String qName,
    Attributes attr) {
        System.out.println("---- uri ---" + uri + "-- localName --" +
        localName + "---- qName ----" + qName);
        System.out.println("---- qName ----" + qName);
        for (int i = 0; i < attr.getLength(); i++) {
            System.out.println("---- attribute value is ---" +
            attr.getValue(i));
        }
    }

    public void startPrefixMapping(String prefix, String uri) {
        System.out.println("--- prefix ---" + prefix + "--- uri ---" +
        uri);
    }
```

```
    public void endPrefixMapping(String prefix) throws SAXException {
        System.out.println("---- end prefix -----" + prefix);
    }

    public void endElement(String uri, String localName, String qName) {
        System.out.println("------- qName ------" + qName);
    }

    public void processingInstruction(String target, String data) throws
SAXException {
        System.out.println("------- data ------" + data);
    }

    public void setDocumentLocator(Locator locator) {
        this.locator = locator;
        if (locator != null) {
            int col = locator.getColumnNumber();
            int line = locator.getLineNumber();
            String publicId = locator.getPublicId();
            String systemId = locator.getSystemId();
            System.out.println("-- col --" + col + "- line --" + line +
                "-- publicId --" + publicId + "-- systemId --" +
                systemId);
        }
    }

    public void skippedEntity(String name) {
        System.out.println("-" + locator.getLineNumber() + "---Skipped
        Entity");
        System.out.println(" --- Name: " + name);
    }

    public void startDocument() throws SAXException {
    }
}
```

Document Object Model (DOM)

The Document Object Model (DOM) is a component of Java API for XML processing used for parsing and creation of XML documents. DOM specification defines a tree-based hierarchical structure for navigating XML documents. The client loads the entire XML document into memory; then it navigates and parses the required portions of the XML document. DOM provides a simple API function for navigation using the parent and child nodes. The DOM API provides support for loading the entire XML document as a stream, transforming it, and using it.

What is the difference between DOM1, DOM2, and DOM3?

The initial DOM standard was recommended by W3C in 1998, and more features and some extensions were added in 2000. The initial version of DOM is called "DOM Level1," the subsequent release is "DOM Level2," and the current release is "DOM Level3." The commonly used terminology in the developer community is DOM1, DOM2, and DOM3.

- DOM Level 1 was published in late 1998. DOM Level 1 allows navigation through an HTML or XML document as well as manipulation of the content in that document.

- DOM Level 2 was published in late 2000. DOM Level 2 extends Level 1 with a number of features such as XML namespace support, filtered views, ranges, events, and so forth.
- DOM Level 3 is the current release of the DOM specification, published in April 2004, and added support for XPath and keyboard event handling, as well as an interface for serializing documents as XML.

The DOM API is defined in the following packages. These packages hold the various classes of DOM API.

- org.w3c.dom—defines the DOM programming interfaces for XML documents, as specified by the W3C
- javax.xml.parsers—defines the "DocumentBuilderFactory" class and the "DocumentBuilder" class, which returns an object that implements the W3C Document interface

The primary interfaces used to manipulate, parse, and validate the XML documents are given below. They are defined in the "org.w3c.dom" package.

- Document—The Document interface represents the entire XML document.
- Node—The Node interface is the primary datatype for the entire Document Object Model. It represents a single node in the document tree.
- NodeList—The NodeList interface provides the abstraction of an ordered collection of nodes.
- Element—The Element interface represents an element in an XML document.
- Attr—The Attr interface represents an attribute in an element object.

Figure 2-5 explains the DOM parsing of an XML document. The DOM parser reads the entire XML document and loads into the system memory.

Figure 2-5: DOM parsing technique

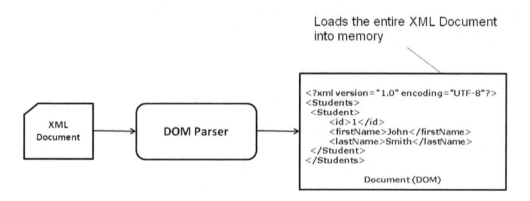

The steps required to parse an XML document using DOM API are given below:

- The application code creates an instance of "javax.xml.parsers.DocumentBuilderFactory" by calling its "newInstance()" method.
- The "newDocumentBuilder()" method of the "DocumentBuilderFactory" instance is used to get the DocumentBuilder object.
- The "DocumentBuilder" class is used to produce a DOM Document object. This document object contains the entire XML tree.

Listing 2-5 has a complete Java program that explains the parsing of an XML document using DOM API.

Listing 2-5: How to parse XML using DOM

```
public class SimpleDOMParser {
    public static void main(String[] args) {
        try {
            // Create a DocumentBuilderFactory
            DocumentBuilderFactory factory =
                    DocumentBuilderFactory.newInstance();

            // Use the factory to create a DocumentBuilder
            DocumentBuilder builder = factory.newDocumentBuilder();

            // Parse the XML file
            Document doc = builder.parse("students.xml");

            // Get a list of all nodes in the document

        } catch(Exception ex) {
            ex.printStackTrace();
        }
    }
}
```

Various methods of "org.w3c.dom.Document" interface are used to navigate through various nodes of the document. Once the instance of "javax.xml.parsers.DocumentBuilder" class is obtained, it can parse the XML with various input sources. The supported input sources are Files, URL's, Input Streams and SAX Input Sources.

Various methods of "org.w3c.dom.Document" interface are used to navigate through various nodes of the document. Once the instance of "javax.xml.parsers.DocumentBuilder" class is obtained, it can parse the XML document with various input sources. The supported input sources are files, URLs, input streams and SAX input sources.

Using the DocumentBuilder Class and Document Interface

How can one get the handle of the "javax.xml.parsers.DocumentBuilder" class and "org.w3c.dom.Document" interface? There are three ways to get the handle of the "DocumentBuilder" class and "Document" interface. The "parse()" method of a "DocumentBuilder" class is used to parse any valid XML document.

CASE 1:

The "newDocumentBuilder()" method of the "DocumentBuilderFactory" class is used to get the instance of DocumentBuilderFactory. The "parse()" method of the "DocumentBuilder" class is used to parse the XML document. The parsing of an XML document using this approach is given below.

```
public void parseXML() throws Exception {
    // Create a DocumentBuilderFactory
    DocumentBuilderFactory factory =
            DocumentBuilderFactory.newInstance();
```

```
    // Use the factory to create a DocumentBuilder
    DocumentBuilder builder = factory.newDocumentBuilder();

    // Parse the XML file
    Document doc = builder.parse("students.xml");

    /* This is the root of the document tree;
        Add your logic here to get the data from XML document */

}
```

CASE 2:

In this approach, a new instance of a DOM document object is created to build a DOM tree using the "newDocument()" method of the "DocumentBuilder" class. The creation of a document object using this approach is given below.

```
public void createEmptyDocument() throws Exception {
    DocumentBuilderFactory factory =
                    DocumentBuilderFactory.newInstance();
    DocumentBuilder builder = factory.newDocumentBuilder();

    /* Creates a new instance of a DOM Document object to build a DOM
        Tree. It is the root of the document tree  */
    Document doc = builder.newDocument();

    // Add your logic here to built an XML
}
```

CASE 3:

In this approach, a new instance is created of a DOM document object to build a DOM tree using the "getDOMImplementation()" method of the "DocumentBuilder" class. The creation of a document object using this approach is given below.

```
private void createXMLUsingDOM() throws Exception {
    DocumentBuilderFactory factory =
                    DocumentBuilderFactory.newInstance();
    DocumentBuilder builder = factory.newDocumentBuilder();
    DOMImplementation domImpl = builder.getDOMImplementation();
    Document document = domImpl.createDocument(null, "students",null);
    // gets the root element

    Element studentsElement = document.getDocumentElement();

    // Add your logic here to built an XML
}
```

The supported method signatures of a "parse()" method is given below. The supported input sources are files, URLs, input streams, and SAX input sources.

```
// Parsing a XML document using "File" input
Document doc = builder.parse("students.xml");

// Parsing a XML document using "InputSource" as input
Document doc1 = builder.parse(new InputSource("students.xml"));
```

```
// Parsing a XML document using "Stream" input
Document doc2 = builder.parse(new InputSource (new
ByteArrayInputStream(myXML.getBytes())));

// Parsing a XML document using URL input
URI uri = new URI("http://localhost:8080/wsbook/demo/student.xml");
Document doc3 = builder.parse(uri.toString());
```

Example 4: How to Parse an XML Document Using DOM2 API

The steps required to parse any valid XML document using DOM parser API are given below.

1. Identify the XML document to be parsed.
2. Create a Java data value object to populate XML data.
3. Create an application-specific parser class using DOM API.

The above-specified steps are described in the following sections.

Step 1: Identify the XML Document to Be Parsed.

Here, I will reuse the XML document that we created in our previous example.

Step 2: Create a Java Data Value Object to Populate XML Data.

The Java object used to populate the XML data is given below.

```
// Student.java
package com.learning.ws.jaxp;

public class Student {
    private String id;
    private String firstName;
    private String lastName;

    // Add getters and setters here
}
```

Step 3: Create an Application-Specific Parser Class Using DOM API.

This class will populate the data extracted from XML document into Java objects. The code provided below is used to parse the XML document and loads it into system memory.

```
DocumentBuilderFactory factory = DocumentBuilderFactory.newInstance();
DocumentBuilder builder = factory.newDocumentBuilder();
Document doc = builder.parse(new InputSource("students.xml"));
```

The code provided below is used to get the root element and its child elements. Iterate over the child elements to extract the data.

```
Node rootElement = doc.getDocumentElement();
NodeList nodeList = rootElement.getChildNodes();
for (int i = 0; i < nodeList.getLength(); i++) {
    // ...
```

```
}
```

Listing 2-6 has the complete Java program that demonstrates the xml parsing using DOM2 API.

Listing 2-6: How to parse an XML document using DOM2 API

```java
// SimpleDOMParser.java
package com.learning.ws.jaxp;

import org.w3c.dom.*;
import org.xml.sax.InputSource;
import javax.xml.parsers.DocumentBuilder;
import javax.xml.parsers.DocumentBuilderFactory;
import javax.xml.transform.TransformerFactory;
import javax.xml.transform.Source;
import javax.xml.transform.Transformer;
import javax.xml.transform.Result;
import javax.xml.transform.dom.DOMSource;
import javax.xml.transform.stream.StreamResult;
import java.util.ArrayList;

public class SimpleDOMParser {
    public static void main(String[] args) {
        try {
            SimpleDOMParser simpleDOMParser = new SimpleDOMParser();
            simpleDOMParser.parseXMLUsingDOM();
        } catch (Exception ex) {
            ex.printStackTrace();
        }
    }

    public void parseXMLUsingDOM() throws Exception {
        // Create a DocumentBuilderFactory
        DocumentBuilderFactory factory =
            DocumentBuilderFactory.newInstance();

        // Use the factory to create a DocumentBuilder
        DocumentBuilder builder = factory.newDocumentBuilder();

        // Parse the XML document
        Document doc = builder.parse(new InputSource("students.xml"));

        // Get the root element
        ArrayList<Student> studentList = new ArrayList<Student>();
        Student student = new Student();
        Node rootElement = doc.getDocumentElement();
        System.out.println("-- Root element name is --" +
                            rootElement.getNodeName());

        // Get all child nodes of a Root Node
        NodeList nodeList = rootElement.getChildNodes();
        for (int i = 0; i < nodeList.getLength(); i++) {
            Node node = nodeList.item(i);
            if (node.getNodeType() == Node.ELEMENT_NODE) {
                String elementName = node.getNodeName();
                System.out.println("-- element name is -- " +
                                    elementName);
```

```
                    student = new Student();
            if (elementName.equalsIgnoreCase("student")) {
                NodeList childNodeList = node.getChildNodes();

                // Looping through all child nodes
                for(int j=0;j<childNodeList.getLength(;j++){
                    Node childNode = childNodeList.item(j);
                    String childNodeName =
                        childNode.getNodeName();
                    String childNodeValue=
                        childNode.getTextContent();

                    /* Build your logic here to get the data
                    From XML document, populate
                    into Java objects.*/
                    if ("id".equalsIgnoreCase(childNodeName)) {
                        student.setId(childNodeValue);
                    } else if ("firstName".equalsIgnoreCase
                        (childNodeName)) {
                        student.setFirstName(childNodeValue);
                    } else if ("lastName".equalsIgnoreCase
                        (childNodeName)) {
                        student.setLastName(childNodeValue);
                    }
                }

                // Add each student object to a list
                studentList.add(student);
            }
        }
    }
}

    // Printing the student data on console
    for (Student studentObj : studentList) {
        System.out.println(" Id: " + studentObj.getId());
        System.out.println(" firstName: " + studentObj.getFirstName());
        System.out.println(" lastName: " + studentObj.getLastName());
    }
}
```

Run the `SimpleDOMParser` class to view the output on the console. The output is shown below.

```
Id: 1
firstName: John
lastName: Smith

Id: 2
firstName: Steve
lastName: Day

Id: 3
firstName: Joe
lastName: Liner
```

Example 5: How to Create an XML Document Using DOM2 API

The steps required for generating an XML document using DOM API is given below.

1. What is the structure of the XML document to be created?
2. Write an XML generator class using DOM API.

The above-specified steps are described in the following sections.

Step 1: What Is the Structure of the XML Document to Be Created?

The structure of an XML document is given below. It is an XML document that represents one student.

```
<?xml version="1.0" encoding="UTF-8" standalone="no"?>
<students>
    <student>
        <id>1</id>
        <firstName>John</firstName>
        <lastName>Smith</lastName>
    </student>
</students>
```

Step 2: Write an XML Generator Class using DOM API

The DOM interface "org.w3c.dom.Document" defines various methods used to generate any XML document. Listing 2-6 has the complete Java program that demonstrates the xml generation using DOM2 API.

Listing 2-6: How to create an XML document using DOM2 API

```java
// SimpleDOMBuilder.java
package com.learning.ws.jaxp;

import org.w3c.dom.Document;
Import org.w3c.dom.Element;
import org.w3c.dom.NodeList;
import org.w3c.dom.Node;
import org.xml.sax.InputSource;
import javax.xml.parsers.DocumentBuilder;
import javax.xml.parsers.DocumentBuilderFactory;
import java.util.ArrayList;

public class SimpleDOMBuilder {
    public static void main(String[] args) {
        try {
            SimpleDOMBuilder simpleDOMBuilder =
                    new SimpleDOMBuilder ();
            simpleDOMParser.createXMLUsingDOM();
        } catch(Exception ex) {
            ex.printStackTrace();
        }
    }

private void createXMLUsingDOM() throws Exception {
```

```
DocumentBuilderFactory factory =
     DocumentBuilderFactory.newInstance();
DocumentBuilder builder = factory.newDocumentBuilder();
DOMImplementation domImpl = builder.getDOMImplementation();
Document document = domImpl.createDocument(null, "students",null);

// Getting the root element
Element studentsElement = document.getDocumentElement();

// Append child elements to the root element
Element studentElement = document.createElement("student");
studentsElement.appendChild(studentElement);

// Append other child elements and set data to it
Element idElement = document.createElement("id");
idElement.setTextContent("1");
studentElement.appendChild(idElement);

Element firstNameElement = document.createElement("firstName");
     firstNameElement.setTextContent("John");
     studentElement.appendChild(firstNameElement);

     Element lastNameElement = document.createElement("lastName");
     lastNameElement.setTextContent("Smith");
     studentElement.appendChild(lastNameElement);

     // Printing the generated XML on console.
     TransformerFactory tranFactory =
                    TransformerFactory.newInstance();
     Transformer aTransformer = tranFactory.newTransformer();
     Source src = new DOMSource(document);
     Result dest = new StreamResult(System.out);
     aTransformer.transform(src, dest);
   }
}
```

Comparison between DOM and SAX

The following table summarizes the comparison between the various technical features of SAX and DOM parsers. Which one to use SAX or DOM? Certainly there is no hard and fast rule; it primarily depends on the application requirement and business need. This section will help you to compare the features, so make your own judgment based on the requirement.

SAX	DOM
SAX is an event-based programming model. For each generated event, a portion of the XML document is parsed.	DOM specification defines a tree-based hierarchical structure for navigating the XML documents.
It does not load the entire document; only a portion of the XML is parsed based on the event generated.	The entire document tree is loaded into the memory.
The memory usage is less because the	If the document size is very large, it

entire document is not loaded into memory.	takes more memory. It uses system memory if the client loads the document.
It is primarily used for parsing the XML documents. Used only for reading XML.	Can be used for both read and write the XML documents.
The size of the XML document is not a constraint. Can be used for small to very big XML documents.	The size of the document depends on system memory. So it is not recommended to parse large documents that consume a lot of memory.
The XML document is parsed sequentially in forward direction from top to bottom. It has to reparse the entire document to get the previously accessed data.	Entire document is loaded into memory, so it is possible edit any element of the XML document.
The main interface used for the SAX parser implements is "org.xml.sax.ContentHandler." This interface has defined all methods that correspond to each generated client event.	The main interface used for the DOM parser implementation is "org.w3c.dom.Document." Various methods of the document interface are used for reading and writing XML documents.

Streaming API for XML (StAX)

Another Java API available for parsing and writing XML documents in the JAXP family is Streaming API for XML (StAX). The points provided below explain the use and capabilities of a StAX parsing technique.

- StAX is an event-based Java API used for both reading and writing of XML documents.
- It uses the pull-based technique to parse XML documents.
- The client code invokes a StAX parser to get the required data from XML documents.
- StAX supports bidirectional parsing, and it can read multiple documents in single thread. StAX was developed to address some of the SAX and DOM limitations.

What is the difference between StAX1 and StAX2?

- StAX1—The core initial version was released by BEA with support from SUN (JSR-173)
- StAX2—This is the extension to the StAX1. Various new interfaces such as "XMLEventReader" and "XMLEventWriter" have been added to provide additional features to read and write XML documents.

The primary packages used for StAX API are given below. These packages hold the different classes of the StAX API.

- `javax.xml.stream`—This package defines the core StAX interfaces used for reading and writing XML.
- `javax.xml.transform.stax`—This package provides StAX-specific transformation APIs.

The classes and interfaces defined in the "javax.xml.stream" package are used to read, write, and validate the XML documents. This package contains the classes and interfaces provided below.

- `EventFilter`—This interface declares a simple filter interface that one can create to filter XMLEventReaders.
- `Location`—Provides information on the location of an event.
- `StreamFilter`—This interface declares a simple filter interface that one can create to filter XMLStreamReaders.
- `XMLEventReader`—This is the top-level interface for parsing XML events.
- `XMLEventWriter`—This is the top-level interface for writing XML documents.
- `XMLReporter`—This interface is used to report nonfatal errors.
- `XMLResolver`—This interface is used to resolve resources during an XML parse.
- `XMLStreamConstants`—This interface declares the constants used in this API.
- `XMLStreamReader`—The XMLStreamReader interface allows forward, read-only access to XML.
- `XMLStreamWriter`—The XMLStreamWriter interface specifies how to write XML.
- `XMLEventFactory`—This interface defines a utility class for creating instances of XMLEvents
- `XMLInputFactory`—This defines an abstract implementation of a factory for getting streams.
- `XMLOutputFactory`—This defines an abstract implementation of a factory for getting `XMLEventWriters` and XMLStreamWriters.

Figure 2-6 explains the StAX parsing of an XML document.

Figure 2-6: StAX parsing technique

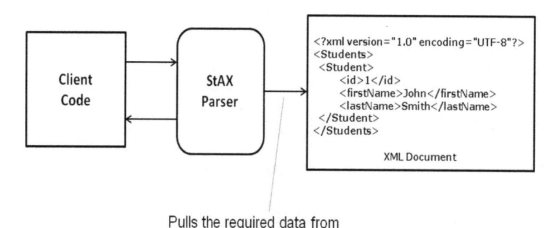

Pulls the required data from
an XML document based on the event

The top-level interface used for reading XML documents using StAX API is "XMLEventReader." This class is used to iterate over the entire XML document and get the required data from XML document. The defined methods of the "XMLEventReader" interface and their significance are given below.

```
public interface XMLEventReader extends Iterator {
    // Get the next XMLEvent
    XMLEvent nextEvent() throws XMLStreamException;

    // Check if there are more events.
```

```
      boolean hasNext();

      // Check the next XMLEvent without reading it from the stream.
      XMLEvent peek() throws XMLStreamException;

      // Reads the content of a text-only element
      String getElementText() throws XMLStreamException;

      /* Skips any insignificant space events until a START_ELEMENT or
          END_ELEMENT is reached.*/
      XMLEvent nextTag() throws XMLStreamException;

      /* Get the value of a feature/property from the underlying
      Implementation */
      Object getProperty(java.lang.String name) throws
                                    IllegalArgumentException;

      // Frees any resources associated with this Reader.
      void close() throws XMLStreamException;
}
```

Similarly, the top-level interface used for writing XML documents is "XMLEventWriter." The significance of each method of the "XMLEventWriter" class is explained with inline comments.

```
public interface XMLEventWriter {
      // Add an event to the output stream
      void add(XMLEvent event)

      // Adds an entire stream to an output stream
      void add(XMLEventReader reader)

      /* Close this writer and free any resources associated with the
          writer.*/
      void close() throws XMLStreamException;

      // Write any cached data to the underlying output mechanism.
      void flush() throws XMLStreamException;

      // few more methods for namespaces, attributes, etc.
}
```

How to Use XMLEventReader and XMLEventWriter Interfaces

The "XMLEventReader" interface is used for reading XML documents. It iterates over the entire XML document and gets the required data from XML. The instance of "XMLEventReader" is obtained by calling the "createXMLEventReader()" method of "XMLInputFactory." Iterate over the XML document using the "hasNext()" method of the "XMLEventReader" interface. The use of "XMLEventReader" for reading an XML document is given below.

```
XMLInputFactory factory = XMLInputFactory.newInstance();
// Setup a new event reader
XMLEventReader eventReader = factory.createXMLEventReader(new
FileInputStream("students.xml"));
while(eventReader.hasNext()) {
      // Write your logic here
```

```
}
```

The "XMLEventWriter" interface is used for writing XML documents. The instance of "XMLEventWriter" is obtained by calling the "createXMLEventWriter()" method of "XMLEventFactory." It will write the generated XML into a document using the "add()" method of "XMLEventWriter." The use of "XMLEventWriter" for generating an XML document is given below.

```
XMLOutputFactory factory  = XMLOutputFactory.newInstance();
XMLEventFactory  xmlEventFactory = XMLEventFactory.newInstance();
XMLEventWriter writer = factory.createXMLEventWriter(new
FileWriter("C:\\output.xml"));
StartDocument startDocument = xmlEventFactory.createStartDocument("UTF-
8", "1.0");
writer.add(startDocument);
```

The below given code examples demonstrates the parsing and XML creating using StAX API.

Example 6: How to Parse an XML Document Using StAX API

The steps required to parse any valid XML document using StAX parser API are given below.

1. Identify the XML document to be parsed.
2. Create a Java data value object to populate XML data.
3. Create an application-specific parser class using StAX API.

The above-specified steps are described in the following sections.

Step 1: Identify the XML Document to Be Parsed.

Here, we will reuse the XML document we created in our previous example.

Step 2: Create a Java Data Value Object to Populate XML Data.

The Java object used to populate the XML data is given below.

```
// Student.java
package com.learning.ws.jaxp;

public class Student {
    private String id;
    private String firstName;
    private String lastName;

    // Add getters and setters here
}
```

Step 3: Create an Application-Specific Parser Class Using StAX API.

The "XMLEventReader" class methods are used to identify the type of event generated. The type of element data that it pulls from the XML document depends on the type of event generated. The element data from the XML document is used to populate the Java object.

The mapping between the XML document and Java object is shown in Figure 2-7. The StAX provided "XMLEventReader" class pulls the required data from XML document based on the client generated event. This data is used to populate the Java object.

Figure 2-7: Mapping between XML and Java class

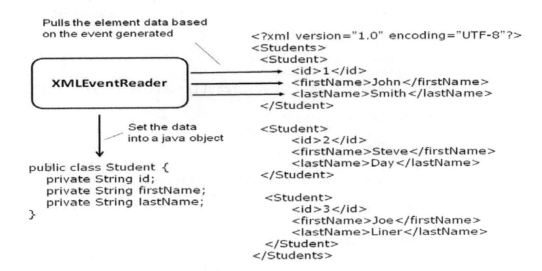

Listing 2-8 has the complete Java code that demonstrates the parsing of an XML document using StAX API. It reads the data from each <Student/> element and sets the values into a Java object.

Listing 2-8: How to parse an XML document using StAX API

```java
// SimpleStaXParser.java
package com.learning.ws.jaxp;

import javax.xml.stream.*;
import javax.xml.stream.events.*;
import java.util.*;
import java.io.FileInputStream;

public class SimpleStaXParser {
    public static void main(String[] args) {
        try {
            SimpleStaXParser simpleStaXParser = new SimpleStaXParser();
            List<Student> studentList =
            simpleStaXParser.getStudentData();

            // Printing the student data on console
            for(Student studentObj : studentList) {
                System.out.println(" Id: " + studentObj.getId());
                System.out.println(" firstName: " +
                            studentObj.getFirstName());
                System.out.println(" lastName: " +
                            studentObj.getLastName());
            }
        } catch (Exception ex) {
            ex.printStackTrace();
        }
    }

    public List<Student> getStudentData() throws Exception {
        // First create a new XMLInputFactory
        XMLInputFactory factory = XMLInputFactory.newInstance();
```

```java
        // Setup a new eventReader
        XMLEventReader eventReader = factory.createXMLEventReader(
            new FileInputStream("C:/students.xml"));

        // List used to add student objects
        Student student = null;
        List<Student> studentsList = new ArrayList<Student>();

        while (eventReader.hasNext()) {
            // Gets the various types of StAX events.
            XMLEvent event = eventReader.nextEvent();
            if (event.getEventType() == XMLEvent.START_ELEMENT) {
                StartElement startElement = event.asStartElement();

                /* If it is a student element we create a student object
                set the data */
                If (startElement.getName().getLocalPart().
                              equalsIgnoreCase("student")) {
                    student = new Student();
                }

                // get data from id element
                if (startElement.getName().getLocalPart().equals("id")) {
                    event = eventReader.nextEvent();
                    student.setId(event.asCharacters().getData());
                    continue;
                }

                // get data from first name element
                if (event.asStartElement().getName().getLocalPart().
                              equals("firstName")) {
                    event = eventReader.nextEvent();
                    student.setFirstName(event.asCharacters().getData());
                    continue;
                }

                // get data from last name element
                if (event.asStartElement().getName().getLocalPart().
                              equals("lastName")) {
                    event = eventReader.nextEvent();
                    student.setLastName(event.asCharacters().getData());
                    continue;
                }
            }

            // Reached the end of student element,add this to the list.
            if(event.getEventType() == XMLEvent.END_ELEMENT) {
                EndElement endElement = event.asEndElement();
                if (endElement.getName().getLocalPart().
                          equalsIgnoreCase("student")) {
                    studentsList.add(student);
                }
            }
        }
        return studentsList;
    }
}
```

Example 7: How to Create an XML Document Using StAX API

The steps required to generate an XML document using StAX API are given below.

1.   What is the structure of the XML document to be created?
2.   Write an XML generator class using StAX API.

The above-specified steps are described in the following sections.

Step 1: What Is the Structure of the XML Document to Be Created?

The structure of the XML document is given below. It is an XML document that represents one student.

```
<?xml version="1.0" encoding="UTF-8" standalone="no"?>
<students>
    <student>
        <id>1</id>
        <firstName>John</firstName>
        <lastName>Smith</lastName>
    </student>
</students>
```

Step 2: Write a XML Generator Class using StAX API

The StAX API-provided "XMLEventWriter" class is used to generate XML documents. Listing 2-9 has the complete Java code that demonstrates the XML generation using StAX API. This code creates the above-provided XML document.

Listing 2-9: How to create an XML document using StAX API

```java
// SimpleStaXParser.java
package com.learning.ws.jaxp;

import javax.xml.stream.*;
import javax.xml.stream.events.*;
import java.util.List;
import java.util.ArrayList;
import java.io.FileInputStream;
import java.io.FileWriter;

public class SimpleStaXParser {
    public static void main(String[] args) {
        try {
            SimpleStaXParser simpleStaXParser = new SimpleStaXParser();

            // Build the XML document using StAX
            simpleStaXParser.buidXMLUsingStax();
        } catch(Exception ex) {
            ex.printStackTrace();
        }
    }

    private void buidXMLUsingStax() throws Exception {
        XMLOutputFactory factory = XMLOutputFactory.newInstance();
```

```java
XMLEventFactory xmlEventFactory =
            XMLEventFactory.newInstance();

XMLEventWriter writer = factory.createXMLEventWriter(new
                       FileWriter("C:\\output.xml"));
StartDocument startDocument =
    xmlEventFactory.createStartDocument("UTF-8", "1.0");
writer.add(startDocument);

// It creates a root element
StartElement rootElement =
        xmlEventFactory.createStartElement("","","students");
writer.add(rootElement);

// It creates an immediate child to root element
StartElement startElement =
        xmlEventFactory.createStartElement("", "", "student");
writer.add(startElement);

// It creates an id element
StartElement idStartElement =
        xmlEventFactory.createStartElement("", "", "id");
writer.add(idStartElement);
Characters id = xmlEventFactory.createCharacters("1");
writer.add(id);
EndElement idEndElement = xmlEventFactory.createEndElement("",
                              "", "id");
writer.add(idEndElement);

// It creates a firstName element
StartElement firstNameStartElement =
    xmlEventFactory.createStartElement("", "", "firstName");
writer.add(firstNameStartElement);
Characters firstName =
            xmlEventFactory.createCharacters("John");
writer.add(firstName);
EndElement firstNameEndElement =
        xmlEventFactory.createEndElement("", "", "firstName");
writer.add(firstNameEndElement);

// It creates a lastName element
StartElement lastNameStartElement =
    xmlEventFactory.createStartElement("", "", "lastName");
writer.add(lastNameStartElement);
Characters lastName =
        xmlEventFactory.createCharacters("Smith");
writer.add(lastName);
EndElement lastNameEndElement =
        xmlEventFactory.createEndElement("", "", "lastName");
writer.add(lastNameEndElement);

writer.flush();
writer.close();
    }
}
```

Comparison between SAX and StAX

The following table summarizes the comparison between the various technical features of SAX and StAX parsers.

StAX	SAX
It uses the pull-based streaming technique to parse XML documents.	It uses the push-based streaming technique to parse the XML documents.
It is used for both reading and writing XML documents.	It is used to read only.
It supports bidirectional and random access.	It supports forward-only sequential access.
Event-based API.	Event-based API; its primary purpose is to read only.
It is possible to skip or ignore the unnecessary XML elements, such as comments.	The entire document is parsed sequentially from beginning to end.
It requires extensions for XML validation.	SAX API has good support for XML validation.

Test Yourself

1. Which of the following Java APIs are considered part of JAXP?
   a) SAX, SAX2, DOM, and JAXB
   b) SAX, SAX2, DOM, and StAX
   c) JAXP,DOM, SAX, and JAXR
   d) JAX-RS, DOM, JAX-RPC, and WSDL
   e) SAAJ, SOAP, DOM, and JAX-WS

2. Which of the snippet of code provided below is correct to parse an XML document using SAX API? Select all correct answers.
   a)
```
SAXParserFactory parserFactory = SAXParserFactory.newInstance();
SAXParser saxParser = parserFactory.newSAXParser();
XMLReader xmlReader = saxParser.getXMLReader();
xmlReader.setContentHandler(xmlHandler);
xmlReader.parse("students.xml");
```

   b)
```
SAXParserFactory parserFactory = SAXParserFactory.newInstance();
XMLReader xmlReader = parserFactory.getXMLReader();
saxParser.setContentHandler(xmlHandler);
saxParser.parse("students.xml");
```

   c)
```
XMLReader xmlReader = XMLReaderFactory.createXMLReader();
xmlReader.setContentHandler(xmlHandler);
xmlReader.readXml("students.xml");
```

   d)

```
SAXParserFactory parserFactory = new SAXParserFactory;
SAXParser saxParser = parserFactory.newSAXParser();
XMLReader xmlReader = saxParser.getXMLReader();
xmlReader.setContentHandler(xmlHandler);
xmlReader.parse("students.xml");
```

e)
```
XMLReader xmlReader = XMLReaderFactory.newXMLReader();
xmlReader.setContentHandler(xmlHandler);
xmlReader.parse("students.xml");
```

3. Select all correct answers. Which of the following code snippets is correct to write an XML document using DOM API?

a)
```
DocumentBuilderFactory factory = DocumentBuilderFactory.newInstance();
DocumentBuilder builder = factory.newDocumentBuilder();
Document doc = builder.newDocument();
```

b)
```
DocumentBuilderFactory factory = new DocumentBuilderFactory();
DocumentBuilder builder = factory.newDocumentBuilder();
DOMImplementation domImpl = builder.getDOMImplementation();
Document document = domImpl.createDocument(null, "students," null);
```

c)
```
DocumentBuilderFactory factory = DocumentBuilderFactory.newInstance();
DocumentBuilder builder = factory.newDocumentBuilder();
DOMImplementation domImpl = builder.getDOMImplementation();
Document document = domImpl.createDocument(null, "students," null);
```

d)
```
DocumentBuilderFactory factory = new DocumentBuilderFactory();
DocumentBuilder builder = factory.newDocumentBuilder();
Document doc = builder.newDocument();
```

e)
```
DocumentBuilderFactory factory = DocumentBuilderFactory.newInstance();
DocumentBuilder builder = factory.newDocumentBuilder();
Document document = builder.createDocument(null, "students", null);
```

4. Which of the following statements is valid w.r.t. to SAX and StAX?
   a) Both SAX and StAX are event-based streaming APIs; the only difference is that StAX can be used for reading and writing the XML documents, but SAX is used only for reading.
   b) SAX loads the entire document in memory, while StAX does not.
   c) SAX uses the push-based technique, whereas StAX uses the pull-based technique for parsing.
   d) SAX is used for JAX-RPC, and StAX is used for JAX-WS.
   e) All are valid statements.

5. What are the supported input sources used to parse an XML document using SAX and DOM?
   a) Files
   b) Input streams

c) URLs
d) SAX input sources
e) All of the above

6. What are the primary interfaces used for reading and writing XML documents using Streaming API for XML?
a) Input Reader and OutputWriter
b) StreamReader and StreamWriter
c) XMLEventReader and XMLEventWriter
d) XMLInputFactory and XMLOutputFactory
e) EventFilter and StreamFilter

7. Referring to the diagram provided below Figure 2-8, which of the following statements is valid?

Figure 2-8: XML parsing

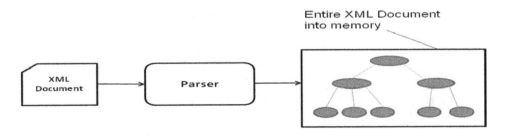

a) This diagram best explains the SAX parsing of an XML document.
b) This diagram best explains the StAX parsing of an XML document.
c) This diagram best explains the DOM parsing of an XML document. The entire XML tree is loaded into the memory so that the client can manipulate the required portions of the XML.
d) None of the parsers is used. The tree structure is not allowed to parse XML documents.
e) All are correct.

8. For the given scenario explained below, which API do you recommend for parsing an XML document?
Your application wants to change the XML tree frequently but also wants to store it for future use.
a) SAX
b) DOM
c) DOM4J
d) JAXP
e) JAXR

9. What is the significance of the "org.xml.sax.helpers.DefaultHandler" class while parsing an XML document?
a) It is used for reading, writing, manipulating, and validating the XML documents.
b) It is an adaptor class for the ContentHandler interface.
c) It is used for storing XML data in any persistent store.
d) It has an empty implementation of the methods defined in the ContentHandler class.
e) It is not related to SAX; it is used in StAX.

10. Insert "YES" and "NO" into the appropriate locations in this table. YES means it supports the given feature, and NO means it does not support that feature.

Statement	SAX	StAX	DOM
Event-based technique used for parsing XML documents			
Used for reading and writing XML documents			
Provides an iterator- and cursor-based API			
Preferred for parsing very large documents.			

11. Which of the following API is most suitable for the pull-based parsing technique?

   a) SAX
   b) SAX2
   c) DOM
   d) DOM2
   e) StAX

Answers to Test Yourself

1. The correct answer is B—SAX, DOM, and StAX are part of the JAXP specification.

2. The correct answers are A and C. Choices B, D, and E do not compile.

3. The correct answers are A and C. "B" and "D" are incorrect because the class "DocumentBuilderFactory" is abstract, so it cannot be instantiated. E is incorrect because there is no "createDocument()" method in the builder class.

4. The correct answers are A and C. Only DOM loads the entire XML document into memory.

5. The correct answer is E. All are valid input sources.

6. The correct answer is C. The StAX2-provided top level interfaces are XMLEventReader and XMLEventWriter

7. The correct answer is C. The entire tree structure is loaded into memory while using DOM parsers.

8. The correct answer is B. DOM is right choice for the given scenario.

9. The correct answers are B and D. The DefultHandler class is an adapter to the ContentHandler interface.

10. The table provided below shows the correct YES and NO responses.

Statement	SAX	StAX	DOM
Event-based technique used for parsing XML documents	YES	YES	NO

Used for reading and writing XML documents	NO	YES	YES
Provides an iterator- and cursor-based API	NO	YES	NO
Preferred for parsing very large documents	YES	YES	NO

11. The correct answer is E.

Chapter 3. DOM4J

There are several open source frameworks available for reading, writing, validating and manipulating XML documents. Majority of these frameworks provide a good support with Java API. They are alternative to SAX and DOM. There is no hard and fast rule which framework to be used in your application; it is totally depends on the application requirement, developers comfort and their prior experience with it. This chapter illustrates the complete use of Document Object Model for Java (Dom4j) framework in application development. The commonly used open-source frameworks currently available in the market for XML processing are listed below.

- Dom4j
- JDOM
- XMLBeans
- Xerces
- XStream
- Woodstox
- AXIOM

All the above-specified frameworks provide similar features; none is superior to the others. As a Web Services developer, it is mandatory to have knowledge of at least one XML framework. Any of these frameworks can be used for reading and writing XML documents.

Approximately 20 frameworks are available for parsing XML documents. Some are vendor specific, and some are open-source, but all provide similar features. These frameworks provide higher-level APIs for processing XML documents.

In this chapter will discuss the following topics:

- How to read, parse, create, write, and compare XML documents using Dom4j
- How to plug in SAX and DOM parses with Dom4j
- Aspects of Dom4j API such as Dom4j helper classes, Dom4j iterator API, and so forth
- How to use Dom4j XPath expressions
- The technical capabilities of Dom4j API

Dom4j is an open-source Java library compatible with JAXP standards. The Dom4j provides a Java API for reading and writing XML documents, and it supports SAX and DOM. The following points summarize the available features of the Dom4j framework.

- Simple and easy-to-use API for reading and writing XML documents
- Easy to plug in with SAX and DOM parsers
- Designed for the Java platform and supports the Java Collections framework
- XPath support for navigation of large XML documents
- Easy to convert API from Java String to XML document and vice versa
- Hides the complexities of JAXP API and provides higher-level API for reading and writing XML documents

Dom4j API is defined in the following core packages. This chapter illustrates the code examples using the classes available in these packages.

- org.dom4j—Defines the Dom4j interfaces together with helper classes.
- org.dom4j.io—Provides input and output via SAX and DOM along with writing Dom4j objects to streams as XML text
- org.dom4j.util—A collection of utility classes for the Dom4j API

How to Plug in the SAX Parser with Dom4j

The Dom4j provides plug-in support for SAX-based parsers. It has the "SAXReader" class, which creates a Dom4j tree object from SAX parsing events. Developers can plug in any JAXP-compatible SAX parser using the Dom4j API. By default, Dom4j uses its own SAX parser unless specifically configured otherwise. Create an instance of the "SAXReader" class and call the "read()" method to get the Dom4j document tree object. Listing 3-1 demonstrates the use of the Dom4j SAX parsing technique.

Listing 3-1: How to plug in SAX parser with Dom4j

```java
// Dom4JExample.java
package com.learning.ws.dom4j;

import org.dom4j.io.SAXReader;
import org.dom4j.Document;
import org.dom4j.Element;
import org.dom4j.Node;
import java.io.*;

public class Dom4JExample {
    public static void main(String[] args) {
        try {
            Dom4JExample dom4j = new Dom4JExample();
            Document document = dom4j. parseXMLUsingSAX();
        } catch (Exception ex) {
            ex.printStackTrace();
        }
    }

    public Document parseXMLUsingSAX() throws Exception {
        // Create an instance of SAXReader class, call read() method
        SAXReader reader = new SAXReader();
        Document document = reader.read(new File("C:\\students.xml"));
        String xmlAsString = document.asXML();

        // Printing the XML document as String
        System.out.println(xmlAsString);
        return document;
    }
}
```

How to Plug in the DOM Parser with Dom4j

Dom4j provides plug-in support for DOM-based parsers. It has a "DOMReader" class; it converts the w3c DOM document into a Dom4j document tree. Create an instance of the "DOMReader" class, and call the "read()" method to get the Dom4j document tree object. Listing 3-2 demonstrates the use of the Dom4j DOM parsing technique.

Listing 3-2: How to plug in DOM parser with Dom4j

```java
// Dom4JExample.java
package com.learning.ws.dom4j;

import org.dom4j.io.DOMReader;
import org.dom4j.Document;
import org.dom4j.Element;
import org.dom4j.Node;
import javax.xml.parsers.DocumentBuilderFactory;
import javax.xml.parsers.DocumentBuilder;
import java.io.*;

public class Dom4JExample {
    public static void main(String[] args) {
        try {
            Dom4JExample dom4j = new Dom4JExample();
            Document document = dom4j. parseXMLUsingDOM ();
        } catch (Exception ex) {
            ex.printStackTrace();
        }
    }

    public Document parseXMLUsingDOM() throws Exception {
        // Create a w3c DOM document
        DocumentBuilderFactory factory =
                DocumentBuilderFactory.newInstance();
            DocumentBuilder builder = factory.newDocumentBuilder();
            org.w3c.dom.Document w3cDOMDocument =
                    builder.parse(new File("C:\\students.xml"));

        // Converts the w3c DOM document to dom4j Document.
        DOMReader reader = new DOMReader();
        org.dom4j.Document document = reader.read(w3cDOMDocument);

        // Printing the XML document as String
        String xmlAsString = document.asXML();
        System.out.println(xmlAsString);
        return document;
    }
}
```

How to Load and Parse XML Documents Using Dom4j

The primary requirement for any XML-based parsing framework is that it be able to read and obtain data from XML documents. Dom4j provides a simple API to load, parse, and navigate in any XML file. A document can be navigated using Dom4j Java-based iterators to obtain any required element data of a document. There is an "elementIterator(…)" method of the "Element" class used for iterating any XML node. Listing 3-3 has the complete Java code that demonstrates how to load and obtain data from an XML document and set it into Java bean objects.

Listing 3-3: How to load and parse XML documents using Dom4j

```java
// Dom4JExample.java
package com.learning.ws.dom4j;

import org.dom4j.io.SAXReader;
import org.dom4j.Document;
import org.dom4j.Element;
import org.dom4j.Node;
import java.io.*;
import java.util.*;

public class Dom4JExample {
    public static void main(String[] args) {
        try {
            Dom4JExample dom4j = new Dom4JExample();
            dom4j.loadAndParseXML();
        } catch (Exception ex) {
            ex.printStackTrace();
        }
    }

    public void loadAndParseXML() throws Exception {
        // Read the XML document
        SAXReader reader = new SAXReader();
        Document document = reader.read(new File("C:\\students.xml"));

        // Getting the root element of the XML document
        Element root = document.getRootElement();

        Student student = null;
        List<Student> studentList = new ArrayList<Student>();

        // Parse the entire document using elementIterator()
        for(Iterator i = root.elementIterator(); i.hasNext(); ) {
            Element element = (Element) i.next();
            if("Student".equalsIgnoreCase(element.getName())) {
                student = new Student();
            }

            // Obtain the required data from the XML, set into java bean
            for(int j = 0, size = element.nodeCount(); j < size; j++ ) {
                Node node = (Node) element.node(j);
                if(node instanceof Element) {
                    if("id".equalsIgnoreCase(node.getName())) {
                        student.setId(node.getText());
                    }
                    if("firstName".equalsIgnoreCase(node.getName())) {
                        student.setFirstName(node.getText());
                    }
                    if("lastName".equalsIgnoreCase(node.getName())) {
                        student.setLastName(node.getText());
                    }
                }
            }

            // Add the student object to a list
```

```
            studentList.add(student);
        }

        // Priting the student data on console
        for(Student studentObj : studentList) {
            System.out.println(" Id: " + studentObj.getId());
            System.out.println(" firstName: " +
                        studentObj.getFirstName());
            System.out.println(" lastName: " +
                        studentObj.getLastName());
        }
    }
}
```

How to Compare Two XML Documents

Dom4j utilities are available in the "org.dom4j.util" package. The common requirement in SOA and Web Services is that the system be able to check the equality of any two nodes of XML documents. In the early days, it was tedious to compare XML documents. However, now the Dom4j utilities package provides a "NodeComparator" class that is capable of comparing the node instances for equality based on their values. Listing 3-4 has the complete Java code that illustrates how to compare two XML documents using the "compare()" method of the "NodeComparator" class.

Listing 3-4: How to compare XML documents using Dom4j

```
// Dom4JExample.java
package com.learning.ws.dom4j;

import org.dom4j.io.SAXReader;
import org.dom4j.Document;
import org.dom4j.DocumentHelper;
import org.dom4j.util.NodeComparator;
import java.io.*;

public class Dom4JExample {
    public static void main(String[] args) {
        try {
            Dom4JExample dom4j = new Dom4JExample();
            dom4j.compareXMLDocuments();
        } catch (Exception ex) {
            ex.printStackTrace();
        }
    }

    public void compareXMLDocuments() throws Exception {
        SAXReader reader = new SAXReader();
        // Read the first document
        Document document1=reader.read(new File("C:\\students1.xml"));

        // Read the second document
        Document document2=reader.read(new File("C:\\students2.xml"));

        // Comparing two documents for equality
        NodeComparator comparator = new NodeComparator();
```

```
            if(comparator.compare(document1, document2) == 0) {
                System.out.println("Both documents are identical.");
            } else {
                System.out.println("Both documents are different.");
            }
        }
    }
}
```

How to Use Dom4j XPath Expressions

Dom4j supports XPath and XSLT transformations. XPath is a technique used for finding required information in an XML document. It uses Dom4j XPath expressions to navigate in any complex XML document. Listing 3-5 has the complete Java code that illustrates how to find and get the text of the <lastName/> element from the "students.xml" file.

Listing 3-5: How to use Dom4j XPath expressions

```java
// Dom4JExample.java
package com.learning.ws.dom4j;

import org.dom4j.io.SAXReader;
import org.dom4j.Document;
import org.dom4j.Element;
import org.dom4j.Node;
import java.io.*;
import java.util.*;

public class Dom4JExample {
    public static void main(String[] args) {
        try {
            Dom4JExample dom4j = new Dom4JExample();
            dom4j.dom4jXPathTest();
        } catch (Exception ex) {
            ex.printStackTrace();
        }
    }

    public void dom4jXPathTest() throws Exception {
        // Read the document
        SAXReader reader = new SAXReader();
        Document document = reader.read(new File("C:\\students.xml"));

        // Printing the list size
        List list = document.selectNodes("//Students");
        System.out.println("------ list ----" + list.size());

        /* Printing the value of tag element lastName -
            /Students/Student/lastName   */
        Node node = document.selectSingleNode("//Students/Student");
        String name = node.valueOf("lastName");
        System.out.println("------ name ----" + name);
    }
}
```

How to Create and Write XML Documents Using Dom4j

Dom4j provides a simple and flexible API for creating and writing XML documents. The Dom4j "XMLWriter" class is used for writing XML into any file; it takes Dom4j documents and formats them to a stream of XML. There are "write()" methods available to write XML documents in many standard formats. The following example illustrates the use of the "XMLWriter" class.

The "parseText(...)" method of the "DocumentHelper" class is used to convert the XML string to a Dom4j document object; the "asXML()" method of the Dom4j "Document" object converts the Dom4j document object to an XML string.

The code snippet below converts the Dom4j document object to an XML string.

```
String xmlString = document.asXML();
System.out.println(xmlString);
```

Similarly, the following code converts the XML string to a Dom4j document.

```
Document documentFromXML = DocumentHelper.parseText(xmlString);
```

Listing 3-6 has the complete Java code that generates an XML document with the given input.

Listing 3-6: How to create XML documents using Dom4j API

```java
// Dom4JExample.java
package com.learning.ws.dom4j;

import org.dom4j.io.SAXReader;
import org.dom4j.io.DOMReader;
import org.dom4j.io.XMLWriter;
import org.dom4j.Document;
import org.dom4j.Element;
import org.dom4j.Node;
import org.dom4j.DocumentHelper;
import org.dom4j.util.NodeComparator;
import javax.xml.parsers.DocumentBuilderFactory;
import javax.xml.parsers.DocumentBuilder;
import java.io.*;
import java.util.*;

public class Dom4JExample {
    public static void main(String[] args) {
        try {
            Dom4JExample dom4j = new Dom4JExample();
            dom4j.createXMLUsingDom4j();
        } catch (Exception ex) {
            ex.printStackTrace();
        }
    }

    public void createXMLUsingDom4j() throws Exception {
        Document document = DocumentHelper.createDocument();
        Element rootElement = document.addElement("students");
        Element studentElement = rootElement.addElement("Student");
        studentElement.addElement("id").addAttribute("country",
```

```
            "usa").addText("1");
        studentElement.addElement("firstName").addText("John");
        studentElement.addElement("lastName").addText("Smith");

        /* Converts the dm4j document to XML string and print on
             Consolev */
        String xmlString = document.asXML();
        System.out.println(xmlString);

        // Convert from String to XML Document
        Document documentFromXML = DocumentHelper.parseText(xmlString);

        // Print the document to output.xml file
        XMLWriter writer = new XMLWriter(new
                FileWriter("c:\\output.xml"));
        writer.write(document);
        writer.close();
    }
}
```

Run the above program and view the output on the console. The XML provided below is generated.

```
<?xml version="1.0" encoding="UTF-8"?>
<students>
  <Student>
    <id country="usa">1</id>
    <firstName>John</firstName>
    <lastName>Smith</lastName>
  </Student>
</students>
```

Test yourself – Objective Type Questions

1. Select all of the correct answers. Which of the following is part of the JXAP specification?

    a) SAX
    b) DOM
    c) Dom4j
    d) SOAP
    e) JAXR

2. Select all of the correct answers. How can one create a dom4j document and get the root element of the document to build/read any XML tree?

    a)
    ```
    Document document = DocumentHelper.createDocument();
    Element rootElement = document.addElement("root");
    ```

    b)
    ```
    Document doc = new DefaultDocument();
    doc.addElement("root");
    ```

```
Element rootElement = doc.getRootElement();
```

c)
```
SAXReader reader = new SAXReader();
Document document = reader.read(new File("C:\\students.xml"));
Element root = document.getRootElement();
```

d)
```
DOMReader reader = new DOMReader();
org.dom4j.Document document = reader.read(w3cDOMDocument);
Element root = document.getRootElement();
```

e) All are valid code snippets.

3. How can one convert a Dom4j document object to a Java string using Dom4j API?

```
a)  String xmlString = document.toString()
b)  Document documentFromXML = DocumentHelper.parseText(xmlString)
c)  String xmlString = document.asXML()
d)  String xmlString = new String(document)
e)  String xmlAsString = document.getXMLString()
```

4. Select all valid answers. How can one read an XML document using Dom4j API?

a)
```
SAXReader reader = new SAXReader();
Document document = reader.read(new File("C:\\students.xml"));
```

b)
```
DOMReader reader = new DOMReader();
DocumentBuilderFactory factory = DocumentBuilderFactory.newInstance();
DocumentBuilder builder = factory.newDocumentBuilder();
org.w3c.dom.Document w3cDOMDocument = builder.parse(new
File("C:\\students.xml"));
org.dom4j.Document document = reader.read(w3cDOMDocument);
```

c)
```
DocumentHelper reader = new DocumentHelper();
Document document = reader.read(new File("C:\\students.xml"));
```

d)
```
NodeReader reader = new NodeReader();
Document document = reader.read(new File("C:\\students.xml"));
```

e) None is valid.

Answers to Test Yourself

1. A and B are the correct answers. The JAXP specification supports the SAX and DOM type of parsers. Dom4j is an XML-based parsing technique, but it is not part of the JAXP specification.

2. The correct answer is E. It explains the various ways of creating an XML document using the Dom4j API.

3. The correct answer is C.

4. A and B are the correct answers. There is no "read()" method available in the "DocumentHelper" class. Option D is an invalid Dom4j code.

We see various types of URLs while browsing the Internet. Why are there various URL patterns? What are they used for? What are the most commonly used URL notations for developing Web applications? Let us review some examples.

Commonly used URL notations for MVC-based Web applications are provided below. Web application frameworks such as Struts, Spring MVC, and JSF follow this kind of notation for developing Web applications.

```
http://localhost:8080/wsbook/demo/getGrades.do
http://localhost:8080/wsbook/demo/getGrades.action
```

Similarly, a typical URL containing a query string is given below. This notation is used to pass the HTML form data query string parameters containing the name and values.

```
http://localhost:8080/wsbook/services/dataservice/student?name=john&id=5
```

The notation used to specify the matrix parameter key value pairs as part of a URI is given below.

```
http://localhost:8080/wsbook/services/bookservice/book/2012;author=john;country=usa
```

Now we have another set of URLs (below). The below provided URL's represent the grades, subjects, topics, and topic content. Let us examine each URL and its output.

```
http://localhost:8080/wsbook/services/gradeservice/grades
http://localhost:8080/wsbook/services/gradeservice/grade/1
http://localhost:8080/wsbook/services/gradeservice/grade/1/subject/Math
http://localhost:8080/wsbook/services/gradeservice/grade/1/subject/Math/topic/Mathematics and art
```

The URL is:

```
http://localhost:8080/wsbook/services/gradeservice/grades
```

Its output is:

```
<grades>
    <grade id="1"
    href="http://localhost:8080/wsbook/services/gradeservice/grade/1"/>
    <grade id="2"
    href="http://localhost:8080/wsbook/services/gradeservice/grade/2"/>
    <grade id="3"
    href="http://localhost:8080/wsbook/services/gradeservice/grade/3"/>
    <grade id="4"
    href="http://localhost:8080/wsbook/services/gradeservice/grade/4"/>
</grades>
```

Now take the URL from the above output to obtain further information about 1st grade.

The URL is:

```
http://localhost:8080/wsbook/services/gradeservice/grade/1
```

Its output is:

```xml
<?xml version="1.0" encoding="UTF-8" ?>
<subjects>

<subject id="Math"
     href="http://localhost:8080/wsbook/services/gradeservice/grade/1/sub
ject/Math"/>

<subject id="Art"
     href="http://localhost:8080/wsbook/services/gradeservice/grade/1/sub
ject/Art"/>

<subject id="Lit"
     href="http://localhost:8080/wsbook/services/gradeservice/grade/1/sub
ject/Lit"/>

</subjects>
```

Now take the URL from the above output to obtain further information about mathematics.

The URL is:

```
http://localhost:8080/wsbook/services/gradeservice/grade/1/subject/Math
```

Its output is:

```xml
<?xml version="1.0" encoding="UTF-8"?>
<topics>

<topic id="Mathematics and art"
href="http://localhost:8080/wsbook/services/gradeservice/grade/1/subject/
Math/topic/Mathematics and art"/>

<topic id="Algebra"
href="http://localhost:8080/wsbook/services/gradeservice/grade/1/subject/
Math/topic/Algebra"/>

<topic id="Calculus"
href="http://localhost:8080/wsbook/services/gradeservice/grade/1/subject/
Math/topic/Calculus"/>

</topics>
```

Now take the URL from the above output to obtain further information about mathematics and art.

The URL is:

```
http://localhost:8080/wsbook/services/gradeservice/grade/1/subject/Math/t
opic/Mathematics and art
```

Its output is:

```
<?xml version="1.0" encoding="UTF-8" ?>
<contents>
    <content id="content"
    href="http://localhost:8080/wsbook/services/gradeservice/grade/1/
    subject/Math/topic/Mathematics and art/content/
    Mathematics and art.pdf"/>
</contents>
```

Clicking on this link will open a PDF document to display the content. The pattern here is that each URL is used to navigate further (to next level) to obtain more information. Each parent resource is mapped to many other sub-resources to obtain next level information. This type of design is called REST. REST stands for representational state transfer.

Java API for Restful Web Services (also called JAX-RS) is a Java specification used for implementing Restful Web services. This specification defines guidelines to develop Web services conforming to REST principles. The JAX-RS is a specification used for developing non-SOAP-based Web services. JAX-RS is part of Java EE.

In this chapter will discuss the following topics:

- REST principles
- The meaning of representational state transfer
- Axiom principles of Web architecture
- REST fundamentals
- REST terminology
- REST advantages
- JAX-RS annotations and its usage
- REST using Spring Framework
- REST implementation examples using Spring, Apache-CXF framework
- REST client design scenarios
- REST service endpoint and URL design scenarios

REST Principles

The word "REST" stands for representational state transfer. *Roy Thomas Fielding* introduced it in his PhD dissertation in 2000. A Restful Web service is HTTP-based that conforms to the principles of REST. Roy's dissertation describes the following six constraints for the REST architecture.

Client-Server—Provide a uniform interface to separate the client and server so that the client and server can be developed independently without altering the interface.

Figure 4-1: Rest principles

Stateless—Communication must be stateless in nature; the server will not store a client-specific state. There is always stateless communication between a client and the server i.e., the output will be the same regardless of who the client is for a given input.

Figure 4-2: Rest principles

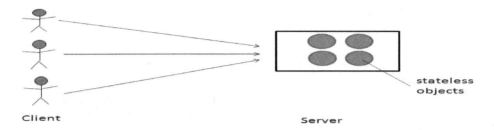

Cacheable—Clients can cache responses, but no client-specific state is stored on the server side. All server-side objects are identical.

Figure 4-3: Rest principles

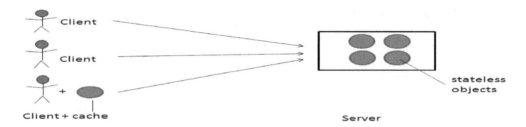

Uniform Interface—Provide a uniform interface between the client and server to decouple the client from a server. In this way, both can be developed independently; this allows the server to cache the data at interface point, this cache is shared across all invoking clients.

Figure 4-4: Rest principles

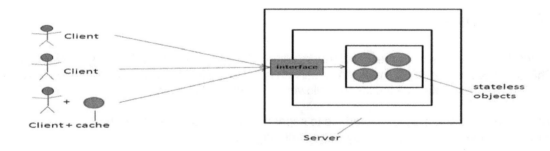

Layered System—This particular feature improves scalability through a load balancer. The load balancer routes the request to the available back-end servers. A client does not know which back-end server it is connected to. There are several ways to implement the layer server architecture that are not addressed here.

Figure 4-5: Rest principles

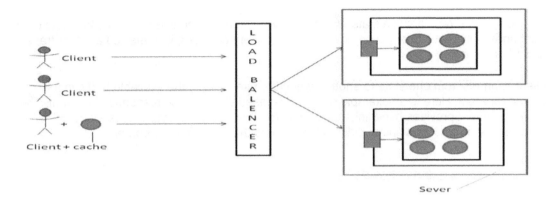

Code on Demand (Optional)—REST enables functionality by downloading and executing the code in the form of applets and Java scripts. This is an optional constraint within REST.

If a service violates any of the above six defined constraints, it cannot be strictly referred to as Restful. The following terms best describes REST:

- REST is an architectural style
- REST is a design pattern
- REST is a certain approach for developing Web services
- REST is a guiding framework for designing Web services
- REST is not a standard, but it is a guiding framework for designing Web standards
- REST is not a tool, not a product, and not technology.

REST Terminology

The following table summarizes the terminology used in REST and their meaning:

Terminology	Meaning
Resource	Sources of specific information
Resource Identifier	URL or URI in HTTP
Representation	HTML document, image file, etc.
RESTful	Web service using HTTP that conforms to the principles of REST.
Resource class	Service endpoint implementation class that uses JAX-RS annotations to expose a Java class as a Web service
Root resource class	A class annotated with @Path. This is the entry point to the class and provides access to class methods
Resource method	Methods of a resource class
Provider	An implementation of JAX-RS extension interface

Why Is It Called Representational State Transfer?

Initially, the browser represents a state. If user performs an action on one hyperlink, the state of the client changes. With each user action, the state of the client changes; it is referred as state transfer of a client from one to another.

The client changes from one state to another when the user selects the available URLs in the response document. Here is an example of a REST-based Web service response document. The response document provides hyperlinks to connect to other sub-resources; the user should continue navigating through various logical URLs to find the final resource content.

Example:

```
<?xml version="1.0" encoding="UTF-8"?>
<subjects>
<subject id="Math"
href="http://localhost:8080/wsbook/services/gradeservice/grade/1/subject/
Math"/>

<subject id="Art"
href="http://localhost:8080/wsbook/services/gradeservice/grade/1/subject/
Art"/>

<subject id="Lit"
href="http://localhost:8080/wsbook/services/gradeservice/grade/1/subject/
Lit"/>

<subject id="Photograpy"
href="http://localhost:8080/wsbook/services/gradeservice/grade/1/subject/
Photograpy"/>
</subjects>
```

Axioms of Web Architecture

An Axiom is an established rule, principle, or law. According to Tim Berners-Lee, the Axioms of Web architecture is defined as follows:

- Axiom 0: Universality 1—Any resource anywhere can be given as a URI.
- Axiom 0a: Universality 2—Any resource of significance should be given as a URI.
- Axiom 1: Global scope—It doesn't matter where you specify a URI; it will always have the same meaning.
- Axiom 2a: Sameness—An URI will repeatedly refer to "the same" thing.
- Axiom 2b: Identity—The significance of identity for a given URI is determined by the person who owns the URI (who first determined what it points to).
- Axiom 3: Non-unique—A URI space does not have to be the only universal space.

These principles explain that each resource on the Web has an URI. The association between URL and Resource is shown in Figure 4-6.

Figure 4-6: Axioms of web architecture

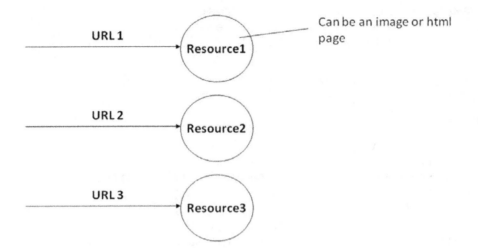

REST Guidelines

The following points briefly explain the basic fundamentals of REST used to develop the REST-based Web services.

- Identify all resources you wish to present as Web services.
- Map service resources to sub-resources to obtain additional information.
- Create a URL for each resource. These resources should be nouns, not verbs.

  Example:

  Do not use this (Note the verb, getGrade)

  ```
  - http://localhost:8080/wsbook/services/gradeservice/getGrade?grade=1
  ```

  Instead, use a noun:

  ```
  - http://localhost:8080/wsbook/services/gradeservice/grade/1
  ```

- Categorize resources based on mode of action (get/modify/add/delete etc.).
  - GET
  - POST
  - PUT
  - DELETE
- Provide a uniform interface between the client and server.
- All resources accessible via HTTP GET should be side-effect free; invoking a GET resource should not modify any other resource.
- Design to reveal data gradually. Don't display everything in a single response document; provide hyperlinks to obtain additional details.

- Use logical URLs instead of physical URLs. The logical URLs are constructed dynamically using the application data. They are not hard coded and they are not physical URLs; creating one thousand resources does not require one thousand physical URLs.
- Communicate statelessly. There will be no client-specific server side cache.
- The REST URLs do not follow the common ".do" or ".action" notation used for Web applications.

REST Advantages

- REST is consistent with Axiom principles of Web architecture.
- REST is Simple, easy to implement, manage, and maintain. No special tools or products are needed for development and deployment.
- REST provides lightweight services.
- REST provides simple and readable service endpoint designs.
- There are no additional testing frameworks/tools needed for testing REST services.
- It is easy to understand what each REST service does simply by examining the URL (i.e., it implements the principle of least surprise).
- There is no need to introduce rules. Rules and priorities are elevated at URL level. "What you see is what you get."
- It's easy to implement high priority—simply assign a faster processing machine to the premier member URL.
- The various URLs are discoverable by search engines and UDDI registries.
- REST architecture improves the scalability of your application.
- Client and server components can be developed independently without altering the interface.
- REST services are portable across the platforms; works well with all platforms (i.e., Windows, Mac, Unix, etc.).
- REST services are interoperable across various technology frameworks; does not matter whether it is Java or .Net.
- REST provides support for multiple content types; not limited to one XML; it can be HTML, SOAP, JSON, and many others.
- REST provides support for annotations; fewer lines to code in your application.
- Low development cost, no special skills or consulting needed for REST services development.

JAX-RS Annotations

JAX-RS provides several annotations for developing restful Web services. These annotations are defined in the "javax.ws.rs" package, and they conform to basic HTTP principles. They include query parameters, path parameters, and matrix parameters defined in the basic URI path. These annotations can be used at field level, method level, class level, and interface level, as well as with method parameters. The following section explains the commonly used annotations for implementing RESTful Web services. Each annotation is demonstrated using a code example.

- @GET
- @POST
- @DELETE
- @PUT
- @Path
- @Produces
- @Consumes

- @Context
- @PathParam
- @QueryParam
- @FormParam
- @MatrixParam
- @DefaultParam

@GET

The method annotated with @GET annotation is similar to HTTP GET request operation; GET requests should be used only for READ-ONLY resources. The get request should not add, modify, or delete any server-side resources. Get is a safe operation and has no side effects. "Safe" means that it should not modify any resource states on the server. An example of the use of the @GET annotation is given below.

```
public interface DocumentManager {
    @GET
    public String getDocument(String id);
}
```

@POST

The method annotated with @POST annotation is similar to HTTP POST request operation; the POST request is used for adding a new resource or to pass long parameters as a query string. The POST operation does have side effects; it will add a new resource. But in general, we use POST for things such as updates and for deleting and adding resources; because of this, the use of DELETE, PUT becomes minimal in Web applications. HTML forms support only GET and POST requests, so we have to improvise to identify DELETE and PUT requests using hidden fields in the HTML form. An example use of @POST annotation is given below.

```
public interface DocumentManager {
    @POST
    public void addDocument(String id);
}
```

@DELETE

The method annotated with @DELETE annotation is similar to HTTP DELETE operation; the DELETE operations are idempotent and used for deleting a resource. Whether you delete a resource at a specific URL once or ten times, the effect is the same. In general, we tunnel the DELETE and PUT requests through POST, because the HTML form supports only GET and POST. An example use of @DELETE annotation is given below.

```
public interface DocumentManager {
    @DELETE
    public void deleteDocument(String id);
}
```

@PUT

The method annotated with @PUT annotation is similar to HTTP PUT; the PUT operations are idempotent and are used for replacing a resource. Whether you replace a resource at a specific URL once or ten times, the effect is the same. An example use of @PUT annotation is given below.

```
public interface DocumentManager {
    @PUT
    public void replaceDocument(String id);
}
```

The use of GET, POST, DELETE, and PUT annotations are given below. Assume that we tunnel the DELETE and PUT requests through the POST operation.

```
public interface DocumentManager {

    @GET
    // This method is used for GET requests.
    public String getDocument(String id);

    @POST
    // This method is used for POST request.
    public void addDocument(String id) ;

    @POST
    /* This method is used to tunnel POST request for DELETE and PUT
        operations. */
    public void deleteOrReplaceDocument(String id);

    @DELETE
    // This method is used for deleting a resource.
    public void deleteDocument(String id);

    @PUT
    // This method is used for replacing a resource.
    public void replaceDocument(String id);

}
```

NOTE: Refer to Example4 for complete working code.

@Path

The @Path annotation is used to identify the entry point of a service and its operation to be executed. This annotation can be used at class and method levels. This annotation looks for an URI path and searches for the exact match at the class and method levels to determine which method of the class should be executed. An example of the use of the @Path annotation is given below.

The URL provided below invokes the "getGrades()" method of "GradeManager" service.

```
http://localhost:8080/wsbook/services/gradeservice/grades
```

It looks for the matching URI path "/gradeservice" at the class level and "/grades" at the method level. The matching operation of a service class will be executed.

```
@Path("/gradeservice/")
public interface GradeManager {
    @GET
    @Path("/grades")
    public String getGrades();
}
```

Similarly, the URL provided below invokes the "getGradeSubjects()" method of "GradeManager" service.

```
http://localhost:8080/wsbook/services/gradeservice/grade/{grade}
```

The service class is given below.

```
@Path("/gradeservice/")
public interface GradeManager {
    @GET
    @Path("/grade/{grade}")
    public String getGradeSubjects(@PathParam("grade") Integer grade) ;
}
```

@Produces

This refers to the type of content a server delivers to the client. The @Produces annotation can be used at the class level and method level. It is allowed to declare more than one content type and is represented as @Produces("application/xml," "plain/text"). If it is declared at the method level and class level, the method-level annotation overrides that of the class level, and it produces the content type declared at the method level. An example of the use of a @Produces annotation is given below.

```
@Path("/gradeservice/")
@Produces("application/xml")
public interface GradeManager {
    @GET
    @Path("/grades")
    @Produces("plain/text")
    public String getGrades();
}
```

At the class level, it is declared to deliver the "application/xml" content type, and at the method level, it produces the "plain/text" content type. The method-level annotation overrides the class-level annotation and sends the "plain/text" content back to the client.

@Consumes

This refers to the type of content a server receives from the client. This annotation can be used at the class level and method level. It is represented as @Consumes("application/xml"), is allowed to declare more than one content type, and is represented as @Consumes("application/xml," "application/html"). An example of the use of the @Consumes annotation is given below.

```
@Path("/loginservice/")
@Consumes("application/x-www-form-urlencoded")
public class AccessManagerImpl {
     @POST
     @Path("/userName/{userName}/password/{password}")
     public void postUserData(MultivaluedMap<String,String> formParams) {
          // Implement your logic here, after getting the form data
          for (String key : formParams.keySet()) {
                    System.out.println("-- value is --" +
               formParams.get(key) );
          }

          // (OR) use this
          for (Map.Entry<String, List<String>> entry :
                                   formParams.entrySet()) {
               System.out.println("---- value ----" + entry.getValue());
          }
     }
}
```

@PathParam

The @PathParam annotation is used at the method level (parameter to method) to obtain the parameter values specified in the REST URL. The parameter name-values of a REST URL are shown in Figure 4-7.

Figure 4-7: PathParam URL notation

http://localhost:8080/wsbook/services/gradeservice/grade/1/subject/Drawing

The example provided below obtains the parameter values of {grade} and {subject} specified in the REST URL.

```
@Path("/gradeservice/")
public interface GradeManager {
     @GET
     @Path("/grade/{grade}/subject/{subject}")
     public String getSubjectTopics(@PathParam("grade") Integer grade,
                              @PathParam("subject") String subject);
     /* value of {grade} maps to Integer grade
          - parameter value "1" assigns to grade */

     /* value of {subject} maps String subject
          - parameter value "Drawing" assigns to subject. */
}
```

@QueryParam

The @QueryParam annotation is used at the method level to obtain the query string values specified in the REST URL. An example use of query string parameter name and value is shown in Figure 4-8.

Figure 4-8: QueryParam URL notation

There are several options to get the query string parameter values. They are listed below.

1. How to get the query string parameters using @Context UriInfo class
2. How to get the query string parameters using @Context HttpServletRequest class
3. How to get the query string parameters using @QueryParam annotation

CASE 1:

How to get the query string parameters using @Context UriInfo

The JAX-RS-provided "UriInfo" class can be used to get the path and query parameters associated with any REST URL. The "getQueryParameters()" method of an "UriInfo" class is used to get the query string parameters of a REST URL. The example below gets the query parameter values specified in the REST URL.

```
@Path("/dataservice/")
@Produces("application/xml")
public class RestDataManagerImpl {
    @GET
    @Path("/restinfo")
    public void getCommmonInfo(@Context UriInfo uriInfo) {
        // Query Parameters
        MultivaluedMap<String, String> queryParams =
                        uriInfo.getQueryParameters();
        for(Map.Entry<String, List<String>> entry :
                            queryParams.entrySet()) {
            // prints [srinivas] and [15]
            System.out.println("-- param value --" + entry.getValue());
        }
    }
}
```

CASE 2:

How to get the query string parameters using @Context HttpServletRequest

The HTTP-provided "HttpServletRequest" class can be used to get the query parameters associated with any REST URL. This is an approach commonly used in Java servlet programming.

The example below gets the query parameter values specified in the REST URL.

```
@Path("/dataservice/")
@Produces("application/xml")
public class RestDataManagerImpl {
    @GET
    @Path("/restinfo")
    public void getCommonInfo(@Context HttpServletRequest req) {
        // Query Parameters
        String name = req.getParameter("name");
        String id = req.getParameter("id");
        System.out.println("-- name and id --" + name + "and" + id);
    }
}
```

CASE 3:

How to get the query string parameters using @QueryParam annotation

The JAX-RS–provided @QueryParam annotation can be used to get the query parameter values associated with any REST URL. The URL provided below specifies the stock symbol as a query string parameter; it invokes the service and returns the stock price.

```
http://localhost:8080/wsbook/services/stockservice/symbol?symbol=GOLD
```

The service code provided below gets the value specified in the above URL using @QueryParam annotation.

```
@Path("/stockservice/")
@Produces("text/plain")
public class StockServiceImpl {
    @GET
    @Path("/symbol")
    public String getStockPrice(@QueryParam("symbol") String symbol) {
        if(symbol.equalsIgnoreCase("GOLD")) {
            return "160.30";
        } else if(symbol.equalsIgnoreCase("XXX")) {
            return "10.0";
        }
        return symbol;
    }
}
```

@FormParam

The @FormParam annotation is used with content type "application/x-www-form-urlencoded" along with the HTTP POST operation. This is used to receive the HTML form data at service endpoint after the client submits the HTML form using the HTTP POST method. An example of the use of @FormParam annotation is given below.

The code provided below receives the individual field's data in method-level variables.

```
@POST
@Path("/userName/{userName}/password/{password}")
public void postUserData(@FormParam("userName") String userName,
                         @FormParam("password") String password) {
    System.out.println("-- userName --" + userName +
                        "--:--" + password);
    // Implement your logic here
}
```

The code provided below receives the entire HTML form data in a map. Iterate the map to get the required values.

```
@POST
@Path("/userName/{userName}/password/{password}")
public void postUserData(MultivaluedMap<String, String> formParams) {
    // Implement the logic here
    for(String key : formParams.keySet()) {
        System.out.println( "-- value is --" + formParams.get(key) );
    }

    // Implement your logic here
}
```

@MatrixParam

This annotation is used at the method level to extract the values of URI matrix parameter key value pairs. An example of the use of @MatrixParam annotation is given below.

```
@Path("/bookservice/")
@Produces("text/plain")
public interface BookService {
    @GET
    @Path("/book/{year}")
    String getBooks(@PathParam("year") String year,
                    @MatrixParam("author") String author,
                    @MatrixParam("country") String country);
}
```

The URL used to invoke the above service is given below.

```
http://localhost:8080/wsbook/services/bookservice/book/2012;author=sriniv
as;country=usa
```

NOTE: Refer to Example5 for complete code.

@Context

This annotation is used at method level (as a method parameter). The @Context annotation is used to get a handle to the `HttpHeaders, UriInfo, Request, HttpServletRequest, HttpServletResponse, SecurityContext, HttpServletConfig,` and `ServletContext` classes. These objects can be used to manipulate the parameter values specified in the REST URL. An example of the use of @Context annotation is given below.

```
@Path("/dataservice/")
@Produces("application/xml")
public class RestDataManagerImpl {
    @GET
    @Path("/contextinfo")
    public void getCommmonInfo(@Context UriInfo uriInfo,
                               @Context HttpHeaders headers,
                               @Context HttpServletRequest req) {
        // Implement your logic here.
        // Refer to Example2 to for complete code.
    }
}
```

To summarize, the use of @PathParam, @QueryParam, @FormParam and @MatrixParam annotations are explained with example URLs.

The @PathParam annotation is used to get the parameter values specified in the REST URL. An example URL of this type given below:

```
http://localhost:8080/wsbook/services/gradeservice/grade/1/subject/Art
```

The @QueryParam annotation is used to get the parameter values specified in the query string. An example URL of this type is given below:

```
http://localhost:8080/wsbook/services/dataservice/restinfo?name=john&id=5
```

The @FormParam annotation is used to get the entire HTML form data submitted through the HTTP POST method.

The @MatrixParam annotation is used to extract the values of URI matrix parameter key value pairs. An example URL of this type is given below.

```
http://localhost:8080/wsbook/services/bookservice/book/2012;author=john
```

@DefaultValue

The @DefaultValue annotation can be used at field level or method level to assign a default value to a variable if it does not find the key value.

Annotation Inheritance with REST

The JAX-RS specification supports the annotation inheritance. It is a very commonly used and is the most powerful feature; every REST developer needs to understand it. There are three ways REST annotations can be inherited.

1. Annotation inheritance by subclassing
2. Annotation inheritance by implementing annotated interfaces

3. Annotation inheritance by subclassing and implementing annotated interfaces

Annotation Rules:

- The annotations declared in the subclass will override the super-class annotations.
- The class will get the inherited annotations of the interface it implements.
- The subclass annotations can only override super-class annotations but cannot completely avoid them from a super class.
- Super class first and interface next - In annotation inheritance by subclassing and implementing annotated interfaces; annotations inherited from a super class will have the highest priority, followed by annotations declared in the interface.

The following example illustrates the use of annotation inheritance by subclassing. There are two scenarios associated with subclassing. The first scenario is that the subclass gets the inherited annotations from a super class; the second scenario is that the subclass will override the super class annotations.

CASE 1:

Let us now discuss the first scenario; the subclass gets the inherited annotations from its super class. The service "StockServiceImpl" class provided below produces the "text/plain" content type.

```
public class StockServiceImpl {
    @GET
    @Path("/symbol/{symbol}")
    @Produces("text/plain")
    public String getStockPrice(@PathParam("symbol") String symbol) {
        System.out.println("---- symbol ----" + symbol);
        if(symbol.equalsIgnoreCase("GLD")) {
            return "1800.30";
        } else if(symbol.equalsIgnoreCase("XXX")) {
            return "10.0";
        }
        return symbol;
    }
}
```

The annotation @Produces is not declared in its subclass "NewStockServiceImpl"; it inherits content type from its super class and produces the "text/plain" content type, provided below.

```
@Path("/stockservice/")
public class NewStockServiceImpl extends StockServiceImpl {
    @GET
    @Path("/symbol/{symbol}")
    public String getStockPrice(@PathParam("symbol") String symbol) {
        if(symbol.equalsIgnoreCase("SLV")) {
            return "32.30";
        } else if(symbol.equalsIgnoreCase("YYYY")) {
            return "10.0";
        }
        return symbol;
    }
}
```

CASE 2:

Let us now discuss the second scenario; the subclass overrides the annotations declared in its super class. The "StockServiceImpl" class produces the "text/plain" content type. The subclass "NewStockServiceImpl" provided below produces a different content type. The subclass annotation overrides the annotation declared in its super class and produces the new content type as "application/xml."

```
@Path("/stockservice/")
public class NewStockServiceImpl extends StockServiceImpl {
    @GET
    @Path("/symbol/{symbol}")
    @Produces("application/xml")
    public String getStockPrice(@PathParam("symbol") String symbol) {
        if(symbol.equalsIgnoreCase("SLV")) {
            return "<price>32.30</price>";
        } else if(symbol.equalsIgnoreCase("YYYY")) {
            return "<price>10.30</price>";
        }
        return symbol;
    }
}
```

CASE 3:

The following example illustrates the use of annotation inheritance by implementing annotated interfaces. The class "BookServiceImpl" implements the "BookService" interface; annotations are declared at the interface level, and the "getBooks()" method of the "BookServiceImpl" class declares all inherited annotations at the interface level and produces the "text/plain" content type.

```
@Path("/bookservice/")
@Produces("text/plain")
public interface BookService {
    @GET
    @Path("/book/{year}")
    String getBooks(@PathParam("year") String year,
                @MatrixParam("author") String author,
                @MatrixParam("country") String country);
}
```

The "BookServiceImpl" class implements the "BookService" interface and declares all inherited annotations at the interface level.

```
public class BookServiceImpl implements BookService {
    public String getBooks(String year, String author, String country) {
        return "year: " + year + " author: " + author + " country: " +
        country;
    }
}
```

CASE 4:

The following example illustrates annotation inheritance by subclassing and implementing annotated interfaces. The interface "StockService" produces the "application/xml" content type.

```java
public interface StockService {
    @Produces("application/xml")
    public String getStockPrice(String symbol);
}
```

The super class "StockServiceImpl" provided below produces the "text/plain" content type.

```java
public class StockServiceImpl {
    @Produces("text/plain")
    public String getStockPrice(String symbol) {
        if(symbol.equalsIgnoreCase("GLD")) {
            return "1800.30";
        } else if(symbol.equalsIgnoreCase("XXX")) {
            return "10.0";
        }
        return symbol;
    }
}
```

The subclass "NewStockServiceImpl" provided below extends the "StockServiceImpl" class and implements the "StockService" interface. It follows the super class first and interface next rule; it gets the inherited annotation from its super class and produces the "text/plain" content type.

```java
@Path("/stockservice/")
public class NewStockServiceImpl extends StockServiceImpl implements
StockService {
    @GET
    @Path("/symbol/{symbol}")
    public String getStockPrice(@PathParam("symbol") String symbol) {
        if(symbol.equalsIgnoreCase("SLV")) {
            return "32.30";
        } else if(symbol.equalsIgnoreCase("YYYY")) {
            return "10.0";
        }
        return symbol;
    }
}
```

REST Code Examples

REST is part of Java specification request. This specification defines a set of guidelines for the development of Web services conforming to REST principles. There are several open-source REST implementation projects available for developing enterprise applications. All these frameworks provide similar features and support Spring framework integration. Some of the commonly used open-source REST implementations are listed below.

- Apache-CXF—Now part of Apache, which is a merger between Celtix and XFire
- Jersey—JAX-RS reference implementation from Sun
- RESTEasy—JBoss's JAX-RS project
- Restlet
- Spring

The following sections explain several REST implementation examples using Spring and Apache-CXF.

NOTE: Refer to Chapter12 for the complete list of jar files required to develop these code examples.

Example 1: REST using Apache-CXF framework

The Apache-CXF framework provides Java API for developing Restful Web services based on the REST architectural style. The steps required to develop a Web service of this type are given below.

1. Create a service endpoint interface.
2. Create a service implementation class.
3. Create dependent helper classes if any are required.
4. Create an Apache-CXF framework-specific configuration file.
5. Create a web.xml file.
6. Create a war file and deploy it in the Tomcat server.
7. Verify the deployment using the REST URL from a browser.
8. Write a client to invoke the deployed service.
9. Log the service request and response.

The above-specified steps are described in the following sections:

Step 1: Create a Service Endpoint Interface

The first step is to create a uniform interface between the client and server. This interface contains all required business methods. The interface provided below contains four business methods associated with corresponding REST URLs. These methods return the list of grades, subjects of each grade, and topics of each subject; finally, they display the content of each topic.

The REST URL paths specified for each method of a service are given below.

- `@Path("/gradeservice/")`—It represents the entry point of a service class or interface.
- `@Path("/grades")`—It represents the entry point for the "getGrades()" method of a service class.
- `@Path("/grade/{grade}")`—It represents the entry point for the "getGradeSubjects()" method of a service class.
- `@Path("/grade/{grade}/subject/{subject}")`—It represents the entry point for the "getSubjectTopics()" method of a service class.
- `@Path("/grade/{grade}/subject/{subject}/topic/{topic}")`—It represents the entry point for the "getTopicContent()" method of a service class.

The @PathParam annotation is used to obtain the values specified in the REST URL.

`@PathParam("grade") Integer grade`—Obtains the {grade} value specified in the REST URL.
`@PathParam("subject") String subject`—Obtains the {subject} value specified in the REST URL.
`@PathParam("topic") String topic`—Obtains the {topic} value specified in the REST URL

The "GradeManager" interface provided below contains all GET operations and produces an "application/xml" content type. Listing 4-1 provides the complete interface code.

Listing 4-1: Rest example using Apache-CXF

```java
// GradeManager.java
package com.learning.ws.rest;

import javax.ws.rs.Path;
import javax.ws.rs.Produces;
import javax.ws.rs.GET;
import javax.ws.rs.PathParam;

@Path("/gradeservice/")
@Produces("application/xml")
public interface GradeManager {
    @GET
    @Path("/grades")
    @Produces("application/xml")
    public String getGrades();

    @GET
    @Path("/grade/{grade}")
    public String getGradeSubjects(@PathParam("grade") Integer grade);

    @GET
    @Path("/grade/{grade}/subject/{subject}")
    public String getSubjectTopics(@PathParam("grade") Integer grade,
                                   @PathParam("subject") String subject);

    @GET
    @Path("/grade/{grade}/subject/{subject}/topic/{topic}")
    public String getTopicContent(@PathParam("grade") Integer grade,
                                  @PathParam("subject") String subject,
                                  @PathParam("topic") String topic);
}
```

Step 2: Create a Service Implementation Class

The implementations of the interface-defined methods are shown in Listing 4-2. A utility class "XMLBuilder" is used for building the response XML for each business method.

Listing 4-2: Service implementation class.

```java
// GradeManagerImpl.java
package com.learning.ws.rest;

import com.learning.util.XMLBuilder;

public class GradeManagerImpl implements GradeManager {
    public String getGrades() {
        return XMLBuilder.getAllGrades();
    }

    public String getGradeSubjects(Integer grade) {
        return XMLBuilder.getAllSubjects(grade);
    }
```

```
    public String getSubjectTopics(Integer grade, String subject) {
        return XMLBuilder.getAllTopics(grade, subject);
    }

    public String getTopicContent(Integer grade,
                                  String subject, String topic) {
        return XMLBuilder.getTopicContent(grade, subject, topic);
    }
}
```

Step 3: Create any Dependent Helper, DAO Classes

The utility class provided below is used to generate the response XML. In the real world, this data comes from a database. The methods of this class are used to build the response XML using Dom4j API.

`public static String getAllGrades()`—Returns the list of grades.

`public static String getAllSubjects(Integer grade)`—Returns the subjects of a given a grade.

`public static String getAllTopics(Integer grade, String subject)`—Returns the topics of a given subject and grade.

`public static String getTopicContent(Integer grade, String subject, String topic)`—Returns the final content of the topic.

Listing 4-3 has the complete Java code used for creating the response XML.

Listing 4-3: Utility class used to create the response XML

```
// XMLBuilder.java
package com.learning.util;

import java.util.List;
import java.util.ArrayList;
import org.dom4j.Document;
import org.dom4j.Element;
import org.dom4j.tree.DefaultDocument;

public class XMLBuilder {
    public static String getAllGrades() {
        Document doc = new DefaultDocument();
        doc.addElement("grades");
        Element rootElement = doc.getRootElement();

        List<String> grades = getGrades();
        for (String grade : grades) {
            Element gradeElement = rootElement.addElement("grade");
            gradeElement.addAttribute("id", grade);

            // Building logical url's
            gradeElement.addAttribute("href",
            "http://localhost:8080/wsbook/services/gradeservice/grade/"
            + grade);
```

```java
        }
        return doc.asXML();
    }

    public static String getAllSubjects(Integer grade) {
        Document doc = new DefaultDocument();
        doc.addElement("subjects");
        Element rootElement = doc.getRootElement();

        // Building logical url's
        List<String> subjects = getSubjects(grade);
        for (String subject : subjects) {
            Element subjectElement = rootElement.addElement("subject");
            subjectElement.addAttribute("id", subject);
            subjectElement.addAttribute("href",
            "http://localhost:8080/wsbook/services/gradeservice/grade/"
            + grade + "/subject/" + subject);
        }
        return doc.asXML();
    }

    public static String getAllTopics(Integer grade, String subject) {
        Document doc = new DefaultDocument();
        doc.addElement("topics");
        Element rootElement = doc.getRootElement();

        // Building logical url's
        List<String> topics = getTopics(subject);
        for (String topic : topics) {
            Element topicElement = rootElement.addElement("topic");
            topicElement.addAttribute("id", topic);
            topicElement.addAttribute("href",
            "http://localhost:8080/wsbook/services/gradeservice/grade/"
            + grade + "/subject/" + subject + "/topic/" + topic);
        }
        return doc.asXML();
    }

    public static String getTopicContent(Integer grade,
                                String subject, String topic) {
        Document doc = new DefaultDocument();
        doc.addElement("content");
        Element rootElement = doc.getRootElement();

        Element contentElement = rootElement.addElement("content");
        contentElement.addAttribute("id", "content");
        contentElement.addAttribute("href",
        "http://localhost:8080/wsbook/services/gradeservice/grade/"
        + grade + "/subject/" + subject + "/topic/" + topic
        + "/content/" + topic + ".pdf");
        return doc.asXML();
    }

    private static List<String> getGrades() {
        List<String> gradesList = new ArrayList<String>();
        gradesList.add("1");
        gradesList.add("2");
```

```java
            gradesList.add("3");
            gradesList.add("4");
            gradesList.add("5");
            gradesList.add("6");
            gradesList.add("10");
            return gradesList;
    }

    private static List<String> getSubjects(Integer grade) {
        List<String> subList = new ArrayList<String>();
        switch (grade) {
            case 10:
                subList.add("Math");
                subList.add("Reading");
                subList.add("Biology");
                return subList;
            case 1:
            case 2:
            case 3:
            case 4:
                subList.add("Math");
                subList.add("Art");
                subList.add("Lit");
                subList.add("Photograpy");
                return subList;
            default:
                subList.add("Java");
                subList.add(".Net");
                return subList;
        }
    }

    private static List<String> getTopics(String subject) {
        List<String> topicList = new ArrayList<String>();
        if ("Java".equalsIgnoreCase(subject)) {
            topicList.add("An Overview of Java");
            topicList.add("Introduction to classes");
            topicList.add("Packages and Interfaces");
            topicList.add("Exception Handling");
            topicList.add("Mutithreading");
            topicList.add("String Handling");
            topicList.add("Colletions Framework");
        }

        if ("Math".equalsIgnoreCase(subject)) {
            topicList.add("Mathematics and art");
            topicList.add("Philosophy of mathematics");
            topicList.add("Algebra");
            topicList.add("Trignometry");
            topicList.add("Calculus");
        }
        return topicList;
    }
}
```

Step 4: Create Apache-CXF Framework-Specific Configuration File

The Apache-CXF framework provides XML-based server-side tags to integrate REST services with the Spring application context. These XML tags seamlessly integrate the Apache-CXF with the Spring framework. The CXF-provided <jaxrs:serviceBeans/> tag is used to register the Java Beans with the Spring container. The complete XML configuration is given below. It is named the applicationContext-cxf.xml.

```xml
<?xml version="1.0" encoding="UTF-8"?>
<beans xmlns="http://www.springframework.org/schema/beans"
    xmlns:xsi="http://www.w3.org/2001/XMLSchema-instance"
    xmlns:jaxrs="http://cxf.apache.org/jaxrs"
    xmlns:cxf="http://cxf.apache.org/core"
    xsi:schemaLocation="http://www.springframework.org/schema/beans
    http://www.springframework.org/schema/beans/spring-beans.xsd
    http://cxf.apache.org/jaxrs
    http://cxf.apache.org/schemas/jaxrs.xsd
    http://cxf.apache.org/core
    http://cxf.apache.org/schemas/core.xsd ">

    <!-- Loads CXF modules from cxf.jar file -->
    <import resource="classpath:META-INF/cxf/cxf.xml"/>
    <import resource="classpath:META-INF/cxf/cxf-extension-soap.xml"/>
    <import resource="classpath:META-INF/cxf/cxf-servlet.xml"/>
    <import resource="classpath:META-INF/cxf/cxf-extension-jaxrs-
    binding.xml"/>

    <jaxrs:server id="gradeservice" address="/">
    <jaxrs:serviceBeans>
        <ref bean="gradeManagerImpl"/>
    </jaxrs:serviceBeans>
    <jaxrs:features>
        <cxf:logging/>
    </jaxrs:features>
    </jaxrs:server>

    <bean id="gradeManagerImpl"
        class="com.learning.ws.rest.GradeManagerImpl"/>
</beans>
```

The following XML is used to enable the user to log on to the server. It prints the request-and-response messages on the server console.

```xml
<jaxrs:features>
    <cxf:logging/>
</jaxrs:features>
```

Step 5: Create a web.xml File

The web.xml file is used for Java Web application-specific configurations. Configure the Apache-CXF–provided transport servlet for routing the request messages. The complete web.xml configurations are given below.

```xml
<?xml version="1.0" encoding="UTF-8"?>
<web-app version="2.4" xmlns="http://java.sun.com/xml/ns/j2ee"
        xmlns:xsi="http://www.w3.org/2001/XMLSchema-instance"
```

```
    xsi:schemaLocation="http://java.sun.com/xml/ns/j2ee
    http://java.sun.com/xml/ns/j2ee/web-app_2_4.xsd">

<display-name>wsbook web application</display-name>
<servlet>
    <servlet-name>wsbook</servlet-name>
    <servlet-class>
        org.springframework.web.servlet.DispatcherServlet
    </servlet-class>
    <load-on-startup>2</load-on-startup>
</servlet>
<servlet-mapping>
    <servlet-name>wsbook</servlet-name>
    <url-pattern>*.action</url-pattern>
</servlet-mapping>
<listener>
    <listener-class>
        org.springframework.web.context.ContextLoaderListener
    </listener-class>
</listener>
<context-param>
    <param-name>contextConfigLocation</param-name>
    <param-value>/WEB-INF/applicationContext-cxf.xml</param-value>
</context-param>
<servlet>
    <servlet-name>CXFServlet</servlet-name>
    <servlet-class>
        org.apache.cxf.transport.servlet.CXFServlet
    </servlet-class>
</servlet>
<servlet-mapping>
    <servlet-name>CXFServlet</servlet-name>
    <url-pattern>/services/*</url-pattern>
</servlet-mapping>
<!-- Welcome Page -->
<welcome-file-list>
<welcome-file>index.vm</welcome-file>
</welcome-file-list>
<mime-mapping>
    <extension>wsdl</extension>
    <mime-type>text/xml</mime-type>
</mime-mapping>
<mime-mapping>
    <extension>xsd</extension>
    <mime-type>text/xml</mime-type>
</mime-mapping>
</web-app>
```

Step 6: Create a War File and Deploy It in Tomcat Server

1. Build a war file using Ant or any other build tool. Make sure the following files are packaged correctly in a war file.

    a) Create a Service endpoint interface
    b) Create a Service endpoint implementation class and its dependent classes
    c) Create an Apache-CXF framework-specific configuration file. (applicationContext-cxf.xml)

d) Create a web.xml configuration file
e) Create a Spring framework-specific configuration file. (wsbook-servlet.xml)
f) All required jar files packaged in "WEB-INF/lib" directory.

The structure of the generated war file is shown below. The diagram provided below shows only a few jar files in "WEB-INF/lib" directory. Refer to Chapter12 for the complete list.

Figure 4-9: war file structure

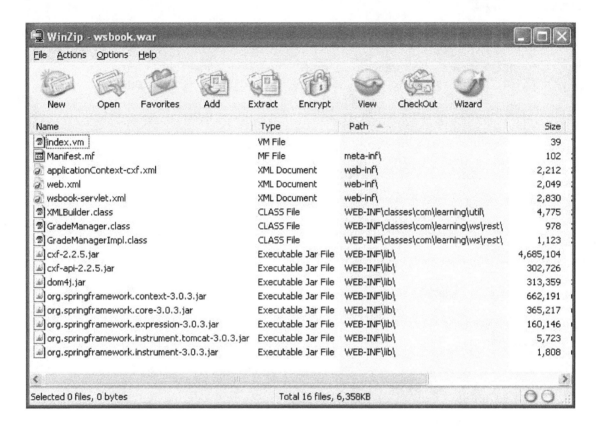

2. Deploy the war file in any Java-compatible servlet container.
   a) Copy the packed war into the "apache-tomcat/webapps" directory.
   b) Start the tomcat server by running the startup.bat batch file available in the "apache-tomcat/bin" directory.
   c) See the server console output and logs; make sure the war file is deployed without any errors.

Step 7: Verify the Service Deployment Using the REST URL from a Browser

Access the deployed service from a Web browser to make sure the service is deployed without any errors. The following URLs will show you the complete XML on the browser.

```
http://localhost:8080/wsbook/services/gradeservice/grades
http://localhost:8080/wsbook/services/gradeservice/grade/1
http://localhost:8080/wsbook/services/gradeservice/grade/1/subject/Math
http://localhost:8080/wsbook/services/gradeservice/grade/1/subject/Math/t
opic/Mathematics and art
```

These URLs are not physical URLs; they are logical URLs. After obtaining the list of grades, use the displayed content to navigate to other available sub-resources.

Step 8: Write a Client to Invoke the Deployed Service

There are several ways to consume the deployed REST service. JAX-RS specification does not define any standard for client invocation. Spring provides a "RestTemplate" class to invoke the deployed REST services. The clients shown below can be used to invoke the deployed REST service.

CASE 1:

Invoke the REST service using standard Java API. The "openConnection()" method of "java.net.URL" class is used to establish the connection and get the required output.

```
private static void invokeService() throws Exception {
    String url1 =
        "http://localhost:8080/wsbook/services/gradeservice/grades";
    URL url = new URL(url1);
    URLConnection conn = url.openConnection();
    conn.setDoOutput(true);

    InputStreamReader isr =
            new InputStreamReader(conn.getInputStream());
    BufferedReader br = new BufferedReader(isr);

    String response;
    while((response = br.readLine()) != null ) {
        System.out.println( response );
    }
    br.close();
}
```

CASE 2:

The Spring framework-provided "RestTemplate" class is used to access the deployed REST service. The use of the Spring framework-provided "RestTemplate" class is given below.

```
private static void invokeServiceUsingSpringAPI () throws Exception {
        RestTemplate restTemplate = new RestTemplate();
        String result = restTemplate.getForObject(
        "http://localhost:8080/wsbook/services/
                gradeservice/grade/{grade}",
                String.class, "1");
        System.out.println("result: " + result);

        Map<String, String> vars = new HashMap<String, String>();
        vars.put("grade", "1");
        vars.put("subject", "Java");

        String result1 = restTemplate.getForObject(
            "http://localhost:8080/wsbook/services/gradeservice/grade/
            {grade}/subject/{subject}",  String.class, vars);
        System.out.println("result1: " + result1);

        Map<String, String> topics = new HashMap<String, String>();
```

```
        vars.put("grade", "1");
        vars.put("subject", "Math");
        vars.put("topic", "Mathematics and art");

        String result2 = restTemplate.getForObject(
            "http://localhost:8080/wsbook/services
            /gradeservice/grade/1/subject/
            {subject}/topic/{topic}", String.class, vars);
    System.out.println("result2: " + result2);
}
```

Step 9: Log the Service Request-and-Response Message

Use the following configuration to log the inbound and outbound messages of a REST service. This information is useful for debugging the REST services.

```
<jaxrs:features>
    <cxf:logging/>
</jaxrs:features>
```

Example 2: How to get Context, Request Information in REST

The @Context annotation is used to get a handle to the `HttpHeaders`, `UriInfo`, `Request`, `HttpServletRequest`, `HttpServletResponse`, `SecurityContext`, `HttpServletConfig`, and `ServletContext` classes. The methods of these objects are used to obtain the data associated with URI and service requests. Data such as the host, post, request headers, parameter names, and parameter values can be obtained using these objects with the @Context annotation. The example provided below demonstrates how to obtain these values.

The steps required to develop a Web service to obtain the HTTP request data are given below.

1. Create a service endpoint interface.
2. Create a service implementation class.
3. Create any dependent helper classes.
4. Create an Apache-CXF framework-specific configuration file.
5. Create a web.xml file.
6. Create a war file and deploy it in the Tomcat server.
7. Verify the deployment using the REST URL from a browser.
8. Write a client to invoke the deployed service.

The above-specified steps are described in the following sections:

Step 1: Create a Service Endpoint Interface

The first step is to define an interface between the client and server. The complete interface code is given below.

`@Context UriInfo`—Used to obtain the URI-specific data such as host, port, and so forth

`@Context HttpHeaders`—Used to obtain the header information such as cookies, locale, and so forth

`@Context HttpServletRequest`—Used to obtain the HTTP request specific data such as parameter names, parameter values, and so forth.

Listing 4-4 demonstrates the use of the @Context annotation with the service endpoint interface.

Listing 4-4: service endpoint interface

```java
// RestDataManager.java
package com.learning.ws.rest;

import javax.ws.rs.Path;
import javax.ws.rs.Produces;
import javax.ws.rs.GET;
import javax.ws.rs.core.Context;
import javax.ws.rs.core.UriInfo;
import javax.ws.rs.core.HttpHeaders;
import javax.servlet.http.HttpServletRequest;

@Path("/dataservice/")
@Produces("text/plain")
public interface RestDataManager {
    @GET
    @Path("/restinfo")
    public String getCommmonInfo(@Context UriInfo uriInfo,
                                 @Context HttpHeaders headers,
                                 @Context HttpServletRequest req);
}
```

Step 2: Create a Service Implementation Class

The implementation of the above-declared interface is shown in Listing 4-5. The output of each method is provided with inline comments along with the code.

Listing 4-5: service implementation class

```java
// RestDataManagerImpl
package com.learning.ws.rest;

import javax.ws.rs.core.*;
import javax.servlet.http.HttpServletRequest;
import java.net.URI;
import java.util.*;

public class RestDataManagerImpl implements RestDataManager {
    public String getCommmonInfo(UriInfo uriInfo,
                                 HttpHeaders headers,
                                 HttpServletRequest req) {

        /* Using @Context UriInfo uriInfo - To get the URI related info
           like, port, host, query parameters etc. */
        String path = uriInfo.getPath();
        System.out.println("---- path ----" + path);

        // Aboslute path
        URI uriPath = uriInfo.getAbsolutePath();
        System.out.println("--- uriPath ---" + uriPath);

        // host and port
        URI requestUri = uriInfo.getRequestUri();
        System.out.println("---- Host and Port ----" +
            requestUri.getHost() + ":" + requestUri.getPort());
```

```java
// Matched uri
List<String> matchedUri = uriInfo.getMatchedURIs();
System.out.println("---- matchedUri ----" + matchedUri);

URI baseUri = uriInfo.getBaseUri();
// http://localhost:8080/wsbook/services/
System.out.println("---- baseUri ----" + baseUri);

UriBuilder uriBuilder = uriInfo.getBaseUriBuilder();
System.out.println("---- name -----" +
                uriBuilder.queryParam("name"));

// Query Parameters
MultivaluedMap<String, String> queryParams =
                uriInfo.getQueryParameters();
System.out.println("--- queryParams ---" +
        queryParams);  //{name=[srinivas], id=[15]}

for(Map.Entry<String, List<String>> entry :
        queryParams.entrySet()) {
    // Prints [srinivas] and [15]
    System.out.println("--- query param ---" +
    entry.getValue());
}

// Path Parameters
MultivaluedMap<String, String> pathParams =
    uriInfo.getPathParameters();
System.out.println("--- pathParams ---" + pathParams);

/* Using HttpHeaders to obtain header information like cookies,
locale etc. */
MultivaluedMap<String, String> requestHeaders =
                            headers.getRequestHeaders();
System.out.println("---- requestHeaders ---" + requestHeaders);

// Obtaining the cookies related information.
Map<String, Cookie> cookie = headers.getCookies();
System.out.println("---- cookie ----" + cookie);

// Obtaining the locale information.
Locale locale = headers.getLanguage();
System.out.println("---- locale ----" + locale);

/* @Context HttpServletRequest req - Obtaining the http request
    parameters values */
String paramName = req.getParameter("name");
System.out.println("---- paramName ----" + paramName);
return path;
    }
}
```

Step 4: Create Apache-CXF Framework-Specific Configuration File

Create an Apache-CXF framework-specific XML configuration file to register the REST Web service class. The complete XML configuration is given below.

```xml
<?xml version="1.0" encoding="UTF-8"?>
<beans xmlns="http://www.springframework.org/schema/beans"
    xmlns:xsi="http://www.w3.org/2001/XMLSchema-instance"
    xmlns:jaxrs="http://cxf.apache.org/jaxrs"
    xmlns:cxf="http://cxf.apache.org/core"
    xsi:schemaLocation="http://www.springframework.org/schema/beans
    http://www.springframework.org/schema/beans/spring-beans.xsd
    http://cxf.apache.org/jaxrs
    http://cxf.apache.org/schemas/jaxrs.xsd
    http://cxf.apache.org/core
    http://cxf.apache.org/schemas/core.xsd ">

    <!-- Loads CXF modules from cxf.jar file -->
    <import resource="classpath:META-INF/cxf/cxf.xml"/>
    <import resource="classpath:META-INF/cxf/cxf-extension-soap.xml"/>
    <import resource="classpath:META-INF/cxf/cxf-servlet.xml"/>
    <import resource="classpath:META-INF/cxf/cxf-extension-jaxrs-
                                            binding.xml"/>

    <jaxrs:server id="gradeservice" address="/">
    <jaxrs:serviceBeans>
        <ref bean="restDataManagerImpl"/>
    </jaxrs:serviceBeans>

    <jaxrs:features>
        <cxf:logging/>
    </jaxrs:features>
    </jaxrs:server>

    <bean id="restDataManagerImpl"
            class="com.learning.ws.rest.RestDataManagerImpl"/>
</beans>
```

Step 5: Create a Web.xml File

Reuse the web.xml file we created in Example1.

Step 6: Create a War File and Deploy It in Tomcat Server

Figure 4-10: war file structure

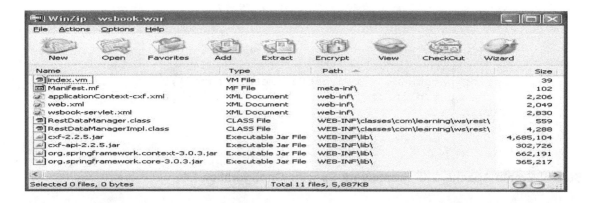

Follow the instructions specified in Example1. The structure of the generated war file is shown in Figure 4-10.

REST Code Examples

Step 7: Verify the Deployment Using the REST URL from a Browser

Invoke the deployed REST service using the following URLs. It will print the data on the server console.

```
http://localhost:8080/wsbook/services/dataservice/restinfo
http://localhost:8080/wsbook/services/dataservice/restinfo?name=john&id=5
```

Example 3: How to Get the Entire HTML Form Data Using REST

This example demonstrates the use of HTML forms with the REST Web service. The client in this scenario is any Web page; it can be HTML, JSP, velocity template, or a freemarker template. The service receives the user-entered data on the Web page, processes it, and sends the response back to the invoking client. The steps required to develop a Web service to get the HTTP POST request data are given below.

1. Create a service endpoint interface.
2. Create a service implementation class.
3. Create Apache-CXF framework specific configuration file.
4. Create a web.xml file.
5. Create a war file and deploy it in the Tomcat server.
6. Write a client to invoke the deployed service.

The above-specified steps are described in the following sections:

Step 1: Create a Service Endpoint Interface

This interface has defined two overloaded methods; which method to use totally depends on the application need. The first method is used to receive the individual field data from an HTML form.

```
@POST
@Path("/userName/{userName}/password/{password}")
public void postUserData(@FormParam("userName")String userName,
                         @FormParam("password")String password);
```

The second method provided below is used to obtain all HTML form data in a key-value map.

```
@POST
@Path("/userName/{userName}/password/{password}")
public void postUserData(MultivaluedMap<String, String> formParams);
```

The service must use the form URL of encoded content type at the service endpoint.

```
@Consumes("application/x-www-form-urlencoded")
```

Listing 4-6 has the complete Java code that demonstrates the service interface.

Listing 4-6: service interface code

```
// AccessManager.java
package com.learning.ws.rest;

import javax.ws.rs.POST;
import javax.ws.rs.Path;
```

```java
import javax.ws.rs.FormParam;
import javax.ws.rs.Consumes;
import javax.ws.rs.core.MultivaluedMap;

@Path("/loginservice/")
@Consumes("application/x-www-form-urlencoded")
public interface AccessManager {
    @POST
    @Path("/userName/{userName}/password/{password}")
    public void postUserData(@FormParam("userName")String userName,
                             @FormParam("password")String password);

    // OR use the below given method, based on the business need.
    @POST
    @Path("/userName/{userName}/password/{password}")
    public void postUserData(MultivaluedMap<String, String> formParams);
}
```

Step 2: Create a Service Implementation Class

The implementation of the above-declared interface is shown in Listing 4-5. It receives the HTML form data and prints it on the console.

Listing 4-7: service implementation class

```java
// AccessManagerImpl.java
package com.learning.ws.rest;

import javax.ws.rs.core.MultivaluedMap;
import java.util.Map;
import java.util.List;

public class AccessManagerImpl implements AccessManager {
    public void postUserData(String userName, String password) {
        // Getting the HTML form data; implement your logic here.
        System.out.println("---- userName ----" + userName +
                    "---- password ----" + password);
    }

    public void postUserData(MultivaluedMap<String,String> formParams) {
        // Getting the HTML form data
        for(String key : formParams.keySet()) {
            System.out.println("-- value is --" + formParams.get(key));
        }
        //OR use this code for getting the form data.
        for(Map.Entry<String, List<String>> entry :
                            formParams.entrySet()) {
            System.out.println("-- value is ---" + entry.getValue());
        }
    }
}
```

Step 3: Create an Apache-CXF Framework-Specific Configuration File

Create an Apache-CXF framework-specific XML configuration file to register the REST Web service class with a Spring container. The complete XML configuration is given below.

```xml
<?xml version="1.0" encoding="UTF-8"?>
<beans xmlns="http://www.springframework.org/schema/beans"
        xmlns:xsi="http://www.w3.org/2001/XMLSchema-instance"
        xmlns:jaxrs="http://cxf.apache.org/jaxrs"
        xmlns:cxf="http://cxf.apache.org/core"
        xsi:schemaLocation="http://www.springframework.org/schema/beans
        http://www.springframework.org/schema/beans/spring-beans.xsd
        http://cxf.apache.org/jaxrs
        http://cxf.apache.org/schemas/jaxrs.xsd
        http://cxf.apache.org/core
        http://cxf.apache.org/schemas/core.xsd ">

        <!-- Loads CXF modules from cxf.jar file -->
        <import resource="classpath:META-INF/cxf/cxf.xml"/>
        <import resource="classpath:META-INF/cxf/cxf-extension-soap.xml"/>
        <import resource="classpath:META-INF/cxf/cxf-servlet.xml"/>
        <import resource="classpath:META-INF/cxf/cxf-extension-jaxrs-
                binding.xml"/>

        <jaxrs:server id="gradeservice" address="/">
            <jaxrs:serviceBeans>
                <ref bean="accessManagerImpl"/>
            </jaxrs:serviceBeans>
            <jaxrs:features>
                <cxf:logging/>
            </jaxrs:features>
        </jaxrs:server>

        <bean id="accessManagerImpl"
            class="com.learning.ws.rest.AccessManagerImpl"/>
</beans>
```

Step 4: Create a web.xml file

Reuse the web.xml file we created in Example1.

Step 5: Create a War File and Deploy It in the Tomcat Server

Figure 4-10: war file structure

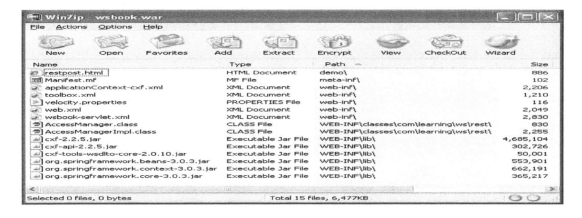

Follow the instructions specified in Example1. The structure of the generated war file is shown in Figure 4-10.

Step 6: Write a Client to Invoke the Deployed Service

In this example, an HTML page is used to submit the request using the POST method. The user entered values in the text fields; "userName" and "password" are passed to the service endpoint class. The form provided below is submitted using a javascript function. The complete HTML form code is given below.

```html
<html>
<head>
    <title>WS REST DEMO</title>
    <script type="text/javascript">
        function submitUserForm() {
            document.forms[0].action = "/wsbook/services/loginservice
            /userName/XXXXX/password/XXXXXXX";
            document.forms[0].submit();
        }
    </script>
</head>
<body>
<form method="post">
    <table align="center">
        <tr>
            <td><label><b>User Id:</b></label></td>
            <td>
                <input type="text" name="userName"
                        id="userName" value="" size="40"/>
            </td>
        </tr>
        <tr>
            <td><label><b>Password:</b></label></td>
            <td>
                <input type="text" name="password"
                        id="password" value="" size="40"/>
            </td>
        </tr>
        <tr>
            <td>
                <a href="javascript:submitUserForm()">1.Log In</a>
            </td>
        </tr>
    </table>
</form>
</body>
</html>
```

Example 4: How to Use GET, POST, DELETE, and PUT

The example provided below demonstrates the use of GET, POST, DELETE, and PUT operations. The steps required to develop a Web service to get the HTTP request data are given below.

1. Create a service endpoint interface.
2. Create a service implementation class.
3. Create an Apache-CXF framework-specific configuration file.
4. Create a web.xml file.
5. Write a client to invoke the deployed service.

6. Create a war file and deploy it in the Tomcat server

The above-specified steps are described in the following sections.

Step 1: Create a Service Endpoint Interface

The interface provided uses four methods for GET, POST, DELETE, and PUT operations. The request for DELETE and PUT are routed through the HTTP POST operation. Listing 4-7 provides the complete Java code.

Listing 4-7: REST example using HTTP GET, POST, DELETE and PUT

```java
// DocumentManager.java
package com.learning.ws.rest;

import javax.ws.rs.*;
@Path("/document/")
@Produces("text/plain")
public interface DocumentManager {
    @GET
    @Path("/read/{id}")
    public String getDocument(@PathParam("id") String id);

    @POST
    @Path("/add/{id}")
    @Consumes("application/x-www-form-urlencoded")
    public void addDocument(@PathParam("id") String id);

    @POST
    @Path("/deleteReplace/{id}")
    @Consumes("application/x-www-form-urlencoded")
    public void deleteOrReplaceDocument(@PathParam("id") String id);

    @DELETE
    public void deleteDocument(String id);

    @PUT
    public void replaceDocument(String id);
}
```

Step 2: Create a Service Implementation Class

The implementation of the above-defined methods in an interface is shown in Listing 4-8. The GET operation is used for reading a document; the POST operation is used for adding a new document; the DELETE operation is used for deleting a document; and the PUT operation is used to replace one document with another.

Listing 4-8: REST service implementation class

```java
// DocumentManagerImpl.java
package com.learning.ws.rest;

public class DocumentManagerImpl implements DocumentManager {
    public String getDocument(String id) {
        // GET operation - implement your logic here to get a document
        System.out.println("---- GET ---" + id);
        return "your document content";
```

```java
    }

    public void addDocument(String id) {
        /* POST operation - implement your logic here to add a new
            Document */
        System.out.println("---- POST ----" + id);
    }

    // Calling DELETE and PUT operations through POST.
    public void deleteOrReplaceDocument(String id) {
        /* DELETE and PUT operations
            -Implement your logic here to delete or replace document */
        deleteDocument(id);
        replaceDocument(id);
    }

    public void deleteDocument(String id) {
        // Implement your logic here to delete a document
        System.out.println("---- DELETE ----");
    }

    public void replaceDocument(String id) {
        // Implement your logic here to replace a document
        System.out.println("---- PUT ----");
    }
}
```

Step 3: Create Apache-CXF Framework-Specific Configuration File

Create an Apache-CXF framework-specific XML configuration file to register the REST Web service class with a Spring container. The complete XML configuration is given below.

```xml
<?xml version="1.0" encoding="UTF-8"?>
<beans xmlns="http://www.springframework.org/schema/beans"
        xmlns:xsi="http://www.w3.org/2001/XMLSchema-instance"
        xmlns:jaxrs="http://cxf.apache.org/jaxrs"
        xmlns:cxf="http://cxf.apache.org/core"
        xsi:schemaLocation="http://www.springframework.org/schema/beans
        http://www.springframework.org/schema/beans/spring-beans.xsd
        http://cxf.apache.org/jaxrs
        http://cxf.apache.org/schemas/jaxrs.xsd
        http://cxf.apache.org/core
        http://cxf.apache.org/schemas/core.xsd ">

    <!-- Loads CXF modules from cxf.jar file -->
    <import resource="classpath:META-INF/cxf/cxf.xml"/>
    <import resource="classpath:META-INF/cxf/cxf-extension-soap.xml"/>
    <import resource="classpath:META-INF/cxf/cxf-servlet.xml"/>
    <import resource="classpath:META-INF/cxf/cxf-extension-jaxrs-
                                        binding.xml"/>

    <jaxrs:server id="documentservice" address="/">
    <jaxrs:serviceBeans>
        <ref bean="documentManagerImpl"/>
    </jaxrs:serviceBeans>
    <jaxrs:features>
```

```
          <cxf:logging/>
      </jaxrs:features>
</jaxrs:server>

      <bean id="documentManagerImpl"
          class="com.learning.ws.rest.DocumentManagerImpl"/>
</beans>
```

Step 4: Create Web.xml File

Reuse the web.xml file we created in Example1.

Step 5: Write a Client to Invoke the Deployed Service

The Web-based client provided below invokes the "deleteOrReplaceDocument()" method of a service endpoint.

The URL provided below invokes the "deleteOrReplaceDocument()" service operation.

```
document.forms[0].action = "/wsbook/services/document/deleteReplace/1";
```

The URL provided below invokes the "addDocument()" service operation.

```
document.forms[0].action = "/wsbook/services/document/add/1";
```

Submit the HTML form provided below and view the output on the server console.

```
<html>
<head>
    <title>REST demo for GET, POST, DELETE and PUT</title>
    <script type="text/javascript">
        function submitUserForm() {
            document.forms[0].action =
                "/wsbook/services/document/deleteReplace/1";
            document.forms[0].submit();
        }
    </script>
</head>
<body>
<form method="post">
    <table align="center">
        <tr>
            <td><label><b>User Id:</b></label></td>
            <td>
                <input type="text" name="userName"
                        id=" documentId" value="" size="40"/>
            </td>
        </tr>
        <tr>
            <td>
                <a href="javascript:submitUserForm()">1.Log In</a>
            </td>
        </tr>
    </table>
</form>
```

```
</body>
</html>
```

Step 6: Create a War File and Deploy It in the Tomcat Server

Follow the instructions specified in Example1. The structure of the generated war file is shown in Figure 4-11.

Figure 4-11: war file structure

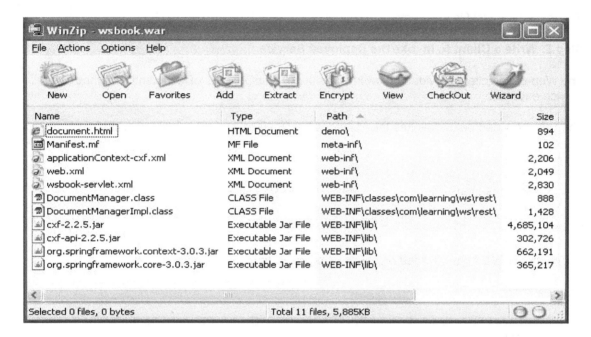

Example 5: How to Use @MatrixParam

The example provided below demonstrates the use of the @MatrixParam annotation while developing REST-based Web services. The steps required to develop a REST Web service to obtain URL data using the @MatrixParam annotation is given below.

1. Create a service endpoint interface.
2. Create a service implementation class.
3. Create an Apache-CXF framework-specific configuration file.
4. Create a web.xml file.
5. Create a war file and deploy it in the Tomcat server.
6. Write a client to invoke the deployed service.

The above-specified steps are described in the following sections.

Step 1: Create a Service Endpoint Interface

The REST interface provided in Listing 4-9 has one service method; it obtains the URL metadata using the @PathParam and @MatrixParam annotations.

Listing 4-9: REST example using @MatrixParam annotation

```
// BookService.java
```

```java
package com.learning.ws.rest;

import javax.ws.rs.*;

@Path("/bookservice/")
@Produces("text/plain")
public interface BookService {
    @GET
    @Path("/book/{year}")
    String getBooks(@PathParam("year") String year,
                    @MatrixParam("author") String author,
                    @MatrixParam("country") String country);
}
```

Step 2: Create a Service Implementation Class

The implementation code of the above-declared method in an interface is shown in Listing 4-10.

Listing 4-10: REST service implementation class

```java
// BookServiceImpl.java
package com.learning.ws.rest;

import javax.ws.rs.MatrixParam;
public class BookServiceImpl implements BookService {
    public String getBooks(String year, String author, String country) {
        return "year: " + year + " author: "
                    + author + " country: " + country;
    }
}
```

Step 3: Create Apache-CXF Framework-Specific Configuration File

Create an Apache-CXF framework-specific XML configuration file to register the REST Web service class with a Spring container. The complete XML configuration is given below.

```xml
<?xml version="1.0" encoding="UTF-8"?>
<beans xmlns="http://www.springframework.org/schema/beans"
        xmlns:xsi="http://www.w3.org/2001/XMLSchema-instance"
        xmlns:jaxrs="http://cxf.apache.org/jaxrs"
        xmlns:cxf="http://cxf.apache.org/core"
        xsi:schemaLocation="http://www.springframework.org/schema/beans
        http://www.springframework.org/schema/beans/spring-beans.xsd
        http://cxf.apache.org/jaxrs
        http://cxf.apache.org/schemas/jaxrs.xsd
        http://cxf.apache.org/core
        http://cxf.apache.org/schemas/core.xsd ">

    <!-- Loads CXF modules from cxf.jar file -->
    <import resource="classpath:META-INF/cxf/cxf.xml"/>
    <import resource="classpath:META-INF/cxf/cxf-extension-soap.xml"/>
    <import resource="classpath:META-INF/cxf/cxf-servlet.xml"/>
    <import resource="classpath:META-INF/cxf/cxf-extension-jaxrs-
                                    binding.xml"/>

    <jaxrs:server id="bookservice" address="/">
```

```
        <jaxrs:serviceBeans>
            <ref bean="bookServiceImpl"/>
        </jaxrs:serviceBeans>
    </jaxrs:server>

    <bean id="bookServiceImpl"
            class="com.learning.ws.rest.BookServiceImpl"/>
</beans>
```

Step 4: Create a Web.xml File

Reuse the web.xml file we created in Example1.

Step 5: Create a War File and Deploy It in the Tomcat Server

Figure 4-12: war file structure

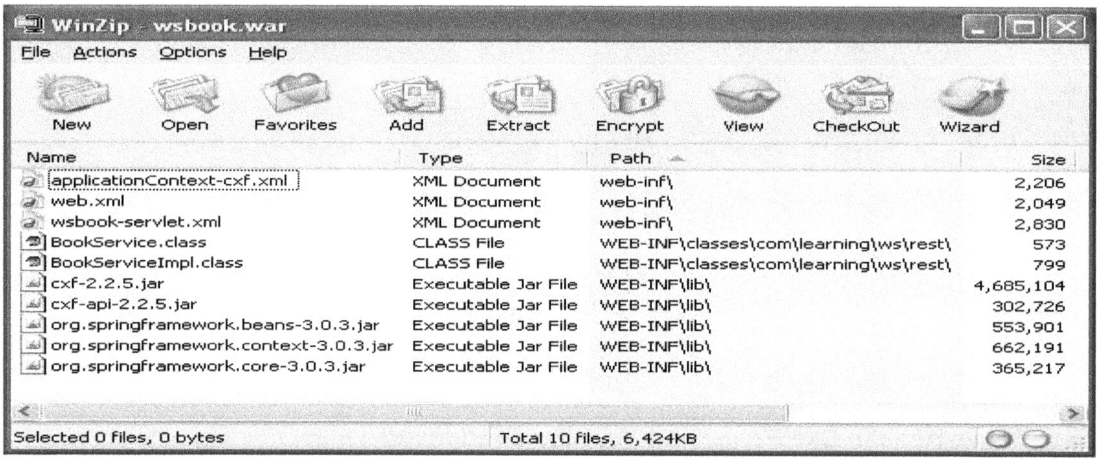

Follow the instructions specified in Example1. The structure of the generated war file is shown in Figure 4-12.

Step 6: Invoke the Deployed Service from Your Browser

The deployed service is ready to invoke from a Web browser. Try the following set of REST URLs and view the output in the browser.

The URL is:

```
http://localhost:8080/wsbook/services/bookservice/book/2012
```

Its output is:

```
    year: 2012 author: null country: null
```

The URL is:

```
http://localhost:8080/wsbook/services/bookservice/book/2012;author=john
```

Its output is:

```
    year: 2012 author: srinivas country: null
```

The URL is:

```
http://localhost:8080/wsbook/services/bookservice/book/2012;author=john;c
ountry=usa
```

Its output is:

```
    year: 2012 author: srinivas country: usa
```


REST Client Design Scenarios

There are several ways a REST client can invoke a deployed REST Web service. The JAX-RS specification does not define a standard for the client API. It is up to the developer to choose a suitable client for his service endpoint. The following client programs can be used to invoke a deployed Web service.

1. How to invoke a REST service using standard Java API
2. How to invoke a REST service using Spring Rest Template
3. How to invoke a REST service from a browser
4. How to invoke a REST service from a Web page

The above-specified client design scenarios are explained in this section.

CASE 1: How to Invoke a REST Service Using Standard Java API

In this approach, the "openConnection()" method of the "java.net.URL" class is used to invoke the Web service endpoint. This approach is generally used for HTTP GET operations. The complete client code is given below.

```java
private static void invokeService() throws Exception {
    // Service endpoint URL
    String restURL =
        "http://localhost:8080/wsbook/services/gradeservice/grades";

    URL url = new URL(restURL);
    URLConnection conn = url.openConnection();
    conn.setDoOutput(true);

    InputStreamReader isr=new InputStreamReader(conn.getInputStream());
    BufferedReader br = new BufferedReader(isr);

    String response;
    while((response = br.readLine()) != null) {
        System.out.println(response);
        // Implement your logic here to build the XML etc.
    }
    br.close();
}
```

CASE 2: How to Invoke a REST Service Using a Spring Rest Template

In this approach, the Spring framework-provided "RestTemplate" class is used to invoke a deployed REST Web service. This approach is generally used for HTTP GET operations. The client code provided below explains the use of the "RestTemplate" class.

```
private static void invokeServiceUsingSpringTemplate() throws Exception {

    /* Invoke the REST service using Spring framework provided
    RestTemplate class. */
    RestTemplate restTemplate = new RestTemplate();

    // Passing single input parameter from client
    String requestURL1 =
    "http://localhost:8080/wsbook/services/gradeservice/grade/{grade}";
    String result = restTemplate.getForObject(requestURL1,
        String.class, "1");
    System.out.println("result: " + result);

    // Passing multiple input parameters from the client
    Map<String, String> vars = new HashMap<String, String>();
    vars.put("grade", "1");
    vars.put("subject", "Java");

    String requestURL2 =
        "http://localhost:8080/wsbook/services/gradeservice/
        grade/{grade}/subject/{subject}";
    String result1 = restTemplate.getForObject(requestURL2,
            String.class, vars);
    System.out.println("result1: " + result1);

    // Passing multiple input parameters from the client
    Map<String, String> topics = new HashMap<String, String>();
    vars.put("grade", "1");
    vars.put("subject", "Math");
    vars.put("topic", "Mathematics and art");

    String requestURL3 =
        "http://localhost:8080/wsbook/services/gradeservice/
            grade/1/subject/{subject}/topic/{topic}";
    String result2 = restTemplate.getForObject(requestURL3,
            String.class, vars);
    System.out.println("result2: " + result2);
}
```

CASE 3: How to Invoke a REST Service from a Browser

In this scenario, use any Web browser to invoke a REST Web service. This approach is generally used for HTTP GET operations. Try the following URLs from your browser and view the results.

```
http://localhost:8080/wsbook/services/gradeservice/grade/1
http://localhost:8080/wsbook/services/gradeservice/grade/1/subject/Math
http://localhost:8080/wsbook/services/gradeservice/grade/1/subject/Math/t
opic/Algebra
http://localhost:8080/wsbook/services/stockservice/symbol?symbol=WFC
```

CASE 4: How to Invoke a REST Service from a Web Page

This approach is used to invoke a deployed REST service from a Web page. Submit the HTML form using the javascript function. This approach is generally used for the HTTP POST operations.

```html
<html>
<head>
<title>WS REST DEMO</title>
<script type="text/javascript">
    function submitUserForm() {
        document.forms[0].action=
            "/wsbook/services/loginservice/userName/XXXX/password/XXX";
        document.forms[0].submit();
    }
</script>
</head>
<body>
    <form method="post">
        <table align="center">
            <tr>
                <td> <label><b>User Id:</b></label></td>
                <td><input type="text" name="userName"
                        id="userName" size="40"/> </td>
            </tr>
            <tr>
                <td> <label><b>Password:</b></label></td>
                <td><input type="text" name="password"
                            id="password" size="40"/> </td>
            </tr>
            <tr>
                <td><b>
                    <a href="javascript:submitUserForm()">
                        1.Log In
                    </a>
                </td>
            </tr>
        </table>
    </form>
</body>
</html>
```

REST Service Endpoint and URL Design Scenarios

The section will explain best practices for designing the service endpoint interface and REST URLs.

CASE 1: How to Design a REST URL

Don't display too much information on one page. Build the URLs logically, and provide links to other resources for additional information. Make sure the user understands the instructions when looking up the URL.

Do not use this, even though it is valid.

```
http://localhost:8080/wsbook/services/gradeservice/grade/GRADE_ID

http://localhost:8080/wsbook/services/gradeservice/grade/GRADE_ID/su
bject/SUB_ID
```

Instead use this, so it is easy for user to navigate from one page to other page. By looking into the URL, user knows the expected output.

```
http://localhost:8080/wsbook/services/gradeservice/grade/1
http://localhost:8080/wsbook/services/gradeservice/grade/1/subject/M
ath
```

Do not use this

```
http://localhost:8080/wsbook/services/gradeservice/getGrade?grade=1
```

Instead use this, use nouns rather than verbs.

```
http://localhost:8080/wsbook/services/gradeservice/grade/1
```

CASE 2: How to Design a Service Endpoint Interface

Provide a uniform interface between the client and service. This is a contact between the client and service endpoint

```
@Path("/gradeservice/")
@Produces("application/xml")
public interface GradeManager {
    @GET
    @Path("/grade/{grade}/subject/{subject}")
    public String getSubjectTopics(@PathParam("grade") Integer grade,
                                   @PathParam("subject") String subject);
}

public class GradeManagerImpl implements GradeManager {
    public String getSubjectTopics(Integer grade, String subject) {
        return XMLBuilder.getAllTopics(grade, subject);
    }
}
```

Do not use this, even though it is a valid service code.

```
@Path("/gradeservice/")
@Produces("application/xml")
public class GradeManagerImpl {
    @GET
    @Path("/grade/{grade}/subject/{subject}")
    public String getSubjectTopics(@PathParam("grade") Integer grade,
                                   @PathParam("subject") String subject) {
        return XMLBuilder.getAllTopics(grade, subject);
    }
}
```

Build and Deployment Instructions

This section explains the steps required to build, package, and deploy the code in any servlet container. The following software tools are used to develop and deploy the code examples.

- Apache-Tomcat—6.0.28
- JDK—1.6
- Ant
- Spring—3
- Apache-CXF—2.2.5
- IDE—Eclipse OR IntelliJ IDEA

Build a war file using Ant or any other build tool. Make sure the following files are packaged correctly in the war file.

- Service endpoint interface
- Service endpoint implementation class
- Any utility classes used for data access, etc.
- Web.xml file
- Spring, Apache-CXF specific configuration files
- Client code—can be a Web page, java class, or simply a browser URL.

Deploy the war file in any servlet container.

- Copy the packaged war file into the "apache-tomcat/webapps" directory.
- Start the Tomcat server using the startup.bat batch file available in the "apache-tomcat/bin" directory.
- View the console output/logs; make sure war file is deployed without any errors.

NOTE: Refer to Chapter12 for detailed build and deployment instructions.

Test Yourself – Objective Type Questions

1. Which one of the following is a valid REST URL? Select correct answer.

   a) http://localhost:8080/wsbook/services/getGrade?id=1
   b) http://localhost:8080/wsbook/services/gradeservice/grade/1
   c) http://localhost:8080/wsbook/services/getGrade.action
   d) http://localhost:8080/wsbook/services/getGrade.do
   e) All are valid.

2. Which of the following are valid REST guidelines?

   a) Create a URL for each resource; these resources should be nouns, not verbs.
   b) In REST it is okay to use the GET request to update the server-side resource.
   c) REST uses logical URLs, not physical URLs; use of a million resources does not require a million physical URLs.
   d) REST does not recommend a uniform interface between the client and server.

e) None of the above statements is valid.

3. Select the correct answer. Which of the following is a valid REST implementation?

a)

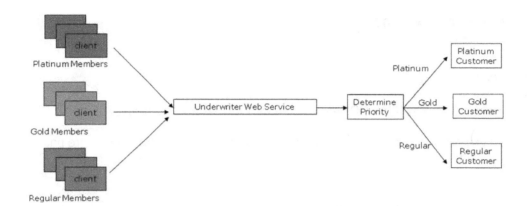

b)

c)

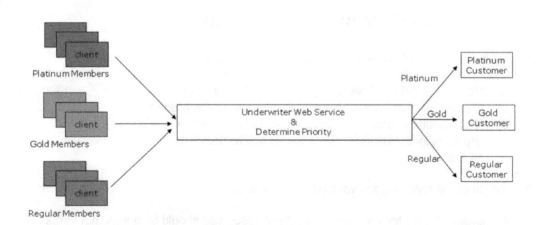

d)

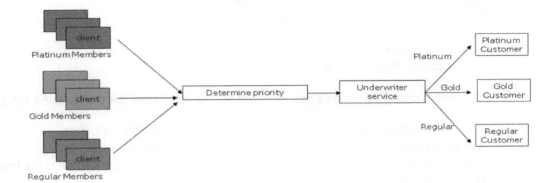

e) All are valid REST implementations

4. Which of the following statements best explains the @Produces annotation used in REST?

    a) It is used to obtain the parameter values specified in a query string.
    b) It is used to receive the HTML form data service endpoint after the client submits the form using the HTTP POST method.
    c) More than one content type can be declared, and it is represented as @Produces ("application/xml," "text/plain").
    d) It is used only at the method level.
    e) It is used only at the class level.

5. Which of the following statements best explains the use of the @Path annotation in REST?

    a) It identifies the entry point to the service and operation.
    b) It can be used at the class level and method level.
    c) It supports the URI template regular expressions.
    d) It supports the annotation inheritance when declared in super class and subclass.
    e) All the above.

6. If a user invokes the REST service using the URL provided below, what is the output of this service? Select the correct answer.

Client URL:

    http://localhost:8080/wsbook/services/dataservice/restinfo

Service Code:

```
@Path("/dataservice/")
@Produces("text/plain")
public class RestDataManagerImpl {
    @GET
    @Path("/restinfo")
    public void getCommmonInfo(@Context UriInfo uriInfo)   {
    URI baseUri = uriInfo.getBaseUri();
        System.out.println("--- baseUri ---" + baseUri);
    }
}
```

a) http://localhost:8080/wsbook/services/dataservice/restinfo
b) http://localhost:8080/wsbook/services/
c) /services/dataservice/restinfo
d) /dataservice/restinfo
e) http://localhost:8080/wsbook

7. Which of the following statements best explains the @FormParam annotation used in REST?

a) It is used to obtain the parameters values specified in the REST URL path.
b) It is used to obtain the parameter values specified in a query string.
c) It is used to receive the HTML form data service endpoint after client submits the form using HTTP POST method
d) It is used as a parameter to a Form Bean
e) It is used for logging the form bean data service endpoint.

8. If a user invokes the REST service using the URL provided below, what is the output of this service? Select the correct answer.

Client URL:

```
http://localhost:8080/wsbook/services/dataservice/restinfo
```

Service Code:

```
@Path("/dataservice/")
@Produces("application/xml")
public class RestDataManagerImpl {
    @GET
    @Path("/restinfo")
    public void getCommmonInfo(@Context UriInfo uriInfo) {
    String path = uriInfo.getPath();
        System.out.println("---- path ----" + path);
    }
}
```

a) /dataservice/restinfo
b) http://localhost:8080/wsbook/services/dataservice/restinfo
c) /wsbook/services/dataservice/restinfo
d) localhost:8080/wsbook/services/dataservice/restinfo
e) http://localhost:8080/wsbook/services/

9. If a user invokes the REST service using the URL provided below, what is the output of this service? Select the correct answer.

Client URL:

```
http://localhost:8080/wsbook/services/loginservice/userName/john/pas
sword/test
```

Service Class:

```
@Path("/loginservice/")
@Produces("plain/text")
public interface AccessManager {
```

```
@POST
@Path("/userName/{userName}/password/{password}")
public String isValidUser(@FormParam("userName") String userName,
                          @FormParam("password") String password);

@POST
@Path("/userName/{userName}/password/{password}")
public String isValidUser(MultivaluedMap<String, String>
                                        formParams);
}
```

a) This code does not work. Overloaded methods are not allowed in REST services.
b) This is a valid service code. The first occurrence of the method will be executed.
c) The code will throw a runtime exception. It works fine during compile time.
d) This is not a valid REST service implementation.
e) None of the above statements is valid.

10. Which of the following annotations is not part of the "javax.ws.rs" package?

a) @Produces
b) @Consumes
c) @Path
d) @Override
e) @Webservice

Answers to Questions

1. B is the correct answer. Use nouns instead of verbs while designing the REST URL's.

2. A and C are correct choices. The choice B is incorrect because GET requests should be side effect free. The choice D is incorrect because REST recommends using an interface between client and service.

3. B is the correct answer. REST recommends identifying each resource with an URI.

4. C is the correct answer. The use of multiple content types is allowed in REST. The choice A is the definition of a @QueryParam annotation and choice B is the definition of a @FormParam annotation.

5. E is the correct answer. All are valid statements w.r.t. @Path annotation. REST supports the annotation inheritance.

6. B is the correct answer. The tutorial Example-2 provides the API details of the REST service.

7. C is the correct answer for the given scenario. It explains the use of @PathParam, @QueryParam and @FormParam annotations while developing the REST web services.

8. A is the correct answer. The tutorial Example-2 provides the API details of the REST service.

9. B is the correct answer. Try this example and see the output. REST allows using overloaded methods but the first occurrence of the method is executed. It does not throw any runtime exception.

10. D and E are correct choices. The @override annotation is part of "java.lang" package and @Webservice annotation belongs to "javax.jws" package used for developing SOAP based web services.

Chapter 5. SOAP

The two entities involved in any Web service development are service provider and service consumer. The service provider implements the business functionality, and consumers use that functionality. But how is the information exchanged between the service provider and the consumers? How do the two applications communicate with each other, and what format do they use for exchanging application data? The specifications that address these details are found in SOAP, which stands for Simple Object Access Protocol. The current version of SOAP is 1.2. The acronym SOAP (Simple Object Access Protocol) is dropped in the SOAP-1.2 version. Version 1.2 has been the W3C standard since 2003.

SOAP is an XML-based message structure used to exchange information between two applications within or outside of an enterprise. SOAP provides a standard XML-based message format for message exchange over the network. As a messaging protocol, SOAP is protocol neutral and can use any other protocol as a transport protocol; SOAP can be transmitted using HHTP, HTTPS, FTP, JMS, SMTP and any other similar protocol. SOAP is an XML-based messaging structure, so it requires a protocol such as HTTP for transmission—an underlying protocol for transferring the messages over the network. The protocol layering of SOAP, HTTP, and TCP/IP is shown in Figure 5-1.

Figure 5-1: Protocol layering

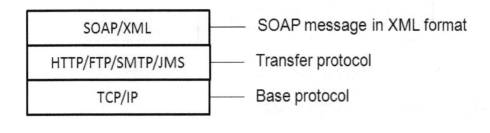

Protocol layering

SOAP is a one-way messaging protocol. SOAP Binding provides a set of rules to transfer the SOAP message on top of another protocol. The commonly used HTTP is a request-and-response protocol; if a user submits a Web page request, this protocol will get the response back to him or her. The XML-based SOAP message can be combined with a protocol such as HTTP to get the responses back using the initial sender connection. SOAP uses the semantics provided by its underlying protocol (SOAP over HTTP) for message transmission, although the generated SOAP message is hidden to the developer. The client-generated SOAP request is wrapped inside the HTTP request and sent to the service endpoint. The service endpoint processes the inbound request and sends the HTTP response, which envelops the SOAP response used to service the invoking clients. The conversion of SOAP to HTTP and vice versa is hidden to the service developer. The Web service development frameworks provide a HTTP-based transport servlet for carrying the SOAP messages over HTTP. The intermediary nodes between the client and the service endpoint can manipulate certain blocks of the SOAP request-and-response messages.

This chapter will discuss the following topics:

- SOAP terminology
- Structure of a SOAP message
- SOAP Binding
- BP (WS-I) standards of a SOAP message
- Comparison of SOAP-1.1 and SOAP-1.2 messages
- The new features of SOAP-1.2

SOAP Terminology

This section explains the terminology commonly used in SOAP while developing Web Services. The SOAP message communication path between sender and receiver is shown in Figure 5-2. The initial sender initiates a SOAP message and passes it through a set of intermediaries (also called nodes) and finally delivers it to the receiver. The receiver receives the incoming message, processes the message, and sends the response back to the sender. The SOAP terminology is defined below.

Figure 5-2: SOAP message communication

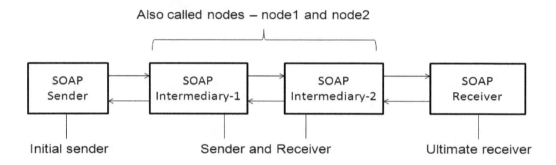

SOAP message communication between sender and receiver

SOAP Node: A SOAP node is the one that processes a SOAP message. The SOAP node can be an initial sender, any intermediary or it can be a final receiver. The intermediary nodes can act as both sender and receiver.

SOAP Sender: A SOAP sender is a SOAP node that transmits a SOAP message.

SOAP Receiver: A SOAP receiver is a SOAP node that receives a SOAP message.

SOAP Message Path: The SOAP message path is the flow of communication between the originator and receiver. It is also called a message chain.

Initial SOAP Sender: The initial SOAP sender is the SOAP node that initiates the SOAP message. This is the starting point of the message in a message path.

Ultimate SOAP Receiver: The ultimate SOAP receiver is the SOAP node that receives the SOAP message at the final destination. This is the end point of the message in a message path.

SOAP Intermediary: The SOAP intermediary is the one that sends and receives the SOAP messages. The two intermediaries configured between initial sender and ultimate receiver is shown in the diagram. The first intermediary receives the soap message from initial sender; passes it to the next intermediary and finally delivers it to the ultimate receiver.

SOAP Intermediary: A SOAP intermediary is not the initiator or final recipient but rather a node along the message path. The two intermediaries configured between the initial sender and ultimate receiver is shown in Figure 5-2. The first intermediary receives the SOAP message from initial sender, passes it to the next intermediary, and finally delivers it to the ultimate receiver.

SOAP Message: A SOAP message is a structured unit of information used for message communication between nodes.

SOAP Envelope: The SOAP envelope is the outermost element of a SOAP message. All other elements are enclosed within the SOAP envelope.

SOAP Header: The SOAP header is an immediate child element of a SOAP envelope. It is an optional element that may not exist for all messages. The SOAP header is processed by configured intermediary SOAP nodes in the message path.

SOAP Body: The SOAP Body contains the actual request and response message targeted for ultimate receiver.

SOAP Fault: The SOAP fault is the immediate child of the SOAP body and contains fault information.

SOAP Block: The SOAP block is a unit of information packaged in the header and body. The two SOAP block forms are the header block and body block.

SOAP Binding: The SOAP binding specifies the set of rules defined to carry the SOAP message on top of another protocol. The SOAP message is layered as shown in Figure 5-3. SOAP supports many underlying protocols such as HTTP, SMTP, and FTP. In general, we use SOAP over HTTP for developing Web services.

Figure 5-3: SOAP Binding over HTTP

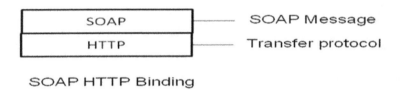

The following table shows the list of namespaces used to represent the soap messages.

Namespace used	URL
This URL represents the namespace of a soap envelope for SOAP-1.1	http://schemas.xmlsoap.org/soap/envelope/
This URL represents the namespace of a soap envelope for SOAP-1.2	http://www.w3.org/2003/05/soap-envelope/
This URL represents the soap encoding namespace for SOAP-1.1	http://schemas.xmlsoap.org/soap/encoding/
This URL represents the soap encoding namespace for SOAP-1.2	http://www.w3.org/2003/05/soap-encoding/
This URL represents the namespace of the XML schema	http://www.w3.org/2001/XMLSchema/

Structure of SOAP Messages (SOAP-1.1 and SOAP-1.2)

The SOAP message is an encoded XML document that contains an outermost <Envelope> element, an optional <Header> element, and a required <Body> element. The body element contains a <Fault> element, which is used for reporting errors. The envelope, header, and body elements should be namespace qualified.

The XML representation of the SOAP message is given below:

```
<soap:Envelope xmlns:soap="http://schemas.xmlsoap.org/soap/envelope/">
  <soap:Header>
    ...
  </soap:Header>
  <soap:Body>
    ...
  </soap:Body>
</soap:Envelope>
```

The structure of a SOAP message is shown in Figure 5-4.

Figure 5-4: Structure of a SOAP message

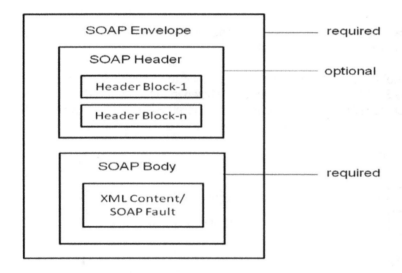

Structure of a SOAP Message

SOAP Envelope

The SOAP envelope is sometimes called a SOAP message. The SOAP envelope is the outermost element of a SOAP message. It contains an optional SOAP header element and a mandatory SOAP body element. The rules applied to a SOAP envelope are given below:

- It must be the outermost element of the SOAP message.
- The element name must be "Envelope"; it is a required element in a SOAP message.
- The attributes of the SOAP envelope element and its child elements must be namespace qualified.

The example skeleton SOAP envelope is given below. Let us review the significance of each element and attribute of the SOAP envelope.

```
<?xml version="1.0"?>
<soap:Envelope xmlns:soap="http://schemas.xmlsoap.org/soap/envelope/"
        soap:encodingStyle="http://schemas.xmlsoap.org/soap/encoding/">
</soap:Envelope>
```

The following attribute represents the namespace URI used to reference the SOAP envelope.

```
xmlns:soap=http://schemas.xmlsoap.org/soap/envelope/
```

The following *encodingStyle* attribute is used to define the data types used in the document.

```
soap:encodingStyle="http://schemas.xmlsoap.org/soap/encoding/">
```

The following element represents the outermost element of a SOAP message; it should be namespace qualified.

```
<soap:Envelope/>
```

SOAP Header

The header element contains application-specific information. The (optional) header element, if it exists, must be the immediate child element of the SOAP envelope. Each sub-element of the SOAP header element is called a header block. A SOAP message header can contain any number of header blocks.

The rules applied to SOAP header elements are given below:

- The element name must be "Header."
- It is an optional element, and if it exists, it must be the immediate child element of the SOAP envelope.
- Any number of header blocks may be used, but each sub-element of the header element must be namespace qualified.
- Each header element must be the immediate child element of the SOAP envelope element.
- A SOAP message should use the SOAP header attributes only in immediate child elements (header blocks) of the SOAP header element.

A SOAP message header block may contain zero or more attributes. These attributes are defined in the default namespace, and its URI is http://www.w3.org/2003/05/soap-envelope. The valid attributes of a SOAP header block are listed below.

- encodingStyle
- role
- mustUnderstand
- relay

The example skeleton SOAP header XML is given below. Let us review the significance of each element and attribute of the SOAP header.

```
<?xml version="1.0"?>
```

```
<soap:Envelope xmlns:soap="http://www.w3.org/2003/05/soap-envelope"
           soap:encodingStyle="http://www.w3.org/2003/05/soap-encoding">
<soap:Header>
    <ws:transaction xmlns:ws="http://wsbook.learning.com/transaction/"
                 soap:mustUnderstand="1">
        567
  </ws:transaction>
</soap:Header>
    ...
</soap:Envelope>
```

The following element represents the SOAP header of a SOAP message.

```
<soap:Header>
```

The following element is the immediate child element of a SOAP header. It is called the SOAP header block.

```
<ws:transaction> ... </ws:transaction>
```

The following attribute represents the namespace used for the SOAP header block.

```
xmlns:ws="http://wsbook.learning.com/transaction/"
```

The above-specified SOAP header block attributes are described in the following section.

SOAP encodingStyle Attribute

The SOAP encodingStyle attribute indicates the encoding rules used to serialize the parts of a SOAP message, represented by a URI. Examples of SOAP encoding URIs are listed below.

```
http://www.w3.org/2003/05/soap-encoding
http://wsbook.learning.com/encoding
http://www.w3.org/2003/05/soap-envelope/soap-encoding/encoding/none
```

The syntax of the encoding style attribute is given below.

```
soap:encodingStyle="URI"
```

The first two URIs represent the standard and custom namespaces used for applying the encoding rules. If no encodingStyle namespace exists for an element and its descendants, the encoding is written as "none," indicating that no encoding rules apply to that element and its descendants.

An example XML code of an envelope using the encodingStyle attribute is given below. Its scope is available to all of its descendants; it is accessible to all header blocks.

```
<soap:Envelope xmlns:soap="http://www.w3.org/2003/05/soap-envelope"
           soap:encodingStyle="http://www.w3.org/2003/05/soap-encoding">
</soap:Envelope>
```

SOAP role Attribute

The SOAP message travels from an initial sender to an ultimate receiver. While on its message path, it passes through a set of intermediary nodes. Some parts of the SOAP message are targeted for the intermediaries in its message path. The role attribute indicates which header block of a SOAP message is targeted for which message node. The syntax of the role attribute is given below. The role attribute is used only for the SOAP header blocks of a SOAP message.

The following attribute is used for soap-1.1.

```
soap:actor="URI"
```

The following attribute is used for soap-1.2.

```
soap:role="URI"
```

The special cases of SOAP roles defined by the SOAP specifications and the significance of each are listed below.

The following role attribute indicates that the SOAP header block is targeted for each available node in its message path. It can be an intermediary or an ultimate receiver.

```
soap:role = "http://www.w3.org/2003/05/soap-envelope/role/next"
```

The following attribute indicates that the nodes must not act on this role.

```
soap:role = "http://www.w3.org/2003/05/soap-envelope/role/none"
```

The following attribute indicates that the message is targeted for the ultimate receiver.

```
soap:role="http://www.w3.org/2003/05/soap-envelope/role/ultimateReceiver"
```

An example XML code of a SOAP header block using its role attribute is given below. The proper methods for using the "manager" role depend on the node implementation.

```
<soap:Header>
    <ws:transaction xmlns:ws="http://wsbook.learning.com/transaction/"
            soap:role=" http://wsbook.learning.com/employee/manager">
            567
    </ws:transaction>
</soap:Header>
```

SOAP mustUnderstand Attribute

The SOAP "mustUnderstand" attribute indicates whether the processing of a SOAP header block is mandatory or optional. The valid values are "true" and "false," and the default value is false unless declared true. The "mustUnderstand" attribute is used only for SOAP header blocks of a SOAP message.

```
soap:mustUnderstand="true|false" OR "0|1"
```

The value "true" indicates the node process that the header block must understand; otherwise, the soap node will throw a SOAP fault.

The value "false" indicates that the processing of the header block is not mandatory.

An example XML code of a SOAP header block using the "mustUnderstand" attribute is given below.

```
<soap:Header>
    <ws:transaction xmlns:ws="http://wsbook.learning.com/transaction/"
                soap: mustUnderstand="1">
        567
    </ws:transaction>
</soap:Header>
```

SOAP relay Attribute

When processing a SOAP header block, the SOAP intermediary removes that header block—as well as unprocessed header blocks—from the SOAP message. However, the unprocessed header block is retained if the relay attribute value is specified as true, and the header block is then relayed to the next available message node in the message path. The relay attribute is used only for SOAP header blocks of a SOAP message. The possible values of a relay attribute are "true" and "false", and the default value is "false." The syntax of the SOAP relay attribute is given below.

```
soap:relay = true|false
```

The value "true" indicates that the header block can be forwarded to the next node in the message path even if it remains unprocessed.

The value "false" indicates that the header block will be removed before the message is forwarded to the next node in the message path.

```
<soap:Header>
    <ws:transaction xmlns:ws="http://wsbook.learning.com/transaction/"
        soap:role=" http://www.w3.org/2003/05/soap-envelope/role/next"
        soap:relay="true">
        567
    </ws:transaction>
</soap:Header>
```

In the above example, the role attribute of the header block is set to next, which means each intermediary node should process this SOAP header block. The header block relay attribute value is true, which indicates the header block can be relayed even if it is processed. So this header block will be processed by all intermediary nodes in the message path.

SOAP Body

The SOAP body contains all valid XML elements. The body of the SOAP message is targeted for the ultimate receiver for processing; however, the SOAP body content may be accessible to the intermediary nodes in its message path. The content of a SOAP body is also called the message payload. It is the actual data used by the Web Service.

The rules applied to the SOAP body element are given below:

- The element name must be "Body."
- It is a mandatory element and must be the immediate child element of the SOAP envelope.
- The local part of the body element must be namespace qualified.
- It is recommended to use namespace prefixes for all sub-elements of a SOAP body element.
- It is recommended to use the SOAP fault sub-element for reporting errors.

The SOAP body XML code of a SOAP message request is given below. The SOAP message request contains input data for the Web service, which is the employee ID used to obtain the employee details from the Web service.

```
<soap:Envelope xmlns:soap="http://schemas.xmlsoap.org/soap/envelope/">
    <soap:Body>
        <ns1:getEmployee xmlns:ns1="http://jaxws.ws.learning.com/">
        <employeeId>823147</employeeId>
        </ns1:getEmployee>
    </soap:Body>
</soap:Envelope>
```

The response sent from the Web service is given below. The body of a response message contains the details of the employee wrapped inside the <getEmployeeResponse/> element.

```
<soap:Envelope xmlns:soap="http://schemas.xmlsoap.org/soap/envelope/">
    <soap:Body>
        <ns1:getEmployeeResponse xmlns:ns1=
                                "http://jaxws.ws.learning.com/">
            <employee>
                <employeeId>823147</employeeId>
                <firstName>John</firstName>
                <lastName>Smith</lastName>
            </employee>
        </ns1:getEmployeeResponse>
    </soap:Body>
</soap:Envelope>
```

The immediate child element of the SOAP body used for reporting errors is the SOAP fault, which is explained in next section.

SOAP Fault

The SOAP fault element of a SOAP message is used to carry the error information. If present, it must be the immediate child element of a SOAP body element. The rules applied to SOAP fault elements are given below.

- The element name must be "Fault."
- The local part of the fault element must be namespace qualified.
- It must be the immediate child element of a SOAP body element. A maximum of one fault element is allowed in a SOAP body.

The XML representation of a SOAP fault element is given below.

```
<soap:Envelope xmlns:soap="http://schemas.xmlsoap.org/soap/envelope/">
    <soap:Body>
        <soap:Fault>
            . . .
        </soap:Fault>
    </soap:Body>
</soap:Envelope>
```

The sub-elements of a SOAP fault element are different in SOAP-1.1 and SOAP-1.2. The sub-elements of a SOAP-1.1 are listed below.

- faultcode
- faultstring
- faultactor
- detail

The XML representation of a SOAP fault and its sub-elements are given below.

```
<soap:Fault xmlns:soap="http://schemas.xmlsoap.org/soap/envelope/">
    <faultcode>soap:Client</faultcode>
    <faultstring>Invalid message format</faultstring>
    <faultactor>http://ws.learning.com/someactor</faultactor>
    <detail>
        <m:msg xmlns:m="http://ws.learning.com/faults/exceptions">
            It has invalid XML elements. I don't understand what it is.
        </m:msg>
    </detail>
</soap:Fault>
```

The faultcode Element

The "faultcode" element is a mandatory element inside the SOAP fault element. This code identifies the type of fault. The children of the SOAP fault element are local to that element, so the code does not require a namespace qualification. The valid fault codes and their meanings are listed below.

Fault Code	Description
Client	The message was not correctly formed by the client, so it cannot be processed. Example: required information was omitted while creating the message.
Server	There was a problem with the server, so message cannot be processed.
VersionMismatch	The processing node found an invalid version of the namespace for the SOAP envelope element.
MustUnderstand	The SOAP header block attribute mustUnderstand set to "1" was not understood.

The faultstring element

The "faultstring" element is a mandatory element inside the SOAP fault element. The fault string element provides a readable explanation of the SOAP fault in text format. An example of a fault string is given below.

```
<faultstring>Invalid message format</faultstring>
```

It is valid to use xml:lang attribute on faultstring element.

```
<faultstring xml:lang="en">Invalid message format</faultstring>
```

The faultactor Element

The "faultactor" element is an optional element inside the SOAP fault element. It indicates which processing node in the message path caused the fault to happen. An example of a "faultactor" is given below.

```
<faultactor>http://ws.learning.com/someactor</faultactor>
```

The detail Element

The "detail" element is required if the contents of the SOAP body are not successfully processed. The detail element contains the application-specific error information related to the SOAP body element. It does not hold any error information related to the SOAP header element. The immediate child elements of the detail element may be namespace qualified. An example of a fault detail is given below.

```
<detail>
    <m:msg xmlns:m="http://ws.learning.com/faults/exceptions">
        It has invalid XML elements. I don't understand what it is?
    </m:msg>
</detail>
```

The SOAP-1.2 defined SOAP fault sub-elements are listed below.

- Code
- Reason
- Node
- Role
- Detail

The XML representation of the SOAP-1.2 SOAP fault is given below. The sub-elements of the SOAP fault element are in bold.

```
<?xml version="1.0"?>
<env:Envelope xmlns:env="http://www.w3.org/2003/05/soap-envelope"
              xmlns:m="http://ws.learning.com/timeouts">
    <env:Body>
        <env:Fault>
            <env:Code>
                <env:Value>env:Sender</env:Value>
                <env:Subcode>
                <env:Value>env:Sender</env:Value>
                </env:Subcode>
            </env:Code>

            <env:Reason>
                <env:Text xml:lang="en-US">
                    Error in Input Data
                </env:Text>
            </env:Reason>

            <env:Node>http://ws.learning.com/failedNode</env:Node>

            <env:Role>
                http://www.w3.org/2003/05/soap-envelope/role/
```

```
        </env:Role>

        <env:Detail>
              <m:maxRelayTime>600</m:maxRelayTime>
        </env:Detail>
      </env:Fault>
    </env:Body>
</env:Envelope>
```

The following section explains the significance of each SOAP fault sub-element.

The Code Element

The <Code/> is a mandatory element inside the SOAP <Fault/> element. It contains a mandatory <value/> element and an optional <Subcode/> element. The element's local name must be "Code," and it must be namespace qualified. This code identifies the type of fault.

An example <Code/> element is given below.

```
<env:Code>
      <env:Value>env:Sender</env:Value>
      <env:Subcode>
            <env:Value>env:Sender</env:Value>
      </env:Subcode>
</env:Code>
```

The valid fault codes and their meanings are listed below.

Fault Code	Description
Sender	The message was not correctly formed or created by the client so it cannot be processed. Example it misses the required mandatory information while creating the message.
Receiver	There was a problem with the server side node so message cannot be processed.
VersionMismatch	The processing node found an invalid version of the namespace for soap envelope element. The local name of the element or namespace did not match.
MustUnderstand	The soap header block attribute "mustUnderstand" set to "true" was not understood.
DataEncodingUnknown	The faulting node did not understand the header element encoding or body element encoding specified using "encodingStyle" attribute.

The Reason element

The <Reason/> is a mandatory element inside the SOAP <Fault/> element. The element's local name must be "Reason," and it must be namespace qualified. The <Reason/> elements contain one or more <Text/> elements that specify the text in different languages. The <Text/> element contains an error message information.

An example of the reason element is given below.

```
<env:Reason>
     <env:Text xml:lang="en-US">Error in Input Data</env:Text>
     <env:Text xml:lang="en">Error in Input Data</env:Text>
</env:Reason>
```

The Node Element

The <Node/> is an optional element inside the SOAP <Fault/> element. The element's local name must be "Node," and it must be namespace qualified. It contains the URI of the SOAP node that generated the fault. An example of a node element is given below.

```
<env:Node>http://ws.learning.com/failedNode</env:Node>
```

The Role Element

The <Role/> is an optional element inside the SOAP <Fault/> element. The element's local name must be "Role," and it must be namespace qualified. The <Role/> element contains a URI; it represents the role of SOAP node that generated the fault.

An example of a role element is given below.

```
<env:Role>
     http://www.w3.org/2003/05/soap-envelope/role/ultimateReceiver
</env:Role>
```

The Detail Element

The <Detail/> is an optional element inside the SOAP <Fault/> element. The element's local name must be "Detail," and it must be namespace qualified. The <Detail/> element can contain one or more child elements that provide additional details about the fault that is occurring. All child elements of the <Detail/> element must be namespace qualified.

An example of a detail element is given below.

```
<env:Detail>
     <m:maxRelayTime>600</m:maxRelayTime>
</env:Detail>
```

SOAP with HTTP

The terminology commonly used in Web service development is SOAP over HTTP or SOAP with HTTP. This terminology does not indicate that SOAP is overriding HTTP; rather, it inherits the semantics provided by HTTP. By nature, SOAP is a one-way messaging protocol, so it requires another protocol, such as HTTP, as a transport protocol. The client-generated SOAP request message wraps inside the HTTP request and sends it to the service; similarly, the SOAP response message is wrapped inside the HTTP response to service the clients. HTTP is a request-and-response protocol used for Web-based applications; SOAP uses HTTP as a transfer protocol for message communication between the client and service.

The steps involved in SOAP message communication between the client and server are listed below.

- The client creates a request to invoke the server.

- The incoming client request is serialized using the SOAP encoder; it converts the client request to a SOAP request and sends it to the HTTP encoder. The structure of the client-generated SOAP message is given below.

```
<soap:Envelope xmlns:soap="http://schemas.xmlsoap.org/soap/envelope/">
    <soap:Body>
        <ns1:getEmployee xmlns:ns1="http://jaxws.ws.learning.com/">
            <employeeId>823147</employeeId>
        </ns1:getEmployee>
    </soap:Body>
</soap:Envelope>
```

- The HTTP encoder wraps the incoming SOAP request; converts the SOAP request to a HTTP request before making a call to Web server because the server understands only HTTP. The structure of the client generated HTTP request message is given below.

```
ID: 1
Address: http://localhost:8080/wsbook/services/employee
Encoding: UTF-8
Content-Type: text/xml
Headers: {SOAPAction=[""], Accept=[*/*]}
Payload:
<soap:Envelope xmlns:soap="http://schemas.xmlsoap.org/soap/envelope/">
    <soap:Body>
        <ns1:getEmployee xmlns:ns1="http://jaxws.ws.learning.com/">
        <employeeId>823147</employeeId>
        </ns1:getEmployee>
    </soap:Body>
</soap:Envelope>
```

In the above HTTP request, the SOAP envelope XML is embedded in the HTTP request. The supported encoding types are UTF-8 and UTF-16. The address header attribute indicates the location of the service. The request must use the "text/xml" as content type, and its SOAPAction header attribute indicates the purpose of the SOAP request. The header payload attribute contains the complete SOAP message in XML format. The regular Web-based applications in this payload section will use the HTML content instead of XML. HTTP carries the XML content of SOAP, however, instead of HTML.

- The server sends the HTTP response back to the HTTP decoder. The response payload XML is embedded in the HTTP response. The structure of the server-generated HTTP response is given below.

```
ID: 1
Encoding: UTF-8
Content-Type: text/xml;charset=UTF-8
```

```
Headers: {content-type=[text/xml;charset=UTF-8], Date=[Thu, 26 Jan
2012 22:21:48 GMT], Content-Length=[303], Server=[Apache-Coyote/1.1]}
Payload:
<soap:Envelope xmlns:soap="http://schemas.xmlsoap.org/soap/envelope/">
   <soap:Body>
        <ns1:getEmployeeResponse xmlns:ns1=
                        "http://jaxws.ws.learning.com/">
            <employee>
                    <employeeId>823147</employeeId>
                    <firstName>John</firstName>
                    <lastName>Smith</lastName>
            </employee>
        </ns1:getEmployeeResponse>
   </soap:Body>
</soap:Envelope>
```

- The HTTP decoder module converts the HTTP response to a SOAP response and sends it to
  the SOAP decoder. The extracted SOAP message from the HTTP response message is given
  below.

```
<soap:Envelope xmlns:soap="http://schemas.xmlsoap.org/soap/envelope/">
   <soap:Body>
        <ns1:getEmployeeResponse xmlns:ns1=
                        "http://jaxws.ws.learning.com/">
            <employee>
                    <employeeId>823147</employeeId>
                    <firstName>John</firstName>
                    <lastName>Smith</lastName>
            </employee>
        </ns1:getEmployeeResponse>
   </soap:Body>
</soap:Envelope>
```

- The SOAP decoder decodes the SOAP response message and passes it to the end client.

Figure 5-5: SOAP message communication

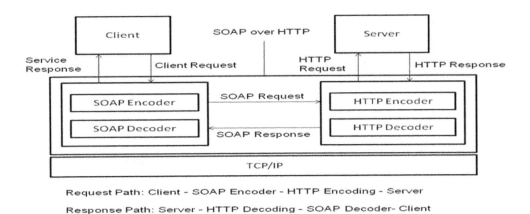

Figure 5-5 shows the request and response paths of this SOAP message communication between
the client and server.

SOAP over HTTP uses the response codes provided by HTTP. The 200-series codes are used to indicate successful processing, and 500-series codes report server-side errors. The 400-series codes indicate invalid client requests, such as invalid XML or content type.

HTTP Status code: 200 OK

This status code indicates that the SOAP message included in the client request has been successfully received and understood. In request-and-response messaging mode, the node will return the successful response back to the client. If there is an error while processing the request, the node will report an error back to the client.

HTTP Status code: 202 Accepted

This status code indicates that the SOAP message included in the client request has been accepted for processing. This does not indicate whether the processing has been completed. This scenario is used for a one-way messaging mode in which the service is not required to send a response back to the client.

HTTP Status code: 400 Bad Request

This status code indicates that the client request has an invalid XML, so the server cannot process it.

HTTP Status code: 415 Unsupported Media Type

This status code indicates that the message contains invalid content type, so the server cannot process the request. The valid content types used for SOAP over HTTP are "text/xml" (SOAP-1.1) and "application/soap+xml" (SOAP-1.2); otherwise, the server will refuse the client request.

HTTP Status code: 500 Internal Server Error

This status code indicates that the server encountered an unexpected exception, so it cannot complete the processing of the request message. In request-and-response messaging mode, it will include this error in the SOAP fault element.

HTTP Status code: 503 Service Unavailable

This status code indicates that the service is down or unavailable to process the request.

SOAP-1.2 Features

This section summarizes the difference between SOAP-1.1 and SOAP-1.2 specifications, also explaining the new features of SOAP-1.2 and the enhanced features of SOAP-1.1.

- The acronym SOAP stands for "Simple Object Access Protocol" and is dropped from version 1.2 because the word "protocol" is misleading; because SOAP is a XML message not a protocol.
- The XML namespaces used for the SOAP envelope and SOAP encoding have been changed in version 1.2.
- The actor attribute of the SOAP-1.1 header block is replaced with the role attribute in SOAP-1.2. SOAP-1.2 has added two new roles.

The URI used for the SOAP-1.1 actor attribute of a header block is given below.

```
soap:actor = "http://www.w3.org/2001/06/soap-envelope/actor/next"
```

The URIs used for the SOAP-1.2 role attribute of a header block is listed below.

```
soap:role="http://www.w3.org/2003/05/soap-envelope/role/next"
soap:role="http://www.w3.org/2003/05/soap-envelope/role/none"
soap:role="http://www.w3.org/2003/05/
                    soap-envelope/role/ultimateReceiver"
```

The header block used for SOAP-1.1 is given below.

```
<soap:Header>
<ws:transaction xmlns:ws="http://wsbook.learning.com/transaction/"
    soap:actor=" http://www.w3.org/2001/06/soap-envelope/actor/next">
        567
</ws:transaction>
</soap:Header>
```

The header block used for SOAP-1.2 is given below.

```
<soap:Header>
    <ws:transaction xmlns:ws="http://wsbook.learning.com/transaction/"
        soap:role="http://www.w3.org/2003/05/soap-envelope/role/next">
        567
    </ws:transaction>
</soap:Header>
```

- The relay <Header/> block attribute is newly added in SOAP-1.2 in addition to its existing actor (role), mustUnderstand, and encodingStyle attributes. The use of the relay attribute in the header block of SOAP-1.2 is given below.

```
<soap:Header>
    <ws:transaction xmlns:ws="http://wsbook.learning.com/transaction/"
            soap:role=" http://www.w3.org/2003/05/soap-
                        envelope/role/next"
            soap:relay="true">
        567
    </ws:transaction>
</soap:Header>
```

- The Fault structure of SOAP-1.2 is changed. One new fault code is added and two existing fault codes are modified.
    - The newly added fault code is "DataEncodingUnknown".
    - The SOAP-1.1 fault code "Client" is renamed to "Sender"
    - The SOAP-1.1 fault code "Server" is renamed to "Receiver"

The XML structure of SOAP-1.1 and SOAP-1.2 <Fault/> element is given below.

SOAP-1.1	SOAP-1.2
env:Fault	env:Fault
Faultcode	env:Code, env:Value, env:Subcode
Faultstring	env:Reason

Faultactor	env:Node, env:Role
Detail	env:Detail

The valid fault codes used for SOAP-1.1 are listed below.

- Client
- Server
- VersionMismatch
- MustUnderstand

The valid fault codes used for SOAP-1.2 are listed below.

- Sender
- Receiver
- VersionMismatch
- MustUnderstand
- DataEncodingUnknown

- SOAP-1.2 added support for version mismatch faults. It provides a mechanism to handle version mismatch faults that occur from receiving the incorrect version of SOAP message requests, such as when the SOAP-1.1 node receives the SOAP-1.2 message or the SOAP-1.2 node receives some version of the message that it does not support. It uses the <Upgrade/> element in the header block to report the version mismatch faults. The <Upgrade/> header block element contains information about the list of supported SOAP message versions.

```
<?xml version="1.0"?>
<soapenv:Envelope
        xmlns:soapenv="http://schemas.xmlsoap.org/soap/envelope/">
    <soapenv:Header>
        <soapenv:Upgrade>
            <soapenv:SupportedEnvelope qname="ns1:Envelope"
                xmlns:ns1="http://www.w3.org/2003/05/soap-
                                        envelope"/>
        </soapenv:Upgrade>
    </soapenv:Header>

    <env:Body>
        <soapenv:Fault>
            <faultcode>soapenv:VersionMismatch</faultcode>
            <faultstring>Version Mismatch</faultstring>
        </soapenv:Fault>
    </soapenv:Body>
</soapenv:Envelope>
```

In the above case, the SOAP-1.2 node received a SOAP-1.1 message; A version mismatch fault was generated, indicating that it supports only the SOAP-1.2 version of the SOAP message. The SOAP-1.2–supported SOAP message URL is provided in the <Upgrade/> header block element.

- SOAP-1.1 specifies the SOAP binding rules only for HTTP. Conversely, SOAP-1.2 defines an abstract binding framework commonly used for all protocols.

- SOAP-1.1 provides support for only the HTTP POST method to carry the messages over the network. SOAP-1.2 provides support for both the HTTP GET and HTTP POST methods. The GET method requests should be idempotent.
- The content type used for SOAP-1.1 binding is "text/xml." It has been changed from "text/xml" to "application/soap+xml" in SOAP-1.2

Basic Profile Standards for SOAP Messaging (1.1 and 1.2)

The basic profile (BP) standards are a specification from the Web services interoperability industry consortium (called WS-I). It provides guidelines for Web services interoperability for SOAP, WSDL, and UDDI. The basic profile interoperability guidelines for SOAP-1.1 and SOAP-1.2 messaging are explained in this section.

- The SOAP envelope must be serialized as XML. The supported character encoding types for message serialization are UTF-8 and UTF-16.
- The structure of the SOAP <Envelope/> must conform to the SOAP-1.1 and SOAP-1.2 specifications. It must have zero or one <Body/> element and may have an optional <Header/> element. The children of the <Body/> element must be namespace qualified. An <Envelope/> element must not contain the document type definition (DTD) and processing instructions (PI).
- The SOAP <Envelope/> element must not have any children elements following the SOAP <Body/> element. The children of the SOAP <Body/> element must be namespace qualified to avoid namespace conflicts.

Invalid SOAP message <Body/> representation:

```
<soap:Envelope xmlns:soap="http://schemas.xmlsoap.org/soap/envelope/">
    <soap:Body>
        <ns1:getEmployee xmlns:ns1="http://jaxws.ws.learning.com/">
            <employeeId>823147</employeeId>
        </ns1:getEmployee>
    </soap:Body>
    <m:data xmlns:m="http://ws.learning.com/data/">
        <m:deptId>FT011</m:deptId>
    </m:data>
</soap:Envelope>
```

Valid SOAP message <Body/> representation:

```
<soap:Envelope xmlns:soap="http://schemas.xmlsoap.org/soap/envelope/">
    <soap:Body>
        <ns1:getEmployee xmlns:ns1="http://jaxws.ws.learning.com/">
            <ns1:employeeId>823147</ns1:employeeId>
            <m:data xmlns:m="http://ws.learning.com/data/">
            <m:deptId>FT011</m:deptId>
            </m:data>
        </ns1:getEmployee>
    </soap:Body>
</soap:Envelope>
```

- The processing of all mandatory header blocks must be completed before the processing of the SOAP message body can begin.

- The BP recommends using literal and non-encoded XML messages. The use of encoded XML introduces interoperability issues, so a SOAP message must not use SOAP encoding schemes for <Envelope/> and <Body/> elements.

Invalid SOAP message representation (BP-WS-I):

```
<soap:Envelope xmlns:soap="http://www.w3.org/2003/05/soap-envelope"
        soap:encodingStyle="http://www.w3.org/2003/05/soap-encoding/">
    <soap:Body>
        <ns1:getEmployee xmlns:ns1="http://jaxws.ws.learning.com/">
            <ns1:employeeId>823147</ns1:employeeId>
        </ns1:getEmployee>
    </soap:Body>
</soap:Envelope>
```

Valid SOAP message representation (BP-WS-I):

```
<soap:Envelope xmlns:soap="http://www.w3.org/2003/05/soap-envelope">
    <soap:Body>
        <ns1:getEmployee xmlns:ns1="http://jaxws.ws.learning.com/">
            <ns1:employeeId>823147</ns1:employeeId>
        </ns1:getEmployee>
    </soap:Body>
</soap:Envelope>
```

- BP standards for SOAP-1.1 Fault:

The local name of the SOAP fault must be "soap:Fault," and it must be the immediate child element of the SOAP message <soap:Body/> element. The namespace qualification is necessary for the SOAP <Fault/> element of a SOAP message. In addition, the <Fault/> message element must not have any child element other than <faultcode/>, <faultstring/>, <faultactor/>, and <detail/> elements.

Invalid SOAP message <Fault/> representation (SOAP-1.1):

```
<soap:Fault xmlns:soap="http://schemas.xmlsoap.org/soap/envelope/">
    <faultcode>soap:Client</faultcode>
    <faultstring>Invalid message format</faultstring>
    <faultactor>http://ws.learning.com/someactor</faultactor>
    <detail>
        <m:msg xmlns:m="http://ws.learning.com/faults/exceptions">
            It has invalid XML elements. I don't understand what it is?
        </m:msg>
    </detail>
    <m1:error xmlns:m1="http://ws.learning.com/faults/exceptions">
        <m1:errorCode>E00120</m1:errorCode>
    </m1:error>
</soap:Fault>
```

Valid SOAP message <Fault/> representation (SOAP-1.1):

```
<soap:Fault xmlns:soap="http://schemas.xmlsoap.org/soap/envelope/">
    <faultcode>soap:Client</faultcode>
    <faultstring>Invalid message format</faultstring>
```

```
        <faultactor>http://ws.learning.com/someactor</faultactor>
        <detail>
            <m:msg xmlns:m="http://ws.learning.com/faults/exceptions">
                It has invalid XML elements. I don't understand what it is?
            </m:msg>
        </detail>
</soap:Fault>
```

The namespace qualification is not necessary for the children of the <soap:Fault/> elements. The <detail/> element can contain any number of child elements, and namespace qualification is not mandatory for the children of the detail fault element.

Invalid SOAP message <Fault/> representation (SOAP-1.1):

```
<soap:Fault xmlns:soap="http://schemas.xmlsoap.org/soap/envelope/">
    <soap:faultcode>soap:Client</soap:faultcode>
    <soap:faultstring>Invalid message format</soap:faultstring>
    <soap:faultactor>http://ws.learning.com/someactor</soap:faultactor>
    <soap:detail>
        <m:msg xmlns:m="http://ws.learning.com/faults/exceptions">
            It has invalid XML elements. I don't understand what it is?
        </m:msg>
    </soap:detail>
</soap:Fault>
```

Valid SOAP message <Fault/> representation (SOAP-1.1):

```
<soap:Fault xmlns:soap="http://schemas.xmlsoap.org/soap/envelope/">
    <faultcode>soap:Client</faultcode>
    <faultstring>Invalid message format</faultstring>
    <faultactor>http://ws.learning.com/someactor</faultactor>
    <detail>
        <m:msg xmlns:m="http://ws.learning.com/faults/exceptions">
            It has invalid XML elements. I don't understand what it is?
        </m:msg>
    </detail>
</soap:Fault>
```

- BP standards for SOAP-1.2 Fault:

The local name of the SOAP fault must be "soap:Fault," and it must be the immediate child element of the SOAP message <soap:Body/> element. The namespace qualification is necessary for the SOAP <Fault/> element and for all of the sub-elements of a SOAP fault message. The <Fault/> message element must not have any child elements other than the <Code/>, <Reason/>, <Node/>, <Role/>, and <Detail/> elements.

Invalid SOAP message <Fault/> representation (SOAP-1.2):

```
<?xml version="1.0"?>
<env:Envelope xmlns:env="http://www.w3.org/2003/05/soap-envelope"
            xmlns:m="http://ws.learning.com/timeouts">
    <env:Body>
        <env:Fault>
            <Code>
                <Value>env:Sender</Value>
```

```
            <Subcode>
            <Value>env:Sender</Value>
            </Subcode>
        </Code>
        <Reason>
            <env:Text xml:lang="en-US">
                Error in Input Data
            </env:Text>
        </Reason>
        <Detail>
            <maxRelayTime>600</maxRelayTime>
        </Detail>
        </env:Fault>
    </env:Body>
</env:Envelope>
```

Valid SOAP message <Fault/> representation (SOAP-1.2):

```
<?xml version="1.0"?>
<env:Envelope xmlns:env="http://www.w3.org/2003/05/soap-envelope"
              xmlns:m="http://ws.learning.com/timeouts">
    <env:Body>
        <env:Fault>
            <env:Code>
                <env:Value>env:Sender</env:Value>
                <env:Subcode>
                    <env:Value>env:Sender</env:Value>
                </env:Subcode>
            </env:Code>
            <env:Reason>
                <env:Text xml:lang="en-US">
                    Error in Input Data
                </env:Text>
            </env:Reason>
            <env:Detail>
                <m:maxRelayTime>600</m:maxRelayTime>
            </env:Detail>
        </env:Fault>
    </env:Body>
</env:Envelope>
```

- The only supported SOAP message binding for SOAP-1.1 is HTTP. The basic profile recommends using the HTTP protocol for message binding for both SOAP-1.1 and SOAP-1.2.
- The HTTP request message for SOAP-1.1 must use the HTTP POST method. The HTTP request for SOAP-1.2 messages supports both the HTTP POST and HTTP GET methods. All HTTP GET requests must be side-effect free, and they are idempotent.

Test Yourself - Objective Type Questions

1. Which of the following definitions specifies the set of rules defined to carry the SOAP message on top of another protocol?
   a) SOAP Encoding
   b) SOAP Block Processing

c) SOAP Binding
d) SOAP Envelope
e) SOAP Intermediary

2. An error occurred while the system was processing the header block elements of a SOAP message. How do you capture the SOAP fault detail information for this scenario? Assume that it is using the SOAP-1.1 message format.
   a) The <detail/> element of the SOAP fault element is used to capture the fault details.
   b) The <faultcode/> element is used to capture the fault details of the SOAP message header block.
   c) Only the ultimate receiver of a SOAP message can handle this scenario.
   d) The detailed error information pertaining to header entries must be carried in the header entries.

3. What is wrong with the following SOAP fault message?

```
<soap:Fault xmlns:soap="http://schemas.xmlsoap.org/soap/envelope/">
    <faultcode>soap:Client</faultcode>
    <faultstring xml:lang="en">Invalid message format</faultstring>
    <faultactor>http://ws.learning.com/someactor</faultactor>
    <detail>
        <m:msg xmlns:m="http://ws.learning.com/faults/exceptions">
        It has invalid XML elements. I don't understand what it is?
        </m:msg>
    </detail>
</soap:Fault>
```

   a) There is nothing wrong with this message. It is a valid SOAP fault message.
   b) The "xml:lang" attribute is not allowed for the SOAP <faultstring/> element.
   c) The sub-elements of the SOAP <Fault/> elements are not namespace qualified.
   d) The sub-elements of the <detail/> element are namespace qualified.
   e) It has an invalid fault code.

4. Select the valid URIs used for SOAP-1.2 role attribute of a SOAP header block.
   a)
   ```
   soap:actor = "http://www.w3.org/2003/05/soap-envelope/actor/next"
   soap:actor = "http://www.w3.org/2003/05/soap-envelope/actor/none"
   soap:actor = "http://www.w3.org/2003/05/soap-envelope/actor/ultimateReceiver"
   ```

   b)
   ```
   soap:role = "http://www.w3.org/2003/05/soap-envelope/role/next"
   soap:role = "http://www.w3.org/2003/05/soap-envelope/role/none"
   soap:role = "http://www.w3.org/2003/05/soap-envelope/role/ultimateReceiver"
   ```

   c)
   ```
   soap:role = "http://www.w3.org/2003/05/soap-envelope/actor/next"
   soap:role = "http://www.w3.org/2003/05/soap-envelope/actor/none"
   soap:role = "http://www.w3.org/2003/05/soap-envelope/actor/ultimateReceiver"
   ```

   d)
   ```
   soap:actor = "http://www.w3.org/2001/06/soap-envelope/actor/next"
   ```

e)
```
soap:actor = "http://www.w3.org/2003/05/soap-envelope/next"
soap:actor = "http://www.w3.org/2003/05/soap-envelope/none"
soap:actor = "http://www.w3.org/2003/05/soap-
envelope/ultimateReceiver"
```

5. Select the optional elements of the SOAP message fault. Assume that the fault is generated using the SOAP-1.2 messaging structure.
   a. Code
   b. faultcode
   c. Reason
   d. Node
   e. faultstring
   f. Role
   g. Detail

   a) a and c
   b) b and e
   c) a, c, d, f, and g
   d) g only
   e) d, e, and g

6. A SOAP message contains many header blocks and uses intermediary nodes to process them. Some of these header blocks are processed by an intermediary, and some are not. You want to retain the unprocessed header blocks of a SOAP message and pass them to the next available node in a message path. How do you achieve this?
   a) Set the header block "relay" attribute value to true.
   b) Set the header block "encodingStyle" attribute value to none.
   c) Set the header block "role" attribute value to ultimateReceiver.
   d) Set the header block "mustUnderstand" attribute value to true.
   e) Set the header block "relay" attribute value to unprocessed.

7. The client sends a message to the server. The client-created message is not correctly formed, so the server is unable to process it. For this scenario, what standard fault code is used to capture the fault?
   a) The fault code used for SOAP-1.1 is "Server" and for SOAP-1.2 is "Receiver."
   b) The fault code used for SOAP-1.1 is "faultdetail" and for SOAP-1.2 is "Detail."
   c) The fault code used for this scenario is "VersionMismatch" for both SOAP-1.1 and SOAP-1.2.
   d) The fault code used for this scenario is "MustUnderstand" for both SOAP-1.1 and SOAP-1.2.
   e) The fault code used for SOAP-1.1 is "Client" and for SOAP-1.2 is "Sender."

8. Select the valid SOAP message body representation as per the basic profile Web services interoperability (WS-I) guidelines.
   a)
```
<soap:Envelope xmlns:soap="http://www.w3.org/2003/05/soap-envelope">
  <soap:Body>
      <ns1:getEmployee xmlns:ns1="http://jaxws.ws.learning.com/">
          <employeeId>823147<employeeId>
      </ns1:getEmployee>
  </soap:Body>
</soap:Envelope>
```

b)
```
<soap:Envelope xmlns:soap="http://www.w3.org/2003/05/soap-envelope">
  <soap:Body>
      <getEmployee xmlns:ns1="http://jaxws.ws.learning.com/">
          <employeeId>823147<employeeId>
      <getEmployee>
  </soap:Body>
</soap:Envelope>
```

c)
```
<soap:Envelope xmlns:soap="http://www.w3.org/2003/05/soap-envelope">
  <soap:Body>
      <getEmployee>
          <employeeId>823147<employeeId>
      <getEmployee>
  </soap:Body>
</soap:Envelope>
```

d)
```
<soap:Envelope xmlns:soap="http://www.w3.org/2003/05/soap-envelope">
  <soap:Body>
      <ns1:getEmployee xmlns:ns1="http://jaxws.ws.learning.com/">
          <ns1:employeeId>823147</ns1:employeeId>
      </ns1:getEmployee>
  </soap:Body>
</soap:Envelope>
```

e)   All are valid SOAP messages.

Answers to the Self-Test

1. The correct answer is C.
    The SOAP Binding specifies the set of rules defined to carry out the SOAP message on top of another protocol. SOAP supports many underlying protocols such as HTTP, SMTP, and FTP in the transfer of messages over the network.

2. The correct answer is D.
    The <detail/> element of a SOAP Fault carries the application-specific error related to the SOAP <Body/> element. It must not be used for carrying information related to the SOAP header entries. The detailed error information pertaining to header entries is carried only in header entries.

3. The correct answer is A.
    It is a valid SOAP fault message. The "xml:lang" attribute can be used to specify the locale-specific text information.

4. The correct answer is B.
    The SOAP-1.2 header blocks support three standard role attributes; they are "next," "none," and "ultimateReceiver." Option D is correct as per the SOAP-1.1 specification.

5. The correct answer is E.

The child elements of a SOAP-1.2 message fault are <Code/>, <Reason/>, <Node/>, <Role/>, and <Detail/>. The <Code/> and <Reason/> elements are mandatory, and the rest are optional. The <faultcode/> and <faultstring/> are the mandatory SOAP fault sub-elements of a SOAP-1.1 messaging structure.

6. The correct answer is A.
    The header block relay attribute "true" value indicates that the header block can be forwarded to the next node in the message path even if it is not processed. This is a standard role introduced in SOAP-1.2 specifications.

7. The correct answer is E.
    This error occurred because the client-created message was not correctly formed. The fault code used in SOAP-1.1 is "soap:Client" and in SOAP-1.2 is "soap:Sender."

8. The correct answer is D.
    As per the BP WS-I guidelines, the SOAP body element and its child elements must be namespace qualified. Thus, for this scenario, the correct answer is D.

Chapter 6. SAAJ

The API used for creating and reading SOAP messages is SAAJ. SAAJ stands for SOAP with Attachments API for Java. SAAJ provides a Java based API that conforms to SOAP-1.1 and 1.2 specifications, Basic Profile standards and SOAP with Attachments specifications. The latest version of the SAAJ is 1.3. The SAAJ provided primary package is "javax.xml.soap". This package contains the required classes used for soap message creation, soap message parsing, sending messages over the Internet and handling attachments.

The SAAJ API can be used for handling soap messages for the following scenarios.

- SAAJ provides an API for creating and reading soap messages
- SAAJ can be used an alternative solution for JAX-WS based web services
- SAAJ can be used for sending soap-based XML messages over the Internet using Java platform.
- SAAJ is the primary API used for JAX-WS message handler implementation.
- SAAJ provides an API for handling soap messages with attachments.

In this chapter will discuss the following topics:

- Creating SOAP Messages using SAAJ API
- Getting data from soap message using SAAJ API
- Using SAAJ with w3c DOM document.
- Invoking web service endpoint using SAAJ API
- Adding attachments to a soap message and reading attachments from soap message using SAAJ API

There are two types of messages that we can create using SAAJ API that conforms to the SOAP specification.

- SOAP message without using Attachments
- SOAP message using Attachments

The XML representation of the SOAP message without any attachments is provided below. It has an optional header element and mandatory envelope and body element. The elements and sub elements of a soap message maps to the SAAJ-provided Java API. Each element of a soap message maps to the corresponding SAAJ-provided Java class or interface.

```
<SOAP-ENV:Envelope xmlns:SOAP-
        ENV="http://schemas.xmlsoap.org/soap/envelope/">
    <SOAP-ENV:Header/>
    <SOAP-ENV:Body/>
</SOAP-ENV:Envelope>
```

The SAAJ-provided "SOAPMessage" class is used to create a soap message. This class represents the XML-based soap message structure based on soap message specification. We can add header, body to the soap message using "SOAPMessage" class provided methods. The following Figure 6-1 shows the structure of a SOAP message without any attachments.

Figure 6-1: SOAP message structure

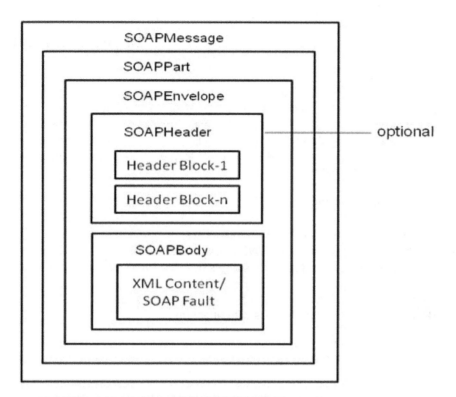

A SOAP Message without attachments

The following table summarizes the mapping between SAAJ API provided Java classes/interfaces and its corresponding mapping to the XML soap message element.

SAAJ API Class/Interface	SOAP message XML Element
SOAPMessage	Represents the entire soap message with empty <Header/> and <Body/> elements
SOAPEnvelope	Represents the soap message <Envelope/> element
SOAPHeader	Represents the soap message <Header/> element
SOAPHeaderElement	Represents the soap <Header/> child elements
SOAPBody	Represents the soap message <Body/>
SOAPBodyElement	Represents the soap <Body/> child elements
SOAPFault	Represents the soap message <Fault/>

The outline XML representation of a SOAP message with attachments is provided below. The attachment section contains any valid MIME content type. We can add XML and non-XML content as an attachment to a soap message.

```
_Part_0_3736006.1328874699062
Content-Type: application/soap+xml; charset=utf-8

<env:Envelope xmlns:env="http://www.w3.org/2003/05/soap-envelope">
```

```
        <env:Header/>
        <env:Body/>
</env:Envelope>
------=_Part_0_3736006.1328874699062
Content-Type: text/plain

------=_Part_0_3736006.1328874699062--
```

The Figure 6-2 shows the structure of a SOAP message with attachments. Adding attachments to a soap message is optional.

Figure 6-2: SOAP message structure with attachments

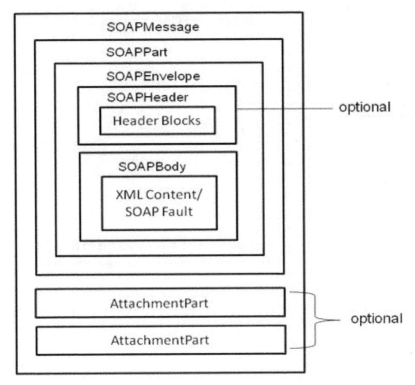

A SOAP Message with attachments

Creating a SOAP Message

The primary class used for creating a soap message using SAAJ API is "SOAPMessage". The "createMessage()" method of the "MessageFactory" class is used to create an instance of a "SOAPMessage" class. The below provided code snippet is used for creating the instance of a soap message. It creates a message that conforms to SOAP-1.1 specification. The SOAPConstants class contains constants pertaining to the soap protocol.

```
MessageFactory factory =
MessageFactory.newInstance(SOAPConstants.SOAP_1_1_PROTOCOL);
SOAPMessage message = factory.createMessage();
```

The below code creates a message that is compatible with SOAP-1.2 specification.

```
MessageFactory factory =
MessageFactory.newInstance(SOAPConstants.SOAP_1_2_PROTOCOL);
SOAPMessage message = factory.createMessage();
```

After creating a soap message we can add the required content to the soap message using SAAJ API.

SOAP Envelope

The soap <Envelope/> element contains the <Header/> and <Body/> elements. The code provided below is used to create an empty soap envelope that conforms to SOAP-1.1 specification.

```
MessageFactory factory =
MessageFactory.newInstance(SOAPConstants.SOAP_1_1_PROTOCOL);
SOAPMessage message = factory.createMessage();
```

The output of the above code is provided below.

```
<SOAP-ENV:Envelope xmlns:SOAP-ENV=
                "http://schemas.xmlsoap.org/soap/envelope/">
    <SOAP-ENV:Header/>
    <SOAP-ENV:Body/>
</SOAP-ENV:Envelope>
```

The code provided below is used to create an empty soap envelope that conforms to SOAP-1.2 specification.

```
MessageFactory factory =
MessageFactory.newInstance(SOAPConstants.SOAP_1_2_PROTOCOL);
SOAPMessage message = factory.createMessage();
```

The output of the above code is provided below.

```
<SOAP-ENV:Envelope xmlns:SOAP-ENV="http://www.w3.org/2003/05/soap-
envelope">
    <SOAP-ENV:Header/>
    <SOAP-ENV:Body/>
</SOAP-ENV:Envelope>
```

The complete code used to print the soap envelope is provided below.

```
public void createMessageEnvelope() throws Exception {
    MessageFactory factory = MessageFactory.newInstance(
                        SOAPConstants.SOAP_1_2_PROTOCOL);
    SOAPMessage message = factory.createMessage();

    // Printing the response message on the console.
    ByteArrayOutputStream out = new ByteArrayOutputStream();
    message.writeTo(out);
    String responseMessage = new String(out.toByteArray());
    System.out.println("----  Message ---" + responseMessage);
```

```
}
```

The code provided below is used to get the soap part using the soap message instance.

```
SOAPMessage message = factory.createMessage();
SOAPPart soapPart = message.getSOAPPart();
```

The code provided below is used to get the soap envelope using the soap part instance.

```
SOAPEnvelope soapEnvelope = soapPart.getEnvelope();
```

The code provided below is used to get the soap header using the soap envelope instance.

```
SOAPHeader soapHeader = soapEnvelope.getHeader();
```

The code provided below is used to get the soap body using the soap envelope instance.

```
SOAPBody soapBody = soapEnvelope.getBody();
```

SOAP Header

The soap message <Header/> element can contain any number of child elements; they are also called as header blocks. The code provided below is used to get the empty soap header conforms to SOAP-1.2 specification.

```
MessageFactory factory = MessageFactory.newInstance(
SOAPConstants.SOAP_1_2_PROTOCOL);
SOAPMessage message = factory.createMessage();
SOAPHeader soapHeader = message.getSOAPPart().getEnvelope().getHeader();
```

Let us now take the following example to demonstrate the use of SAAJ API for creating a soap message header. The soap header contains two header blocks "<ws:transaction/>" and "<log:logger/>". The header block "<ws:transaction/>" has three attributes "mustUnderstand", "relay" and "role". The "<log:logger/>" header block has one attribute "role".

```
<env:Envelope xmlns:env="http://www.w3.org/2003/05/soap-envelope">
    <env:Header>
        <ws:transaction xmlns:ws="http://saaj.ws.learning.com/"
                env:mustUnderstand="true"
                env:relay="true"
                env:role="http://www.w3.org/2003/05/soap-
                                    envelope/role/next">
            567
        </ws:transaction>

        <log:logger xmlns:log="http://saaj.ws.learning.com/"
            env:role="http://www.w3.org/2003/05/soap-
                                    envelope/role/next"/>
    </env:Header>
    <env:Body/>
</env:Envelope>
```

The SAAJ API can be used to create the above soap header message. The "addHeaderElement()" method of a "SOAPHeader" instance is used to add child elements to the soap message header.

The complete code example is provided below:

```java
public SOAPMessage createMessageHeader() throws Exception {
    /* Creates a soap message that is compatible with SOAP-1.2
        Specification */
    MessageFactory factory =
    MessageFactory.newInstance(SOAPConstants.SOAP_1_2_PROTOCOL);
    SOAPMessage message = factory.createMessage();
    SOAPHeader soapHeader =
        message.getSOAPPart().getEnvelope().getHeader();

    // Adding an element to a soap header; called as header block.
    QName qName = new QName("http://saaj.ws.learning.com/",
                                "transaction", "ws");
    SOAPHeaderElement soapHeaderElement =
                                soapHeader.addHeaderElement(qName);

    // Adding attributes to the header block
    soapHeaderElement.setAttribute("xmlns:ws",
                        "http://wsbook.learning.com/transaction/");
    soapHeaderElement.setRole("http://www.w3.org/2003/05/soap-
                                envelope/role/next");
    soapHeaderElement.setRelay(true);
    soapHeaderElement.setMustUnderstand(true);
    soapHeaderElement.setTextContent("567");

    // Adding another header block to a soap header
    QName logQName = new QName("http://saaj.ws.learning.com/",
                                "logger", "log");
    SOAPHeaderElement logSOAPHeaderElement =
                soapHeader.addHeaderElement(logQName);
    logSOAPHeaderElement.setAttribute("xmlns:log",
                    "http://wsbook.learning.com/logger/");
    logSOAPHeaderElement.setRole("http://www.w3.org/2003/05/soap-
                                envelope/role/next");

    // Printing the response message on the console.
    ByteArrayOutputStream out = new ByteArrayOutputStream();
    message.writeTo(out);
    String responseMessage = new String(out.toByteArray());
    System.out.println("----  Message ----" + responseMessage);
    return message;
}
```

SOAP Body

The soap message <Body/> element can contain any number of child elements also called as body blocks. The code provided below is used to get the empty soap body conforms to SOAP-1.2 specification.

```java
MessageFactory factory = MessageFactory.newInstance(
SOAPConstants.SOAP_1_2_PROTOCOL);
```

```
SOAPMessage message = factory.createMessage();
SOAPBody soapBody = message.getSOAPPart().getEnvelope().getBody();
```

The code provided below adds a root element to the soap body block.

```
QName qName = new QName("http://saaj.ws.learning.com/",
                       "getEmployeeRequest", "ns1");
SOAPBodyElement soapBodyElement = soapBody.addBodyElement(qName);
```

The code provided below adds a child element "<employeeId/>" to the root element and sets a value to it.

```
QName employeeId = new QName("employeeId");
SOAPElement soapElement = soapBodyElement.addChildElement(employeeId);
soapElement.addTextNode("666666");
```

Let us now take the following example to demonstrate the use of SAAJ API for creating a soap message body. The soap body contains one header block "<ns1:getEmployeeRequest/>"; it is used for creating the input request for the web service.

```
<env:Envelope xmlns:env="http://www.w3.org/2003/05/soap-envelope">
    <env:Header/>
    <env:Body>
        <ns1:getEmployeeRequest xmlns:ns1=
                "http://saaj.ws.learning.com/">
            <employeeId>666666</employeeId>
        </ns1: getEmployeeRequest>
    </env:Body>
</env:Envelope>
```

The SAAJ API can be used to create the above soap body. The "addBodyElement()" method of a "SOAPBody" instance is used to add child elements to the soap message body.

The code example is provided below.

```
public SOAPMessage createMessageBody() throws Exception {
    /* Creates a soap message that is compatible with SOAP-1.2
    Specification */
    MessageFactory factory = MessageFactory.newInstance(
            SOAPConstants.SOAP_1_2_PROTOCOL);
    SOAPMessage message = factory.createMessage();
    SOAPBody soapBody = message.getSOAPPart().getEnvelope().getBody();

    // Adding an element to soap body; called as body block.
    QName qName = new QName("http://saaj.ws.learning.com/",
                "getEmployeeRequest", "ns1");
    SOAPBodyElement soapBodyElement = soapBody.addBodyElement(qName);

    // Adding a child element to the body block.
    QName employeeId = new QName("employeeId");
    SOAPElement soapElement =
            soapBodyElement.addChildElement(employeeId);
    soapElement.addTextNode("666666");

    // Printing the response message on the console.
```

```
ByteArrayOutputStream out = new ByteArrayOutputStream();
message.writeTo(out);
String responseMessage = new String(out.toByteArray());
System.out.println("----  Message ----" + responseMessage);

return message;
}
```

SOAP Fault

The structure of the soap message fault is redesigned in SOAP-1.2 specification. The soap-1.1 complaint <Fault/> element can contain four immediate child elements; they are <faultcode/>, <faultstring>, <faultactor> and <detail/>. The code provided below is used to get the empty soap fault conforms to SOAP-1.1 specification.

```
// Creates a soap message that conforms to SOAP-1.1 specification
MessageFactory factory =
MessageFactory.newInstance(SOAPConstants.SOAP_1_1_PROTOCOL);
SOAPMessage message = factory.createMessage();

// Adding a soap fault to the soap body.
SOAPBody soapBody = message.getSOAPPart().getEnvelope().getBody();
SOAPFault soapFault = soapBody.addFault();
```

Let us now take the following example to demonstrate the use of SAAJ API for creating a soap message fault element. If it exists, the <Fault/> element must be the immediate child element of a <Body/> element. The complete SOAP-1.1 compatible soap <Fault/> message is given below.

```
<SOAP-ENV:Envelope xmlns:SOAP-
        ENV="http://schemas.xmlsoap.org/soap/envelope/">
    <SOAP-ENV:Header/>
    <SOAP-ENV:Body>
        <SOAP-ENV:Fault>
            <faultcode>SOAP-ENV:Server</faultcode>
            <faultstring>Service not available</faultstring>
            <faultactor>http://ws.learning.com/someactor</faultactor>
            <detail>I dont understand what it is?</detail>
        </SOAP-ENV:Fault>
    </SOAP-ENV:Body>
</SOAP-ENV:Envelope>
```

The "addFault()" method of a "SOAPBody" instance is used to add fault element to the soap message body. The Java code used to create the above-specified soap fault message is provided below.

```
public void createMessageFaultSOAP11() throws Exception {
    /* Creates a soap message that is compatible with SOAP-1.1
        Specification */
    MessageFactory factory = MessageFactory.newInstance(
        SOAPConstants.SOAP_1_1_PROTOCOL);
    SOAPMessage message = factory.createMessage();

    // Adding a soap fault to the soap body.
    SOAPBody soapBody = message.getSOAPPart().getEnvelope().getBody();
```

```
        SOAPFault soapFault = soapBody.addFault();

        // Adding child elements to the soap fault.
        QName faultName = new QName(
                SOAPConstants.URI_NS_SOAP_1_1_ENVELOPE, "Server");
        soapFault.setFaultCode(faultName);
        soapFault.setFaultString("Service not available");
        soapFault.setFaultActor("http://ws.learning.com/someactor");
        Detail detail = soapFault.addDetail();
        detail.setTextContent("I dont understand what it is?");

        // Printing the response message on the console.
        ByteArrayOutputStream out = new ByteArrayOutputStream();
        message.writeTo(out);
        String responseMessage = new String(out.toByteArray());
        System.out.println("----  Message ----" + responseMessage);
}
```

The complete SOAP-1.2 compatible soap <Fault/> message is given below. The soap-1.2 complaint <Fault/> element can contain five immediate child elements; they are <Code/>, <Reason>, <Role> and <Detail/> and <Node/>.

```
<env:Envelope xmlns:env="http://www.w3.org/2003/05/soap-envelope">
    <env:Header/>
    <env:Body>
        <env:Fault>
            <env:Code>
                <env:Value>env:Sender</env:Value>
            </env:Code>
            <env:Reason>
                <env:Text xml:lang="en-US">
                    Invalid input XML
                </env:Text>
            </env:Reason>
            <env:Role>http://ws.learning.com/someactor</env:Role>
            <env:Detail>Error in Input Data</env:Detail>
        </env:Fault>
    </env:Body>
</env:Envelope>
```

The Java code used to create the above-specified soap fault message is provided below.

```
public SOAPMessage createMessageFaultSOAP12() throws Exception {
    /* Creates a soap message that is compatible with SOAP-1.2
    Specification */
    MessageFactory factory = MessageFactory.newInstance(
            SOAPConstants.SOAP_1_2_PROTOCOL);
    SOAPMessage message = factory.createMessage();

    // Adding a soap fault to the soap body.
    SOAPBody soapBody = message.getSOAPPart().getEnvelope().
        getBody();
    SOAPFault soapFault = soapBody.addFault();

    // Adding child elements to the soap fault.
    QName faultName = new QName(
```

```
          SOAPConstants.URI_NS_SOAP_1_2_ENVELOPE, "Sender");
    soapFault.setFaultCode(faultName);
    soapFault.addFaultReasonText("Invalid input XML", Locale.US);
    soapFault.setFaultRole("http://ws.learning.com/someactor");
    Detail detail = soapFault.addDetail();
    detail.setTextContent("Error in Input Data");

    // Printing the response message on the console.
    ByteArrayOutputStream out = new ByteArrayOutputStream();
    message.writeTo(out);
    String responseMessage = new String(out.toByteArray());
    System.out.println("---  Message ---" + responseMessage);

    return message;
}
```

Getting the content of a SOAP Message

We discussed how to create a SOAP message using SAAJ API in our previous section. How to read a soap message using SAAJ will be explained in this section.

SOAP Envelope

The code provided below gets a soap message envelope from a soap message that conforms to SOAP-1.2 specification.

```
MessageFactory factory =
MessageFactory.newInstance(SOAPConstants.SOAP_1_2_PROTOCOL);
SOAPMessage message = factory.createMessage();
SOAPPart soapPart = message.getSOAPPart();
SOAPEnvelope soapEnvelope = soapPart.getEnvelope();
```

The simplified version of the above code to get the soap envelope is provided below.

```
MessageFactory factory =
MessageFactory.newInstance(SOAPConstants.SOAP_1_2_PROTOCOL);
SOAPMessage message =
factory.createMessage().getSOAPPart().getEnvelope();
```

SOAP Header

The "getChildElements()" method of a "SOAPHeader" object is used to get the available header blocks of a soap message. The code provided below gets a soap header blocks from a soap message.

```
private void readSOAPHeader() throws Exception {
    // Getting the soap header from a soap message.
    SOAPMessage saopMessage = createMessageHeader();
    SOAPHeader soapHeader = saopMessage.getSOAPPart().getEnvelope().
                           getHeader();
```

```
Iterator iterator = soapHeader.getChildElements();

// Getting first header block
SOAPHeaderElement transactionElement = (SOAPHeaderElement)
            iterator.next();
String headerBlockName = transactionElement.getNodeName();
String value = transactionElement.getValue();
System.out.println("----- Header Block Name ----" +
                    headerBlockName + "---- value ----" + value);

// Getting first header block attributes
boolean mustUnderstand = transactionElement.getMustUnderstand();
String role = transactionElement.getRole();
boolean relay = transactionElement.getRelay();
System.out.println("---- mustUnderstand---" + mustUnderstand);
System.out.println("------ role ----" + role);
System.out.println("----- relay ----" + relay);

// Getting second header block and its attributes.
String loggerHeaderBlockName = "";
String loggerRole = "";
while (iterator.hasNext()) {
    SOAPHeaderElement loggerElement = (SOAPHeaderElement)
                                        iterator.next();
    loggerHeaderBlockName = loggerElement.getNodeName();
    loggerRole = loggerElement.getRole();
}
System.out.println("---- logger role ----" + loggerRole);
System.out.println("---- Header Block Name ----" +
                            loggerHeaderBlockName);
}
```

SOAP Body

The "getChildElements()" method of a "SOAPBody" object is used to get the available body blocks of a soap message. The code provided below gets a soap body blocks from a soap message.

```
private void readSOAPBody() throws Exception {
    // Getting the soap body from a soap message.
    SOAPMessage saopMessage = createMessageBody();
    SOAPBody soapBody = saopMessage.getSOAPPart().getEnvelope().
                        getBody();

    // Getting the soap body element and its contents
    Iterator iterator = soapBody.getChildElements();
    SOAPBodyElement bodyElement = (SOAPBodyElement) iterator.next();
    System.out.println("---- Body Element Name---" +
            bodyElement.getNodeName());

    String employeeId = null;
    if (soapBody.getElementName().getLocalName().equals("Body")) {
        for(Element result : getElements(bodyElement.
                    getElementsByTagName("employeeId"))) {
            employeeId = getNamedElement(result,
                            "employeeId").getTextContent();
```

```
            }
        }
        System.out.println("----- employeeId ------" + employeeId);
}
```

SOAP Fault

The "getFault()" method of a "SOAPBody" object is used to get soap fault of a soap message. The code provided below gets soap fault related information from a soap message.

```
private void readSOAPFault() throws Exception {
    // Getting the soap fault from a soap message.
    SOAPMessage saopMessage = createMessageFaultSOAP12();
    SOAPFault soapFault = saopMessage.getSOAPPart().getEnvelope().
                        getBody().getFault();

    // Getting the fault information from fault message
    String code = soapFault.getFaultCode();
    String reason = soapFault.getFaultReasonText(Locale.US);
    String role = soapFault.getFaultRole();
    Detail detail = soapFault.getDetail();
    String conetnt = detail.getTextContent();
}
```

Creating SOAP message using w3c DOM Document

The SAAJ provides a way to create a soap message using the JAXP-provided Source objects. The supported source objects are listed below.

- SAXSource
- DOMSource
- StreamSource

We can add the Source objects directly to a "SOAPPart" object. Let us now take the following XML; name it as "employee.xml". We will create a "SOAPPart" object using the below provided XML.

```
<SOAP-ENV:Envelope xmlns:SOAP-
            ENV="http://schemas.xmlsoap.org/soap/envelope/">
    <SOAP-ENV:Header/>
    <SOAP-ENV:Body>
        <ns1:getEmployeeRequest xmlns:ns1=
                        "http://saaj.ws.learning.com/">
            <employeeId>666666</employeeId>
        </ns1:getEmployeeRequest>
    </SOAP-ENV:Body>
</SOAP-ENV:Envelope>
```

The "setContent()" method of a "SOAPPart" object is used to add a DOM source to a "SOAPPart" object. The complete method code used to create a soap message using DOM source is provided below.

```
private void createSOAPPartUsingDOM() throws Exception {
    // Creating a DOM document using request XML.
    DocumentBuilderFactory factory = DocumentBuilderFactory.
                                               newInstance();
    factory.setNamespaceAware(true);
    DocumentBuilder builder = factory.newDocumentBuilder();
    Document w3cDocument = builder.parse("employee.xml");
    DOMSource domSource = new DOMSource(w3cDocument);

    /* Creates a soap message that is compatible with SOAP-1.1
    Specification   */
    MessageFactory messageFactory = MessageFactory.newInstance(
            SOAPConstants.SOAP_1_1_PROTOCOL);
    SOAPMessage message = messageFactory.createMessage();
    SOAPPart soapPart = message.getSOAPPart();

    // Adding DOM source to soap part object.
    soapPart.setContent(domSource);

    // Printing the entire message on the console.
    ByteArrayOutputStream out = new ByteArrayOutputStream();
    message.writeTo(out);
    String responseMessage = new String(out.toByteArray());
    System.out.println("----  Message ----" + responseMessage);
}
```

The SAAJ provides a way to create a soap message by adding the document directly to a soap message body. The body of XML is provided below and named it as "employeebody.xml".

```
<ns1:getEmployeeRequest xmlns:ns1="http://saaj.ws.learning.com/">
    <employeeId>666666</employeeId>
</ns1:getEmployeeRequest>
```

The "addDocument()" method of a "SOAPBody" object is used to add a DOM source to a "SOAPBody" object. In this scenario it adds the content to body of a soap message. The complete method code used to create a soap message using DOM source is provided below.

```
private void createSOAPBodyUsingDOM() throws Exception {
    // Creating a DOM document using request XML.
    DocumentBuilderFactory factory =
                  DocumentBuilderFactory.newInstance();
    factory.setNamespaceAware(true);
    DocumentBuilder builder = factory.newDocumentBuilder();
    Document w3cDocument = builder.parse("employeebody.xml");

    /* Creates a soap message that is compatible with SOAP-1.2
    specification */
    MessageFactory messageFactory = MessageFactory.newInstance(
                  SOAPConstants.SOAP_1_2_PROTOCOL);
    SOAPMessage message = messageFactory.createMessage();

    // Adding DOM source to soap message body.
    SOAPBody soapBody = message.getSOAPBody();
    soapBody.addDocument(w3cDocument);

    // Printing the response message on the console.
```

```
        ByteArrayOutputStream out = new ByteArrayOutputStream();
        message.writeTo(out);
        String responseMessage = new String(out.toByteArray());
        System.out.println("---- Message ----" + responseMessage);
}
```

To summarize there are two different ways we can create a soap message using JAXP provided Source object.

- By adding the DOM source to SOAPPart object
- The other way is adding the DOMSource to SOAPBody object

Sending SOAP Message

The SAAJ API can be used to send messages over the network and get the response back to the client. SAAJ provides an API to invoke the web service endpoint operations in a request-response messaging mode. An example implementation of the SAAJ API to send messages is provided below.

The structure of the web service endpoint operation is provided below.

```
<xs:element name="getEmployee" type="getEmployee" />
<xs:complexType name="getEmployee">
    <xs:sequence>
        <xs:element minOccurs="0" name="employeeId" type="xs:string" />
    </xs:sequence>
</xs:complexType>
```

The generated XML soap input request message is provided below. The web service takes employee id as input parameter; and it provides the employee details as a response. The below provided XML is named as inputdata.xml.

```
<ns1:getEmployee xmlns:ns1="http://jaxws.ws.learning.com/">
    <employeeId>666666</employeeId>
</ns1:getEmployee>
```

The SAAJ API used to invoke the web service endpoint operation is provided below. The "call()" method of the "SOAPConnection" object is used to send-and-receive a message from the deployed web service.

```
private void callWebService() throws Exception {
    SOAPConnectionFactory  soapConnectionFactory =
            SOAPConnectionFactory.newInstance();
    SOAPConnection  soapConnection =
            soapConnectionFactory.createConnection();

    // Web service endpoint URL
    URL endpoint = new
            URL("http://localhost:8080/wsbook/services/employee");

    // Creating a w3c DOM document.
    DocumentBuilderFactory factory =
            DocumentBuilderFactory.newInstance();
```

```
        factory.setNamespaceAware(true);
        DocumentBuilder builder = factory.newDocumentBuilder();
        Document w3cDocument = builder.parse("inputdata.xml");

        // Creating the request SOAP Message using SAAJ API.
        MessageFactory messageFactory = MessageFactory.newInstance(
                SOAPConstants.SOAP_1_1_PROTOCOL);
        SOAPMessage message = messageFactory.createMessage();
        SOAPBody soapBody = message.getSOAPBody();
        soapBody.addDocument(w3cDocument);

        // Calling the service endpoint to get the response.
         SOAPMessage response = soapConnection.call(message, endpoint);

        // Printing the response message on the console.
        ByteArrayOutputStream out = new ByteArrayOutputStream();
        response.writeTo(out);
        String responseMessage = new String(out.toByteArray());
        System.out.println("---  Message ---" + responseMessage);

        // Closing the connection
        soapConnection.close();
}
```

NOTE: This topic is further discussed in web services development using Apache-CXF.

Adding Attachments to a SOAP Message

The soap message body can contain only XML content type; but the attachment part can contain both XML and non-XML content type. The "createAttachmentPart()" method of a "SOAPMessage" object is used for creating an attachment. The code provided below adds a plain text attachment to a soap message.

```
public SOAPMessage createMessageWithAttachment() throws Exception {
    /* Creates a soap message that is compatible with SOAP-1.2
    specification */
    MessageFactory factory = MessageFactory.newInstance(
        SOAPConstants.SOAP_1_2_PROTOCOL);
    SOAPMessage message = factory.createMessage();
    SOAPPart soapPart = message.getSOAPPart();
    SOAPEnvelope soapEnvelope = soapPart.getEnvelope();
    SOAPBody soapBody = soapEnvelope.getBody();

    // Creating the soap message body
     QName qName = new QName("http://saaj.ws.learning.com/",
                "getEmployeeRequest", "ns1");
    SOAPBodyElement  soapBodyElement =
                soapBody.addBodyElement(qName);
    QName employeeId = new QName("employeeId");
    SOAPElement  soapElement =
            soapBodyElement.addChildElement(employeeId);
    soapElement.addTextNode("666666");
```

```
        // Creating an attachment.
        AttachmentPart attachment = message.createAttachmentPart();
        String stringContent = "Update home address of an employee whose
                    id is: 666666 - " +
                "2500 W.ROUNDBOUT CIR, CHANDLER, AZ, USA";

        // Id used to identify an attachment
        attachment.setContentId("home_address_update");

        // Setting the content type. It is using plain text.
        attachment.setContent(stringContent, "text/plain");

        // Addting attachment to a soap message
        message.addAttachmentPart(attachment);

        // Printing the response message on the console.
        ByteArrayOutputStream out = new ByteArrayOutputStream();
        message.writeTo(out);
        String responseMessage = new String(out.toByteArray());
        System.out.println("----  Message ---- =" + responseMessage);

        return message;
}
```

The output of the above method is provided below. The soap message request contain two parts; the first part is a soap message body which is of type "application/soap+xml" and second part is an attachment part which is of type "text/plain".

```
_Part_0_14867177.1328811785082
Content-Type: application/soap+xml; charset=utf-8

<env:Envelope xmlns:env="http://www.w3.org/2003/05/soap-envelope">
    <env:Header/>
    <env:Body>
        <ns1:getEmployeeRequest
                xmlns:ns1="http://saaj.ws.learning.com/">
            <employeeId>666666</employeeId>
        </ns1:getEmployeeRequest>
    </env:Body>
</env:Envelope>
------=_Part_0_14867177.1328811785082
Content-ID: home_address_update
Content-Type: text/plain

Update home address of an employee whose id is: 666666 - 2500 W.ROUNDBOUT
CIR, CHANDLER, AZ, USA
------=_Part_0_14867177.1328811785082—
```

We created a soap message with attachment. The following section will explain how to read an attachment content using SAAJ API. The "getAttachments()" method of a "SOAPMessage" object can be used to get the all attachment parts of a soap message. The code provided below reads the attachment we created in our previous example and prints the data on console.

```
private void readSOAPMessageAttachments() throws Exception {
    // Getting the soap message that contain attachments.
```

```
SOAPMessage saopMessage =createMessageWithAttachment();
Iterator iterator = saopMessage.getAttachments();

/* Iterating over the attachments to get the required attachment
data.*/
Object content = "";
while(iterator.hasNext()) {
    AttachmentPart attachment = (AttachmentPart) iterator.next();
    String contentId = attachment.getContentId();
    String contentType = attachment.getContentType();
    if("text/plain".equalsIgnoreCase(contentType)) {
        content = attachment.getContent();
    }
}
System.out.println("--- attachment content is ---" + content);
}
```

The above method prints the below provided output on the console.

```
----- attachment content is ------
Update home address of an employee whose id is: 666666 - 2500 W.ROUNDBOUT
CIR, CHANDLER, AZ, USA
```

Test Yourself - Objective Type Questions

1. Which of the following are valid ways of getting a SOAP message body? Select all correct
    answers.

    a)
    ```
    MessageFactory factory =
    MessageFactory.newInstance(SOAPConstants.SOAP_1_1_PROTOCOL);
    SOAPMessage message = factory.createMessage();
    SOAPBody soapBody = message.getSOAPPart().getEnvelope().getBody();
    ```

    b)
    ```
    MessageFactory factory =
    MessageFactory.newInstance(SOAPConstants.SOAP_1_1_PROTOCOL);
    SOAPMessage message = factory.createMessage();
    SOAPBody soapBody = message.getSOAPBody();
    ```

    c)
    ```
    MessageFactory factory =
    MessageFactory.newInstance(SOAPConstants.SOAP_1_1_PROTOCOL);
    SOAPMessage message = factory.createMessage();
    SOAPBody soapBody = message.getSOAPPart().getSOAPBody();
    ```

    d)
    ```
    MessageFactory factory =
    MessageFactory.newInstance(SOAPConstants.SOAP_1_1_PROTOCOL);
    SOAPMessage message = factory.createMessage();
    SOAPBody   soapBody =
    message.getSOAPPart().getEnvelope().getSOAPBody();
    ```

e)   All are valid.

2.   Which of the following are the valid outline structures of a SOAP message? Select all correct answers.

a)

```
SOAPMessage
   SOAPPart
      SOAPEnvelope
         SOAPHeader
         SOAPBody
      AttachmentPart
```

b)

```
SOAPMessage
   SOAPPart
      SOAPEnvelope
         SOAPHeader
         SOAPBody
         AttachmentPart
```

c)

```
SOAPMessage
   SOAPPart
      AttachmentPart
      SOAPEnvelope
         SOAPHeader
         SOAPBody
```

d)

```
SOAPMessage
   SOAPPart
      SOAPEnvelope
         SOAPHeader
         SOAPBody
```

e)

```
SOAPMessage
   SOAPPart
      SOAPEnvelope
         SOAPHeader
         SOAPBody
   AttachmentPart
```

3.   The below given code snippet creates a SOAP message that conforms to SOAP-1.2 specification. Select the correct code snippet.

a)
```
MessageFactory factory =
MessageFactory.newInstance(SOAPConstants.SOAP_1_1_PROTOCOL);
SOAPMessage message = factory.createMessage();
```

b)

```
MessageFactory factory =
MessageFactory.newInstance(SOAPConstants.SOAP_1_2_PROTOCOL);
SOAPMessage message = factory.createMessage();
```

c)
```
MessageFactory factory = MessageFactory.newInstance();
SOAPMessage message = factory.createMessage();
```

d)
```
MessageFactory factory = MessageFactory.newInstance();
SOAPMessage message =
factory.createMessage(SOAPConstants.SOAP_1_2_PROTOCOL);
```

e) All are valid.

Answers to Test Yourself

1. A and B are the correct choices. The choice "C" is incorrect because there is no "getSOAPBody()" method on "SOAPPart" object. Similarly the choice "D" is incorrect because there is no "getSOAPBody()" method on SOAPEnvelope object.

2. D and E are the correct choices. The choice "D" represents a SOAP message without attachments and choice "E" represents the SOAP message with attachment.

3. B is the correct answer. The "SOAPConstants" class contains a constant "SOAP_1_2_PROTOCOL" used for creating a SOAP-1.2 compatible soap message.

Chapter 7. WSDL

In the world of Web services, we deal with clients and service endpoints. The service endpoint provides the implementation of the business functionality, and the client invokes the service endpoint to obtain the required business data. To invoke the service endpoint, the client has to know certain details about the Web service endpoint, such as the service location, operation name, input parameters, return values, exceptions, and so forth. How does one share these abstract and concrete details of the service endpoint with the calling client? The specification used to document the details of the Web service endpoint structure is WSDL; WSDL stands for Web Services Description Language, pronounced as "wiz-dul." WSDL provides a common language and terminology to understand the deployed Web service endpoint using XML.

The current version of WSDL is 2.0, but many Web services development frameworks still provide support only for the previous version of WSDL, which is 1.1.

This chapter will discuss the following topics:

- The structure of WSDL-1.1 and 2.0 documents
- The relationship between the various elements of the WSDL document.
- The mapping between WSDL and Java objects.
- The available message exchange patterns in WSDL-1.1 and 2.0
- The available Web service messaging modes in WSDL-1.1 and 2.0
- Comparison between WSDL-1.1 and 2.0

Introduction

Web Services Description Language (WSDL) is an XML-based document used to describe the structure of the Web service endpoint, providing the "what," "how," and "where" details. It provides details such as the operation's name, the input parameters and return value anticipated, how the messages are exchanged between the client and the service endpoint, and where it is located. Web service clients use this information to invoke the deployed Web service.

The WSDL document is a kind of contract between the service provider and service consumer. It educates the service consumers about the service endpoint and its abstract functionality. WSDL provides a common vocabulary between the service provider and consumer. Many Web services development frameworks provide tools to generate WSDL from Java classes, and vice versa.

There are two ways a Web service is generally developed. The first approach is to write a WSDL document and then use this WSDL to generate the Web service endpoint interface and its dependent classes. Various Web service development frameworks provide tools to generate Java objects for a given WSDL document. This approach is called the contract-first development. The second approach is to write the Java code first and then generate a WSDL document from the Java code using the tools provided in the framework. This approach is called code-first development. In the code-first approach, the generation of WSDL document is sometimes optional; the Java containers will generate a WSDL document after deploying the Web service.

The WSDL documents are based extensively on XML; one disadvantage of this is that sometimes it is tedious to edit various sections of very large WSDL documents; so this requires more attention.

Structure of a WSDL Document

The WSDL document contains various sections, and each section defines specific information about the Web service endpoint. One section of the document is used for type declarations, one section is used for defining the interface and its operations; and the final section provides the implementation details of the Web service. The structure of the WSDL-2.0 document is slightly modified from its earlier version, which is WSDL-1.1. The following sections will address the structure of the WSDL document in greater detail.

WSDL-1.1

The WSDL-1.1 document describes the Web service in two stages; one is abstract and one is concrete. The "<definitions/>" element is the topmost root element of the WSDL-1.1 document; all other elements are child elements of this element. The abstract section contains *types*, *messages*, and *port type* definitions; the concrete section contains *binding* and *service* details. Figure 7-1 shows the structure of a WSDL-1.1 document.

Figure 7-1: WSDL-1.1 document structure

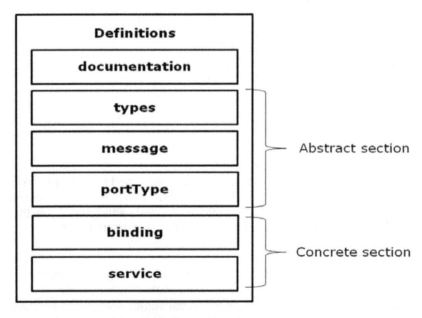

WSDL1.1 document structure

The names of various objects defined in WSDL-1.1 are given below.

- Definitions
- Documentation
- Types
- Messages
- Port Type
- Binding
- Service

The *Definitions* element is the topmost root element of the WSDL document. This is used to declare all required namespaces used throughout the document.

The *Documentation* element contains the textual information about the Web service, its purpose and function, and its constraints and limitations.

The *Types* element is used to define the information related to request, response, and fault types. Inline or external XML schemas represent this information.

The *Messages* element corresponds to operations of a Web service endpoint. The message element contains *parts* that map to request-and-response types.

The *Port-type* element is used to define the Web service endpoint interface. It contains abstract operations and defines the functionality service provided by the operations.

The *Binding* element assigns a message format and style for the operations defined in the port type. It defines the message transmission protocol and how messages are exchanged.

The *Service* element defines locations of the Web service and where the service is available.

Now let us review a sample WSDL to understand each section of the WSDL document in detail. The Web service defined in WSDL has one operation: "getEmployee()"; It returns the details of the employee for a given employee id. The complete WSDL document is given below:

```
<?xml version="1.0" encoding="UTF-8"?>
<wsdl:definitions name="employeeService"
            targetNamespace="http://jaxws.ws.learning.com/"
            xmlns:tns="http://jaxws.ws.learning.com/"
            xmlns:soap="http://schemas.xmlsoap.org/wsdl/soap/"
            xmlns:wsdl="http://schemas.xmlsoap.org/wsdl/"
            xmlns:xsd="http://www.w3.org/2001/XMLSchema">

    <wsdl:documentation>
        This document describes the employee web service.
    </wsdl:documentation>

    <wsdl:types>
        <xs:schema targetNamespace="http://jaxws.ws.learning.com/"
                xmlns="http://jaxws.ws.learning.com/"
                xmlns:xs="http://www.w3.org/2001/XMLSchema">
        <xs:complexType name="employee">
            <xs:sequence>
                <xs:element minOccurs="0"
                    name="employeeId" type="xs:string"/>
                <xs:element minOccurs="0"
                    name="firstName" type="xs:string"/>
                <xs:element minOccurs="0"
                    name="lastName" type="xs:string"/>
                <xs:element minOccurs="0"
                    name="address" type="xs:string"/>
            </xs:sequence>
        </xs:complexType>
        <xs:element name="EmployeeFault" type="EmployeeFault"/>
        <xs:complexType name="EmployeeFault">
            <xs:sequence/>
        </xs:complexType>
```

```xml
        <xs:element name="getEmployee" type="getEmployee"/>
        <xs:complexType name="getEmployee">
        <xs:sequence>
                <xs:element minOccurs="0" name="employeeId"
                                    type="xs:string"/>
            </xs:sequence>
        </xs:complexType>
            <xs:element name="getEmployeeResponse"
                        type="getEmployeeResponse"/>
        <xs:complexType name="getEmployeeResponse">
            <xs:sequence>
                <xs:element minOccurs="0" name="return"
                                    type="employee"/>
            </xs:sequence>
        </xs:complexType>
    </xs:schema>
</wsdl:types>

<wsdl:message name="getEmployee">
    <wsdl:part element="tns:getEmployee" name="parameters"/>
</wsdl:message>
<wsdl:message name="getEmployeeResponse">
    <wsdl:part element="tns:getEmployeeResponse"
                name="parameters"/>
</wsdl:message>
<wsdl:message name="EmployeeFault">
    <wsdl:part element="tns:EmployeeFault" name="EmployeeFault"/>
</wsdl:message>

<wsdl:portType name="EmployeeService">
    <wsdl:operation name="getEmployee">
        <wsdl:input message="tns:getEmployee" name="getEmployee"/>
        <wsdl:output message="tns:getEmployeeResponse"
                name="getEmployeeResponse"/>
    </wsdl:operation>
</wsdl:portType>

<wsdl:binding name="employeeServiceSoapBinding"
                    type="tns:EmployeeService">
<soap:binding style="document"
            transport="http://schemas.xmlsoap.org/soap/http"/>
    <wsdl:operation name="getEmployee">
        <soap:operation soapAction="" style="document"/>
            <wsdl:input name="getEmployee">
                <soap:body use="literal"/>
            </wsdl:input>
            <wsdl:output name="getEmployeeResponse">
                <soap:body use="literal"/>
            </wsdl:output>
    </wsdl:operation>
</wsdl:binding>

<wsdl:service name="employeeService">
    <wsdl:port binding="tns:employeeServiceSoapBinding"
            name="EmployeeServicePort">
        <soap:address
        location="http://localhost:8080/wsbook/services/employee"/>
```

```
        </wsdl:port>
    </wsdl:service>
</wsdl:definitions>
```

Let us review each section of the WSDL document and determine its meaning and significance.

Section 1: WSDL definitions -

The *definitions* element is the topmost root element for any WSDL-1.1 document and is the container for all other WSDL elements. The *definitions* part of WSDL is used to declare the namespaces related to WSDL, SOAP, and XML that are used in this service definition. Let us take the WSDL *definitions* section to analyze the declared namespaces.

```
<wsdl:definitions name="employeeService"
                  targetNamespace="http://jaxws.ws.learning.com/"
                  xmlns:tns="http://jaxws.ws.learning.com/"
                  xmlns:soap="http://schemas.xmlsoap.org/wsdl/soap/"
                  xmlns:wsdl="http://schemas.xmlsoap.org/wsdl/"
                  xmlns:xsd="http://www.w3.org/2001/XMLSchema">
    ...
</wsdl:definitions>
```

This following code specifies the name of the Web service definitions. This element does not have any technical significance.

```
<wsdl:definitions name="employeeService"
```

The below given XML is the target namespace for this WSDL document. The target namespace value is the same as a Java package name but in reverse order.

```
targetNamespace="http://jaxws.ws.learning.com/"
```

The below given XML is an actual namespace to be used in this document with the "tns:" prefix in "QNames" to refer to the target namespace of this service. The URI of this is same as that of the target namespace.

```
xmlns:tns="http://jaxws.ws.learning.com/"
```

The below given XML is the namespace of the actual SOAP specification.

```
xmlns:soap="http://schemas.xmlsoap.org/wsdl/soap/"
```

The below given XML is the namespace of the actual WSDL specification.

```
xmlns:wsdl="http://schemas.xmlsoap.org/wsdl/"
```

The below given XML is the namespace of the actual XML schema specification.

```
xmlns:xsd="http://www.w3.org/2001/XMLSchema">
```

Section 2: WDSL documentation - < documentation/>

The *documentation* part of the WSDL is used to provide comments about the Web service in human readable text format. These comments are similar to class-level comments we provide in

---

Java, explaining the purpose of this service, its limitations, and its constraints. This section does not have any technical significance.

Section 3: WDSL types -

This section contains the data type definitions using the XML schema definition language. The XML complex data type definitions for request, response, and faults are defined in this section of the WSDL document.

The XML *types* defined in this example is given below.

```
<wsdl:definitions>
    ...
    <wsdl:types>
        <xs:schema targetNamespace="http://jaxws.ws.learning.com/"
                xmlns="http://jaxws.ws.learning.com/"
                xmlns:xs="http://www.w3.org/2001/XMLSchema">
            <xs:complexType name="employee">
                <xs:sequence>
                    <xs:element minOccurs="0" name="employeeId"
                            type="xs:string"/>
                    <xs:element minOccurs="0" name="firstName"
                            type="xs:string"/>
                    <xs:element minOccurs="0" name="lastName"
                            type="xs:string"/>
                    <xs:element minOccurs="0" name="address"
                            type="xs:string"/>
                </xs:sequence>
            </xs:complexType>
            <xs:element name="EmployeeFault" type="EmployeeFault"/>
            <xs:complexType name="EmployeeFault">
                <xs:sequence/>
            </xs:complexType>
            <xs:element name="getEmployee" type="getEmployee"/>
            <xs:complexType name="getEmployee">
                <xs:sequence>
                    <xs:element minOccurs="0" name="employeeId"
                            type="xs:string"/>
                </xs:sequence>
            </xs:complexType>
            <xs:element name="getEmployeeResponse"
                    type="getEmployeeResponse"/>
            <xs:complexType name="getEmployeeResponse">
                <xs:sequence>
                    <xs:element minOccurs="0" name="return"
                            type="employee"/>
                </xs:sequence>
            </xs:complexType>
        </xs:schema>
    </wsdl:types>
</wsdl:definitions>
```

The below given XML schema target namespace we created for employee Web service.

```
<xs:schema targetNamespace="http://jaxws.ws.learning.com/"
```

The below given XML schema default namespace we created for employee web service.

```
xmlns="http://jaxws.ws.learning.com/"
```

The below given XML is the namespace of the actual XML schema specification.

```
xmlns:xs="http://www.w3.org/2001/XMLSchema">
```

The below given XML is the declaration for XML schema complex types. The request, response, and fault data types are defined in this section.

```
<xs:complexType>
    . . .
</xs:complexType>
```

Section 4: WDSL message - <message/>

The *message* acts as a holder for the WSDL *part* of the element used to represent the request, response, and fault data types to be communicated.

Figure 7-2: Relation between message, part and types

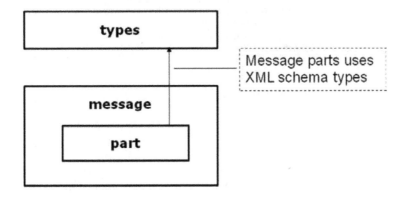

Relation between message, part and types

The WSDL *messages* and *parts* defined in this example are provided below.

```
<wsdl:definitions>
    . . .
    <wsdl:message name="getEmployee">
        <wsdl:part element="tns:getEmployee" name="parameters"/>
    </wsdl:message>
    <wsdl:message name="getEmployeeResponse">
        <wsdl:part element="tns:getEmployeeResponse"name="parameters"/>
    </wsdl:message>
    <wsdl:message name="EmployeeFault">
        <wsdl:part element="tns:EmployeeFault" name="EmployeeFault"/>
    </wsdl:message>
</wsdl:definitions>
```

The following element represents the message types used for request, response, and fault types of a Web service operation.

```
<wsdl:message name="...">
```

The following *part* elements represent the data type of the request, response, and fault types and refer to the XML complex types defined in the *types* section of WSDL document.

```
<wsdl:part element="tns:getEmployee" name="parameters"/>
<wsdl:part element="tns:getEmployeeResponse" name="parameters"/>
<wsdl:part element="tns:EmployeeFault" name="EmployeeFault"/>
```

Section 5: WDSL port type -

This represents the abstract interface definition of the service endpoint and defined operations. Each operation defined in *port type* has input and output elements; they refer to the message types defined in the *messages* section of the WSDL document. The relationship between port type, operation, and message types are shown Figure 7-3

Figure 7-3: Relation between port type, operation and message.

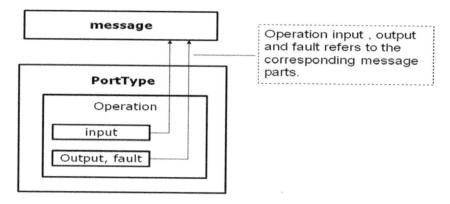

Relation between port type, operation and message

The WSDL *port type* defined in this example is given below.

```
<wsdl:definitions>
    ...
    <wsdl:portType name="EmployeeService">
        <wsdl:operation name="getEmployee">
            <wsdl:input message="tns:getEmployee" name="getEmployee"/>
            <wsdl:output message="tns:getEmployeeResponse"
                        name="getEmployeeResponse"/>
        </wsdl:operation>
    </wsdl:portType>
</wsdl:definitions>
```

The following element represents the endpoint interface. The "name" attribute of the "portType" element represents the name of the endpoint interface.

```
<wsdl:portType name="EmployeeService">
```

Structure of a WSDL Document

The following element represents the operation defined in the endpoint interface. The "name" attribute of the "operation" element represents the name of the operation.

```
<wsdl:operation name="getEmployee">
```

The following element represents the method input parameter. The "message" attribute of the "input" element refers to the WSDL message *part* type; the optional "name" attribute refers to the name of the WSDL input element.

```
<wsdl:input message="tns:getEmployee" name="getEmployee"/>
```

The following element represents the method return value. The "message" attribute of the "output" element refers to the WSDL message *part* type, the optional "name" attribute refers to the name of the WSDL output element.

```
<wsdl:output message="tns:getEmployeeResponse"
             name="getEmployeeResponse"/>
```

Section 6: WDSL binding - <binding/>

The *binding* specifies the interface, SOAP message exchange pattern, and protocol used to transfer the SOAP message. It defines how the message is transmitted between the client and service endpoint. The relation between WSDL *binding* and its *port type* are shown in Figure 7-4.

Figure 7-4: Relation between binding and port type.

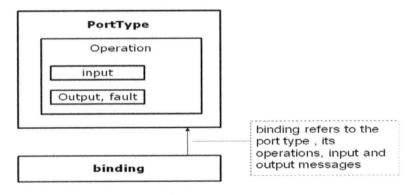

Relation between binding and port type

The WSDL *binding* definition is given below.

```
<wsdl:definitions>
     ......
    <wsdl:binding name="employeeServiceSoapBinding"
                  type="tns:EmployeeService">
        <soap:binding style="document"
                  transport="http://schemas.xmlsoap.org/soap/http"/>
        <wsdl:operation name="getEmployee">
            <soap:operation soapAction="" style="document"/>
            <wsdl:input name="getEmployee">
            <soap:body use="literal"/>
            </wsdl:input>
            <wsdl:output name="getEmployeeResponse">
```

```
                        <soap:body use="literal"/>
                    </wsdl:output>
                </wsdl:operation>
            </wsdl:binding>
        </wsdl:definitions>
```

The following element specifies the WSDL binding used for the interface. The "name" attribute of the "binding" element represents the binding name used for the port type. The "type" attribute of the binding element represents the port type defined for the service.

```
<wsdl:binding name="employeeServiceSoapBinding"
              type="tns:EmployeeService">
```

The following "style" attribute of the SOAP binding element represents the message formatting style, which is "RPC" or "Document." The "transport" attribute of the binding element represents the protocol used to transfer the message, which is SOAP over HTTP.

```
<soap:binding style="document"
              transport="http://schemas.xmlsoap.org/soap/http"/>
```

The child elements of the "<wsdl:binding>" element are operation, input and output. These elements maps directly to the corresponding child elements of the "<wsdl:portType>" operation, input and output.

```
<wsdl:operation name="getEmployee">
    <soap:operation soapAction="" style="document"/>
    <wsdl:input name="getEmployee">
        <soap:body use="literal"/>
    </wsdl:input>
    <wsdl:output name="getEmployeeResponse">
        <soap:body use="literal"/>
    </wsdl:output>
</wsdl:operation>
```

The following element represents the name of the operation.

```
<wsdl:operation name="getEmployee">
```

The following element represents the message formatting style used for the SOAP message between the client and service endpoint operation.

```
<soap:operation soapAction="" style="document"/>
```

The following element represents the binding used for input parameter values. It specifies what type of encoding the "<soap:body>" of the input message is using, which is "Literal" or "SOAP/Encoded."

```
<wsdl:input name="getEmployee">
    <soap:body use="literal"/>
</wsdl:input>
```

The following element represents the binding used for the method return value. It specifies what type of encoding the "<soap:body>" of the return message is using, which is "Literal" or "SOAP/Encoded."

```
<wsdl:output name="getEmployeeResponse">
    <soap:body use="literal"/>
</wsdl:output>
```

Section 7: WDSL service -

This section of the WSDL represents the collections of the service endpoints. The "Port" element of the service is used to specify the binding used and the location of the Web service endpoint. The relationship between the service and binding is shown in Figure 7-5.

Figure 7-5: Relation between service, Port and binding.

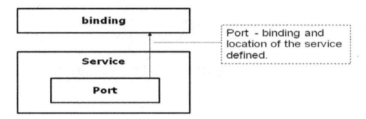

Relation between Service, Port and binding

The WSDL *service* definition is given below.

```
<wsdl:definitions>
    ...
    <wsdl:service name="employeeService">
        <wsdl:port binding="tns:employeeServiceSoapBinding"
                name="EmployeeServicePort">
            <soap:address
            location="http://localhost:8080/wsbook/services/employee"/>
        </wsdl:port>
    </wsdl:service>
</wsdl:definitions>
```

The following element represents the name of the service.

```
<wsdl:service name="employeeService">
```

The following "binding" attribute of the "port" element represents the binding used, and the "name" attribute represents the name of the binding. The name should be unique if you use multiple bindings for the same service.

```
<wsdl:port binding="tns:employeeServiceSoapBinding"
            name="EmployeeServicePort">
```

The "location" attribute of the "<soap:addrees>" element represents the service endpoint address.

```
<soap:address location="http://localhost:8080/wsbook/services/employee"/>
```

The following WSDL code snippet shows how to use multiple bindings for the same service endpoint. The three ports defined for the service endpoint use the SOAP-1.1, SOAP-1.2, and HTTP bindings.

```
<wsdl:service name="employeeService">
    <wsdl:port name="employeeServiceHttpSoap11Endpoint"
            binding="ns:employeeServiceSoap11Binding">
        <soap:address location="http://localhost:8080/axis2/services/
            employeeService.employeeServiceHttpSoap11Endpoint/"/>
    </wsdl:port>

    <wsdl:port name="employeeServiceHttpSoap12Endpoint"
            binding="ns:employeeServiceSoap12Binding">
        <soap12:address location="http://localhost:8080/axis2/
            services/
            employeeService.employeeServiceHttpSoap12Endpoint/"/>
    </wsdl:port>

    <wsdl:port name="employeeServiceHttpEndpoint"
            binding="ns:employeeServiceHttpBinding">
        <http:address location="http://localhost:8080/axis2/
            services/employeeService.employeeServiceHttpEndpoint/"/>
    </wsdl:port>
</wsdl:service>
```

WSDL-2.0

The WSDL-2.0 document describes the Web service in two stages; one is abstract, and one is concrete. The "<description/>" element is the topmost root element of the WSDL-2.0 document; all other elements are its child elements. The abstract section contains *types* and *interface* definitions; the concrete section contains *binding* and *service* details. The following Figure 7-6 shows the structure of a WSDL-2.0 document.

Figure 7-6: Structure of WSDL-2.0 document.

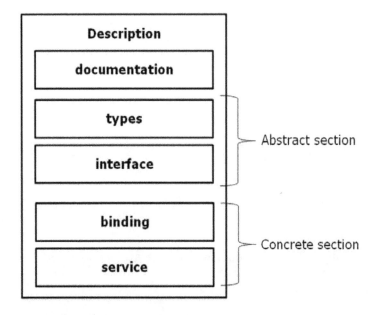

WSDL2 document structure

The names of various objects defined in WSDL-2.0 are given below.

- Description
- Documentation
- Types
- Interface
- Binding
- Service

The *Description* element is the topmost root element of the WSDL document. This is used for declaring all required namespaces used throughout the document.

The *Documentation* element contains the textual information about the Web service, its purpose, use, and its function.

The *Types* element defines the information related to request, response, and fault types. Inline or external XML schemas are used to represent this information.

The *Interface* element defines the Web service endpoint interface. It contains abstract operations and faults. It defines the functionality of the web service operations.

The *Binding* element refers to the message format and style defined in the interface and defines the transmission protocol. It defines how messages are exchanged.

The *Service* element defines the location of the Web service, including the service endpoint.

Now let us review a sample WSDL to understand each section of the WSDL document in detail. The Web service defined in WSDL has one operation: "getEmployee()"; It returns the details of the employee for a given employee id. The complete WSDL document is given below:

```xml
<?xml version="1.0" encoding="UTF-8"?>
<description xmlns="http://www.w3.org/ns/wsdl"
    targetNamespace="http://jaxws.ws.learning.com/2012/wsdl/empService"
    xmlns:tns="http://jaxws.ws.learning.com/2012/wsdl/empService"
    xmlns:empns="http://jaxws.ws.learning.com/2012/schemas/empService"
    xmlns:wsoap="http://www.w3.org/ns/wsdl/soap"
    xmlns:soap="http://www.w3.org/2003/05/soap-envelope/"
    xmlns:wsdlx="http://www.w3.org/ns/wsdl-extensions">

    <documentation>
        This document describes the employee web service.
    </documentation>

    <types>
        <xs:schema xmlns:xs="http://www.w3.org/2001/XMLSchema"
            targetNamespace=
            "http://jaxws.ws.learning.com/2012/schemas/empService"
            xmlns=
            "http://jaxws.ws.learning.com/2012/schemas/empService">

            <xs:complexType name="employee">
                <xs:sequence>
                    <xs:element minOccurs="0" name="employeeId"
                        type="xs:string"/>
                    <xs:element minOccurs="0" name="firstName"
```

```
                                type="xs:string"/>
                    <xs:element minOccurs="0" name="lastName"
                                type="xs:string"/>
                    <xs:element minOccurs="0" name="address"
                                type="xs:string"/>
                </xs:sequence>
            </xs:complexType>

            <xs:element name="getEmployee" type="getEmployee"/>
            <xs:complexType name="getEmployee">
                <xs:sequence>
                    <xs:element minOccurs="0" name="employeeId"
                                    type="xs:string"/>
                </xs:sequence>
            </xs:complexType>

            <xs:element name="EmployeeFault" type="EmployeeFault"/>
            <xs:complexType name="EmployeeFault">
                <xs:sequence/>
            </xs:complexType>

            <xs:element name="getEmployeeResponse"
                    type="getEmployeeResponse"/>
                <xs:complexType name="getEmployeeResponse">
                    <xs:sequence>
                        <xs:element minOccurs="0" name="return"
                            type="employee"/>
                    </xs:sequence>
            </xs:complexType>
        </xs:schema>
</types>

<interface name="EmployeeServiceInterface">
    <fault name="employeeFault" element="empns:EmployeeFault"/>
    <operation name="getEmployee"
            pattern="http://www.w3.org/ns/wsdl/in-out"
                    style="http://www.w3.org/ns/wsdl/style/iri"
                    wsdlx:safe="true">
            <input messageLabel="In" element="empns:getEmployee"/>
            <output messageLabel="Out"
                    element="empns:getEmployeeResponse"/>
            <outfault ref="tns:employeeFault" messageLabel="Out"/>
        </operation>
</interface>

<binding name="employeeServiceSOAPBinding"
        interface="tns:EmployeeServiceInterface"
        type="http://www.w3.org/ns/wsdl/soap"
        wsoap:protocol=
        "http://www.w3.org/2003/05/soap/bindings/HTTP/">
    <fault ref="tns:employeeFault" wsoap:code="soap:Sender"/>
    <operation ref="tns:getEmployee"
    wsoap:mep="http://www.w3.org/2003/05/soap/mep/soap-response"/>
</binding>

<service name="employeeService"
        interface="tns:EmployeeServiceInterface">
```

```
        <endpoint name="employeeServiceEndpoint"
                binding="tns:employeeServiceSOAPBinding"
                address=
            "http://localhost:8080/wsbook/services/employeeService"/>
    </service>
</description>
```

Let us review each section of the WSDL document to determine its meaning and significance.

Section 1: WSDL Description -

The *description* is the topmost root element in any WSDL-2.0 document and is the container for all other WSDL elements. This section of the WSDL is used to declare the namespaces related to WSDL and XML to be used in this particular service description. Let us review the WSDL description to analyze the declared namespaces.

```
<description xmlns="http://www.w3.org/ns/wsdl"
    targetNamespace="http://jaxws.ws.learning.com/2012/wsdl/empService"
    xmlns:tns="http://jaxws.ws.learning.com/2012/wsdl/empService"
    xmlns:empns="http://jaxws.ws.learning.com/2012/schemas/empService"
    xmlns:wsoap="http://www.w3.org/ns/wsdl/soap"
    xmlns:soap="http://www.w3.org/2003/05/soap-envelope/"
    xmlns:wsdlx="http://www.w3.org/ns/wsdl-extensions">
    ...
</description>
```

The below given XML is the XML namespace for the WSDL-2.0 specification used as the default namespace for this document.

```
xmlns="http://www.w3.org/ns/wsdl"
```

The below given XML is the target namespace for this WSDL document. Its value is same as the Java package name but in reverse order.

```
targetNamespace="http://jaxws.ws.learning.com/2012/wsdl/empService"
```

The below given XML is an actual namespace to be used in this document with the "tns:" prefix; in "QNames," it is used to refer to the target namespace of this service. Its URI is the same as that of the target namespace.

```
xmlns:tns="http://jaxws.ws.learning.com/2012/wsdl/empService"
```

This namespace declaration in the WSDL description allows us to refer to the XML message *types* defined in the XML schema. In this example, the prefix "empns:" QName is used to refer to the *types* defined in the inline XML schema of the WSDL document.

```
xmlns:empns="http://jaxws.ws.learning.com/2012/schemas/empService"
```

The following namespace used to refer to the SOAP binding extensions.

```
xmlns:wsoap="http://www.w3.org/ns/wsdl/soap"
```

The following namespace used to refer to the SOAP message specification.

Structure of a WSDL Document   175

```
xmlns:soap="http://www.w3.org/2003/05/soap-envelope/"
```

The following namespace used to refer to the WSDL extensions.

```
xmlns:wsdlx="http://www.w3.org/ns/wsdl-extensions"
```

Section 2: WDSL documentation - < documentation/>

The *documentation* section of the WSDL is used to provide comments about the Web service in human readable text format. This is similar to the class-level comments we provide in Java. It explains the purpose of this service and its constraints. It has no technical significance.

Section 3: WDSL types -

This section of the WSDL defines the request, response, and fault message types used in these service operations. In the Java world, it represents the parameter values, return types, and exceptions of an operation. This particular example uses the inline XML schema; thus, the XML schema is part of the WSDL document. The user can also import the XML schema import mechanism to use external schemas. The definition of the message types follows the standard XML schema syntax. The message types defined in this example are given below.

```
<description xmlns="http://www.w3.org/ns/wsdl"
      targetNamespace="http://jaxws.ws.learning.com/2012/wsdl/empService"
      xmlns:tns="http://jaxws.ws.learning.com/2012/wsdl/empService"
      xmlns:empns="http://jaxws.ws.learning.com/2012/schemas/empService">
      ...
<types>
      <xs:schema xmlns:xs="http://www.w3.org/2001/XMLSchema"
            targetNamespace=
            "http://jaxws.ws.learning.com/2012/schemas/empService"
            xmlns=
            "http://jaxws.ws.learning.com/2012/schemas/empService">

      <xs:complexType name="employee">
            <xs:sequence>
                  <xs:element minOccurs="0" name="employeeId"
                        type="xs:string"/>
                  <xs:element minOccurs="0" name="firstName"
                        type="xs:string"/>
                  <xs:element minOccurs="0" name="lastName"
                              type="xs:string"/>
                        <xs:element minOccurs="0" name="address"
                              type="xs:string"/>
                  </xs:sequence>
      </xs:complexType>

      <xs:element name="getEmployee" type="getEmployee"/>
      <xs:complexType name="getEmployee">
            <xs:sequence>
                  <xs:element minOccurs="0" name="employeeId"
                        type="xs:string"/>
            </xs:sequence>
      </xs:complexType>

      <xs:element name="EmployeeFault" type="EmployeeFault"/>
      <xs:complexType name="EmployeeFault">
```

```
                <xs:sequence/>
            </xs:complexType>

            <xs:element name="getEmployeeResponse"
                        type="getEmployeeResponse"/>
            <xs:complexType name="getEmployeeResponse">
                <xs:sequence>
                    <xs:element minOccurs="0" name="return"
                                type="employee"/>
                </xs:sequence>
            </xs:complexType>
        </xs:schema>
    </types>
</description>
```

The below given namespace declaration in the WSDL description will allow us to refer to the XML message types defined in the XML schema. In this example, the prefix "empns:" QName refers to the types defined in the inline XML schema of the WSDL document.

```
xmlns:empns="http://jaxws.ws.learning.com/2012/schemas/empService"
```

The below given XML is the namespace of the actual XML schema specification.

```
xmlns:xs="http://www.w3.org/2001/XMLSchema"
```

The below given XML is the XML schema target namespace we created for the employee Web service.

```
targetNamespace="http://jaxws.ws.learning.com/2012/schemas/empService"
```

The below given XML is the XML schema default namespace that we created for the employee Web service.

```
xmlns="http://jaxws.ws.learning.com/2012/schemas/empService">
```

Section 4: WDSL interface -

This section of the WSDL defines the abstract interface and its abstract operations. Each operation of the interface specifies the messaging style and message exchange pattern used to transfer the messages between client and service.

```
<description xmlns="http://www.w3.org/ns/wsdl"
    targetNamespace="http://jaxws.ws.learning.com/2012/wsdl/empService"
    xmlns:tns="http://jaxws.ws.learning.com/2012/wsdl/empService"
    xmlns:empns="http://jaxws.ws.learning.com/2012/schemas/empService"
    xmlns:wsdlx="http://www.w3.org/ns/wsdl-extensions">
    ...
    <interface name="EmployeeServiceInterface">
        <fault name="employeeFault" element="empns:EmployeeFault"/>
        <operation name="getEmployee"
                pattern="http://www.w3.org/ns/wsdl/in-out"
                style="http://www.w3.org/ns/wsdl/style/iri"
                wsdlx:safe="true">
            <input messageLabel="In" element="empns:getEmployee"/>
            <output messageLabel="Out"
```

```
                    element="empns:getEmployeeResponse"/>
            <outfault ref="tns:employeeFault" messageLabel="Out"/>
        </operation>
    </interface>
</description>
```

The below given XML is the namespace used to refer to the WSDL extensions.

```
xmlns:wsdlx="http://www.w3.org/ns/wsdl-extensions"
```

The below given XML represents the name of the abstract interface that declares the operations and faults.

```
<interface name="EmployeeServiceInterface">
```

The below given "name" attribute represents the fault name used by the operation, and the "element" attribute represents the fault message type defined in the XML schema.

```
<fault name="employeeFault" element="empns:EmployeeFault"/>
```

The below given "name" attribute represents the operation name.

```
<operation name="getEmployee"
```

The below given "pattern" attribute represents the type of message exchange pattern used. In this example, we have the request-and-response pattern, so this is the in-out pattern.

```
pattern="http://www.w3.org/ns/wsdl/in-out"
```

The below given "style" attribute represents the messaging style of the operation, which is IRI.

```
style="http://www.w3.org/ns/wsdl/style/iri"
```

The operation is marked safe without any side effects using the below given XML. It does not force the user to perform some other activity while invoking this operation.

```
wsdlx:safe="true"
```

The below given "messageLabel" attribute of the input element represents the input message. The "element" attribute represents the input message type used by the operation, which is defined in the XML schema.

```
<input messageLabel="In" element="empns:getEmployee"/>
```

The below given "messageLabel" attribute of the output element represents the output message. The "element" attribute represents the return message type of the operation, which is defined in the XML schema.

```
<output messageLabel="Out" element="empns:getEmployeeResponse"/>
```

The below given XML element represent the output fault of the operation. It references the fault message, which is defined in this interface.

```
<outfault messageLabel="Out" ref="tns:employeeFault"/>
```

The relation between *types* and *interface* is shown in Figure 7-7.

Figure 7-7: Relation between types, interface and operation

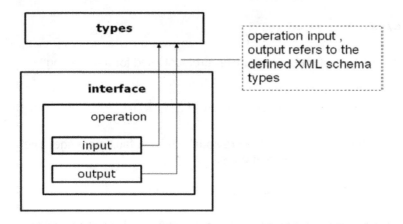

Relation between types, interface and operation

Section 5: WDSL binding -

This section of the WSDL represents how messages can be exchanged. It also specifies the message format (an example is the SOAP envelope) and protocol used (an example is the HTTP for transport) for transferring the message. The binding has to be specified for each operation and fault type defined in the service interface.

```
<description xmlns="http://www.w3.org/ns/wsdl"
     targetNamespace="http://jaxws.ws.learning.com/2012/wsdl/empService"
     xmlns:tns="http://jaxws.ws.learning.com/2012/wsdl/empService"
     xmlns:empns="http://jaxws.ws.learning.com/2012/schemas/empService"
     xmlns:wsoap="http://www.w3.org/ns/wsdl/soap"
     xmlns:soap="http://www.w3.org/2003/05/soap-envelope/"
     xmlns:wsdlx="http://www.w3.org/ns/wsdl-extensions">
     . . .

     <binding name="employeeServiceSOAPBinding"
          interface="tns:EmployeeServiceInterface"
          type="http://www.w3.org/ns/wsdl/soap"
          wsoap:protocol="http://www.w3.org/2003/05/soap/bindings/HTTP/">
          <fault ref="tns:employeeFault" wsoap:code="soap:Sender"/>
          <operation ref="tns:getEmployee"
                    wsoap:mep="http://www.w3.org/2003/05/soap/mep/soap-
                                                 response"/>
     </binding>
</description>
```

The below given "name" attribute represents the name used for this binding.

```
<binding name="employeeServiceSOAPBinding"
```

The below given "interface" attribute represents the service endpoint interface name used for specifying the message format and message transmission protocol.

```
interface="tns:EmployeeServiceInterface"
```

The below given XML represents the type of message format used.

```
type="http://www.w3.org/ns/wsdl/soap"
```

The below given XML represents the type of message transfer protocol used for transferring messages.

```
wsoap:protocol="http://www.w3.org/2003/05/soap/bindings/HTTP/">
```

The below given XML specifies the binding details for the previously defined fault message. The attribute "wsoap:code" is used to specify the SOAP fault code.

```
<fault ref="tns:employeeFault" wsoap:code="soap:Sender"/>
```

The below given XML specifies the binding details for the previously defined abstract operation. The attribute "wsoap:mep" specifies the implementation of the message exchange pattern defined for the interface operation "getEmployee," which is in-out.

```
<operation ref="tns:getEmployee"
    wsoap:mep="http://www.w3.org/2003/05/soap/mep/soap-response"/>
```

The relationship between *interface* and *binding* is shown in Figure 7-8.

Figure 7-8: Relationship between interface and binding

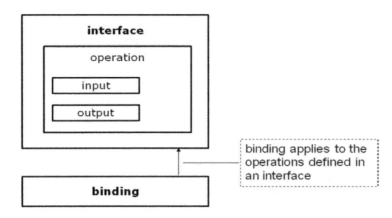

Relation between interface and binding

Section 6: WDSL service -

This section of the WSDL document specifies the location of the Web service endpoint. In addition, each endpoint references the binding defined in the previous section.

```
<description xmlns="http://www.w3.org/ns/wsdl"
```

```
        targetNamespace="http://jaxws.ws.learning.com/2012/wsdl/empService"
        xmlns:tns="http://jaxws.ws.learning.com/2012/wsdl/empService"
        xmlns:empns="http://jaxws.ws.learning.com/2012/schemas/empService"
        xmlns:wsoap="http://www.w3.org/ns/wsdl/soap"
        xmlns:soap="http://www.w3.org/2003/05/soap-envelope/"
        xmlns:wsdlx="http://www.w3.org/ns/wsdl-extensions">
        ...
        <service name="employeeService"
                interface="tns:EmployeeServiceInterface">
            <endpoint name="employeeServiceEndpoint"
                binding="tns:employeeServiceSOAPBinding"
                address=
                "http://localhost:8080/wsbook/services/employeeService"/>
        </service>
</description>
```

The below given "name" attribute represents the service name. The "interface" attribute represents the name of the interface, which is defined in the interface section.

```
<service name="employeeService" interface="tns:EmployeeServiceInterface">
```

The below given "name" attribute represents the service endpoint name. The "binding" attribute represents the binding used for this endpoint, which references the binding defined in the previous section. The "address" attribute represents the location of the Web service deployment.

```
<endpoint name="employeeServiceEndpoint"
        binding="tns:employeeServiceSOAPBinding"
        address=
        "http://localhost:8080/wsbook/services/employeeService"/>
```

The relationships between *binding*, *service*, and *endpoint* are shown in Figure 7-9.

Figure 7-9: Relationships between binding, service, and endpoint

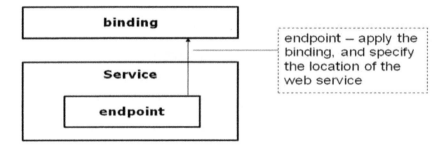

Relation between Service, endpoint and binding

WSDL to Java Mapping Details

The following table shows the WSDL code snippet and its corresponding equivalent Java code for WSDL-1.1 and 2.0. This comparison helps the developer visualize how WSDL maps to the endpoint interface, interface methods, input parameters, return values, and exceptions declared in an operation.

WSDL-1.1

WSDL code	Equivalent Java code

`<wsdl:portType name="EmployeeService">`
`</wsdl:portType>`
	`public interface EmployeeService {`
	`}`
	Port type name maps to an interface name.

`<wsdl:operation name="getEmployee">`
 	
`<wsdl:input message="tns:getEmployee"`
      `name="getEmployee"/>`
 	
  `<wsdl:output`
     `message="tns:getEmployeeResponse"`
     `name="getEmployeeResponse"/>`
 	
`</wsdl:operation>`
	getEmployee() – maps to operation name
	
	String employeeId – maps to method parameters
	
	Employee – maps to method return value
	
	The complete method signature is given below:
	`public Employee getEmployee`
	`(String employeeId)`

`<xs:complexType name="employee">`
 `<xs:sequence>`
  `<xs:element minOccurs="0"`
       `name="employeeId"`
       `type="xs:string"/>`
 	
  `<xs:element minOccurs="0"`
       `name="firstName"`
       `type="xs:string"/>`
 	
  `<xs:element minOccurs="0"`
       `name="lastName"`
       `type="xs:string"/>`
 	
  `<xs:element minOccurs="0" name="address"`
       `type="xs:string"/>`
 `</xs:sequence>`
 	
`</xs:complexType>`
	`public class Employee {`
	
	  `private String employeeId;`
	
	. `private String firstName;`
	
	  `private String lastName;`
	
	. `private String address;`
	
	  `//add getter and setter methods`
	`}`
	
	XML schema complex type maps to Employee Java bean object. This is the method's return value.

`<xs:complexType name="getEmployee">`
 `<xs:sequence>`
  `<xs:element minOccurs="0"`
       `name="employeeId"`
       `type="xs:string"/>`
 `</xs:sequence>`
`</xs:complexType>`
	`getEmployee (String employeeId)`
	
	The XML schema complex type maps to the Java method input parameter, which is employeeId.

`<xs:complexType name="EmployeeFault">`	Maps to exception.

WSDL code	Equivalent Java code
`<xs:sequence/>` `</xs:complexType>`	Example: throws EmployeeFault

WSDL-2.0

WSDL code	Equivalent Java code

`<interface name="EmployeeServiceInterface">`
`</interface>`
	`public interface EmployeeServiceInterface {`
	`}`
	interface name maps to java interface name.

`<operation name="getEmployee"`
`    pattern="http://www.w3.org/ns/wsdl/in-out"`
`    style="http://www.w3.org/ns/wsdl/style/iri"`
`    wsdlx:safe="true">`
 	
`    <input messageLabel="In"`
`        element="empns:getEmployee"/>`
 	
`    <output messageLabel="Out"`
`      element="empns:getEmployeeResponse"/>`
 	
`    <outfault messageLabel="Out"`
`            ref="tns:employeeFault"/>`
 	
`</operation>`
	getEmployee() – maps to operation name
	
	String employeeId – maps to method parameters
	
	Employee – maps to method return value
	
	throws EmployeeFault – maps to exception
	
	The complete method signature is given below:
	
	`public Employee getEmployee`
	`(String employeeId) throws EmployeeFault;`

`<xs:complexType name="employee">`
`  <xs:sequence>`
`    <xs:element minOccurs="0"`
`            name="employeeId"`
`            type="xs:string"/>`
 	
`    <xs:element minOccurs="0"`
`            name="firstName"`
`            type="xs:string"/>`
 	
`    <xs:element minOccurs="0"`
`            name="lastName"`
`            type="xs:string"/>`
 	
`    <xs:element minOccurs="0"`
`            name="address"`
`            type="xs:string"/>`
`  </xs:sequence>`
`</xs:complexType>`
	`public class Employee {`
	
	`    private String employeeId;`
	
	`    private String firstName;`
	
	`    private String lastName;`
	
	`    private String address;`
	
	`    //add getter and setter methods`
	`}`
	
	XML schema complex type maps to Employee java bean object. This is the method's return value.

`<xs:complexType name="getEmployee">`	getEmployee(**String employeeId**)

```
<xs:sequence>
   <xs:element minOccurs="0"
              name="employeeId"
              type="xs:string"/>
</xs:sequence>
</xs:complexType>
```

The XML schema complex type maps to the Java method input parameter, which is employee id.

Message Exchange Patterns (MEP)

This specifies the sequence of WSDL message types (input, output, and fault) for each operation. The message exchange patterns specify how a Web service client invokes the service endpoint and how the service endpoint should respond to the client. It specifies the pattern of the endpoint method invocation, indicating whether it is one-way, synchronous, asynchronous, and so forth.

WSDL-1.1 Message Exchange Patterns

The WSDL-1.1 service endpoint supports four types of message exchange patterns, listed below. They represent the type of messages or faults exchanged between the client and service endpoint.

- One-way messaging
- Request-response messaging
- Solicit-response messaging
- Notification messaging

One way messaging pattern—The endpoint operation receives only an input request message.

The one-way message exchange pattern between the client and service endpoint is shown in Figure 7-10.

Figure 7-10: One way messaging

The WSDL representation of the one-way message pattern is given below.

```
<wsdl:portType name="EmployeeService">
    <wsdl:operation name="deleteEmployee">
        <wsdl:input message="tns:deleteEmployee"
                    name="deleteEmployee"/>
    </wsdl:operation>
</wsdl:portType>
```

Request-response messaging pattern—The endpoint operation receives an input request and sends the response back to the client.

Figure 7-11: Request-response messaging

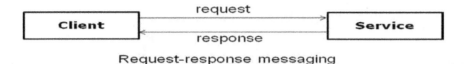

Request-response messaging

The WSDL representation of the request-response message pattern is given below.

```
<wsdl:portType name="EmployeeService">
    <wsdl:operation name="getEmployee">
        <wsdl:input message="tns:getEmployee" name="getEmployee"/>
        <wsdl:output message="tns:getEmployeeResponse"
                name="getEmployeeResponse"/>
        <wsdl:fault message="tns:EmployeeFault" name="EmployeeFault"/>
    </wsdl:operation>
</wsdl:portType>
```

Solicit-response messaging pattern—The endpoint operation sends an output message and waits for an input request message from the client.

Figure 7-12: Solicit-response messaging

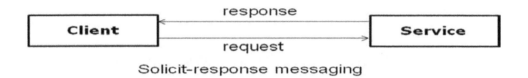

Solicit-response messaging

The WSDL representation of the solicit-response message pattern is given below.

```
<wsdl:portType name="EmployeeService">
    <wsdl:operation name="getEmployee">
        <wsdl:output message="tns:getEmployeeResponse"
                name="getEmployeeResponse"/>
        <wsdl:input message="tns:getEmployee" name="getEmployee"/>
        <wsdl:fault message="tns:EmployeeFault" name="EmployeeFault"/>
    </wsdl:operation>
</wsdl:portType>
```

Notification message pattern—The endpoint operation sends only an output message.

Figure 7-13: Notification messaging

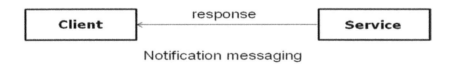

Notification messaging

The WSDL representation of the notification message pattern is given below.

```
<wsdl:portType name="EmployeeService">
    <wsdl:operation name="getEmployee">
        <wsdl:output message="tns:getEmployeeResponse"
                     name="getEmployeeResponse"/>
    </wsdl:operation>
</wsdl:portType>
```

WSDL-2.0 Message Exchange Patterns

They define the way, how the service endpoint is called and how the service endpoint should respond back to the client. The WSDL-2.0 has defined eight types of message exchange patterns, listed below.

There are four inbound message exchange patterns, listed below.

In-Only—The service endpoint operation receives only inbound messages and does not respond or send a fault back to the client.

Figure 7-14: In-only messaging

In-Only messaging

The WSDL representation of the in-only message exchange pattern is given below.

```
<operation name="opDeleteEmployee"
           pattern="http://www.w3.org/ns/wsdl/in-only"
           style="http://www.w3.org/ns/wsdl/style/iri">
    <input messageLabel="In" element="empns:getEmployee"/>
</operation>
```

Robust-In-Only—The service endpoint operation receives only inbound messages; however, it can send a fault back to the client.

Figure 7-15: Robust-in-only messaging

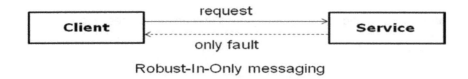

Robust-In-Only messaging

The WSDL representation of the robust-in-only message exchange pattern is given below.

```
<operation name="opDeleteEmployee"
           pattern="http://www.w3.org/ns/wsdl/robust-in-only"
           style="http://www.w3.org/ns/wsdl/style/iri">
    <input messageLabel="In" element="empns:getEmployee"/>
```

```
        <outfault messageLabel="Out" ref="tns:employeeFault"/>
</operation>
```

In-Out—The service endpoint operation receives inbound messages and sends a response back to the client. If an error occurs during the response to the client, it will send a fault message to the client.

Figure 7-16: In-out messaging

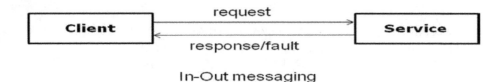

In-Out messaging

The WSDL representation of the in-out message exchange pattern is given below.

```
<operation name="getEmployee"
        pattern="http://www.w3.org/ns/wsdl/in-out"
        style="http://www.w3.org/ns/wsdl/style/iri">
    <input messageLabel="In" element="empns:getEmployee"/>
    <output messageLabel="Out" element="empns:getEmployeeResponse"/>
    <outfault messageLabel="Out" ref="tns:employeeFault"/>
</operation>
```

In-Optional-Out—The service endpoint operation receives inbound messages; the response is optional in this scenario.

Figure 7-17: In-optional-out messaging

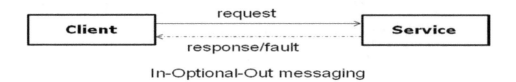

In-Optional-Out messaging

The WSDL representation of the in-optional-out message exchange pattern is given below.

```
<operation name="opDeleteEmployee"
        pattern="http://www.w3.org/ns/wsdl/in-optional-out"
        style="http://www.w3.org/ns/wsdl/style/iri">
    <input messageLabel="In" element="empns:getEmployee"/>
    <output messageLabel="Out" element="empns:getEmployeeResponse"/>
</operation>
```

There are four outbound message exchange patterns, listed below.

Out-Only—The service endpoint operation produces an outbound message; it does not receive response or fault back from the client.

Figure 7-18: Out-only messaging

Out-Only messaging

The WSDL representation of the out-only message exchange pattern is given below.

```
<operation name="opSendMessage"
            pattern="http://www.w3.org/ns/wsdl/out-only"
            style="http://www.w3.org/ns/wsdl/style/iri">
    <output messageLabel="Out" element="empns:getEmployeeResponse"/>
</operation>
```

Robust-Out-Only—The service endpoint operation produces an outbound message; in this case, it may receive a fault back from the client.

Figure 7-19: Robust-out-only messaging

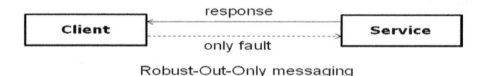

Robust-Out-Only messaging

The WSDL representation of the robust-out-only message exchange pattern is given below.

```
<operation name="opSendMessage"
          pattern="http://www.w3.org/ns/wsdl/robust-out-only"
          style="http://www.w3.org/ns/wsdl/style/iri">
    <output messageLabel="Out" element="empns:getEmployeeResponse"/>
    <infault messageLabel="In" ref="tns:employeeFault"/>
</operation>
```

Out-In—The service endpoint operation produces an outbound message and receives a response back from the client.

Figure 7-20: Out-in messaging

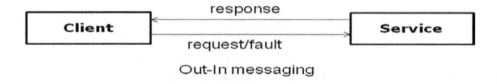

Out-In messaging

The WSDL representation of the out-in message exchange pattern is given below.

```
<operation name="opSendMessage"
          pattern="http://www.w3.org/ns/wsdl/out-in"
```

```
            style="http://www.w3.org/ns/wsdl/style/iri">
    <output messageLabel="Out" element="empns:getEmployeeResponse"/>
    <input messageLabel="In" element="empns:getEmployee"/>
</operation>
```

Out-Optional-In—The service endpoint operation produces an outbound message; the client response is optional in this scenario.

Figure 7-21: Out-optional-in messaging

The WSDL representation of the out-optional-in message exchange pattern is given below.

```
<operation name="opSendMessage"
            pattern="http://www.w3.org/ns/wsdl/out-optional-in"
            style="http://www.w3.org/ns/wsdl/style/iri">
    <output messageLabel="Out" element="empns:getEmployeeResponse"/>
</operation>
```

Web Service Messaging Modes

The message mode of a Web service specifies how the inbound-and-outbound SOAP messages are formatted while communicating between the client and service endpoint. Each Web service endpoint operation has to specify the message formatting, which is later used in WSDL binding. The WSDL binding specifies how a Web service endpoint is bound to a SOAP message protocol. The WSDL binding specifies the formatting style (SOAP) and transport (HTTP) used to transfer the message. There are four message modes defined in WSDL-1.1 and three defined in WSDL-2.0. The details of the supported message modes are discussed in this section.

WSDL-1.1

The valid types of message styles used for WSDL binding are "document" and "remote procedure call" (RPC), and they use "literal" or "encoded" binding. The valid combinations are given below.

- RPC/literal
- Document/literal
- RPC/encoded
- Document/encoded

The basic profile standards for Web services interoperability prohibits the use of encoded message types due to interoperability issues, so the use of RPC/encoded and Document/encoded messaging styles are limited.

RPC/Literal: In the RPC style, each part of the message is a method parameter or return value. In the example provided below, the method parameter uses the String Java types "empId" and "state," which map to the equivalent XML data type of "xsd:string." Each Java type has a corresponding XML data type defined for mapping and follows the same rule for the response part of the message. This message formatting style is called "RPC" messaging.

The code below shows the WSDL structure of request and response:

```
<wsdl:message name="getEmployerInformation">
    <wsdl:part name="empId" type="xsd:string" />
    <wsdl:part name="state" type="xsd:string" />
</wsdl:message>
<wsdl:message name="getEmployerInformationResponse">
    <wsdl:part name="return" type="xsd:string" />
</wsdl:message>
```

The code below shows the WSDL interface definition using the above-defined *parts* of the message.

```
<wsdl:portType name="EmployeeService">
    <wsdl:operation name="getEmployerInformation">
        <wsdl:input message="tns:getEmployerInformation"
                name="getEmployerInformation"/>
        <wsdl:output message="tns:getEmployerInformationResponse"
                name="getEmployerInformationResponse"/>
    </wsdl:operation>
</wsdl:portType>
```

Document/Literal: In the document style, each part of the message maps to the XML complex type defined in the XML schema, which is available in WSDL *types* section. In the example provided below, the WSDL element "getEmployerInformation" refers to the XML schema complex type "getEmployerInformation," which is defined in this WSDL. This message formatting style is called "Document" messaging.

The code below shows the XML schema defined for request-and-response messages:

```
<wsdl:types>
    <xs:schema targetNamespace="http://jaxws.ws.learning.com/"
            xmlns="http://jaxws.ws.learning.com/"
            xmlns:xs="http://www.w3.org/2001/XMLSchema">

    <xs:element name="getEmployerInformation"
            type="getEmployerInformation"/>
        <xs:complexType name="getEmployerInformation">
        <xs:sequence>
            <xs:element minOccurs="0" name="empId" type="xs:string"/>
            <xs:element minOccurs="0" name="state" type="xs:string"/>
        </xs:sequence>
    </xs:complexType>

    <xs:element name="getEmployerInformationResponse"
            type="getEmployerInformationResponse"/>
        <xs:complexType name="getEmployerInformationResponse">
        <xs:sequence>
            <xs:element minOccurs="0" name="return" type="xs:string"/>
        </xs:sequence>
```

```
            </xs:complexType>
        </xs:schema>
</wsdl:types>
```

The code below shows the WSDL message *parts* of request-and-response messages:

```
<wsdl:message name="getEmployerInformation">
    <wsdl:part element="tns:getEmployerInformation" name="parameters"/>
</wsdl:message>
<wsdl:message name="getEmployerInformationResponse">
    <wsdl:part element="tns:getEmployerInformationResponse"
            name="parameters"/>
</wsdl:message>
```

The code below shows the WSDL interface definition using the above-defined *parts* of the message.

```
<wsdl:portType name="EmployeeService">
    <wsdl:operation name="getEmployerInformation">
        <wsdl:input message="tns:getEmployerInformation"
                name="getEmployerInformation"/>
        <wsdl:output message="tns:getEmployerInformationResponse"
                name="getEmployerInformationResponse"/>
    </wsdl:operation>
</wsdl:portType>
```

WSDL-2.0

The valid messaging styles used for WSDL-2.0 service binding are "RPC," "IRI," and "Multipart." Each operation declared in an interface uses one of these message styles, which is later used while binding the SOAP messages. Each message style is represented with an URI and is specified as the "style" attribute of an "<operation/>" element.

RPC: This message style is represented by an URI "http://www.w3.org/ns/wsdl/style/rpc". The RPC style is applied by specifying the value of "style" attribute in the "<operation/>" element of an interface element. The representation of a RPC message style as used in WSDL with a service operation is given below.

```
<interface name="EmployeeServiceInterface">
    <fault name="employeeFault" element="empns:EmployeeFault"/>
    <operation name="getEmployee"
            pattern="http://www.w3.org/ns/wsdl/in-out"
            style="http://www.w3.org/ns/wsdl/style/rpc"
            wsdlx:safe="true">
        <input messageLabel="In" element="empns:getEmployee"/>
        <output messageLabel="Out"
            element="empns:getEmployeeResponse"/>
        <outfault ref="tns:employeeFault" messageLabel="Out"/>
    </operation>
</interface>
```

The rules applied to an RPC message style are given below.

• The RPC message style is used with "in-only" and "in-out" message exchange patterns.

- The input and output elements must be in the same namespace. The input and output elements provided below belong to the same namespace.

```
<input messageLabel="In" element="empns:getEmployee"/>
<output messageLabel="Out" element="empns:getEmployeeResponse"/>
```

- The input element name must be the same as that of the interface operation name.
- The input and output elements cannot have any local attributes.
- The input and output elements can have only local element children.
- The input and output elements cannot contain multiple children with the same name.

The example representation of input and output elements in WSDL is given below:

```
<input messageLabel="In" element="empns:getEmployee"/>
<output messageLabel="Out" element="empns:getEmployeeResponse"/>
```

The corresponding XML schema definition for the input and output elements is given below:

```
<types>
    <xs:schema xmlns:xs="http://www.w3.org/2001/XMLSchema"
        targetNamespace=
        "http://jaxws.ws.learning.com/2012/schemas/empService"
        xmlns=
        "http://jaxws.ws.learning.com/2012/schemas/empService">

        <xs:complexType name="employee">
            <xs:sequence>
                <xs:element minOccurs="0" name="employeeId"
                        type="xs:string"/>
                <xs:element minOccurs="0" name="firstName"
                        type="xs:string"/>
                <xs:element minOccurs="0" name="lastName"
                        type="xs:string"/>
                <xs:element minOccurs="0" name="address"
                        type="xs:string"/>
            </xs:sequence>
        </xs:complexType>

        <xs:element name="getEmployee" type="getEmployee"/>
        <xs:complexType name="getEmployee">
            <xs:sequence>
                <xs:element minOccurs="0" name="employeeId"
                        type="xs:string"/>
            </xs:sequence>
        </xs:complexType>

        <xs:element name="getEmployeeResponse"
                    type="getEmployeeResponse"/>
        <xs:complexType name="getEmployeeResponse">
            <xs:sequence>
                <xs:element minOccurs="0" name="return"
                                    type="employee"/>
            </xs:sequence>
        </xs:complexType>
    </xs:schema>
```

```
</types>
```

IRI: This message style is represented by the following URI: "http://www.w3.org/ns/wsdl/style/iri."
The IRI style is applied by specifying the value of the "style" attribute in the "<operation/>" element
of an interface element. The representation of the IRI message style as used in WSDL with a
service operation is given below.

```
<operation name="getEmployee"
        pattern="http://www.w3.org/ns/wsdl/in-out"
        style="http://www.w3.org/ns/wsdl/style/iri"
        wsdlx:safe="true">
   <input messageLabel="In" element="empns:getEmployee"/>
   <output messageLabel="Out" element="empns:getEmployeeResponse"/>
</operation>
```

The rules applied to the IRI message style are given below.

- The input element name must be same as the interface operation name.
- The input element cannot have any local attributes.
- The input element can only have local element children.
- The input element cannot contain the multiple children with the same name.

Multipart: This message style is represented by an URI "http://www.w3.org/ns/wsdl/style/multipart."
The multipart style is applied by specifying the value of "style" attribute in the "<operation/>"
element of an interface element. The representation of the multipart message style as used in
WSDL with a service operation is given below.

```
<operation name="getEmployee"
        pattern="http://www.w3.org/ns/wsdl/in-out"
        style="http://www.w3.org/ns/wsdl/style/multipart"
        wsdlx:safe="true">
   <input messageLabel="In" element="empns:getEmployee"/>
   <output messageLabel="Out" element="empns:getEmployeeResponse"/>
</operation>
```

The rules applied to a multipart message style are given below.

- The input element name must be same as the interface operation name.
- The input element cannot have any local attributes.
- The input element can have only local element children.
- The input element cannot contain multiple children with the same name.

Comparison between WSDL-1.1 and 2.0

The following table summarizes the comparison between WSDL-1.1 and 2.0. Many new features
are included to address the limitations of the WSDL-1.1 specification.

Feature	WSDL-1.1	WSDL-2.0
WSDL namespace declaration	http://schemas.xmlsoap.org/wsdl/	http://www.w3.org/ns/wsdl
WSDL Structure—various	Definitions	Description

objects defined	Types Messages and parts Port Type Binding Service and port	Types Interface Binding Service and endpoint *Messages* and *PortType* are replaced with *interface* in WSDL-2.0
Message exchange patterns (mep)	One-way Request-response Solicit-response Notification	In-only Robust-in-only In-out In-optional-out Out-only Robust-out-only Out-in Out-optional-in
Message modes	RPC/literal Document/literal	RPC IRI Multiform
Importing WSDL definitions	Supports wsdl:import	Supports both wsdl:import and wsdl:include
Interface inheritance	N/A	Newly introduced in WSDL-2.0. One interface can extend one or more interfaces.
Creating custom message exchanges patterns	N/A	Newly introduced in WSDL-2.0.
Supports RESTful services	N/A	Included in WSDL-2.0

Test Yourself — Objective Questions

1. Which of the following object definitions correctly describes the structure of WSDL-2.0?

   a) description, definition, types, messages, port type, and binding
   b) definitions, types, messages, port type, binding, and service
   c) definitions, types, messages, parts, interface, and endpoint
   d) description, types, interface, binding, and service
   e) types, messages, parts, interface, service, and endpoint

2. Which of the following is the valid message exchange patterns used for inbound messaging as per the WSDL-2.0 specification?

   a) Out-only, Robust-out-only, Out-in, Out-optional-in
   b) One-way, request-response, solicit-response, notification
   c) In-only, Robust-in-only, In-out, In-optional-out
   d) RPC/literal, Document/literal, RPC/encoded, Document/encoded
   e) In-only, Out-only, In-out, Out-in

3. Referring to the WSDL operation definition provided below, which of the following statements is valid according to WSDL 1.1 specifications?

```
<wsdl:portType name="EmployeeService">
   <wsdl:operation name="getEmployee">
       <wsdl:output message="tns:getEmployeeResponse"
                 name="getEmployeeResponse"/>
       <wsdl:input message="tns:getEmployee" name="getEmployee"/>
       <wsdl:fault message="tns:EmployeeFault" name="EmployeeFault"/>
   </wsdl:operation>
</wsdl:portType>
```

a) The sequence of the WSDL message elements best explains the solicit-response type of message exchange pattern.
b) The sequence of the WSDL message elements best explains the request-response type of message exchange pattern.
c) The sequence of the WSDL message elements best explains the one-way type of message exchange pattern.
d) The sequence of the WSDL message elements best explains the event type of message exchange pattern.
e) None of the above is correct.

4. Which of the following are valid message styles used for WSDL-1.1 binding according to basic profile standards of Web service interoperability?

a) RPC/literal
b) Document/literal
c) In-out
d) IRI
e) Multipart

5. Which of the following is a valid representation of the RPC-based messaging style used according to WSDL-2.0 specifications?

a)
```
<operation name="getEmployee"
           pattern="http://www.w3.org/ns/wsdl/in-out"
           style="http://www.w3.org/ns/wsdl/style/rpc"
           wsdlx:safe="true">
    . . .
</operation>
```

b)
```
<operation name="getEmployee"
           pattern="http://www.w3.org/ns/wsdl/Robust-Out-Only"
           style="http://www.w3.org/ns/wsdl/style/rpc"
           wsdlx:safe="true">
    . . .
</operation>
```

c)
```
<operation name="getEmployee"
           pattern="http://www.w3.org/ns/wsdl/Robust-In-Only"
           style="http://www.w3.org/ns/wsdl/style/rpc"
           wsdlx:safe="true">
    . . .
</operation>
```

d)

```
<operation name="getEmployee"
           pattern="http://www.w3.org/ns/wsdl/in-only"
           style="http://www.w3.org/ns/wsdl/style/rpc"
           wsdlx:safe="true">
    ...
</operation>
```

e) All are valid.

6. Which of the URIs provided below is a valid representation of the messaging style used for service binding in an operation?

a) http://www.w3.org/ns/wsdl/in-only
b) http://www.w3.org/ns/wsdl/style/rpc
c) http://www.w3.org/ns/wsdl/style/multipart
d) http://www.w3.org/ns/wsdl/in-out
e) http://www.w3.org/ns/wsdl/out-only

Answers to Test Questions

1. D is the correct answer.
The structure of WSDL-2.0 is different from that of WSDL-1.1. The *message* and *part* elements of WSDL are completely removed in WSDL-2.0. The *port type* of the WSDL-1.1 is replaced with the *interface* element in WSDL-2.0. Choice B represents the structure of the WSDL-1.1 document. All other combinations are invalid.

2. C is the correct answer.
There are eight message exchange patterns defined in the WSDL-2.0 specification; four are used for inbound messaging and four are used for outbound messaging. So C is the correct answer. Choice B is valid for WSDL-1.1. Choice A is valid for outbound messaging. All other combinations are invalid.

3. A is the correct answer.
The endpoint operation sends an output message and waits for an input request message from the client. The order of WSDL elements is output, input, and fault. So A is the correct answer.

4. A and B are correct.
Choices D and E are valid according to WSDL-2.0 specifications. Choice C is invalid because it is a message exchange pattern.

5. A and D are correct.
The RPC message style is used with "in-only" and "in-out" message exchange patterns.

6. B and C are correct.
Choices A, D, and E are incorrect because they represent the message exchange patterns. The valid messaging styles used for WSDL-2.0 binding are "RPC," "IRI," and "Multipart."

Chapter 8. JAX-WS

Java API for XML Web services (JAX-WS) is a Java specification (JSR-224) for implementing Web services using Java and XML. The JAX-WS specification defines a set of Java API for the development of Web services using the XML-based SOAP protocol. JAX-RPC (JSR 101) was Sun's previous version of the Web services specification. JAX-WS is a successor to Java API for the Remote Procedure Call (JAX-RPC); it is newly architected for developing Web services. JAX-WS is part of the Java EE platform. JAX-WS provides new enhancements and features for developing Web services using annotations.

In this chapter will discuss the following topics:

- JAX-WS fundamentals and its architecture
- JAX-WS advantages and disadvantages
- JAX-WS terminology
- JSR-181 annotations and its use
- JSR-222 annotations and its use
- JSR-224 annotations and its use
- JSR-250 annotations and its use

JAX-WS Fundamentals and Its Architecture

The Web service endpoint uses JAX-WS runtime, and it can be deployed in any Java-compatible Web container. The client uses JAX-WS API to communicate with the service endpoint with the XML-based SOAP protocol. It supports both one-way and request-and-response message types. The complexity of the SOAP-related functionality is hidden to the application developer; it is handled internally by the JAX-WS runtime. The application developer will not construct the SOAP messages; JAX-WS runtime converts the HTTP requests to SOAP requests, and vice versa. Thus, the application developer can focus on service endpoint interface and its implementation.

JAX-WS API provides an exhaustive set of powerful annotations for Web services development. JAX-WS simplified the complexity of deployment descriptors and metadata defined in XML files by using a simplified annotation-based programming model. Instead of obtaining the metadata from XML files, the metadata related to the client and service can be declared using JAX-WS annotations.

Basic profile is a specification for the Web service interoperability industry consortium (called WS-I); it provides guidelines for Web services specifications such as SOAP and WSDL. The objective of these guidelines is to promote interoperability of the Web services across multiple languages and platforms. JAX-WS supports the basic profile standards and guidelines to provide interoperable services, so non-Java clients can invoke the JAX-WS service endpoints.

The Figure 8-1 shows the communication between the Web service client and service endpoint deployed in any Java-compatible Web container. The client invokes the service using JAX-WS API. It sends a SOAP message to the service endpoint; then the service endpoint receives the message, processes it, and sends the response back to the client.

Figure 8-1: JAX-WS Architecture

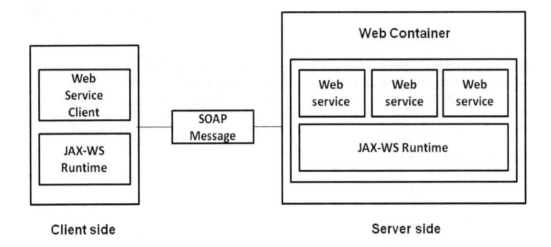

JAX-WS Advantages

- It uses the annotation-based programming model.
- JAX-WS is a successor to Java API for XML Remote Procedure Call (JAX-RPC), a simplified programming model compared to JAX-RPC. It eliminated some of the complexities of the JAX-RPC programming model.
- It enables simplified application development, targeted for junior and mid-level developers. It improves developer productivity.
- It supports WS-I basic profile guidelines to provide better interoperability of the Web services.
- It simplified the use of message handlers.
- It separates the data-binding technology and Web services programming model. There is a different set of annotations available for binding (JAXB) and Web services development.
- No separate deployment descriptors are needed as were required in previous versions of Web services development (JAX-RPC). Deployment descriptors are replaced with annotations, so we can declare the metadata using annotations along with the Web service code.
- It enables rapid development; it is easy to develop a Web service that exposes existing business functionality to external applications to meet the business needs.
- JAX-WS provides tools to generate Java objects from WSDL and vice versa.
- It is easy to expose a POJO class as a Web service endpoint.
- It supports both synchronous and asynchronous message processing.
- It provides support for both static and dynamic clients.

JAX-WS Disadvantages

- A switch from JAX-RPC to JAX-WS requires lot of code rewrite. There is no standard way to migrate from JAX-RPC to JAX-WS.
- It is suitable for Java 1.5 and higher.

JAX-WS Annotations

JAX-WS provides several annotations for developing XML-based Web services. These annotations can be used at field level, method level, class level, and interface level and can also be used as a method parameter. The following section explains the annotations commonly used for implementing the JAX-WS–based Web services. The Java specification requests (JSRs) used for defining these annotations are JSR-181, JSR-222, JSR-224, and JSR-250.

JSR 181—The annotations defined in this JSR represent the Web services metadata. These annotations are replacements for the metadata defined in deployment descriptors and XML files in previous releases (JAX-RPC) of Web services. These annotations are used to control the mapping between Java and WSDL. The annotations provided below are defined in JSR 181.

- javax.jws.WebService
- javax.jws.WebMethod
- javax.jws.Oneway
- javax.jws.WebParam
- javax.jws.WebResult
- javax.jws.HandlerChain
- javax.jws.soap.SOAPBinding
- javax.jws.soap.SOAPMessageHandlers—Deprecated in JSR 181-2.0 with no replacement.

JSR 222—The annotations defined in this JSR generate the XML documents from the Java bean classes, and vice versa, using JAX-WS API. The annotations provided below are defined in JSR 222.

- javax.xml.bind.annotation.XmlRootElement
- javax.xml.bind.annotation.XmlAccessorType
- javax.xml.bind.annotation.XmlType
- javax.xml.bind.annotation.XmlElement
- javax.xml.bind.annotation.XmlElementWrapper
- javax.xml.bind.annotation.XmlAttribute
- javax.xml.bind.annotation.XmlAccessorOrder

JSR 250—The annotations defined in this JSR are used for resource injection and life cycle management. These are the commonly used annotations for Web development using the Java servlet container. The annotations provided below are defined in JSR 250.

- javax.annotation.Resource
- javax.annotation.PostConstruct
- javax.annotation.PreDestroy

JSR 224—The annotations provided below are generated from WSDL using the JAX-WS binding utilities. The unmarshaling technique is used to generate Java classes from WSDL. These annotations are declared to the generated Java classes during its unmarshaling from WSDL. The annotations provided below are defined in JSR 224.

- javax.xml.ws.RequestWrapper
- javax.xml.ws.ResponseWrapper
- javax.xml.ws.WebEndpoint
- javax.xml.ws.WebFault

- javax.xml.ws.WebServiceClient
- javax.xml.ws.WebServiceProvider
- javax.xml.ws.WebServiceRef
- javax.xml.ws.BindingType
- javax.xml.ws.ServiceMode

NOTE: JSR-224 annotations are generated automatically using the "WSDL2Java" utility, which is used in Web services development. The chapters, Apache-CXF and Axis2 explain the details of the "WSDL2Java" utility.

Web Service Metadata Annotations (JSR-181)

This section will help you to understand the Web services metadata annotations defined in the JSR-181 specification.

@javax.jws.WebService

The @WebService annotation is used at class level or interface level. This annotation is declared to a service endpoint interface or service implementation class to convert it to a Web service. The definition of the @WebService annotation is given below.

```
package javax.jws;

public @interface WebService {
    java.lang.String name() default "";
    java.lang.String targetNamespace() default "";
    java.lang.String serviceName() default "";
    java.lang.String portName() default "";
    java.lang.String wsdlLocation() default "";
    java.lang.String endpointInterface() default "";
}
```

The example provided below demonstrates the use of the @WebService annotation. The service implementation class is annotated with the member values provided below.

```
@WebService(name="EmployeeService",
            targetNamespace="http://jaxws.ws.learning.com/",
            serviceName="employeeService",
            portName="EmployeeServicePort",
            wsdlLocation="",
            endpointInterface="com.learning.ws.jaxws.EmployeeService")
```

Let us now examine the WSDL document to understand how these members of the annotation are mapped to various WSDL elements. The following example illustrates the mapping between members of the @Webservice annotation and the corresponding WSDL elements.

name: This member value of the @WebService annotation is mapped to the "name" of WSDL element "<wsdl:portType/>." The mapping between "name" and the generated WSDL is given below.

Annotation declaration is:

```
@WebService(name="EmployeeService")
```

The generated WSDL mapping is:

```
<wsdl:portType name="EmployeeService">
```

targetNamespace: This member value of the @WebService annotation is mapped to the XML namespace used for WSDL and XML elements. If not specified, it uses the package name as the default target namespace. The mapping between "targetNameSpace" and the generated WSDL is given below.

Annotation declaration is:

```
@WebService(targetNamespace="http://jaxws.ws.learning.com/")
```

The generated WSDL mapping is:

```
<wsdl:definitions name="employeeService"
             targetNamespace=http://jaxws.ws.learning.com/
  and

<xs:schema targetNamespace="http://jaxws.ws.learning.com/"
```

portName: This member value of the @WebService annotation is mapped to the "name" attribute of the "<wsdl:port/>" element in WSDL. The mapping between "portName" and the generated WSDL is given below.

Annotation declaration is:

```
@WebService(portName="EmployeeServicePort")
```

The generated WSDL mapping is:

```
<wsdl:port binding="tns:employeeServiceSoapBinding"
        name="EmployeeServicePort">
```

wsdlLocation: This member value of the @WebService annotation is mapped to the "location" of the predefined WSDL file. It is not mandatory to use this; the user may not always have access to predefined WSDL while defining the endpoint interface. The mapping between the "wsdlLocation" and the generated WSDL is given below.

Annotation declaration is:

```
@WebService(wsdlLocation="")
```

The generated WSDL mapping is:

```
<soap:address location=
     "http://localhost:8080/wsbook/services/employee"/>
```

serviceName: This member value of the @WebService annotation is mapped to the "name" attribute of the "<wsdl:service/>" element in WSDL. The mapping between "serviceName" and the generated WSDL is given below.

Annotation declaration is:

```
@WebService(serviceName="employeeService")
```

The generated WSDL mapping is:

```
<wsdl:service name="employeeService">
```

endpointInterface: This member value of the @WebService annotation refers to the service endpoint interface the service class is implementing. This annotation can be used only at the service class level. This member value of the @WebService annotation is mapped to WSDL port-type bindings.

Annotation declaration is:

```
@WebService(endpointInterface="com.learning.ws.jaxws.EmployeeService")
```

The generated WSDL mapping is:

```
<wsdl:binding name="employeeServiceSoapBinding"
              type="tns:EmployeeService">
```

The @WebService annotation should be declared to a service endpoint interface without any member values. The member values "serviceName" and "endpointInterface" are assigned while declaring the annotation to its service implementation class. It is not mandatory that the service implementation class implement an endpoint interface.

This is Valid:

```
@WebService
public interface EmployeeService {
    String getEmployeeAddressInfo(String employeeId) throws Exception;
}

@WebService(endpointInterface="com.learning.ws.jaxws.EmployeeService",
            serviceName="employeeService")
public class EmployeeServiceImpl implements EmployeeService {

    public EmployeeServiceImpl() {}

    public String getEmployeeAddressInfo(String employeeId)
    throws Exception {
        // Implement your logic here to get the address.
        return "3943 W.Roundabout CIR, Chandler, Arizona, 85226";
    }
}
```

This is Valid:

```
@WebService
public interface EmployeeService {
```

```
        void deleteEmployee(String employeeId);
}

@WebService(endpointInterface="com.learning.ws.jaxws.EmployeeService",
        serviceName="employeeService")
public class EmployeeServiceImpl {
    public EmployeeServiceImpl() {}

    void deleteEmployee(String employeeId) {
        ...
    }
}
```

This does not allow the user to declare the annotation member "endpointInterface" at service endpoint interface (SEI) level; it will compile fine, but it will throw a runtime exception. The following combinations of the service endpoint interface and service implementation class are invalid.

Invalid use of @WebService annotation:

```
@WebService(endpointInterface="com.learning.ws.jaxws.EmployeeService",
            serviceName="employeeService")
public interface EmployeeService {
    void deleteEmployee(String employeeId);
}

public class EmployeeServiceImpl implements EmployeeService {
    public EmployeeServiceImpl() {}
}
```

Invalid use of @WebService annotation:

```
@WebService(endpointInterface="com.learning.ws.jaxws.EmployeeService",
            serviceName="employeeService")
public interface EmployeeService {
    void deleteEmployee(String employeeId);
}

@WebService
public class EmployeeServiceImpl {
    public EmployeeServiceImpl() {}
}
```

NOTE: The invalid scenarios provided above will throw an exception while invoking the service endpoint. The generated exception message is: "javax.xml.ws.WebServiceException: Attributes 'portName,' 'serviceName,' and 'endpointInterface' are not allowed in the @WebService annotation of an SEI."

@javax.jws.WebMethod

The @WebMethod annotation is used at method level. It customizes the web service method, whether to expose as a service method or not. The definition of @WebMethod annotation is given below.

```
public @interface WebMethod {
    java.lang.String operationName() default "";
    java.lang.String action() default "";
    boolean exclude() default false;
}
```

The following example demonstrates the use of the @WebMethod annotation. The service endpoint interface method is annotated with the following member values.

```
@WebMethod(operationName="getEmployeeAddress",
        exclude=false,
        action="employee")
```

By default, if undeclared, the operation name takes the endpoint interface method name "getEmployeeAddressInfo" as the "name" attribute of the "<wsdl:operation/>" element. In this case, the "name" attribute of the "<wsdl:operation/>" element is "getEmployeeAddress." The use of the @WebMethod annotation is given below.

```
@WebService
public interface EmployeeService {
    @WebMethod(operationName="getEmployeeAddress",
            exclude=false,
            action="employee")
    String getEmployeeAddressInfo(String employeeId) throws Exception;
}
```

Let us now examine the WSDL document to understand how these members of the @WebMethod annotation are mapped to various WSDL elements. The following example illustrates the mapping among members of the @WebMethod annotation and the corresponding WSDL elements.

operationName: This member value of the @WebMethod annotation is mapped to the "name" attribute of the "<wsdl:operation/>" element. The mapping between "operationName" and the generated WSDL is given below.

Annotation declaration is:

```
@WebMethod(operationName="getEmployeeAddress")
```

The generated WSDL mapping is:

```
<wsdl:operation name="getEmployeeAddress">
```

exclude: The default value is "false," specifying that the method should be excluded from the service endpoint interface. Thus, clients cannot invoke this operation. The mapping between "exclude" and the generated WSDL is given below.

Annotation declaration is:

```
@WebMethod(exclude=true)
```

The generated WSDL mapping is:

It does not have a precise WSDL mapping. This operation will disappear (no longer available) from the generated WSDL.

NOTE: Set value of *exclude* to "true" and try to invoke the Web service operation using the service client; it will throw an exception, and the generated message is: "javax.xml.ws.WebServiceException: Could not find 'wsdl:binding' operation info for Web method getEmployeeAddressInfo."

action: The default value is empty, specifying the value of the "soapAction" attribute of the "<soap:operation/>" element. The mapping between "action" and the generated WSDL is given below.

Annotation declaration is:

```
@WebMethod(action="employee")
```

The generated WSDL mapping is:

```
<soap:operation soapAction="employee" style="document"/>
```

@javax.jws.Oneway

This annotation is used at the method level of a service endpoint interface. In general, it is used for void methods; the service endpoint does not have to send a response back to the client. This annotation does not have any members. The definition of the @Oneway annotation is given below.

```
public @interface Oneway {
}
```

The use of the @Oneway annotation in the service endpoint operation is given below.

```
@WebService
public interface EmployeeService {
    @Oneway
    void deleteEmployee(String employeeId);
}
```

@javax.jws.WebParam

This annotation is used with the method parameters of a service endpoint interface to map the request elements of "<wsdl:part/>" of the generated WSDL. The definition of the @WebParam annotation is given below.

```
public @interface WebParam {
    java.lang.String name() default "";
    java.lang.String partName() default "";
    java.lang.String targetNamespace() default "";
    javax.jws.WebParam.Mode mode() default javax.jws.WebParam.Mode.IN;
    boolean header() default false;
}
```

The following example demonstrates the use of the @WebParam annotation. The service endpoint interface method parameter is annotated with the member values provided below.

```
String getEmployeeAddressInfo(@WebParam(name="empId",
                mode=Mode.IN,
                partName="empParam",
                targetNamespace="empParam",
                header=true) String  employeeId) throws Exception;
```

By default, if undeclared, the method parameter name takes the endpoint interface method parameter name "employeeId" as the "name" attribute of the "<wsdl:part/>" element. In this case, the "name" attribute of the "<wsdl:part/>" element is "empId." The use of the @WebParam annotation is given below.

```
@WebService
public interface EmployeeService {
    String getEmployeeAddressInfo(@WebParam(name="empId",
            mode= Mode.IN,
            partName="empParam",
            targetNamespace="empParam",
            header=true) String employeeId) throws Exception;
}
```

Let us now examine the WSDL document to understand how these members of the annotation are mapped to various WSDL elements. The example provided below illustrates the mapping between members of the @WebParam annotation and the corresponding generated WSDL elements.

name: This member value of the @WebParam annotation is mapped to the "element" attribute value of the "<wsdl:part/>" element in WSDL. The mapping between "name" and the generated WSDL is given below.

Annotation declaration is:

```
String getEmployeeAddressInfo(@WebParam(name="empId") String employeeId)
throws Exception;
```

The generated WSDL mapping is:

```
<wsdl:part element="ns1:empId" name="empParam"/>
```

mode: This specifies the type of parameter mode. The valid values are "Mode.IN," "Mode.OUT," and "Mode.INOUT." The parameter mode "IN" is used for read-only, and other two are used to write. The default parameter mode is "Mode.IN" unless specified otherwise.

Annotation declaration is:

```
    String getEmployeeAddressInfo(@WebParam(name="empId", mode= Mode.IN)
    String employeeId) throws Exception;
```

partName: This member value of the @WebParam annotation is mapped to the "name" attribute value of a "<wsdl:part/>" element in the generated WSDL. The mapping between the "partName" and the generated WSDL is given below.

Annotation declaration is:

```
    String getEmployeeAddressInfo(@WebParam(name="empId",
                mode= Mode.IN,
```

```
                         partName="empParam",
                         targetNamespace="empParam",
                         header=true) String employeeId) throws Exception;
```

The generated WSDL mapping is:

```
     <wsdl:part element="ns1:empId" name="empParam"/>
```

header: The default value is "false," specifying that the parameter should not be passed as part of the SOAP header. If it is "true," it will be included in the SOAP header.

Annotation declaration is:

```
     String getEmployeeAddressInfo(@WebParam(name="empId",
                         mode= Mode.IN,
                         partName="empParam",
                         targetNamespace="empParam",
                         header=true) String employeeId) throws Exception;
```

targetNamespace: The default value is the service's namespace, specifying the namespace for the method parameter.

Annotation declaration is:

```
     String getEmployeeAddressInfo(@WebParam(name="empId",
                         mode=Mode.IN,
                         partName="empParam",
               targetNamespace="http://com.learning.ws/empParam",
               header=true) String employeeId) throws Exception;
```

The generated WSDL mapping is:

```
     <xsd:schema attributeFormDefault="unqualified"
             elementFormDefault="unqualified"
             targetNamespace="http://com.learning.ws/empParam"
             xmlns:tns="http://com.learning.ws/empParam"
             xmlns:xsd="http://www.w3.org/2001/XMLSchema">
        <xsd:element name="empId" nillable="true" type="xsd:string"/>
     </xsd:schema>
```

@javax.jws.WebResult

This annotation is used with the methods of a service endpoint interface to map the response elements of "<wsdl:part/>" in the generated WSDL. The definition of the @WebResult annotation and its properties is given below.

```
public @interface WebResult {
    java.lang.String name() default "";
    java.lang.String partName() default "";
    java.lang.String targetNamespace() default "";
    boolean header() default false;
}
```

The following example demonstrates the use of the @WebResult annotation. The service endpoint interface method is annotated with the following parameter values.

```
@WebResult(name="addressMessage", partName="addressMessagePart",
           targetNamespace="addressMessage", header=true)
```

By default it uses "return" unless the method is annotated with the "name" attribute of the "<wsdl:part/>" response element as "addressMessage." The use of the @WebResult annotation is given below.

```
@WebService
public interface EmployeeService {
    @WebResult(name="addressMessage", partName="addressMessagePart",
               targetNamespace="addressMessage", header=true)
    String getEmployeeAddressInfo(String employeeId) throws Exception;
}
```

Let us now examine the WSDL document to understand how these members of the annotation are mapped to various WSDL elements. The following example illustrates the mapping between members of the @WebResult annotation and the corresponding WSDL elements.

The following section explains the properties of the @WebParam annotation.

name: This specifies the "element" attribute value of the "<wsdl:part/>" response element in WSDL. The mapping between "name" and the generated WSDL is given below.

Annotation declaration is:

```
@WebResult(name="addressMessage", partName="addressMessagePart",
           targetNamespace="addressMessage", header=true)
```

The generated WSDL mapping is:

```
<wsdl:message name="getEmployeeAddressResponse">
    <wsdl:part element="ns2:addressMessage" name="addressMessagePart"/>
</wsdl:message>
```

partName: This member value of the annotation is mapped to the "<wsdl:part/>" response element's "name" attribute value in WSDL. The mapping between "partName" and the generated WSDL is given below.

Annotation declaration is:

```
@WebResult(name="addressMessage", partName="addressMessagePart",
           targetNamespace="addressMessage", header=true)
```

The generated WSDL mapping is:

```
<wsdl:message name="getEmployeeAddressResponse">
    <wsdl:part element="ns2:addressMessage" name="addressMessagePart" />
</wsdl:message>
```

header: The default value is "false," specifying that the parameter should not be passed as part of the SOAP header. If it is "true," it will be included in the SOAP header.

Annotation declaration is:

```
@WebResult(name="addressMessage", partName="addressMessagePart",
            targetNamespace="addressMessage", header=true)
```

targetNamespace: This uses the namespace of the service as the default value unless specified otherwise. It specifies the namespace for the method's return value.

Annotation declaration is:

```
@WebResult(name="addressMessage", partName="addressMessagePart",
        targetNamespace="http://com.learning.com/addressMessage",
        header=true)
```

The generated WSDL mapping is:

```
<xsd:schema attributeFormDefault="unqualified"
            elementFormDefault="unqualified"
            targetNamespace="http://com.learning.com/addressMessage"
            xmlns:tns="http://com.learning.com/addressMessage"
            xmlns:xsd="http://www.w3.org/2001/XMLSchema">
    <xsd:element name="addressMessage" nillable="true"
                type="xsd:string"/>
</xsd:schema>
```

@javax.jws.HandlerChain

This annotation is declared with the service endpoint interface or service implementation class. Handlers are used to customize the incoming SOAP request or outgoing SOAP response from the Web service endpoint. Handlers can be configured on the client side as well as the server side. The definition of the @HandlerChain annotation and its properties is given below.

```
public @interface HandlerChain {
    String file();
}
```

The following example demonstrates the use of the @HandlerChain annotation. The service endpoint interface is annotated with the member value provided below.

The following code uses the physical path on the server to locate the configuration file.

```
@HandlerChain(file="http://localhost:8080/wsbook/demo/handlerchain.xml")
```

The following code uses the relative path to locate the configuration file.

```
@HandlerChain(file="../../demo/handlerchain.xml")
```

file: This specifies the location of the externally defined XML file containing the details of the handler classes used to customize the incoming and outgoing SOAP messages.

The use of the @HandlerChain annotation with the service endpoint interface is given below.

```
@HandlerChain(file="http://localhost:8080/wsbook/demo/handlerchain.xml")
```

```
public interface EmployeeService {
    Employee getEmployee(String employeeId) throws Exception;
}
```

NOTE: Web service development frameworks provide their own implementations to support the handler classes intercepting SOAP messages. This topic is covered extensively in Web services development using CXF, Axis2, and Spring-WS.

@javax.jws.soap.SOAPBinding

This annotation provides the details of the SOAP binding used while deploying the Web service. This annotation can be declared at interface level or at method level. The definition of the @SOAPBinding annotation and its properties is given below.

```
public @interface SOAPBinding {
    javax.jws.soap.SOAPBinding.Style style() default
                    javax.jws.soap.SOAPBinding.Style.DOCUMENT;
    javax.jws.soap.SOAPBinding.Use use() default
                    javax.jws.soap.SOAPBinding.Use.LITERAL;
    javax.jws.soap.SOAPBinding.ParameterStyle parameterStyle() default
            javax.jws.soap.SOAPBinding.ParameterStyle.WRAPPED;
}
```

The following example demonstrates the use of the @SOAPBinding annotation. The service endpoint interface method is annotated with the following parameter values.

```
@SOAPBinding(style=Style.DOCUMENT,
                parameterStyle=ParameterStyle.WRAPPED,
                use=Use.LITERAL)
public interface EmployeeService {
}
```

style: This specifies the style of the message; the valid values are "DOCUMENT" and "RPC." In the DOCUMENT style, the body of the SOAP message is a single valid XML document. In RPC, each part of the message is a method parameter or return value, similar to RMI method calls. WSI-BP (basic profile standards for Web services interoperability) prohibits RPC- and DOCUMENT-style operations in the same service endpoint. The default service endpoint uses the DOCUMENT style unless specified otherwise.

Valid usage:

```
@SOAPBinding(style=Style.RPC,
                parameterStyle=ParameterStyle.WRAPPED, use=Use.LITERAL)
@WebService
public interface EmployeeService {
    String getEmployeeAddressInfo(@WebParam(name="empId", mode= Mode.IN)
    String employeeId) throws Exception;
}
```

Valid usage:

```
@SOAPBinding(style=Style.DOCUMENT,
```

```
                      parameterStyle=ParameterStyle.WRAPPED, use=Use.LITERAL)
@WebService
public interface EmployeeService {
    String getEmployeeAddressInfo(@WebParam(name="empId", mode= Mode.IN)
                                  String employeeId) throws Exception;
}
```

Invalid Usage:

```
@SOAPBinding(style=Style.DOCUMENT,
             parameterStyle=ParameterStyle.BARE, use=Use.LITERAL)
@WebService
public interface EmployeeService {
    @SOAPBinding(style=Style.RPC,
             parameterStyle=ParameterStyle.BARE, use=Use.LITERAL)
    String getEmployeeAddressInfo(@WebParam(name="empId",mode= Mode.IN)
                                  String employeeId) throws Exception;
}
```

Invalid Usage:

```
@WebService
public interface EmployeeService {
    @SOAPBinding(style=Style.RPC, parameterStyle=ParameterStyle.BARE,
                 use=Use.LITERAL)
    String getEmployeeAddressInfo(@WebParam(name="empId", mode= Mode.IN)
                                  String employeeId) throws Exception;
}
```

NOTE: The invalid scenarios depicted above will throw a runtime exception while invoking the Web service endpoint. The exception message is given as follows: "javax.xml.ws.WebServiceException: java.lang.RuntimeException: WSI-BP prohibits RPC- and DOCUMENT-style operations in the same service."

---

use: This specifies the formatting style of the SOAP message; the valid values are "literal" and "encoded." The basic profile standards for Web services interoperability do not recommend using an encoded messaging style due to its interoperability issues. Unless annotated, the service endpoint interface uses Document/Literal with the "WRAPPED" parameter style by default.

The four possible combinations are listed below.

- RPC/Literal
- Document/Literal
- RPC/encoded
- Document/encoded

parameterStyle: This signifies whether the SOAP message is wrapped into a single root element, with each method parameter a sub-element to the wrapped element, or method parameters represent the entire message body. The valid values are "wrapped" and "bare."

The example provided below shows a resulting WSDL for a RPC/LITERAL message style:

```
<wsdl:message name="deleteEmployee">
    <wsdl:part name="arg0" type="xsd:string" />
</wsdl:message>
<wsdl:message name="getEmployeeAddressInfo">
    <wsdl:part name="empId" type="xsd:string" />
</wsdl:message>
```

The example provided below shows a resulting WSDL for a DOCUMENT/LITERAL message style:

```
<wsdl:message name="deleteEmployee">
    <wsdl:part element="tns:deleteEmployee" name="parameters"/>
</wsdl:message>
<wsdl:message name="getEmployeeAddressInfo">
    <wsdl:part element="tns:getEmployeeAddressInfo" name="parameters"/>
</wsdl:message>
```

The example provided below shows a resulting WSDL for a DOCUMENT/LITERAL message binding:

```
<wsdl:binding name="employeeServiceSoapBinding"
            type="tns:EmployeeService">
    <soap:binding style="document"
                transport="http://schemas.xmlsoap.org/soap/http"/>
    <wsdl:operation name="getEmployeeAddressInfo">
    <soap:operation soapAction="" style="document" />
        <wsdl:input name="getEmployeeAddressInfo">
            <soap:body use="literal" />
        </wsdl:input>
        <wsdl:output name="getEmployeeAddressInfoResponse">
            <soap:body use="literal" />
        </wsdl:output>
    </wsdl:operation>
    <wsdl:operation name="deleteEmployee">
    <soap:operation soapAction="" style="document" />
        <wsdl:input name="deleteEmployee">
            <soap:body use="literal" />
        </wsdl:input>
        <wsdl:output name="deleteEmployeeResponse">
            <soap:body use="literal" />
        </wsdl:output>
    </wsdl:operation>
</wsdl:binding>
```

The example provided below shows a resulting WSDL for a RPC/LITERAL message binding:

```
<wsdl:binding name="employeeServiceSoapBinding"
            type="tns:EmployeeService">
    <soap:binding style="rpc"
                transport="http://schemas.xmlsoap.org/soap/http"/>

    <wsdl:operation name="getEmployeeAddressInfo">
        <soap:operation soapAction="" style="rpc"/>
            <wsdl:input name="getEmployeeAddressInfo">
                <soap:body namespace="http://jaxws.ws.learning.com/"
                        use="literal"/>
            </wsdl:input>
```

```
                    <wsdl:output name="getEmployeeAddressInfoResponse">
                        <soap:body namespace="http://jaxws.ws.learning.com/"
                                   use="literal"/>
                    </wsdl:output>
            </wsdl:operation>

            <wsdl:operation name="deleteEmployee">
                <soap:operation soapAction="" style="rpc"/>
                <wsdl:input name="deleteEmployee">
                    <soap:body namespace="http://jaxws.ws.learning.com/"
                               use="literal"/>
                </wsdl:input>
                <wsdl:output name="deleteEmployeeResponse">
                    <soap:body namespace="http://jaxws.ws.learning.com/"
                               use="literal"/>
                </wsdl:output>
            </wsdl:operation>
        </wsdl:binding>
```

@javax.jws.soap.SOAPMessageHandlers

This annotation was discontinued in JSR 181-2.0 with no replacement. This annotation cannot be combined with the @HandlerChain annotation.

XML Generation using JAXB Annotations (JSR-222)

Java API for XML Binding (JAXB) provides the ability to marshal the Java objects into XML and vice versa. The Web service endpoint annotations and JAXB annotations are separated. The commonly used JAXB annotations are discussed in this section.

@javax.xml.bind.annotation.XmlRootElement

This annotation is used with top-level class or enum types. Its value is mapped to an XML element in an XML document. The definition of the @XMLRootElement annotation and its properties is given below.

```
public @interface XmlRootElement {
    String namespace() default "##default";
    String name() default "##default";
}
```

The following example demonstrates the use of the @XMLRootElement annotation. The class "EmployeeCollection" is annotated with the following parameter values.

```
@XmlRootElement(name="employees")
public class EmployeeCollection {
    private Collection<Employee> empList = new ArrayList<Employee>();

    // provide getters and setters
}
```

The resulting XML is:

```xml
<?xml version="1.0" encoding="UTF-8" standalone="yes"?>
<employees>
    <!- the outer element is created and we
    can enclose other elements to this.-->
</employees>
```

@javax.xml.bind.annotation.XmlElement

This annotation is used with Java bean properties and class-level fields. Its value is mapped to the local element in an XML schema complex type derived from a Java bean property. The definition of the @XmlElement annotation and its properties is given below.

```java
public @interface XmlElement {
    String name() default "##default";
    boolean nillable() default false;
    boolean required() default false;
    String namespace() default "##default";
    String defaultValue() default "\u0000";
    Class type() default DEFAULT.class;
}
```

The following example demonstrates the use of the @XmlElement annotation. The method "getZip()" is annotated, and the name assigned to it is "zipCode." By default, it uses the Java bean property name as its element name. The following code renames the element name from "<zip>" to "</zipCode>"

```java
@XmlRootElement(name="address")
public class Address {
    private String zip;
    // renaming from zip to zipCode
    @XmlElement(name = "zipCode")
    public String getZip() {
        return zip;
    }

    public void setZip(String zip) {
        this.zip = zip;
    }
}
```

The resulting XML is:

```xml
<address>
    <zipCode>85226</zipCode>
</address>
```

@javax.xml.bind.annotation.XmlType

This annotation is used with top-level class or enum types. It maps the class or enum type to an XML schema *simple* or *complex* type. The definition of the @XmlType annotation and its properties is given below:

```
public @interface XmlType {
    String name() default "##default";
    String[] propOrder() default {""};
    String namespace() default "##default" ;
    Class factoryClass() default DEFAULT.class;
    String factoryMethod() default "";
}
```

The following example demonstrates the use of the @XmlType annotation. The "Address" class is annotated with the annotation property "propOrder." This property maintains the order of XML elements in the <xs:sequence/> element.

The below code maps to a *complex* type "xs:element" with a customized order of Java bean properties.

```
@XmlType(propOrder = {"street", "city", "zip"})
```

The below code maps to a *complex* type with xs:all.

```
@XmlType(propOrder = {}) - maps to a complex type with xs:all
```

The following code generates an XML; the resulting XML elements "street," "city," and "zip" maintain the same order as specified in the @XmlType.

```
@XmlRootElement(name="address")
@XmlType(propOrder = {"street", "city", "zip"})
public class Address {
    private String zip;
    private String street;
    private String city;

    // Add getters and setters
}
```

The resulting XML is:

```
<address>
    <street>Roundabout cir</street>
    <city>Chandler</city>
    <zip>85226</zip>
</address>
```

@javax.xml.bind.annotation.XmlAccessorType

This specifies whether the fields and properties are serialized. The definition of the @XmlAccessorType annotation and its properties is given below.

```
public @interface XmlAccessorType {
    XmlAccessType value() default XmlAccessType.PUBLIC_MEMBER;
}
```

The below given class is annotated with @XmlAccessorType annotation.

```
@XmlAccessorType
public class Address {
    private String street;
    private String city;
    private String zip;
    private String country;

    // Add getters and setters here
}
```

@javax.xml.bind.annotation.XmlAttribute

This maps the Java bean property to the XML schema attribute. This annotation can be used with a Java bean property or field. The definition of the @XmlAttribute annotation and its properties is given below.

```
public @interface XmlAttribute {
    String name() default "##default";
    boolean required() default false;
    String namespace() default "##default";
}
```

The following example demonstrates the use of the @XmlAttribute annotation. The method "getCountry()" provided below is annotated with the @XmlAttribute.

```
@XmlRootElement(name="address")
@XmlType(propOrder = {"street", "city", "zip"})
public class Address {
    private String zip;
    private String street;
    private String city;
    private String country;

    @XmlAttribute(name="country")
    public String getCountry() {
        return country;
    }

    // Add getters and setters
}
```

The resulting XML is:

```
<address country="USA">
    <street>Roundabout cir</street>
    <city>Chandler</city>
    <zipCode>85226</zipCode>
</address>
```

@javax.xml.bind.annotation.XmlElementWrapper

This annotation is primarily used to generate a wrapper element around an existing XML element. In general, it is used along with Java collections to produce a wrapper XML element around the Java collections. This annotation can be used with a Java bean property or field. The definition of the @XmlElementWrapper annotation and its properties is given below.

```
public @interface XmlElementWrapper {
     String name() default "##default";
     String namespace() default "##default";
     boolean nillable() default false;
     boolean required() default false;
}
```

The following example demonstrates the use of the @XmlElementWrapper annotation. The method "getAddressList()" is annotated with the "name" annotation property. It creates a wrapper element "<homeAddress/>" around the "<address/>" element.

```
@XmlRootElement(name="employee")
public class Employee {
     private String zip;
     private String street;
     private String city;
     private String country;
     private Collection<Address> addressList = new ArrayList<Address>();

     @XmlElement(name="address")
     @XmlElementWrapper(name="homeAddress")
     public Collection<Address> getAddressList() {
          return addressList;
     }

     public void setAddressList(Collection<Address> addressList) {
          this.addressList = addressList;
     }
}
```

The resulting XML is:

```
<homeAddress>
     <address country="USA">
          <street>Roundabout cir</street>
          <city>Chandler</city>
          <zipCode>85226</zipCode>
     </address>
</homeAddress>
```

@javax.xml.bind.annotation.XmlAccessorOrder

This annotation is used to control the ordering of fields and properties in a class. The definition of the @XmlAccessorOrder annotation and its properties is given below.

```
public @interface XmlAccessorOrder {
     XmlAccessOrder value() default XmlAccessOrder.UNDEFINED;
```

```
}
```

The following example demonstrates the use of the @XmlAccessorOrder annotation. The address class provided below is annotated with @XmlAccessorOrder

```
@XmlType(propOrder = {"street", "city", "zip"})
@XmlAccessorOrder(XmlAccessOrder.ALPHABETICAL)
@XmlAccessorType
public class Address {
    private String street;
    private String city;
    private String zip;
}
```

Example 1: XML generation using JAXB annotations.

The code example provided below demonstrates the use of all of the JAXB annotations we have discussed so far. The steps required for generating an XML document using JAXB annotations are given below.

1. Create an Address class with the required attributes.
2. Create an Employee class with the required attributes.
3. Create an Employee Collection class to hold all employee details.
4. Create a main class for marshaling the Java objects into an XML.

The steps provided above are described in the following sections:

Step 1: Create an Address Class with Required Attributes

The Address class is annotated with various JAXB annotations to generate the XML document. @XmlElement renames the element from "<zip>" to "<zipCode>." @XmlType generates the elements in sequence. Refer to the generated XML to see the complete XML document. Listing 8-1 has Java code that demonstrates the XML generation using JAXB annotations.

Listing 8-1: XML generation using JAXB annotations

```
// Address.java
package com.learning.util;

import javax.xml.bind.annotation.*;

@XmlRootElement(name="address")
@XmlType(propOrder = {"street", "city", "zip"})
@XmlAccessorOrder(XmlAccessOrder.ALPHABETICAL)
@XmlAccessorType
public class Address {
    private String street;
    private String zip;
    private String city;
    private String country;

    public String getStreet() {
        return street;
    }
```

```
        public void setStreet(String street) {
            this.street = street;
        }

        public String getCity() {
            return city;
        }

        public void setCity(String city) {
            this.city = city;
        }

        // Renaming the element from zip to zipCode.
        @XmlElement(name = "zipCode", nillable=true, required=true)
        public String getZip() {
            return zip;
        }

        public void setZip(String zip) {
            this.zip = zip;
        }

        @XmlAttribute(name="country")
        public String getCountry() {
            return country;
        }

        public void setCountry(String country) {
            this.country = country;
        }
}
```

Step 2: Create an Employee Class with Required Attributes

The Employee class is annotated with various JAXB annotations to generate the XML document. The @XmlRootElement generates the outer level XML element "<employee/>." The @XmlElementWrapper wraps the "<address/>" element with the "<homeAddress/>" element. Refer to the generated XML to see the complete XML document. Listing 8-2 has Java code that demonstrates use of JAXB annotations.

Listing 8-2: Java class using JAXB annotations

```
// Employee.java
package com.learning.util;

import javax.xml.bind.annotation.*;
import java.util.Collection;
import java.util.ArrayList;

@XmlRootElement(name="employee")
// Controls the ordering of fields and properties in a class
@XmlAccessorOrder(XmlAccessOrder.ALPHABETICAL)
public class Employee {

    private static final long serialVersionUID = 1L;
    private String employeeId;
    private String lastName;
```

```
    private String firstName;
    private Address address;
    private Collection<Address> addressList = new ArrayList<Address>();

    // Add your getters and setters here for above fields
    @XmlElement(name="address")
    @XmlElementWrapper(name="homeAddress")
    public Collection<Address> getAddressList() {
        return addressList;
    }

    public void setAddressList(Collection<Address> addressList) {
        this.addressList = addressList;
    }
}
```

Step 3: Create an Employee Collection Class to Hold the Complete Employee Details

The EmployeeCollection class holds the complete data structure we created in this example. The @XmlRootElement generates the top-level root element "<employees/>" of the XML document. Refer to the generated XML to see the complete XML document. Listing 8-3 has Java code that demonstrates use of JAXB annotations.

Listing 8-3: Java class using JAXB annotations

```
// EmployeeCollection.java
package com.learning.util;

import javax.xml.bind.annotation.XmlRootElement;
import javax.xml.bind.annotation.XmlElement;
import java.util.*;

@XmlRootElement(name="employees")
public class EmployeeCollection {
    private Collection<Employee> empList = new ArrayList<Employee>();

    @XmlElement(name="employee", type=Employee.class)
    public Collection<Employee> getEmpList() {
        return empList;
    }

    public void setEmpList(Collection<Employee> empList) {
        this.empList = empList;
    }
}
```

Step 4: Create a Main Java Class for Marshalling the Java Objects into an XML.

The "JaxbXMLBuilder" is the main class used for generating the XML, and writes it on the console. The Java bean classes are populated with the required data to generate the XML document. The "createMarshaller()" method of "JAXBContext" is used to generate the XML. It marshals the data populated in Java bean classes and creates the XML document. Listing 8-4 has a complete Java code used to demonstrate the XML creation using JAXB annotations.

Listing 8-4: Creating xml using JAXB annotations

```java
// JaxbXMLBuilder.java
package com.learning.util;

import javax.xml.bind.JAXBContext;
import javax.xml.bind.Marshaller;
import java.io.StringWriter;
import java.util.List;
import java.util.Collection;
import java.util.ArrayList;

public class JaxbXMLBuilder {
    public static void main(String args[]) {
        try {
            JaxbXMLBuilder builder = new JaxbXMLBuilder();
            builder.generateXML();
        } catch(Exception ex) {
            ex.printStackTrace();
        }
    }

    private void generateXML() throws Exception {
        /* holds the list of employees */
        Collection<Employee> empList = new ArrayList<Employee>();

        /* holds the list of employee addresses */
        Collection<Address> addressList = new ArrayList<Address>();

        /* holds the complete data structure */
        EmployeeCollection coll = new EmployeeCollection();

        /* Setting the employee data */
        Employee employee = new Employee();
        Address address = new Address();
        employee.setEmployeeId("1");
        employee.setFirstName("John");
        employee.setLastName("McCoy");

        /* Setting the address data */
        address = new Address();
        address.setCity("Chandler");
        address.setStreet("Roundabout cir");
        address.setZip("85226");
        address.setCountry("USA");
        addressList = new ArrayList<Address>();
        addressList.add(address);
        employee.setAddressList(addressList);
        empList.add(employee);

        employee = new Employee();
        employee.setEmployeeId("2");
        employee.setFirstName("John");
        employee.setLastName("Smith");
        empList.add(employee);

        address = new Address();
```

```
            address.setCity("Reading");
            address.setStreet("Malting Place");
            address.setZip("RG67QG");
            address.setCountry("UK");
            addressList = new ArrayList<Address>();
            addressList.add(address);
            employee.setAddressList(addressList);

            /* collection holds the complete data structure used for XML
            generation*/
            coll.setEmpList(empList);

            /* generates XML, writes it to console using createMarshaller()
            method*/
            StringWriter writer = new StringWriter();
            JAXBContext context =
                JAXBContext.newInstance(EmployeeCollection.class);
            Marshaller m = context.createMarshaller();
            m.marshal(coll, writer);
            System.out.println(writer);
        }
}
```

The <employees/> element is the root element to the entire document; the <homeAddress/> element wraps the <address/> element. The generated XML is given below.

```
<?xml version="1.0" encoding="UTF-8" standalone="yes"?>
<employees>
    <employee>
        <homeAddress>
            <address country="USA">
                <street>Roundabout cir</street>
                <city>Chandler</city>
                <zipCode>85226</zipCode>
            </address>
        </homeAddress>
        <employeeId>1</employeeId>
        <firstName>John</firstName>
        <lastName>McCoy</lastName>
    </employee>

    <employee>
        <homeAddress>
            <address country="UK">
                <street>Malting Place</street>
                <city>Reading</city>
                <zipCode>RG67QG</zipCode>
            </address>
        </homeAddress>
        <employeeId>2</employeeId>
        <firstName>John</firstName>
        <lastName>Smith</lastName>
    </employee>
</employees>
```

Common Annotations (JSR-250)

@javax.annotation.Resource

This annotation can be applied at class level, method level, or filed level and obtains the information related to the Web services context, message context, JNDI names, user principle, and role. This information is used in service endpoints to perform the required application functionality. The definition of the @Resource annotation and its properties is given below.

```
public @interface Resource {
    String name() default "";
    String description() default "";
    AuthenticationType authenticationType() default
                            AuthenticationType.CONTAINER;
    boolean shareable() default true;
    String mappedName() default "";
    Class type() default java.lang.Object.class;
}
```

The following example demonstrates the use of the @Resource annotation. In this example, the @Resource annotation is applied to the *field* of a service endpoint.

```
@WebService(name="EmployeeService",
        endpointInterface="com.learning.ws.jaxws.EmployeeService")
public class EmployeeServiceImpl implements EmployeeService {

    @Resource
    private WebServiceContext context;

    public EmployeeServiceImpl() {}

    @WebMethod(operationName="getEmployee")
    public Employee getEmployee(String employeeId) throws Exception {
        if(context != null) {
            System.out.println("-- UserPrincipal --" +
                context.getUserPrincipal());
        System.out.println(" --- isUserInRole --" +
                context.isUserInRole("admin"));
        MessageContext messageContext = context.getMessageContext();
        System.out.println(" ---- SERVLET_REQUEST ----  " +
                messageContext.SERVLET_REQUEST);
        }

        Employee emp = new Employee();
        emp.setEmployeeId(employeeId);
        emp.setFirstName("John");
        emp.setLastName("Smith");

        return emp;
    }
}
```

@javax.annotation.PostConstruct

This annotation is used at the method level to perform the required initialization. The method annotated with the @PostConstruct is called after the default constructor. The annotated method *must* be invoked before the class is put into service. Within any given service, only one method can be annotated with this annotation. The definition of the @PostConstruct annotation is given below.

```
public @interface PostConstruct {
}
```

The following example demonstrates the use of the @PostConstruct annotation. In this case, the @PostConstruct annotation is applied to the "init()" method of a service endpoint to perform any required initialization.

```
@WebService(name="EmployeeService",
        endpointInterface="com.learning.ws.jaxws.EmployeeService")
public class EmployeeServiceImpl implements EmployeeService {
    public EmployeeServiceImpl() {
        System.out.println("--- Constructor called ---");
    }

    @PostConstruct
    private void init() {
        System.out.println("-- Perform required initialization --");
    }
}
```

@javax.annotation.PreDestroy

This annotation is used at method level to perform cleanup activities such as releasing the resources the process is holding. The method annotated with @PreDestroy is a callback method managed by the container. The definition of the @PreDestroy annotation is given below.

```
public @interface PreDestroy {
}
```

The following example demonstrates the use of the @PreDestroy annotation. In this case, the @PreDestroy annotation is applied to the "doCleanUp()" method of a service endpoint to perform the required cleanup activity.

```
@WebService(name="EmployeeService",
        endpointInterface="com.learning.ws.jaxws.EmployeeService")
public class EmployeeServiceImpl implements EmployeeService {

    public EmployeeServiceImpl() {
        System.out.println("---- Constructor called ----");
    }

    @PreDestroy
    private void doCleanUp() {
        System.out.println("-- Perform clean-up after you are done with
        it -");
    }
}
```

```
}
```

JAX-WS Annotations (JSR-224)

The annotations provided below are declared to the generated Java classes during the process of unmarshaling from WSDL. The Web service framework utilities generate the Java classes from WSDL. The "WSDL2Java" utility generates the annotations and dependent classes provided below.

@javax.xml.ws.BindingType

This annotation is declared at the service implementation class to specify the type of SOAP binding to use when publishing the Web service. If not specified, the default SOAP binding value is "SOAP1.1/HTTP." The definition of the @BindingType annotation is given below.

```
public @interface BindingType {
    String value() default "";
}
```

The following example demonstrates the use of the @BindingType annotation. The service implementation class is annotated with the @BindingType annotation. It uses the SOAP1.2/HTTP binding.

```
@WebService(name="EmployeeService",
        endpointInterface="com.learning.ws.jaxws.EmployeeService")
@BindingType(javax.xml.ws.soap.SOAPBinding.SOAP12HTTP_BINDING)
public class EmployeeServiceImpl implements EmployeeService {
    // service class methods.
}
```

Let us now examine the WSDL document to understand how these members of the annotation are mapped to various WSDL elements. The member value of the @BindingType annotation maps to the "transport" attribute of the SOAP "binding" element. The generated WSDL given below shows the difference between SOAP12HTTP_BINDING and SOAP11HTTP_BINDING. The following example illustrates the mapping between members of the @BindingType annotation and the corresponding WSDL elements.

The service endpoint (using soap-1.2 binding) implementation class code is:

```
@WebService(name="EmployeeService",
    endpointInterface="com.learning.ws.jaxws.EmployeeService")
@BindingType(javax.xml.ws.soap.SOAPBinding.SOAP12HTTP_BINDING)
public class EmployeeServiceImpl implements EmployeeService {
    // service class methods.
}
```

Generated WSDL is:

```
<wsdl:binding name="employeeServiceSoapBinding"
            type="tns:EmployeeService">
    <soap12:binding style="document"
            transport="http://www.w3.org/2003/05/soap/bindings/HTTP/"/>
```

```
<wsdl:operation name="getEmployee">
    <soap12:operation soapAction="" style="document"/>
    <wsdl:input name="getEmployee">
        <soap12:body use="literal"/>
    </wsdl:input>
    <wsdl:output name="getEmployeeResponse">
        <soap12:body use="literal"/>
    </wsdl:output>
</wsdl:operation>
<wsdl:operation name="getEmployeeAddress">
    <soap12:operation soapAction="" style="document"/>
    <wsdl:input name="getEmployeeAddress">
        <soap12:body use="literal"/>
    </wsdl:input>
    <wsdl:output name="getEmployeeAddressResponse">
        <soap12:body use="literal"/>
    </wsdl:output>
</wsdl:operation>
<wsdl:operation name="getEmployerInformation">
    <soap12:operation soapAction="" style="document"/>
    <wsdl:input name="getEmployerInformation">
        <soap12:body use="literal"/>
    </wsdl:input>
    <wsdl:output name="getEmployerInformationResponse">
        <soap12:body use="literal"/>
    </wsdl:output>
</wsdl:operation>
<wsdl:operation name="deleteEmployee">
    <soap12:operation soapAction="" style="document"/>
    <wsdl:input name="deleteEmployee">
        <soap12:body use="literal"/>
    </wsdl:input>
    <wsdl:output name="deleteEmployeeResponse">
        <soap12:body use="literal"/>
    </wsdl:output>
</wsdl:operation>
</wsdl:binding>
```

Let us now change the binding type to SOAP1.1/HHTP and observe the changes in the generated WSDL. This is the default implementation if the class is not annotated.

The service endpoint (using soap-1.1 binding) implementation class code is:

```
@WebService(name="EmployeeService",
        endpointInterface="com.learning.ws.jaxws.EmployeeService")
@BindingType(javax.xml.ws.soap.SOAPBinding. SOAP11HTTP_BINDING)
public class EmployeeServiceImpl implements EmployeeService {
    // service class methods.
}
```

Generated WSDL is:

```
<wsdl:binding name="employeeServiceSoapBinding"
            type="tns:EmployeeService">
    <soap:binding style="document"
                transport="http://schemas.xmlsoap.org/soap/http"/>
```

```
<wsdl:operation name="getEmployee">
<soap:operation soapAction="" style="document"/>
    <wsdl:input name="getEmployee">
        <soap:body use="literal"/>
    </wsdl:input>
    <wsdl:output name="getEmployeeResponse">
        <soap:body use="literal"/>
    </wsdl:output>
</wsdl:operation>
<wsdl:operation name="getEmployeeAddress">
<soap:operation soapAction="" style="document"/>
    <wsdl:input name="getEmployeeAddress">
        <soap:body use="literal"/>
    </wsdl:input>
    <wsdl:output name="getEmployeeAddressResponse">
        <soap:body use="literal"/>
    </wsdl:output>
</wsdl:operation>
<wsdl:operation name="getEmployerInformation">
    <soap:operation soapAction="" style="document"/>
    <wsdl:input name="getEmployerInformation">
        <soap:body use="literal"/>
    </wsdl:input>
    <wsdl:output name="getEmployerInformationResponse">
        <soap:body use="literal"/>
    </wsdl:output>
</wsdl:operation>
<wsdl:operation name="deleteEmployee">
<soap:operation soapAction="" style="document"/>
    <wsdl:input name="deleteEmployee">
        <soap:body use="literal"/>
    </wsdl:input>
    <wsdl:output name="deleteEmployeeResponse">
        <soap:body use="literal"/>
    </wsdl:output>
</wsdl:operation>
</wsdl:binding>
```

@javax.xml.ws.RequestWrapper

This annotation is applied to the methods of a service endpoint interface. JAXB maps the
"localName" to the operation name, "targetNamespace" to the namespace of the service endpoint
interface, and "className" to request wrapper bean that it generates during the unmarshaling
process from XML to Java beans. The definition of the @RequestWrapper annotation is given
below.

```
public @interface RequestWrapper {
    public String localName() default "";
    public String targetNamespace() default "";
    public String className() default "";
}
```

The following example demonstrates the use of the @RequestWrapper annotation. The service
endpoint method is generated with the @RequestWrapper annotation. The following WSDL snippet
of the XML schema generates the service endpoint interface method.

```
<xs:element name="getEmployee" type="getEmployee"/>

<xs:complexType name="getEmployee">
    <xs:sequence>
        <xs:element minOccurs="0" name="employeeId" type="xs:string"/>
    </xs:sequence>
</xs:complexType>

<wsdl:message name="getEmployee">
    <wsdl:part element="tns:getEmployee" name="parameters" />
</wsdl:message>
```

Above-specified XML generates the below provided service endpoint interface. The element name "getEmployee" maps to the "localName," using the default target namespace of the SEI, and using the "getEmployee" XML complex type to generate the Java bean wrapper class "com.learning.ws.jaxws.wsdl2java.GetEmployee."

```
@WebService(targetNamespace = "http://jaxws.ws.learning.com/",
            name="EmployeeService")
public interface EmployeeService {
    @RequestWrapper(localName = "getEmployee",
        targetNamespace = "http://jaxws.ws.learning.com/",
        className = "com.learning.ws.jaxws.wsdl2java.GetEmployee")
    public Employee getEmployee(@WebParam(name = "employeeId",
                targetNamespace = "") java.lang.String employeeId);
}
```

@javax.xml.ws.ResponseWrapper

This annotation is applied to the methods of a service endpoint interface. JAXB maps the "localName" to the operation name, "targetNamespace" to the namespace of the service endpoint interface, and "className" to the response wrapper bean it generated during the unmarshaling process from XML to Java beans. The definition of the @ResponseWrapper annotation is given below.

```
public @interface ResponseWrapper {
    public String localName() default "";
    public String targetNamespace() default "";
    public String className() default "";
}
```

The following example demonstrates the use of the @ResponseWrapper annotation. The service endpoint method is generated with the @ResponseWrapper annotation. The following WSDL snippet of the XML schema generates the service endpoint interface method.

```
<xs:complexType name="employee">
    <xs:sequence>
        <xs:element minOccurs="0" name="employeeId" type="xs:string"/>
        <xs:element minOccurs="0" name="firstName" type="xs:string"/>
        <xs:element minOccurs="0" name="lastName" type="xs:string"/>
    </xs:sequence>
</xs:complexType>

<xs:element name="getEmployeeResponse" type="getEmployeeResponse"/>
```

```
<xs:complexType name="getEmployeeResponse">
    <xs:sequence>
        <xs:element minOccurs="0" name="return" type="employee"/>
    </xs:sequence>
</xs:complexType>

<wsdl:message name="getEmployeeResponse">
    <wsdl:part element="tns:getEmployeeResponse" name="parameters"/>
</wsdl:message>
```

The above-specified XML generates the below provided service endpoint interface. The element name "getEmployeeResponse" maps to the "localName"; it uses the default target namespace of the SEI, and uses the "getEmployeeResponse" XML complex type to generate the Java bean wrapper class "com.learning.ws.jaxws.wsdl2java.GetEmployeeResponse."

```
@WebService(targetNamespace = "http://jaxws.ws.learning.com/",
            name = "EmployeeService")
public interface EmployeeService {
    @RequestWrapper(localName = "getEmployee",
            targetNamespace = "http://jaxws.ws.learning.com/",
            className = "com.learning.ws.jaxws.wsdl2java.GetEmployee")
    @ResponseWrapper(localName = "getEmployeeResponse",
    targetNamespace = "http://jaxws.ws.learning.com/",
    className = "com.learning.ws.jaxws.wsdl2java.GetEmployeeResponse")
    public com.learning.ws.jaxws.wsdl2java.Employee getEmployee(
                @WebParam(name = "employeeId", targetNamespace = "")
                java.lang.String employeeId );
}
```

@javax.xml.ws.WebServiceClient

This annotation is specified in a generated service class. The information specified in this annotation is used to identify the name of the Web service endpoint in a WSDL document. The definition of the @WebServiceClient annotation is given below.

```
public @interface WebServiceClient {
    String name() default "";
    String targetNamespace() default "";
    String wsdlLocation() default "";
}
```

The example provided below demonstrates the use of the @WebServiceClient annotation. The WSDL provided below generates the service class.

```
<wsdl:service name="employeeService">
    ...
</wsdl:service>
```

The generated service class for the above-specified WSDL is given below. The "name" attribute of the "<wsdl:service/>" element maps to the "name" element of the @WebServiceClient annotation. This information is useful for client to invoke the web service endpoint.

The generated service class for the WSDL specified above is given below. The "name" attribute of the "<wsdl:service/>" element maps to the "name" element of the @WebServiceClient annotation. This information helps the client to invoke the Web service endpoint.

```
@WebServiceClient(name = "employeeService",
wsdlLocation = "file:/C:/projects/Learning/book_ws/build/employee.wsdl",
targetNamespace = "http://jaxws.ws.learning.com/")
public class EmployeeService_Service extends Service {

}
```

@javax.xml.ws.WebEndpoint

This annotation is declared to the "getPort()" methods of a generated service class. The information specified in this annotation identifies the "<wsdL:port/>" name of the Web service endpoint specified inside the "<wsdl:service/>" element. The definition of the @WebEndpoint annotation is given below.

```
public @interface WebEndpoint {
    String name() default "";
}
```

The example provided below demonstrates the use of the @WebEndpoint annotation. The WSDL provided below is used to generate the service class.

```
<wsdl:port binding="tns:employeeServiceSoapBinding"
        name="EmployeeServicePort">
    <soap:address
        location="http://localhost:8080/wsbook/services/employee"/>
</wsdl:port>
```

The generated service class for the above-specified WSDL is given below. The "name" attribute of the "<wsdl:port/>" element maps to the "name" element of the @WebEndpoint annotation.

```
public class EmployeeService_Service extends Service {
    @WebEndpoint(name = "EmployeeServicePort")
    public EmployeeService getEmployeeServicePort() {
            return super.getPort(EmployeeServicePort,
                EmployeeService.class);
        }

        @WebEndpoint(name = "EmployeeServicePort")
        public EmployeeService
        getEmployeeServicePort(WebServiceFeature... features) {
            return super.getPort(EmployeeServicePort,
                EmployeeService.class, features);
    }
}
```

@javax.xml.ws.ServiceMode

This annotation indicates whether a provider implementation wishes to work with the entire SOAP message or only the message payload. To work with the entire SOAP message, it is written as <soap:envelope/>; to use only the message payload, it is written as <soap:body/>. The service mode is used by the dispatch client while invoking the Web service endpoint. Dispatch objects have two message modes:

- javax.xml.ws.Service.Mode.MESSAGE—Indicates the entire SOAP message.
- javax.xml.ws.Service.Mode.PAYLOAD—Indicates only the message payload.

By default, the PAYLOAD service mode is used. The definition of the @ServiceMode annotation is given below.

```
public @interface ServiceMode {
    public Service.Mode value() default Service.Mode.PAYLOAD;
}
```

The example provided below demonstrates the use of the service mode. The "Dispatch" client provided below is used to invoke a Web service endpoint using the "MESSAGE" service mode.

```
private void testCreateDispatch() throws Exception {
    URL url = new
            URL("http://localhost:8080/wsbook/services/employee?wsdl");
    QName qname = new QName("http://jaxws.ws.learning.com/",
                    "employeeService");
    Service service = Service.create(url, qname);
    QName portName = new QName("http://jaxws.ws.learning.com/",
                        "EmployeeServicePort");

    Dispatch<SOAPMessage> dispatch =
            service.createDispatch(portName, SOAPMessage.class,
                        Service.Mode.MESSAGE);

    // Use Dispatch as BindingProvider
    BindingProvider bp = (BindingProvider) dispatch;

    // Obtain a SAAJ MessageFactory
    MessageFactory factory = ((SOAPBinding)
                        bp.getBinding()).getMessageFactory();

    // Create SOAPMessage Request - Input to the web service endpoint
    SOAPMessage request = factory.createMessage();

    // SOAP Body for Input request
    SOAPBody body = request.getSOAPBody();

    // Build the soap:Body request payload
    QName payloadName =
            new QName("http://localhost:8080/wsbook/services/employee",
            "getEmployee", "ns1");

    SOAPBodyElement payload = body.addBodyElement(payloadName);
    SOAPElement message = payload.addChildElement("employeeId");
    message.addTextNode("12345678");
```

```
/* Invoke the endpoint synchronously, Invoke Endpoint Operation
        and read response */
SOAPMessage response = dispatch.invoke(request);

// Process the web service response using SAAJ api.
```
}

NOTE: Dispatch client is a low-level API used to invoke the Web services. Apache-CXF chapter explains the details of Message Mode, Dispatch client, and Provider-based Web service implementation.

@javax.xml.ws.WebFault

This annotation is generated by the JAXB while mapping the <wsdl:fault/> messages to the Java exception classes. It handles the exceptions for the service endpoint interface methods. The definition of the @WebFault annotation is given below.

```
public @interface WebFault {
    public String name() default "";
    public String targetNamespace() default "";
    public String faultBean() default "";
}
```

The example provided below demonstrates the use of the @WebFault annotation. The WSDL provided below is used to generate the service class.

```
<wsdl:message name="EmployeeFault">
    <wsdl:part element="tns:EmployeeFault" name="EmployeeFault" />
</wsdl:message>

<wsdl:operation name="getEmployee">
    <wsdl:input message="tns:getEmployee" name="getEmployee"/>
    <wsdl:output message="tns:getEmployeeResponse"
                 name="getEmployeeResponse"/>
    <wsdl:fault message="tns:EmployeeFault" name="EmployeeFault"/>
</wsdl:operation>
```

The generated exception class for the above-specified WSDL is given below. Only the snippet of the code is provided below to demonstrate the use of the @WebFault annotation.

```
@WebFault(name = "EmployeeFault",
        targetNamespace = "http://jaxws.ws.learning.com/")
public class EmployeeFault_Exception extends Exception {
    public static final long serialVersionUID = 20111225073204L;
    private com.learning.ws.jaxws.wsdl2java.EmployeeFault
                                    employeeFault;
    public EmployeeFault_Exception() {
        super();
    }

    public EmployeeFault_Exception(String message) {
```

```
        super (message) ;
    }
}
```

@javax.xml.ws.WebServiceProvider

This annotation is supported only in classes that implement the "javax.xml.ws.Provider" interface.
@WebServiceProvider and @WebService annotations are mutually exclusive, so both annotations
cannot be present in one service endpoint; one or the other must be used.

The definition of the @WebServiceProvider annotation is given below.

```
public @interface WebServiceProvider {
    String wsdlLocation() default "";
    String serviceName() default "";
    String targetNamespace() default "";
    String portName() default "";
}
```

The following are the valid object types used to implement the "javax.xml.ws.Provider" interface.

- javax.xml.transform.Source
- javax.xml.soap.SOAPMessage
- javax.activation.DataSource

The valid implementations of the "javax.xml.ws.Provider" interface service modes are "Message"
and "Payload" Mode. The following Web service uses a valid SOAP binding provider
implementation using the "MESSAGE" mode. The request and response should be a valid
"SOAPMessage."

```
@WebServiceProvider(serviceName="employeeServiceProvider")
@ServiceMode(value= Service.Mode.MESSAGE)
public class EmployeeServiceProvider implements Provider<SOAPMessage> {
    // ...
}
```

The following Web service endpoint uses the "PAYLOAD" mode; the request and response should
be a valid "DOMSource."

```
@WebServiceProvider(serviceName="employeeServiceProvider")
@ServiceMode(value= Service.Mode.PAYLOAD)
public class EmployeeServiceProvider implements Provider<DOMSource> {
    // ...
}
```

The following Web service endpoint implementation class demonstrates the use of the
@WebServiceProvider annotation. The service endpoint class must implement the "invoke()"
method; it receives a SOAPMessage from Web service client and returns the response as a
SOAPMessage. The request-and-response type is a SOAPMessage.

```
@WebServiceProvider(serviceName="employeeServiceProvider")
@ServiceMode(value= Service.Mode.MESSAGE)
public class EmployeeServiceProvider implements Provider<SOAPMessage> {
```

```
    public EmployeeServiceProvider() {}
    public SOAPMessage invoke(SOAPMessage request) {
        // implement your logic here and return the response.
    }
}
```

NOTE: The details of the Dispatch client and Provider-based web service implementations are explained in Apache-CXF chapter

---

@javax.xml.ws.Action

The action annotation is applied to the methods of an SEI. It specifies the association among the input, output, and fault messages of a WSDL operation with the specified WS-Addressing Action codes of an annotated method. The definition of the @Action annotation is given below.

```
public @interface Action {
    String input() default "";
    String output() default "";
    FaultAction[] fault() default { };
}
```

The use @Action annotation with the SEI is given below.

```
@WebService
public interface EmployeeService {
    @WebMethod(operationName="getEmployeeAddress")
    @Action(input="employeeId", output="address")
    String getEmployeeAddressInfo(@WebParam(name="empId", mode= Mode.IN)
            String employeeId) throws Exception;
}
```

The generated WSDL is given below. It maps to the "wsaw:Action" attribute values of the <wsdl:input/> and <wsdl:output/> elements of a WSDL operation.

```
<wsdl:operation name="getEmployeeAddress">
    <wsdl:input message="tns:getEmployeeAddress"
        name="getEmployeeAddress" wsaw:Action="employeeId"/>
    <wsdl:output message="tns:getEmployeeAddressResponse"
        name="getEmployeeAddressResponse" wsaw:Action="address"/>
</wsdl:operation>
```

Test Yourself — Objective Questions

1. Select all correct answers. Which of the Web service messaging styles provided below does WSI-BP recommend?
    a) RPC/LITERAL
    b) RPC/ENCODED
    c) DOCUMENT/LITERAL
    d) DOCUMENT/ENCODED

---

e) All are valid.

2. Which of the annotations provided below is used for methods having only the void return type?
   a) @WebService
   b) @SOAPBinding
   c) @WebParam
   d) @HandlerChain
   e) @Oneway

3. Select all correct answers. Which of the Web service endpoint declarations provided below is valid and will run without any errors?

   a)
```
@SOAPBinding(style=Style.RPC, parameterStyle=ParameterStyle.WRAPPED,
use=Use.LITERAL)
@WebService
public interface EmployeeService {
      String getEmployeeAddressInfo(@WebParam(name="empId",
                        mode= Mode.IN)
                        String employeeId) throws Exception;
}
```

   b)
```
@SOAPBinding(style=Style.DOCUMENT,
parameterStyle=ParameterStyle.WRAPPED, use=Use.LITERAL)
@WebService
public interface EmployeeService {
      String getEmployeeAddressInfo(@WebParam(name="empId",
                        mode= Mode.IN)
                        String employeeId) throws Exception;
}
```

   c)
```
@WebService
public interface EmployeeService {
      String getEmployeeAddressInfo(@WebParam(name="empId",
               mode= Mode.IN) String employeeId) throws Exception;
}
```

   d)
```
@SOAPBinding(style=Style.DOCUMENT, parameterStyle=ParameterStyle.BARE,
use=Use.LITERAL)
@WebService
public interface EmployeeService {
  @SOAPBinding(style=Style.RPC,parameterStyle=ParameterStyle.BARE,
               use=Use.LITERAL)
      String getEmployeeAddressInfo(@WebParam(name="empId",
               mode= Mode.IN) String employeeId) throws Exception;
}
```

   e)
```
@WebService
public interface EmployeeService {
      @SOAPBinding(style=Style.RPC,
               parameterStyle=ParameterStyle.BARE, use=Use.LITERAL)
```

```
        String getEmployeeAddressInfo(@WebParam(name="empId",
            mode= Mode.IN) String employeeId) throws Exception;
    }
```

4. Which of the SEI method parameter modes provided below is used for write purposes?
    a) Mode.IN
    b) Mode.WRITE
    c) Mode.OUT
    d) Mode.INOUT
    e) Mode.WRITEONLY

5. Which of the SEI and implementations provided below employs an invalid use of the @WebService annotation?

    a)
```
@WebService
public interface EmployeeService {
  void deleteEmployee(String employeeId);
}

@WebService(endpointInterface="com.learning.ws.jaxws.EmployeeService",
            serviceName="employeeService")
public class EmployeeServiceImpl implements EmployeeService {
        public EmployeeServiceImpl() {}
        public void deleteEmployee(String employeeId) {
            // ...
        }
}
```

    b)
```
@WebService
public interface EmployeeService {
        void deleteEmployee(String employeeId);
}

@WebService(endpointInterface="com.learning.ws.jaxws.EmployeeService",
            serviceName="employeeService")
public class EmployeeServiceImpl {
        public EmployeeServiceImpl() {}
        public void deleteEmployee(String employeeId) {
            // ...
        }
}
```

    c)
```
@WebService(endpointInterface="com.learning.ws.jaxws.EmployeeService",
            serviceName="employeeService")
public interface EmployeeService {
        void deleteEmployee(String employeeId);
}

@WebService
public class EmployeeServiceImpl implements EmployeeService {
        public EmployeeServiceImpl() {}
        public void deleteEmployee(String employeeId) {
            // ...
```

```
        }
    }
```

d) All are valid

e) All are invalid

6. Which of the annotations provided below is used for life cycle management of a Web service to perform initialization and cleanup activities? The annotated methods are invoked automatically by the container; clients do not need to invoke them.
   a) @WebService
   b) @Action
   c) @PostConstruct
   d) @PreDestroy
   e) @XMLRootElement

7. From the options provided below, select a suitable JAXB annotation to generate a wrapper element around an existing XML element.
   a) javax.xml.bind.annotation.XmlRootElement
   b) javax.xml.bind.annotation.XmlAccessorType
   c) javax.xml.bind.annotation.XmlType
   d) javax.xml.bind.annotation.XmlElement
   e) javax.xml.bind.annotation.XmlElementWrapper

Answers to Test Questions

1. The correct choices are A and C. The basic profile guidelines for Web services interoperability (WSI-BP) prohibit the use of encoded messaging style due to interoperability issues.

2. The correct choice is E. The annotation @Oneway is used only with methods of a void return type. All other annotations have no restrictions on method signature.

3. The correct choices are A, B, and C. Choice D is invalid because the Document and RPC styles are not both allowed for the same service endpoint. Choice E is invalid because the service endpoint uses Document/Literal with the WRAPPED parameter style by default. Option C is correct because it uses the default SOAP binding.

4. The correct choices are C and D. The valid values are Mode.IN, Mode.OUT, and Mode.INOUT. The parameter mode IN is used for read-only, and other two are used to write.

5. The correct choice is C; it is invalid because it does not allow you to use the annotation member "endpointInterface" at the service endpoint interface (SEI) level.

6. The correct answers are C and D. The annotations defined in JSR-250 are used for life cycle management. The @PostConstruct and @PreDestroy annotated methods are automatically invoked by the servlet container.

7. The correct answer is E.

Apache-CXF is a most popular open-source framework used for developing fully featured Web Services conforming to JAX-WS standards. This project is derived from combining the two open-source projects "**C**eltix" and "**XF**ire". The name CXF is derived from two projects "**C**eltix" and "**XF**ire". The combined project is now available with Apache Software Foundation. This chapter illustrates the Web Services development using Apache-CXF framework.

In this chapter will discuss the following topics:

- The "code-first" and "contract-first" Web services development using Apache-CXF.
- The Provider-based web services development.
- The Web service client, endpoint design scenarios.
- The use of SOAP message handlers.
- How to configure a SOAP handler chain to a web service client and endpoint
- Build and Deployment instructions for Tomcat.
- The CXF framework tools and utilities.

There are several open-source Web Services frameworks available to implement JAX-WS conformant web services. The commonly used open-source Web service frameworks are listed below.

- JAX-WS (RI) – A reference implementation from Sun
- Apache-CXF
- Apache-Axis2
- Spring Web Services (Spring-WS)
- JBoss-WS

Prerequisite and Setting up the Environment

- The jar files required to develop the CXF-based Web Services are provided along with the CXF distribution. Download the CXF framework from apache website.
- Make sure you use the correct version of jar files to avoid the class loader jar file version mismatch related exceptions.
- The complete distribution is available in the form of jar files. So no additional software needed for development.
- The complete list of jar files required for CXF Web service development is provided in Chapter12.

Apache-CXF Advantages

- CXF provides good support for various Web Services standards like SOAP, WSDL and WS-I Basic profile.
- CXF provides support for various client side programming models to invoke the deployed service endpoint. It provides support for static and dynamic clients.

- CXF extensions available to configure the SOAP message handlers and interceptors.
- CXF provides a simple logging mechanism to log request-and-response SOAP messages.
- CXF provides support for both "code-first" and "contract-first" type of web service development models.
- CXF provides a seamless integration with Spring framework. The Spring and CXF XML tags can co-exist in the same configuration file. Both look similar.
- Using CXF, It is easy to expose existing business functionality as a Web service to other applications to meet the application-specific business need.
- CXF provided services are easy to plug into the already exiting application code.
- CXF follows simple syntax; so it is easy to learn.
- CXF provides wide range of annotations for Web services development.
- CXF provides support for JAX-RS and JAX-WS standards. It is possible to develop REST-based and SOAP-based Web service endpoint using CXF framework
- CXF provides support for various Java specification requests like JSR-181 (meta data annotations), JSR-224 (JSR-WS), JSR-311 (JAX-RS), and JSR-222 (JAXB)
- CXF provides support for multiple data formats like JSON, XML, and SOAP.

Apache-CXF Disadvantages

- Not backwardly compatible with their older versions like XFire. It requires code rewrite.
- It is suitable for Java versions 1.5 and above.

Development Methodologies

The following sections illustrate the web services development using CXF framework. There are two different ways we can develop Web Services using CXF.

- Write Java interface-first, and expose it as a Web Service
- Write WSDL document-first; generate Java classes using CXF-provided framework tools.

Example 1: Java First Development (Also Called Code First)

In this approach we start the development with Java interface and its implementation class by declaring "@WebService" annotation to mark it as a Web Service. The steps required to develop a Web Service of this type are provided below.

1. Create a service endpoint interface
2. Create a service implementation class
3. Create a CXF configuration file
4. Create a web.xml file
5. Create a war file and deploy into a Tomcat server
6. Verify the WSDL document
7. Write a client to invoke the deployed service

The above-specified steps are described in the following sections:

This is an employee web service; for a given employee id, it provides the employee details.

Step 1: Create a Service Endpoint Interface

The only required annotation at the service endpoint interface is "@WebService". All other annotations are optional; other annotations I used it here for sake of developers to get familiar with them. The significance of each annotation is explained in Chapter8 with code examples. The below provided service endpoint interface "EmployeeService" has four methods. Listing 9-1 has a Java code that demonstrates the POJO-based web service implementation.

Listing 9-1: Developing POJO-based web service

```
// EmployeeService.java
package com.learning.ws.jaxws;

import javax.jws.WebParam.Mode;
import javax.jws.*;

@WebService
public interface EmployeeService {
    @WebMethod(operationName="getEmployee")
    Employee getEmployee(@WebParam (name="employeeId")
                    String employeeId) throws EmployeeFault;

    @WebMethod(operationName="getEmployeeAddress")
    String getEmployeeAddressInfo(@WebParam(name="empId", mode= Mode.IN)
                    String employeeId) throws Exception;

    String getEmployerInformation(@WebParam(name="empId", mode= Mode.IN)
        String employeeId, @WebParam(name="state", mode= Mode.IN)
        String state) throws Exception;

    @WebMethod(operationName="deleteEmployee")
    void deleteEmployee(@WebParam (name="employeeId") String
                        employeeId);
}
```

The below provided "Employee" Java bean class is used for data population:

```
// Employee.java
package com.learning.ws.jaxws;

public class Employee {

    private static final long serialVersionUID = 1L;
    private String employeeId;
    private String lastName;
    private String firstName;

    // Generate getters and setters for the above
}
```

Step 2: Create a Service Implementation Class

The service implementation class "EmployeeServiceImpl" is declared with "@WebService" annotation to mark it as a Web Service. The above interface-defined methods are implemented in its implementation class. They are shown in Listing 9-2.

Listing 9-2: POJO-based web service implementation class.

```java
// EmployeeServiceImpl.java
package com.learning.ws.jaxws;

import javax.jws.*;
import javax.xml.ws.*;

@WebService(name="EmployeeService",
            serviceName="employeeService",
            endpointInterface="com.learning.ws.jaxws.EmployeeService")
public class EmployeeServiceImpl implements EmployeeService {

    public Employee getEmployee(String employeeId) throws EmployeeFault{

        if(employeeId == null) {
            throw new EmployeeFault("Invalid input received");
        }

        Employee emp = new Employee();
        emp.setEmployeeId(employeeId);
        emp.setFirstName("John");
        emp.setLastName("Smith");

        return emp;
    }

    public String getEmployeeAddressInfo(String employeeId)
    throws Exception {
        /* Implement your logic here to get the employee address,
        here the hard coded return value is used.*/
        String address = "3943 Roundabout CIR, Chandler,Arizona,85226";
        return address;
    }

    public void deleteEmployee(String employeeId) {
        System.out.println("--- Delete Employee ---" + employeeId);
        // Implement your logic here to delete an employee.
    }

    public String getEmployerInformation(String employeeId,
                String state) throws Exception {
        // Implement your logic here
        String employer = "Bank of Chandler, Chandler, Arizona, 85226";
        return employer;
    }
}
```

Step 3: Create a CXF Configuration File

Apache-CXF provides XML-based tags to configure the Web service endpoint with JAX-WS runtime. CXF tags look similar to Spring framework bean tags. Both Spring and CXF tags can co-exist in the same configuration file. Configure the Web service endpoint using "<jaxws:endpoint/>" tag. The use of CXF-provided "<jaxws:endpoint/>" tag is given below.

```xml
<jaxws:endpoint id="employee"
            implementor="com.learning.ws.jaxws.EmployeeServiceImpl"
```

```
                    address="/employee">
</jaxws:endpoint>
```

This XML tag "<jaxws:endpoint/>" contains the details of web service implementation class and web service binding address. The complete XML file is provided below; named the "applicationContext-jaxws.xml".

```
<?xml version="1.0" encoding="UTF-8"?>
<beans xmlns="http://www.springframework.org/schema/beans"
        xmlns:xsi="http://www.w3.org/2001/XMLSchema-instance"
        xmlns:jaxws="http://cxf.apache.org/jaxws"
        xmlns:cxf="http://cxf.apache.org/core"
        xsi:schemaLocation="http://www.springframework.org/schema/beans
        http://www.springframework.org/schema/beans/spring-beans.xsd
        http://cxf.apache.org/jaxws
        http://cxf.apache.org/schemas/jaxws.xsd
        http://cxf.apache.org/core
        http://cxf.apache.org/schemas/core.xsd ">

    <!-- Loads CXF modules from cxf.jar file -->
    <import resource="classpath:META-INF/cxf/cxf.xml"/>
    <import resource="classpath:META-INF/cxf/cxf-extension-soap.xml"/>
    <import resource="classpath:META-INF/cxf/cxf-servlet.xml"/>
    <import resource="classpath:META-INF/cxf/cxf-extension-jaxrs-
    binding.xml"/>

    <!-- Configure the web service endpoint -->
    <jaxws:endpoint id="employee"
            implementor="com.learning.ws.jaxws.EmployeeServiceImpl"
            address="/employee">
    </jaxws:endpoint>
</beans>
```

Step 4: Create a web.xml File

Configure the spring context listener and CXF transport servlet in web.xml. The complete web.xml file is provided below.

```
<?xml version="1.0" encoding="UTF-8"?>
<web-app version="2.4" xmlns="http://java.sun.com/xml/ns/j2ee"
    xmlns:xsi="http://www.w3.org/2001/XMLSchema-instance"
    xsi:schemaLocation="http://java.sun.com/xml/ns/j2ee
    http://java.sun.com/xml/ns/j2ee/web-app_2_4.xsd">

<display-name>Web Services Application</display-name>
<listener>
    <listener-class>
        org.springframework.web.context.ContextLoaderListener
    </listener-class>
</listener>

<context-param>
    <param-name>contextConfigLocation</param-name>
    <param-value>/WEB-INF/applicationContext-jaxws.xml</param-value>
</context-param>
```

```
<servlet>
    <servlet-name>CXFServlet</servlet-name>
    <servlet-class>
        org.apache.cxf.transport.servlet.CXFServlet
    </servlet-class>
</servlet>

<servlet-mapping>
    <servlet-name>CXFServlet</servlet-name>
    <url-pattern>/services/*</url-pattern>
</servlet-mapping>

<mime-mapping>
    <extension>wsdl</extension>
    <mime-type>text/xml</mime-type>
</mime-mapping>
<mime-mapping>
    <extension>xsd</extension>
    <mime-type>text/xml</mime-type>
    </mime-mapping>
</web-app>
```

The following provided configurations initialize the root application context. This is the boot strap listener to start up the Spring root web application context and it loads all files specified in the <param-value/> into the context.

```
<listener>
    <listener-class>
        org.springframework.web.context.ContextLoaderListener
    </listener-class>
</listener>
<context-param>
    <param-name>contextConfigLocation</param-name>
    <param-value>/WEB-INF/applicationContext-jaxws.xml</param-value>
</context-param>
```

Configure the CXF transport servlet in web.xml. All Web Service requests routes through this transport servlet; it converts the HTTP request to SOAP request and vice versa.

```
<servlet>
    <servlet-name>CXFServlet</servlet-name>
    <servlet-class>
        org.apache.cxf.transport.servlet.CXFServlet
    </servlet-class>
</servlet>
<servlet-mapping>
    <servlet-name>CXFServlet</servlet-name>
    <url-pattern>/services/*</url-pattern>
</servlet-mapping>
```

Step 5: Create a war File and Deploy it in Tomcat Server.

1. Build a war file using Ant or any other build tool. Make sure the following files are packaged correctly in war file.

   a. Service endpoint interface

b.   Service endpoint implementation class
c.   Any utility classes used for data access.
d.   web.xml file
e.   CXF configuration file (applicationContext-jaxws.xml) file.

The structure of the war file is shown Figure 9-1.

Figure 9-1: Structure of a war file

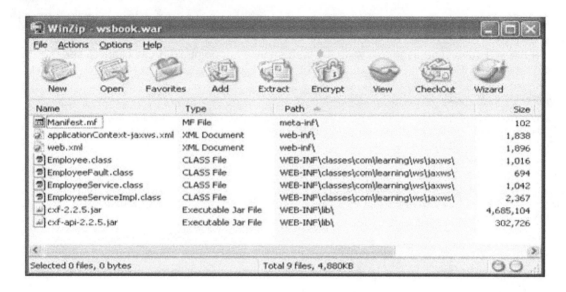

NOTE: The above provided Figure 9-1 shows only a few jar files in "WEB-INF/lib" directory. Refer to Chapter12 for the complete list.

---

2.   Deploy the war file in any servlet container.

a.   Copy the packed war into "apache-tomcat/webapps" directory
b.   Start the tomcat sever by running the "startup.bat" batch file available in "apache-tomcat/bin" directory
c.   See the server console output and logs; make sure war file is deployed without any errors.

Step 6: Verify the WSDL Document

Access the WSDL file from web browser to make sure service is deployed without any errors. Use the below given URL to view the complete WSDL.

```
http://localhost:8080/wsbook/services/employee?wsdl
```

Step 7: Write a Client to Invoke the Deployed Service

The following used to specify the location of the WSDL:

```
URL url = new URL("http://localhost:8080/wsbook/services/employee?wsdl");
```

The below provided "Service.create()" method is used to create an instance of "Service" object. It takes two parameters. The first parameter is service URI, second parameter is service name.

```
QName qname = new QName("http://jaxws.ws.learning.com/",
                        "employeeService");
Service service = Service.create(url, qname);
```

This is used to get the binding port to invoke the methods defined in the service endpoint interface.

```
EmployeeService employeeService = service.getPort(EmployeeService.class);
```

Listing 9-3 has a Java code used to invoke the web service endpoint. Run this client to see the output.

Listing 9-3: Client to invoke the service endpoint

```java
// TestClient.java
package com.learning.ws.jaxws;

import java.net.URL;
import javax.xml.namespace.QName;
import javax.xml.ws.Service;

public class TestClient {
    public static void main(String args[]) throws Exception {
        try {
            TestClient client = new TestClient ();
            client.invokeEmployeeService();
        } catch(Exception ex) {
            ex.printStackTrace();
        }
    }

    private void invokeEmployeeService() throws Exception {
        // Location of the wsdl
        URL url = new URL("http://localhost:8080/
                wsbook/services/employee?wsdl");

        /* 1st argument is service URI - maps to targetNamespace in
        Wsdl, 2nd argument is service name - maps to <wsdl:service/>
        element's name attribute in wsdl */
        QName qname = new QName("http://jaxws.ws.learning.com/",
                "employeeService");
        Service service = Service.create(url, qname);

        // Get the service port - maps to <wsdl:portType/> in wsdl
        EmployeeService employeeService =
            service.getPort(EmployeeService.class);

        // Invoke the service endpoint methods.
        String address =
            employeeService.getEmployeeAddressInfo("823147");
        System.out.println("Address is: " + address);

        Employee emp = employeeService.getEmployee("133334");
        System.out.println("Employee Id:" + emp.getEmployeeId() +
```

```
             "-- First Name --" + emp.getFirstName() + "-- Last Name --"
                + emp.getLastName());
        }
}
```

Example 2: WSDL First Development (Also Called Contract First)

In this approach developer first creates a WSDL document, also called contract; this WSDL is used for generating the Java service endpoint interface and its dependent classes. The steps required to develop a Web Service of this type are given below.

1. Create a WSDL file
2. Generate service endpoint Java classes using WSDL2Java tool
3. Create a CXF configuration file
4. Create a web.xml file
5. Create a war file and deploy it in Tomcat server
6. Verify the WSDL document
7. Write a client to invoke the deployed service

The above-specified steps are described in the following sections:

Step 1: Create a WSDL File

Apache-CXF provides tools to generate the Java classes from WSDL. The following WSDL is used for generating the Java classes using "org.apache.cxf.tools.wsdlto.WSDL2Java" utility; available with CXF framework. The complete WSDL file is provided below.

```xml
<?xml version="1.0" encoding="UTF-8"?>
<wsdl:definitions name="employeeService"
        targetNamespace="http://jaxws.ws.learning.com/"
        xmlns:ns1="http://cxf.apache.org/bindings/xformat"
        xmlns:soap="http://schemas.xmlsoap.org/wsdl/soap/"
        xmlns:tns="http://jaxws.ws.learning.com/"
        xmlns:wsdl="http://schemas.xmlsoap.org/wsdl/"
        xmlns:xsd="http://www.w3.org/2001/XMLSchema">
    <wsdl:types>
        <xs:schema attributeFormDefault="unqualified"
            elementFormDefault="unqualified"
            targetNamespace="http://jaxws.ws.learning.com/"
            xmlns="http://jaxws.ws.learning.com/"
            xmlns:xs="http://www.w3.org/2001/XMLSchema">
        <xs:complexType name="employee">
            <xs:sequence>
                <xs:element minOccurs="0" name="employeeId"
                                    type="xs:string"/>
                <xs:element minOccurs="0" name="firstName"
                                    type="xs:string"/>
                <xs:element minOccurs="0" name="lastName"
                                    type="xs:string"/>
            </xs:sequence>
        </xs:complexType>
        <xs:element name="EmployeeFault" type="EmployeeFault" />
        <xs:complexType name="EmployeeFault">
            <xs:sequence />
        </xs:complexType>
```

```xml
<xs:element name="getEmployeeAddress"
        type="getEmployeeAddress"/>
<xs:complexType name="getEmployeeAddress">
    <xs:sequence>
        <xs:element minOccurs="0" name="empId"
                            type="xs:string"/>
    </xs:sequence>
</xs:complexType>
<xs:element name="getEmployeeAddressResponse"
        type="getEmployeeAddressResponse"/>
    <xs:complexType name="getEmployeeAddressResponse">
        <xs:sequence>
            <xs:element minOccurs="0" name="return"
                                type="xs:string"/>
        </xs:sequence>
    </xs:complexType>
<xs:element name="getEmployee" type="getEmployee"/>
<xs:complexType name="getEmployee">
    <xs:sequence>
        <xs:element minOccurs="0" name="employeeId"
                                type="xs:string"/>
    </xs:sequence>
</xs:complexType>
    <xs:element name="getEmployeeResponse"
                    type="getEmployeeResponse"/>
<xs:complexType name="getEmployeeResponse">
    <xs:sequence>
        <xs:element minOccurs="0" name="return"
                                type="employee"/>
    </xs:sequence>
</xs:complexType>
<xs:element name="getEmployerInformation"
            type="getEmployerInformation"/>
<xs:complexType name="getEmployerInformation">
    <xs:sequence>
        <xs:element minOccurs="0" name="empId"
                                type="xs:string"/>
        <xs:element minOccurs="0" name="state"
                                type="xs:string"/>
    </xs:sequence>
</xs:complexType>
<xs:element name="getEmployerInformationResponse"
            type="getEmployerInformationResponse"/>
<xs:complexType name="getEmployerInformationResponse">
    <xs:sequence>
        <xs:element minOccurs="0" name="return"
                                type="xs:string"/>
    </xs:sequence>
</xs:complexType>
<xs:element name="deleteEmployee" type="deleteEmployee"/>
<xs:complexType name="deleteEmployee">
    <xs:sequence>
        <xs:element minOccurs="0" name="employeeId"
                                type="xs:string"/>
    </xs:sequence>
</xs:complexType>
<xs:element name="deleteEmployeeResponse"
```

```
                type="deleteEmployeeResponse"/>
        <xs:complexType name="deleteEmployeeResponse">
            <xs:sequence/>
        </xs:complexType>
    </xs:schema>
</wsdl:types>

<wsdl:message name="deleteEmployee">
    <wsdl:part element="tns:deleteEmployee" name="parameters"/>
</wsdl:message>
<wsdl:message name="EmployeeFault">
    <wsdl:part element="tns:EmployeeFault" name="EmployeeFault" />
</wsdl:message>
<wsdl:message name="getEmployee">
    <wsdl:part element="tns:getEmployee" name="parameters"/>
</wsdl:message>
<wsdl:message name="deleteEmployeeResponse">
    <wsdl:part element="tns:deleteEmployeeResponse"
                name="parameters"/>
</wsdl:message>
<wsdl:message name="getEmployerInformationResponse">
<wsdl:part element="tns:getEmployerInformationResponse"
        name="parameters"/>
</wsdl:message>
<wsdl:message name="getEmployeeAddress">
    <wsdl:part element="tns:getEmployeeAddress" name="parameters"/>
</wsdl:message>
<wsdl:message name="getEmployeeResponse">
    <wsdl:part element="tns:getEmployeeResponse"
                name="parameters"/>
</wsdl:message>
    <wsdl:message name="getEmployerInformation">
    <wsdl:part element="tns:getEmployerInformation"
                name="parameters"/>
</wsdl:message>
<wsdl:message name="getEmployeeAddressResponse">
        <wsdl:part element="tns:getEmployeeAddressResponse"
                name="parameters"/>
</wsdl:message>

<wsdl:portType name="EmployeeService">
    <wsdl:operation name="getEmployeeAddress">
        <wsdl:input message="tns:getEmployeeAddress"
                name="getEmployeeAddress"/>
        <wsdl:output message="tns:getEmployeeAddressResponse"
                name="getEmployeeAddressResponse"/>
    </wsdl:operation>
    <wsdl:operation name="getEmployee">
        <wsdl:input message="tns:getEmployee" name="getEmployee"/>
        <wsdl:output message="tns:getEmployeeResponse"
            name="getEmployeeResponse"/>
    </wsdl:operation>
    <wsdl:operation name="getEmployerInformation">
        <wsdl:input message="tns:getEmployerInformation"
            name="getEmployerInformation"/>
        <wsdl:output message="tns:getEmployerInformationResponse"
            name="getEmployerInformationResponse"/>
```

```
            </wsdl:operation>
            <wsdl:operation name="deleteEmployee">
                <wsdl:input message="tns:deleteEmployee"
                            name="deleteEmployee"/>
                <wsdl:output message="tns:deleteEmployeeResponse"
                            name="deleteEmployeeResponse"/>
                <wsdl:fault message="tns:EmployeeFault"
                                name="EmployeeFault" />
            </wsdl:operation>
    </wsdl:portType>

    <wsdl:binding name="employeeServiceSoapBinding"
                type="tns:EmployeeService">
        <soap:binding style="document"
                transport="http://schemas.xmlsoap.org/soap/http"/>
        <wsdl:operation name="getEmployee">
            <soap:operation soapAction="" style="document"/>
                <wsdl:input name="getEmployee">
                    <soap:body use="literal"/>
                </wsdl:input>
                <wsdl:output name="getEmployeeResponse">
                    <soap:body use="literal"/>
                </wsdl:output>
        </wsdl:operation>
        <wsdl:operation name="getEmployeeAddress">
            <soap:operation soapAction="" style="document"/>
                <wsdl:input name="getEmployeeAddress">
                    <soap:body use="literal"/>
                </wsdl:input>
                <wsdl:output name="getEmployeeAddressResponse">
                    <soap:body use="literal"/>
                </wsdl:output>
        </wsdl:operation>
        <wsdl:operation name="getEmployerInformation">
            <soap:operation soapAction="" style="document"/>
                <wsdl:input name="getEmployerInformation">
                    <soap:body use="literal"/>
                </wsdl:input>
                <wsdl:output name="getEmployerInformationResponse">
                    <soap:body use="literal"/>
                </wsdl:output>
        </wsdl:operation>
        <wsdl:operation name="deleteEmployee">
            <soap:operation soapAction="" style="document"/>
                <wsdl:input name="deleteEmployee">
                    <soap:body use="literal"/>
                </wsdl:input>
                <wsdl:output name="deleteEmployeeResponse">
                    <soap:body use="literal"/>
                </wsdl:output>
        </wsdl:operation>
    </wsdl:binding>

    <wsdl:service name="employeeService">
        <wsdl:port binding="tns:employeeServiceSoapBinding"
                name="EmployeeServicePort">
            <soap:address
```

```
                location="http://localhost:8080/wsbook/services/employee"/>
            </wsdl:port>
        </wsdl:service>

</wsdl:definitions>
```

Step 2: Generate Service Endpoint Java Classes using WSDL2Java Utility

The "WSDL2Java" utility takes the WSDL input; and generates the fully annotated Java classes to implement the Web service. There are three different ways we can generate code using "WSDL2Java" utility.

- Using command line
- Using Ant build tool
- Using Maven CXF Maven plug-in.

Using command line:

Specify the physical location of WSDL file as input to generate the Java classes.

Example:

```
wsdl2java employee.wsdl
```

Specify the package for the generated classes

```
wsdl2java -p com.learning.ws.jaxws employee.wsdl
```

Using Ant Build Tool:

Add the below provided Ant target to your application build script. Refer to the Build and Deployment instructions (Chapter12) to view the complete Ant script to build this application. This Ant target generates and compiles the JAX-WS/JAXB code. This "build-wsdl2java" ant target takes many optional arguments; and only required argument for code generation is "wsdl-path".

```
<!-- Apache-CXF Ant target - To Generate and compile JAX-WS/JAXB code
     from WSDL -->
<target name="build-wsdl2java">
    <echo message="Running WSDL2Java task"/>
    <delete quiet="true" dir="${build-gen}"/>
    <mkdir dir="${build-gen}"/>
    <java classpathref="build.classpath" fork="true"
        classname="org.apache.cxf.tools.wsdlto.WSDLToJava">

        <!-- -d parameter sets the output root directory for
        generated files -->
        <arg value="-d"/>
        <arg value="${source.dir}"/>

        <!-- -p parameter specifies the complete package name of the
        generated code -->
        <arg value="-p"/>
        <arg value="${package-name}"/>

        <!-- -validate parameter used for WSDL validation before
```

```
            generation -->
            <arg value="-validate"/>

            <!-- actual input WSDL -->
            <arg value="${wsdl-path}"/>
        </java>

        <!-- Compile the generated code -->
        <mkdir dir="${build-gen}/bin"/>
        <javac srcdir="${source.dir}" destdir="${build-gen}/bin"
                                  debug="true">
            <classpath>
                <path refid="build.classpath"/>
            </classpath>
        </javac>
    </target>
</target>
```

The above provided Ant target generates the following list of Java files in the specified location. Make sure, all generated files use the correct package name before going for service endpoint implementation.

- DeleteEmployee.java
- DeleteEmployeeResponse.java
- Employee.java
- EmployeeFault.java
- EmployeeFault_Exception.java
- **EmployeeService.java**
- EmployeeService_Service.java
- GetEmployee.java
- GetEmployeeAddress.java
- GetEmployeeAddressResponse.java
- GetEmployeeResponse.java
- GetEmployerInformation.java
- GetEmployerInformationResponse.java
- ObjectFactory.java
- package-info.java

Now write your service endpoint implementation class to implement the application specific business logic; and make sure it implements the generated endpoint interface "EmployeeService.java". In this example "EmployeeServiceImpl.java" class is used to implement the business functionality; and this class implements the auto-generated methods defined in the interface "EmployeeService.java". Listing 9-4 has the complete service implementation class code.

Listing 9-4: Web service implementation class

```
// EmployeeServiceImpl.java
package com.learning.ws.jaxws.wsdl2java;

@WebService(name="EmployeeService",
            serviceName="employeeService",
            endpointInterface="
            com.learning.ws.jaxws.wsdl2java.EmployeeService")
public class EmployeeServiceImpl implements EmployeeService {

    public Employee getEmployee(String employeeId) throws EmployeeFault{
```

```
        System.out.println("--- employeeId ---" + employeeId);
        if(employeeId == null) {
            throw new EmployeeFault("Invalid input received");
        }

        Employee emp = new Employee();
        emp.setEmployeeId(employeeId);
        emp.setFirstName("John");
        emp.setLastName("Smith");

        return emp;
    }

    public String getEmployeeAddressInfo(String employeeId) throws
    Exception {
    /* Implement your logic here to get the employee address, here I
    have hard coded the value. */
        return "3943 Roundabout CIR, Chandler, Arizona, 85226";
    }

    public void deleteEmployee(String employeeId) {
        // Implement your logic here to delete an employee.
    }

    public String getEmployerInformation(String employeeId,
        String state) throws Exception {
        // Implement your logic here…
        return "Bank of Chandler, Chandler, Arizona, 85226";
    }
}
```

Step 3: Create a CXF Configuration File

Apache-CXF uses Spring framework to configure of Web Service endpoints. We can integrate the CXF-provided XML tags with Spring framework provided "<bean/>" tags. The complete XML used for this example is provided below. It is named the "applicationContext-jaxws.xml".

```
<?xml version="1.0" encoding="UTF-8"?>
<beans xmlns="http://www.springframework.org/schema/beans"
    xmlns:xsi="http://www.w3.org/2001/XMLSchema-instance"
    xmlns:jaxws="http://cxf.apache.org/jaxws"
    xmlns:cxf="http://cxf.apache.org/core"
    xsi:schemaLocation="http://www.springframework.org/schema/beans
    http://www.springframework.org/schema/beans/spring-beans.xsd
    ttp://cxf.apache.org/jaxws
    http://cxf.apache.org/schemas/jaxws.xsd
    http://cxf.apache.org/core
    http://cxf.apache.org/schemas/core.xsd ">

    <!-- Loads CXF modules from cxf.jar file -->
    <import resource="classpath:META-INF/cxf/cxf.xml"/>
    <import resource="classpath:META-INF/cxf/cxf-extension-soap.xml"/>
    <import resource="classpath:META-INF/cxf/cxf-servlet.xml"/>
    <import resource="classpath:META-INF/cxf/cxf-extension-jaxrs-
    binding.xml"/>
```

```
<jaxws:endpoint id="EmployeeService" implementor=
            "com.learning.ws.jaxws.wsdl2java.EmployeeServiceImpl"
            wsdlLocation="WEB-INF/wsdl/employee.wsdl"
            address="/employeeService"/>
```

```
</beans>
```

Now let us go through "<jaxws:endpoint/>" tag parameters to have the better understanding of the service endpoint.

```
<jaxws:endpoint id="EmployeeService"
            implementor=
            "com.learning.ws.jaxws.wsdl2java.EmployeeServiceImpl"
            wsdlLocation="WEB-INF/wsdl/employee.wsdl"
            address="/employeeService"/>
```

- id – Id used for this endpoint.
- implementor – It specifies the service endpoint implementation class
- wsdlLocation – It specifies the location of the WSDL file available at runtime
- address – It maps to "<wsdl:service name="employeeService">" of WSDL. It specifies the service endpoint name.

Step 4: Create a web.xml file

Configure the Spring context listener and CXF transport servlet in web.xml. Re-use the same web.xml file we created in Example1. The complete web.xml file is provided below.

```
<?xml version="1.0" encoding="UTF-8"?>
<web-app version="2.4" xmlns="http://java.sun.com/xml/ns/j2ee"
    xmlns:xsi="http://www.w3.org/2001/XMLSchema-instance"
    xsi:schemaLocation="http://java.sun.com/xml/ns/j2ee
    http://java.sun.com/xml/ns/j2ee/web-app_2_4.xsd">

<display-name>Web Services Application</display-name>
<listener>
<listener-class>
    org.springframework.web.context.ContextLoaderListener
    </listener-class>
</listener>
<context-param>
    <param-name>contextConfigLocation</param-name>
    <param-value>
        /WEB-INF/applicationContext-jaxws.xml
    </param-value>
</context-param>

<servlet>
    <servlet-name>CXFServlet</servlet-name>
        <servlet-class>
            org.apache.cxf.transport.servlet.CXFServlet
        </servlet-class>
</servlet>
<servlet-mapping>
    <servlet-name>CXFServlet</servlet-name>
        <url-pattern>/services/*</url-pattern>
```

```
        </servlet-mapping>
</web-app>
```

Step 5: Create a war file and deploy it in Tomcat server

1. Build a war file using Ant or any other build tool. Make sure the following files are packaged correctly in war file.
    a. All generated class files including endpoint interface
    b. Service endpoint implementation class
    c. Any utility classes used for data access etc.
    d. web.xml file
    e. CXF configuration file (applicationContext-jaxws.xml) file.
    f. WSDL file.

2. Deploy the war file in any servlet container.
    a. Copy the packed war into "apache-tomcat/webapps" directory
    b. Start the tomcat sever by running the "startup.bat" batch file available in "apache-tomcat/bin" directory
    c. See the server console output and logs; make sure war file is deployed without any errors.

NOTE: The below provided Figure 9-2 shows only a few jar files in "WEB-INF/lib" directory. Refer to Chapter12 for the complete list.

The structure of the war file is shown Figure 9-2.

Figure 9-2: Structure of a war file

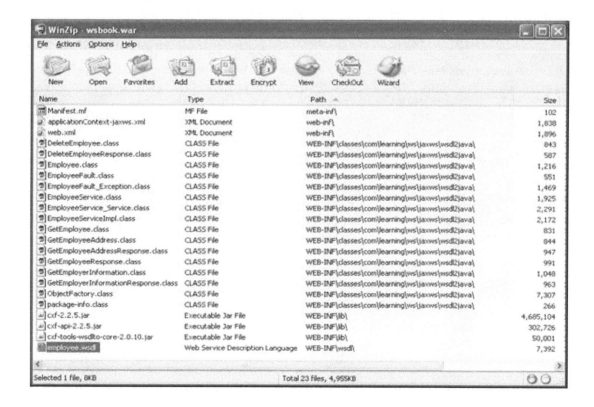

Step 6: Verify the WSDL Document

Access the WSDL file from web browser to make sure service is deployed without any errors. Use the below given URL to view the complete WSDL.

```
http://localhost:8080/wsbook/services/employeeService?WSDL
```

Step 7: Write a Client to Invoke the Deployed Web Service.

There are several ways we can invoke the deployed Web Service. In this example we use the "WSDL2Java" generated classes to invoke the web service endpoint methods. Listing 9-5 has the Web service client used to invoke deployed web service.

Listing 9-5: Web service client code

```java
// Client.java
package com.learning.ws.jaxws.wsdl2java;

import javax.xml.ws.BindingProvider;

public class Client {
    public static void main(String args[]) throws Exception {
        try {
            Client client = new Client();
            client.invokeService();
        } catch(Exception ex) {
            ex.printStackTrace();
        }
    }

    private void invokeService() throws Exception {
        // create the client stub using tool generated classes.
        EmployeeService_Service service = new
                        EmployeeService_Service();
        EmployeeService stub = service.getEmployeeServicePort();

        // Service endpoint URL
        String target =
            "http://localhost:8080/wsbook/services/employeeService";
        BindingProvider provider = (BindingProvider) stub;
        provider.getRequestContext().
            put(BindingProvider.ENDPOINT_ADDRESS_PROPERTY, target);

        // Invoking the endpoint method - getEmployeeAddress()
        String address = stub.getEmployeeAddress("823147");
        System.out.println("Address  is : " + address);

        // Invoking the endpoint method - getEmployee()
        Employee emp = stub.getEmployee("133334");
        System.out.println("Employee Id:" + emp.getEmployeeId() +
        "-- First Name --" + emp.getFirstName() + "-- Last Name --" +
            emp.getLastName());
    }
}
```

The generated "EmployeeService_Service" class for the above-specified WSDL is given below. The name attribute of the "<wsdl:service/>" element maps to the "name" attribute of the "@WebServiceClient" annotation. This web service client uses this information to invoke the Web Service endpoint.

```
@WebServiceClient(name = "employeeService",
    wsdlLocation =
        "file:/C:/projects/Learning/book_ws/build/employee.wsdl",
    targetNamespace = "http://jaxws.ws.learning.com/")
public class EmployeeService_Service extends Service {

}
```

Let us now take the below provided code to understand it better. This gives the handle to the web service endpoint stub; this stub can be used to invoke the service endpoint operations.

```
EmployeeService_Service service = new EmployeeService_Service();
EmployeeService stub = service.getEmployeeServicePort();
```

After accessing the client stub; use "javax.xml.ws.BindingProvider" interface to get access to the protocol binding, associated context objects for request-and-response processing.

```
String target = "http://localhost:8080/wsbook/services/employeeService";
BindingProvider provider = (BindingProvider) stub;
provider.getRequestContext().put(BindingProvider.ENDPOINT_ADDRESS_PROPERTY, target);
```

NOTE: Web service client is used to invoke the deployed web service endpoint. In Example1 the "Service.create()" method is used to invoke the service endpoint; in this example "WSDL2Java" generated stub classes are used to invoke the service endpoint.

Example 3: An Alternative to Service Endpoint Interface (Using Provider interface)

The *Provider* interface provides an alternative to service endpoint interfaces (SEI) for implementing Web Services. In this case the developer needs to work with low level message API's like SOAP messages, and DOM sources; so we have to learn the details of the structure of request-response messages; and API's used to manipulate these messages. The Provider-based service endpoint implementation class must satisfy the following conformance rules:

- The following provided valid object types the "javax.xml.ws.Provider" interface must support.
  - javax.xml.transform.Source
  - javax.xml.soap.SOAPMessage
  - javax.activation.DataSource
- The Provider interface must use concrete Java type parameter like Provider<Source>, and Provider<SOAPMessage>. It is not allowed to use generic type like Provider<T>
- The Provider-based service endpoint implementation class must have a default public constructor.
- The service endpoint implementation class must implement Provider interface of valid type.
- The service endpoint implementation class must use "@WebServiceProvider" annotation to mark it as a Web Service.

- The messaging mode of the Provider service is configured using "@ServiceMode" annotation. This is optional, by default it uses "PAYLOAD" service mode.

The steps required to develop-and-run the Web Service of this type are given below.

1. Create a Provider-based service implementation class
2. Create a web.xml file
3. Create a CXF configuration file
4. Create a war file and deploy it in Tomcat server
5. Verify the WSDL document
6. Create a *Dispatch* client to invoke the deployed service

The above-specified steps are described in the following sections:

Step 1: Create a "Provider" Based Service Implementation Class

Make sure the Provider-based web service endpoint implementation class follows the conformance rules listed above. In this example the Provider implementation class satisfies to the following conformance rules.

- The endpoint implementation class implements the "Provider<SOAPMessage>" interface.
- The endpoint implementation class has public default constructor.
- The annotation "@WebServiceProvider" is declared to mark it as Web Service.

```
@WebServiceProvider(serviceName="employeeServiceProvider")
@ServiceMode(value= Service.Mode.MESSAGE)
public class EmployeeServiceProvider implements Provider<SOAPMessage> {
    // Default public constructor
    public EmployeeServiceProvider() {}
}
```

For each client request "invoke()" method of the service endpoint is called; and this is the entry point to the web service endpoint. It receives the client request; processes it; sends the response back to the invoking client. Listing 9-6 demonstrates the Provider-based Web service implementation.

Listing 9-6: Provider-based web service implementation class

```
// EmployeeServiceProvider.java
package com.learning.ws.jaxws;

import org.w3c.dom.Element;
import org.w3c.dom.NodeList;
import javax.xml.soap.*;
import javax.xml.ws.Provider;
import javax.xml.ws.Service;
import javax.xml.ws.ServiceMode;
import javax.xml.ws.WebServiceProvider;
import java.util.*;
import java.io.ByteArrayOutputStream;

@WebServiceProvider(serviceName="employeeServiceProvider")
@ServiceMode(value= Service.Mode.MESSAGE)
public class EmployeeServiceProvider implements Provider<SOAPMessage> {
```

```java
    // Default public constructor
    public EmployeeServiceProvider() {}

    // invoke method - this is called for each request
    public SOAPMessage invoke(SOAPMessage request) {
        SOAPMessage response = null;
        try {
            //Printing the input request message.
            ByteArrayOutputStream out = new ByteArrayOutputStream();
            request.writeTo(out);
            String requestMessage = new String(out.toByteArray());
            System.out.println("--request Message--" + requestMessage);

            SOAPBody requestBody = request.getSOAPBody();
            Iterator iterator = requestBody.getChildElements();
            SOAPBodyElement bodyElement = (SOAPBodyElement)
                            iterator.next();
            String employeeId = null;
            if(requestBody.getElementName().
                    getLocalName().equals("Body")) {
                for(Element result : getElements(bodyElement.
                getElementsByTagName("employeeId"))) {
                    employeeId = getNamedElement(result,
                    "employeeId").getTextContent();
                    System.out.println(" employeeId -" + employeeId);
                }
            }

            // Implement your logic here based on input data received.
            MessageFactory mf = MessageFactory.newInstance();
            SOAPFactory sf = SOAPFactory.newInstance();
            if(employeeId != null &&
                employeeId.equalsIgnoreCase("12345678")) {
                // Creating the response message
                response = mf.createMessage();
                SOAPBody respBody = response.getSOAPBody();
                SOAPElement responseElement =
                    respBody.addChildElement("getEmployeeResponse");
                SOAPElement firstNameContent =
                    responseElement.addChildElement("firstName");
                firstNameContent.setValue("John");
                SOAPElement lastNameContent =
                responseElement.addChildElement("lastName");
                lastNameContent.setValue("Smith");
                response.saveChanges();
            }

            // Printing the output response message.
            ByteArrayOutputStream out1 = new ByteArrayOutputStream();
            response.writeTo(out1);
            String responseMessage = new String(out1.toByteArray());
            System.out.println("- Response Message -" +
                            responseMessage);
            return response;
        } catch(Exception ex) {
            ex.printStackTrace();
        }
```

```
        return response;
    }

    // Utility method used for SOAP message processing
    private static List<Element> getElements(NodeList nodes) {
    List<Element> result = new ArrayList<Element>(nodes.getLength());
    for(int i = 0; i < nodes.getLength(); i++) {
        Node node = (Node) nodes.item(i);
        if(node instanceof Element) {
                result.add((Element)node);
            }
        }
        return result;
    }

    // Utility method used for SOAP message processing
    private static Element getNamedElement(Element element,
    String name) {
        if(!element.getNodeName().equals(name))
            throw new IllegalArgumentException("Expected " + name +
                ",but got " + element.getNodeName());
        return element;
        }
}
```

Step 2: Create a web.xml File

Re-use the previously created web.xml file.

Step 3: Create a CXF Configuration File

Re-use the previously created "applicationContext-jaxws.xml" file. Add the below provided endpoint configuration.

```
<jaxws:endpoint id="employeeServiceProvider"
        implementor="com.learning.ws.jaxws.EmployeeServiceProvider"
        address="/employeeServiceProvider"/>
```

Step 4: Create a war File and Deploy it in Tomcat Server

1. Build a war file using Ant or any other build tool. Make sure the following files are packaged correctly in war file.

    a. Service endpoint implementation class
    b. Any utility classes used for data access etc.
    c. web.xml file
    d. CXF configuration file (applicationContext-jaxws.xml) file.

2. Deploy the war file in any servlet container.

    a. Copy the packed war into "apache-tomcat/webapps" directory
    b. Start the tomcat sever by running the "startup.bat" batch file available in "apache-tomcat/bin" directory
    c. See the server console output and logs; make sure war file is deployed without any errors.

The structure of the war file is shown in Figure 9-3.

Figure 9-3: Structure of a war file

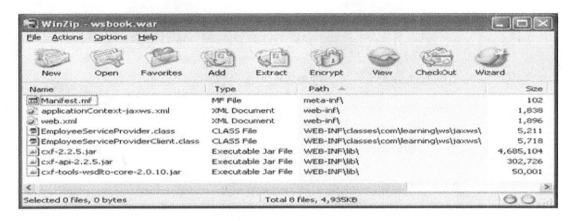

Step 5: Verify the WSDL Document

Access the WSDL file from web browser to make sure service is deployed without any errors. Use the below provided URL to view the complete WSDL.

```
http://localhost:8080/wsbook/services/employeeServiceProvider?WSDL
```

Step 6: Create a "Dispatch" Client to Invoke the Deployed Service

The dynamic client API for JAX-WS is called the *Dispatch* client (javax.xml.ws.Dispatch). The higher level JAX-WS API's hides the message communication between client and service endpoint interfaces. The conversions between XML to Java classes are hidden to the developer; but in some scenarios it is essential to work with lower level messages. The Dispatch client is an XML-oriented messaging client used to work with lower messages. It works with two message modes.

- javax.xml.ws.Service.Mode.MESSAGE – In this mode the *Dispatch* client provides complete message including <soap:Envelope/>, <soap:Header/>, and <soap:Body/>
- javax.xml.ws.Service.Mode.PAYLOAD – In this mode the *Dispatch* client provides only <soap:Body/>. The JAX-WS runtime adds the <soap:Envelope/> and <soap:Header/> to the soap message.

The below provided *Dispatch* client is used to invoke the deployed web service endpoint. The Java code is provided in Listing 9-7.

Listing 9-7: Dispatch client

```java
// EmployeeServiceProviderClient.java
package com.learning.ws.jaxws;

import org.w3c.dom.Element;
import org.w3c.dom.NodeList;
import javax.xml.namespace.QName;
import javax.xml.ws.Service;
import javax.xml.ws.Dispatch;
import javax.xml.ws.BindingProvider;
import javax.xml.ws.soap.SOAPBinding;
import javax.xml.soap.*;
```

```java
import java.net.URL;
import java.util.*;
import java.io.ByteArrayOutputStream;

public class EmployeeServiceProviderClient {

    public static void main(String args[]) throws Exception {
        try {
            EmployeeServiceProviderClient client = new
                              EmployeeServiceProviderClient();
            client.invokeProvider();
        } catch(Exception ex) {
            ex.printStackTrace();
        }
    }

    private void invokeProvider() throws Exception {
        // Service endpoint URL used to create a service instance
        URL url = new URL("http://localhost:8080/wsbook/
            services/employeeServiceProvider?wsdl");
        QName qname = new QName("http://jaxws.ws.learning.com/",
                    "employeeServiceProvider");
        Service service = Service.create(url, qname);
        QName portName = new QName("http://jaxws.ws.learning.com/",
                    "EmployeeServiceProviderPort");

        // Create a dispatch instance
        Dispatch<SOAPMessage> dispatch = service.createDispatch(
            portName,SOAPMessage.class, Service.Mode.MESSAGE);
            System.out.println("-- dispatch --" + dispatch.toString());

        // Use Dispatch as BindingProvider
        BindingProvider bp = (BindingProvider) dispatch;

        // create a request message
        MessageFactory factory = ((SOAPBinding)
        bp.getBinding()).getMessageFactory();
        SOAPMessage request = factory.createMessage();

        // Request message Body
        SOAPBody body = request.getSOAPBody();

        // Compose the soap:Body payload
        QName payloadName = new QName("http://localhost:8080/wsbook/
                services/employeeServiceProvider", "invoke", "ns1");
        SOAPBodyElement payload = body.addBodyElement(payloadName);
        SOAPElement message = payload.addChildElement("employeeId");
        message.addTextNode("12345678");

        // invoke the service endpoint.
        SOAPMessage replyMessage = dispatch.invoke(request);

        // Printing the response message on the console.
        ByteArrayOutputStream out = new ByteArrayOutputStream();
        replyMessage.writeTo(out);
        String responseMessage = new String(out.toByteArray());
        System.out.println("-- reply Message --" + responseMessage);
```

```java
            // process the response to obtain the data.
            SOAPBody responseBody = replyMessage.getSOAPBody();
            for(Element result : getElements(responseBody.
                getElementsByTagName("getEmployeeResponse"))) {
                List<Element> resultDataChildren =
                    getElements(result.getChildNodes());
                String firstName = getNamedElement(
                resultDataChildren.get(0), "firstName").getTextContent();
                String lastName = getNamedElement(
                resultDataChildren.get(1), "lastName").getTextContent();
                System.out.println("-- firstName ---" + firstName + "—
                                    lastName ---" + lastName);
            }
        }

    private static List<Element> getElements(NodeList nodes) {
        List<Element> result = new
                ArrayList<Element>(nodes.getLength());
        for(int i = 0; i < nodes.getLength(); i++) {
            Node node = (Node) nodes.item(i);
            if(node instanceof Element) {
                result.add((Element)node);
            }
        }
        return result;
    }

    private static Element getNamedElement(Element element,
    String name) {
        if(!element.getNodeName().equals(name))
            throw new IllegalArgumentException("Expected " + name
            + ",but got " + element.getNodeName());
            return element;
        }
}
```

Examine the below provided request-and-response messages while invoking the *Provider* service endpoint. The web service request message is provided below.

```xml
<SOAP-ENV:Envelope xmlns:SOAP-
ENV="http://schemas.xmlsoap.org/soap/envelope/">
  <SOAP-ENV:Header/>
  <SOAP-ENV:Body>
    <ns1:invoke xmlns:ns1=
    "http://localhost:8080/wsbook/services/employeeServiceProvider">
      <employeeId>12345678</employeeId>
    </ns1:invoke>
  </SOAP-ENV:Body>
</SOAP-ENV:Envelope>
```

The web service response message is provided below.

```xml
<SOAP-ENV:Envelope xmlns:SOAP-
ENV="http://schemas.xmlsoap.org/soap/envelope/">
  <SOAP-ENV:Header/>
```

```
<SOAP-ENV:Body>
  <getEmployeeResponse>
     <firstName>John</firstName>
     <lastName>Smith</lastName>
  </getEmployeeResponse>
</SOAP-ENV:Body>
</SOAP-ENV:Envelope>
```

Example 4: Composite Endpoints (Single Endpoint for JAX-RS and JAX-WS)

In this approach a single service endpoint can be used for both SOAP and REST-based endpoint. A single service class is supporting both REST and SOAP-based annotations at the same time using JAX-WS, JAX-RS runtimes.

Figure 9-4: Composite endpoint

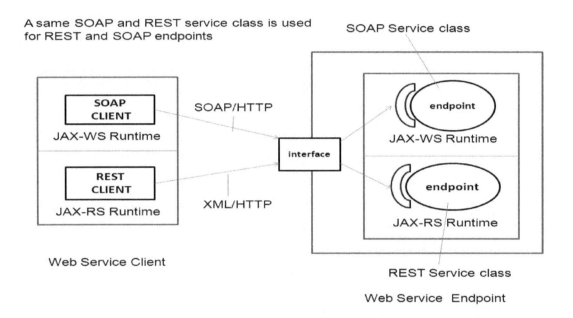

This endpoint implementation class uses the annotations declared with its service endpoint interface. An endpoint class is loaded into SOAP and REST runtime environments to service the clients. Apache-CXF supports the sharing of both REST and SOAP-based annotations for the same endpoint interface.

The steps required to develop a web service of this type are given below.

1. Create a service endpoint interface
2. Create a service implementation class
3. Create a CXF configuration file
4. Create a web.xml file
5. Create a war file and deploy into a Tomcat server
6. Verification of the deployment.
7. Write a client to invoke the deployed service

The above-specified steps are described in the following sections:

Step 1: Create a Service Endpoint Interface

Define a service endpoint interface. This interface is annotated with JAX-WS and JAX-RS-provided annotations. The "@Webservice" annotation is declared with the interface to mark it as a SOAP-based endpoint; and "@Path" annotation is declared with the class and method to identify the entry point for the REST-based endpoint.

Listing 9-8 has the service endpoint interface code.

Listing 9-8: Endpoint interface code

```java
// GradeManager.java
package com.learning.ws.jaxws.composite;

import javax.ws.rs.Path;
import javax.ws.rs.Produces;
import javax.ws.rs.GET;
import javax.ws.rs.PathParam;
import javax.jws.WebService;

@WebService
@Path("/compositegradeservice/")
@Produces("application/xml")
public interface GradeManager {
    @GET
    @Path("/grade/{grade}")
    public String getGradeSubjects(@PathParam("grade")Integer grade);
}
```

Step 2: Create a Service Implementation Class

This class implements the methods defined in the interface. This service endpoint class is annotated with "@Webservice" annotation.

The endpoint implementation class code is provided in Listing 9-9.

Listing 9-9: Endpoint implementation class

```java
// GradeManagerImpl.java
package com.learning.ws.jaxws.composite;

import com.learning.util.XMLBuilder;
import javax.jws.WebService;

@WebService(name = "GradeManagerService",
    endpointInterface="com.learning.ws.jaxws.composite.GradeManager")
public class GradeManagerImpl implements GradeManager {
    public String getGradeSubjects(Integer grade) {
        return XMLBuilder.getAllSubjects(grade);
    }
}
```

NOTE: Re-use the XMLBuilder utility class we created in JAX-RS chapter.

Step 3: Create a CXF Configuration File

Apache-CXF provides XML tags to configure the Web Service endpoint with JAX-WS and JAX-RS runtimes. Both Spring and CXF tags can co-exist in the same configuration file. Configure the SOAP-based web service endpoint using "<jaxws:endpoint/>" tag; and REST-based endpoint using "<jaxrs:serviceBeans>" tag. The Spring container loads the service implementation class into corresponding SOAP and REST runtime environments.

The use of CXF tags "<jaxws:endpoint/>", "<jaxrs:serviceBeans>" are provided below.

```xml
<?xml version="1.0" encoding="UTF-8"?>
<beans xmlns="http://www.springframework.org/schema/beans"
       xmlns:xsi="http://www.w3.org/2001/XMLSchema-instance"
       xmlns:jaxws="http://cxf.apache.org/jaxws"
       xmlns:jaxrs="http://cxf.apache.org/jaxrs"
       xmlns:cxf="http://cxf.apache.org/core"
       xsi:schemaLocation="http://www.springframework.org/schema/beans
       http://www.springframework.org/schema/beans/spring-beans.xsd
                http://cxf.apache.org/jaxws
                http://cxf.apache.org/schemas/jaxws.xsd
                http://cxf.apache.org/jaxrs
                http://cxf.apache.org/schemas/jaxrs.xsd
                http://cxf.apache.org/core
                http://cxf.apache.org/schemas/core.xsd ">

    <!-- Loads CXF modules from cxf.jar file -->
    <import resource="classpath:META-INF/cxf/cxf.xml"/>
    <import resource="classpath:META-INF/cxf/cxf-extension-soap.xml"/>
    <import resource="classpath:META-INF/cxf/cxf-servlet.xml"/>
    <import resource="classpath:META-INF/cxf/cxf-extension-jaxrs-
binding.xml"/>

    <!-- Loading the JAX-RS endpoint -->
    <jaxrs:server id="restGradeService" address="/">
        <jaxrs:serviceBeans>
            <ref bean="gradeManagerImpl"/>
        </jaxrs:serviceBeans>

        <jaxrs:features>
            <cxf:logging/>
        </jaxrs:features>
    </jaxrs:server>

    <!-- Loading the JAX-WS endpoint -->
    <jaxws:endpoint id="jaxwsGradeService"
                implementor="#gradeManagerImpl"
                address="/jaxwsGradeService"/>

    <!-- Spring bean used as a service endpoint -->
    <bean id="gradeManagerImpl"
        class="com.learning.ws.jaxws.composite.GradeManagerImpl"/>

</beans>
```

The below given configuration is used to load the service implementation class into JAX-RS runtime.

```
<jaxrs:server id="restGradeService" address="/">
    <jaxrs:serviceBeans>
        <ref bean="gradeManagerImpl"/>
    </jaxrs:serviceBeans>
</jaxrs:server>
```

The below given configuration is used to load the service implementation class into JAX-WS runtime.

```
<jaxws:endpoint id="jaxwsGradeService"
            implementor="#gradeManagerImpl"
            address="/jaxwsGradeService"/>
```

The service endpoint implementation class is loaded into the Spring container. The same class is used for both SOAP and REST runtimes.

```
<bean id="gradeManagerImpl"
    class="com.learning.ws.jaxws.composite.GradeManagerImpl"/>
```

Step 4: Create a web.xml File

Configure the spring context listener and CXF transport servlet in web.xml. The complete web.xml file is provided below.

```
<?xml version="1.0" encoding="UTF-8"?>
<web-app version="2.4" xmlns="http://java.sun.com/xml/ns/j2ee"
        xmlns:xsi="http://www.w3.org/2001/XMLSchema-instance"
        xsi:schemaLocation="http://java.sun.com/xml/ns/j2ee
        http://java.sun.com/xml/ns/j2ee/web-app_2_4.xsd">

    <display-name>wsbook Web Application</display-name>

    <listener>
        <listener-class>
            org.springframework.web.context.ContextLoaderListener
        </listener-class>
    </listener>

    <context-param>
        <param-name>contextConfigLocation</param-name>
        <param-value>
            /WEB-INF/applicationContext-composite.xml
        </param-value>
    </context-param>

    <servlet>
        <servlet-name>CXFServlet</servlet-name>
            <servlet-class>
                org.apache.cxf.transport.servlet.CXFServlet
        </servlet-class>
    </servlet>

    <servlet-mapping>
        <servlet-name>CXFServlet</servlet-name>
        <url-pattern>/services/*</url-pattern>
    </servlet-mapping>
```

```
</web-app>
```

Step 5: Create a war File and Deploy it in Tomcat Server

1. Build a war file using Ant or any other build tool. Make sure the following files are packaged correctly in war file.

   a. Service endpoint interface
   b. Service endpoint implementation class
   c. Any utility classes used for data access etc.
   d. web.xml file
   e. CXF configuration file (applicationContext-jaxws.xml) file.

2. Deploy the war file in any servlet container.

   a. Copy the packed war into "apache-tomcat/webapps" directory
   b. Start the tomcat sever by running the "startup.bat" batch file available in "apache-tomcat/bin" directory
   c. See the server console output and logs; make sure war file is deployed without any errors.

The structure of the generated war file is shown Figure 9-5.

Figure 9-5: Composite endpoint war file structure

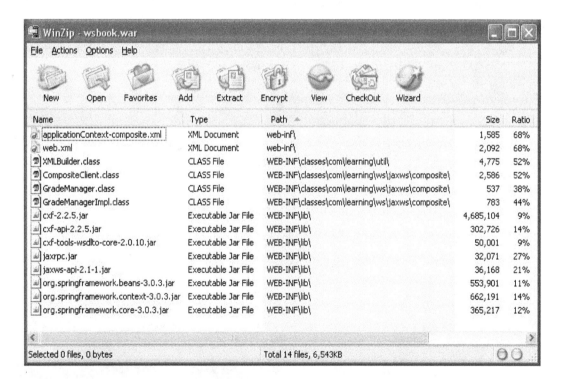

Step 6: Verification of the Deployment.

Verify the deployment to make sure the service is deployed without any errors.

The below provided URL can be used to test the SOAP service endpoint. It displays the complete WSDL.

```
http://localhost:8080/wsbook/services/jaxwsGradeService?wsdl
```

The below given URL can be used to test the REST service endpoint. It displays the XML.

```
http://localhost:8080/wsbook/services/compositegradeservice/grade/1
```

Step 7: Write a Client to Invoke the Deployed Service

There are several ways a client can invoke the deployed service endpoint. This example uses the following clients.

- How to invoke the service endpoint using JAX-WS proxy client (for SOAP endpoint)
- How to invoke the service endpoint using REST client (for REST endpoint)

CASE 1: How to Invoke the Service Endpoint Using JAX-WS Proxy Client

The below provided JAX-WS proxy client cab be used to invoke the SOAP-based service endpoint.

```java
private void invokeSOAPEndpoint() throws Exception {
    URL url = new URL("http://localhost:8080/wsbook/services/
            jaxwsGradeService?wsdl");
    QName qname = new QName("http://composite.jaxws.ws.learning.com/",
                        "GradeManagerImplService");
    Service service = Service.create(url, qname);
    GradeManager gradeManager = service.getPort(GradeManager.class);

    String subjects = gradeManager.getGradeSubjects(1);
    System.out.println("--- subjects is --- " + subjects);
}
```

CASE 2: How to Invoke the Service Endpoint Using REST Client

The below provided JAX-RS client can be used to invoke the REST-based service endpoint.

```java
private void invokeRestEndpoint() throws Exception {
    RestTemplate restTemplate = new RestTemplate();
    String result = restTemplate.getForObject("http://localhost:8080/
            wsbook/services/compositegradeservice/grade/{grade}",
            String.class, "1");
    System.out.println("--- result is ---" + result);
}
```

The complete client code is provided below.

```java
// CompositeClient.java
package com.learning.ws.jaxws.composite;

import org.springframework.web.client.RestTemplate;
import javax.xml.namespace.QName;
import javax.xml.ws.Service;
import java.net.URL;
```

```
public class CompositeClient {

    public static void main(String args[]) throws Exception {
        try {
            CompositeClient client = new CompositeClient();
            client.invokeSOAPEndpoint();
            client.invokeRestEndpoint();
        } catch(Exception ex) {
            ex.printStackTrace();
        }
    }

    private void invokeSOAPEndpoint() throws Exception {
        URL url = new URL("http://localhost:8080/wsbook/services/
            jaxwsGradeService?wsdl");
        QName qname = new
            QName("http://composite.jaxws.ws.learning.com/",
                "GradeManagerImplService");
        Service service = Service.create(url, qname);
        GradeManager gradeManager =
                service.getPort(GradeManager.class);

        String subjects = gradeManager.getGradeSubjects(1);
        System.out.println("--- subjects is --- " + subjects);

    }

    private void invokeRestEndpoint() throws Exception {
        RestTemplate restTemplate = new RestTemplate();
        String result =
            restTemplate.getForObject("http://localhost:8080/
            wsbook/services/compositegradeservice/grade/{grade}",
            String.class, "1");
        System.out.println("---- result is ---- " + result);
    }
}
```

Web Service Endpoint Design Scenarios

There are two different ways we can mark the Java class or interface as a Web Service. The one way is using "@WebService" annotation and another way is Provider-based web service implementation using "@WebServiceProder" annotation. The @WebService, @WebServiceProder annotations are mutually exclusive; so both cannot be used for the same service endpoint. This section demonstrates the various Web service endpoint design options for implementing web services.

Implementing SEI with @WebService Annotation

The only mandatory annotation required to mark a class or interface as a web service is "@WebService"; all other annotations are optional. The metadata declared with the "@WebService" annotation is mapped to the "<wsdl:service/>" element of the generated WSDL.

The steps required to develop a Web Service of this type are given below.

1. Declare @WebService annotation with the SEI and its implementation class.
2. The annotation metadata values of "serviceName", "endpointInterface" are assigned while declaring the service implementation class.

The below provided code example explains the use "@WebService" annotation:

```
@WebService
public interface EmployeeService {
    String getEmployeeAddressInfo(String  employeeId) throws Exception;
}


@WebService(endpointInterface="com.learning.ws.jaxws.EmployeeService",
            serviceName="employeeService")
public class EmployeeServiceImpl  implements  EmployeeService {
    public EmployeeServiceImpl() {}

    public String getEmployeeAddress(String employeeId)
    throws Exception {
        // Implement your logic here to get the address.
        return "3943 W.Roundabout CIR, Chandler, Arizona, 85226";
    }
}
```

Implementing SEI of type RPC/LITERAL style

This type of web service endpoint is created by declaring the "@SOAPBinding" annotation with "style = Style.RPC" and "use = Use.LITERAL". It specifies the type of message formatting the web service endpoint is using during deployment. In case of "RPC/LITERAL" style each message part is a method parameter or return value. The parameter and return values maps to the corresponding standard Java types.

The below provided code example explains the use "RPC/LITERAL" messaging style.

```
@WebService
@SOAPBinding(style = Style.RPC, use = Use.LITERAL)
public interface EmployeeService {
    String getEmployerInformation(@WebParam(name="empId")
        String employeeId, @WebParam(name="state") String state)
        throws Exception;
}
```

And its implementation is provided below.

```
@WebService(name="EmployeeService",
            serviceName="employeeService",
            endpointInterface="com.learning.ws.jaxws.EmployeeService")
public class EmployeeServiceImpl implements EmployeeService {
    public  String  getEmployerInformation(String employeeId, String
        state) throws Exception {
        return "Bank of Chandler, Chandler, Arizona, 85226";
    }
}
```

The generated WSDL is provided below. The endpoint method input parameters "empId" and "state" mapped to "<wsdl:part/>" elements in WSDL.

```
<wsdl:message name="getEmployerInformation">
    <wsdl:part name="empId" type="xsd:string" />
    <wsdl:part name="state" type="xsd:string" />
</wsdl:message>
```

Implementing SEI of type DOCUMENT/LITERAL style

This type of web service endpoint is created by declaring the "@SOAPBinding" annotation with "style = Style.DOCUMENT" and "use = Use.LITERAL". If you don't annotate the service endpoint by default it uses "DOCUMENT/LITERAL" messaging style. In case of "DOCUMENT/LITERAL" style the input parameters and return values are wrapped in a single XML element.

The below provided code example explains the use "DOCUMENT/LITERAL" messaging style.

```
@WebService
@SOAPBinding(style = Style. DOCUMENT, use = Use.LITERAL)
public interface EmployeeService {
String getEmployerInformation(@WebParam(name="empId") String employeeId,
            @WebParam(name="state") String state) throws Exception;
}
```

And its implementation is provided below.

```
@WebService(name="EmployeeService",
        serviceName="employeeService",
        endpointInterface="com.learning.ws.jaxws.EmployeeService")
public class EmployeeServiceImpl implements EmployeeService {
    public String getEmployerInformation(String employeeId, String
    state) throws Exception {
        return "Bank of Chandler, Chandler, Arizona, 85226";
    }
}
```

The generated WSDL is provided below. The endpoint method input parameters "empId" and "state" are wrapped in a "<getEmployerInformation/>" element.

```
<xs:element name="getEmployerInformation"
        type="getEmployerInformation"/>
<xs:complexType name="getEmployerInformation">
    <xs:sequence>
        <xs:element minOccurs="0" name="empId" type="xs:string" />
        <xs:element minOccurs="0" name="state" type="xs:string" />
    </xs:sequence>
</xs:complexType>

<wsdl:message name="getEmployerInformation">
    <wsdl:part element="tns:getEmployerInformation" name="parameters"/>
</wsdl:message>
```

Implementing Provider-based Web Service Endpoint

The service endpoint implementation class is declared with "@WebServiceProvider" annotation and implements "javax.xml.ws.Provider" interface to mark it as a Web Service. This type of web service endpoint is used to operate with low level XML-oriented messages. The Dispatch type of binding provider is used to invoke this service endpoint.

The below provided code example explains the use "@WebServiceProvider" annotation and "javax.xml.ws.Provider" interface:

```
@WebServiceProvider(serviceName="employeeServiceProvider")
@ServiceMode(value= Service.Mode.MESSAGE)
public class EmployeeServiceProvider implements Provider<SOAPMessage> {
    // Default public constructor
    public EmployeeServiceProvider() {}

    // invoke method - this is called for each client request
    public SOAPMessage invoke(SOAPMessage request) {
        // Implement your logic here and send the response back
    }
}
```

Web Service Client Design Scenarios

There are several ways a client can access the deployed web service endpoint. This section illustrates the various client design scenarios to access a deployed web service endpoint. The JAX-WS provides two types of client programming models to access the web service endpoint.

- Static client programming model
- Dynamic client programming model

The *static client* programming model for JAX-WS is the called the *Proxy* client. The Proxy client invokes a Web Service based on a Service Endpoint Interface (SEI); which must be provided. The JAX-WS runtime hides the complexities of XML to Java class conversions.

The *dynamic client* programming model for JAX-WS is called the *Dispatch* client. The Dispatch client is an XML messaging oriented client, the data is sent in either "PAYLOAD" or "MESSAGE" mode. Dispatch client operates with low level messages using SAAJ and JAXP API's.

Figure 9-6: Proxy and Dispatch client

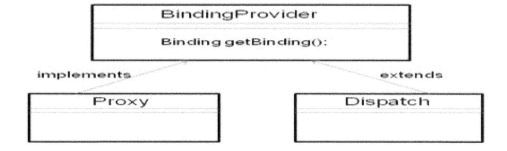

The Figure 9-6 is a class diagram shows the relationship between Proxy client, Dispatch client and Binding Provider.

Now let us see how various types of client API's are used to invoke a deployed Web Service endpoint. The following Web Service client types are covered in this section.

1. Creating a client using WSDL2Java Generated stub (stub clients)
2. Creating a client using JAX-WS Proxy
3. Creating a client using Apache-CXF provided "ProxyFactoryBean" class
4. Creating a client using JAX-WS Dispatch API
5. Creating a SOAP client to invoke the Web Service endpoint

Creating a Client using WSDL2Java Generated Stub

This type of Web Service client can also be called as static stub clients. The "WSDL2Java" utility generates client classes using WSDL files. It provides a strongly typed Java interface through which you can invoke the service endpoint operations. One major drawback with this approach is; the client classes have to be generated each and every time if there is a change in WSDL. Let us now see the following code example to demonstrate the use of stub clients. The "getPort()" methods of a service endpoint provides stub instance, by which we can invoke all service endpoint operations.

```
private static void invokeService() throws Exception {
    // Create the client stub
    EmployeeService_Service service = new EmployeeService_Service();
    EmployeeService stub = service.getEmployeeServicePort();

    // Invoking the endpoint method - getEmployeeAddress()
    String address = stub.getEmployeeAddress("823147");
}
```

Creating a Client using JAX-WS Proxy

The Proxy client can access the service endpoint interface operations during runtime without generating the static stub classes. The Proxy clients are not thread safe, thread synchronization techniques can be used to make it thread safe.

Let us now see the following code example to demonstrate the use of Proxy clients. The "Service.create()" method is used to create the service instances. The "getPort()" method of a service class instance is used to get the handle of the service endpoint interface by which we can invoke the service endpoint operations.

```
private void invokeService () throws Exception {
    // Service endpoint URL
    URL url = new URL
            ("http://localhost:8080/wsbook/services/employee?wsdl");

    // 1st argument service URI; 2nd argument is service name
    QName qname = new QName("http://jaxws.ws.learning.com/",
                                "employeeService");
    Service service = Service.create(url, qname);
```

```
EmployeeService  employeeService =
                    service.getPort(EmployeeService.class);
String address = employeeService.getEmployeeAddress("823147");
}
```

Creating a Client using CXF-Provided "JaxWsProxyFactoryBean" Class

Apache-CXF frame work provides a simple client API to invoke the deployed web services using "JaxWsProxyFactoryBean" class. This is also a Proxy type client, does not need to generate the stub classes to invoke the service endpoint operations.

The below provided code example explains the use of "JaxWsProxyFactoryBean" class to invoke the service endpoint operations.

```
private void invokeService() throws Exception {
    JaxWsProxyFactoryBean factory = new JaxWsProxyFactoryBean();
    factory.setServiceClass(EmployeeService.class);
    factory.setAddress("http://localhost:8080/wsbook/services/employee")
    EmployeeService client = (EmployeeService) factory.create();
    String data = client. getEmployeeAddress("823147");
    System.out.println("---- Server said: ----" + data);
}
```

Creating a Client using JAX-WS Dispatch API

The dynamic client API (javax.xml.ws.Dispatch) for JAX-WS is called the *Dispatch* client. The Dispatch client creates the XML messages of types "SOAPMessage" or "Source" objects; and dispatches them to the service endpoint method. The data is sent in either PAYLOAD or MESSAGE mode. The service endpoint method processes the request; and sends the response back to the client.

Let us now examine below provided client code to demonstrate the use of Dispatch client. This client uses "invoke()" method of the dispatch object to invoke the service endpoint interface.

```
private void invokeProvider() throws Exception {
    // serice endpoint URL used to create a service instance
    URL url = new URL("http://localhost:8080/wsbook/services/
        employeeServiceProvider?wsdl");
    QName qname = new QName("http://jaxws.ws.learning.com/",
                "employeeServiceProvider");
    Service service = Service.create(url, qname);

    // Port name
    QName portName = new QName("http://jaxws.ws.learning.com/",
        "EmployeeServiceProviderPort");

    // Create a dispatch instance
    Dispatch<SOAPMessage> dispatch = service.createDispatch(portName,
                SOAPMessage.class, Service.Mode.MESSAGE);

    // Use Dispatch as BindingProvider
    BindingProvider bp = (BindingProvider) dispatch;
```

```
    // create a request message
    MessageFactory factory = ((SOAPBinding)
                    bp.getBinding()).getMessageFactory();
    SOAPMessage request = factory.createMessage();

    // Request message Body
    SOAPBody body = request.getSOAPBody();

    // Compose the soap:Body payload
    QName payloadName = new QName("http://localhost:8080/wsbook/
                services/employeeServiceProvider", "invoke", "ns1");
    SOAPBodyElement payload = body.addBodyElement(payloadName);
    SOAPElement message = payload.addChildElement("employeeId");
    message.addTextNode("12345678");

    // Invoke the service endpoint.
    SOAPMessage replyMessage = dispatch.invoke(request);
}
```

Creating a SOAP Client to Invoke the Web Service Endpoint

A SOAP client can be used to invoke the deployed service endpoint. The SAAJ API is used to send messages over the network; and get the response back to the client. SAAJ provides an API to invoke the Web Service endpoint operations in a request-response messaging mode. An example implementation of the SOAP client is provided below.

The below provided XML is used for the input request (inputdata.xml).

```
<ns1:getEmployee xmlns:ns1="http://jaxws.ws.learning.com/">
    <employeeId>666666</employeeId>
</ns1:getEmployee>
```

The "call()" method of the "SOAPConnection" object can be used to send-and-receive a SOAP message from the deployed Web Service.

```
private void invokeService() throws Exception {
    SOAPConnectionFactory  soapConnectionFactory =
                SOAPConnectionFactory.newInstance();
    SOAPConnection  soapConnection =
                soapConnectionFactory.createConnection();

    // Web service endpoint URL
    URL endpoint = new URL("http://localhost:8080/wsbook/
                services/employee");

    // Creating a w3c DOM document.
    DocumentBuilderFactory factory =
                DocumentBuilderFactory.newInstance();
    factory.setNamespaceAware(true);
    DocumentBuilder builder = factory.newDocumentBuilder();
    Document w3cDocument = builder.parse("inputdata.xml");

    // Creating the request SOAP Message using SAAJ API.
    MessageFactory messageFactory = MessageFactory.newInstance(
            SOAPConstants.SOAP_1_1_PROTOCOL);
```

```
SOAPMessage message = messageFactory.createMessage();
SOAPBody soapBody = message.getSOAPBody();
soapBody.addDocument(w3cDocument);

// Calling the service endpoint to get the response.
SOAPMessage response = soapConnection.call(message, endpoint);

// Printing the response message on the console.
ByteArrayOutputStream out = new ByteArrayOutputStream();
response.writeTo(out);
String responseMessage = new String(out.toByteArray());
System.out.println("---  Message ---" + responseMessage);

// Closing the connection
soapConnection.close();
}
```

Logging SOAP Messages Using CXF

The very common requirement in web services development is, logging of the request-and-response messages. It is very essential that every web service developer should know how to debug and log SOAP messages. Apache-CXF provides several logging mechanisms to log incoming-and-outgoing messages with client and server. The "in", "out" and "fault" interceptors can be used to log the messages with client and server. "LoggingOutInterceptor" can be used to log the outbound soap messages and "LoggingInInterceptor" can be used to log the inbound soap messages.

Logging Messages at Client Side

The below provided code can be used log outbound-and-inbound log messages.

```
Client client = ClientProxy.getClient(employeeService);
client.getInInterceptors().add(new LoggingInInterceptor());
client.getOutInterceptors().add(new LoggingOutInterceptor());
```

The below provided example demonstrates the use of logging interceptors at client side.

```
private void invokeService() throws Exception {
    URL url = new URL("http://localhost:8080/
                wsbook/services/employee?wsdl");
    QName qname = new QName("http://jaxws.ws.learning.com/",
                    "employeeService");
    Service service = Service.create(url, qname);
    EmployeeService employeeService =
                service.getPort(EmployeeService.class);

    // logs the outbound and inbound soap messages.
    Client client = ClientProxy.getClient(employeeService);
    client.getInInterceptors().add(new LoggingInInterceptor());
    client.getOutInterceptors().add(new LoggingOutInterceptor());

    // Invoke your service endpoint operations
```

```
        String address = employeeService.
                    getEmployeeAddressInfo("823147");
        System.out.println("Address is: " + address);
}
```

The below provided example demonstrates the use of logging interceptors at client side using "JaxWsProxyFactoryBean" class.

```
private void invokeService() throws Exception {
    JaxWsProxyFactoryBean factory = new JaxWsProxyFactoryBean();

    // logs the outbound and inbound soap messages.
    factory.getInInterceptors().add(new LoggingInInterceptor());
    factory.getOutInterceptors().add(new LoggingOutInterceptor());
    factory.setServiceClass(EmployeeService.class);

    factory.setAddress("http://localhost:8080/wsbook/
                        services/employee");
    EmployeeService client = (EmployeeService) factory.create();

    // Invoke your service endpoint operations
    String data = client.getEmployeeAddressInfo("823147");
}
```

Logging Messages at Web Service Endpoint

Apache-CXF provides annotation based logging mechanism to log the inbound-and-outbound soap messages at the service endpoint interface. The following example demonstrates the use of logging interceptors at server side. The service endpoint implementation class is annotated to log soap messages on the server console.

```
@WebService(name="EmployeeService",
        serviceName="employeeService",
        endpointInterface="com.learning.ws.jaxws.EmployeeService")
@InInterceptors(interceptors =
"org.apache.cxf.interceptor.LoggingInInterceptor")
@OutInterceptors(interceptors =
"org.apache.cxf.interceptor.LoggingOutInterceptor")

public class EmployeeServiceImpl implements EmployeeService {
    // ...
}
```

JAX-WS Message Handler Framework

In this chapter we discussed Web service client and endpoint implementation scenarios. All the time we deal with soap messages of a client and service endpoint. Is it possible to process the outbound/inbound messages on its way from client to service endpoint? Certainly yes, the JAX-WS provides a flexible message handler framework for soap message processing. In general, handlers are used for various purposes such as logging messages, validating header information, validating the message content, and so forth.

There are two types of handlers defined in JAX-WS:

- Logical Handlers
- Protocol Handlers

Logical handlers are protocol independent; works only with message payloads and message context properties. Logical Handlers are the handlers that implements "javax.xml.ws.handler.LogicalHandler" interface. Logical Handlers cannot change the protocol specific information like <header/>. It can change only the actual payload (body) of the message.

Protocol handlers are specific to a particular protocol; and works with entire protocol message and message context properties. Protocol Handlers are the handlers that implement "javax.xml.ws.handler.Handler" interface or any protocol specific interface that is derived from "javax.xml.ws.handler.Handler" interface. Protocol handlers can alter full message including the <header/> element.

The Figure 9-7 shows the Handler class hierarchy. The handler interfaces "LogicalHandler" and "SOAPHandler" extends the "Handler" interface. These handlers has three life cycle methods "handleMessage()", "handleFault()" and "close()" which will be discussed in this section.

Figure 9-7: Handler class hierarchy

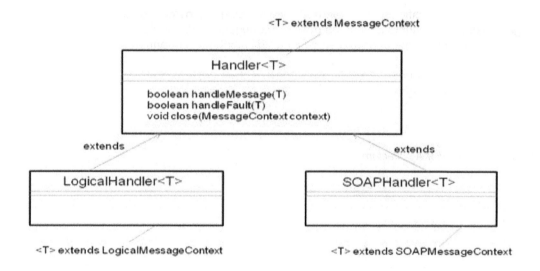

The below provided code explains the use of "SAOPHandler" interface using soap message context.

```
public class ValidationHandler implements SOAPHandler<SOAPMessageContext>
{
    // Life cycle methods to be added.
}
```

These message handlers can be attached to the client as well as the service endpoint. It is possible to add more than one message handler called as "handler chain". These handlers are executed for outbound-and-inbound messages in a specific order. The complete message context is available in handlers for processing. The Figure 9-8 shows the use of protocol handler chain between client and service endpoint.

Figure 9-8: Protocol handler chain

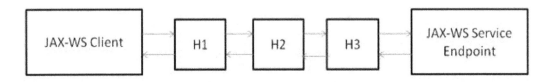

If the Logical handlers are included in a handler chain along with Protocol handlers, all logical handlers will be executed first followed by protocol handlers. The Figure 9-9 shows the use of logical handlers and protocol handlers in a handler chain between client and service endpoint.

Figure 9-9: Handler chain ordering – "L" and "H" are used for Logical and Protocol handlers.

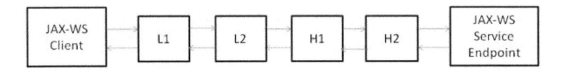

This handler chain can be configured programmatically or using deployment descriptors. JAX-WS provided "@HandlerChain" annotation can be used for configuring the handler chains. The below provided service endpoint interface is annotated using "@HandlerChain" annotation.

```
@HandlerChain(file="http://localhost:8080/wsbook/demo/handlerchain.xml")
public interface EmployeeService {
    Employee getEmployee(String employeeId) throws Exception;
}
```

Figure 9-10: JAX-WS Handler Architecture

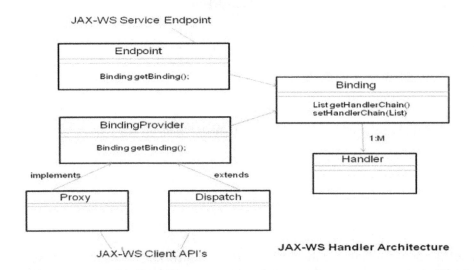

The inbound messages are processed by the handlers prior to the binding provider (Proxy or Dispatch) processing; and outbound messages are processed after the binding provider processing. The JAX-WS handler architecture is shown in Figure 9-10

JAX-WS Message Handler Framework

SOAP Handler Life Cycle Management

The JAX-WS runtime is responsible for handler life cycle management. Also JAX-WS runtime is responsible for creation of the handler instances as specified in deployment descriptors, injecting any dependent resources, invocation of the container specific callback methods like "postConstruct()" and "postDestroy()". For each client request it invokes the life cycle methods of a handler class for outbound-and-inbound messages. There are three methods each protocol message handler class has to implement, they are "handleMessage()", "handleFault()" and "close()". The message context is passed to all the available handlers in a handler chain. The order of execution of the life cycle methods of a handler class is listed below.

- The life cycle of soap handler begins, when JAX-WS runtime start the creation of a handler instance. The default constructor of the handler class is first invoked.
- JAX-WS runtime injects any context specific resources using "javax.annotation.Resource".
- JAX-WS runtime invokes a method that is annotated with "@PostConstruct()" annotation, if exists any. This method is used to perform required initialization.
- The handler instance will be created and it is in ready state.
- The handler instance processes the inbound-and-outbound messages using "handleMessage()", "handleFault()" and "close()" methods. It ends the handler life cycle.
- JAX-WS runtime invokes a method that is annotated with "@PreDestroy()" annotation, if there is any. This method is used to perform cleanup activities like releasing the resources the process is holding.
- Finally the handler instance is available for garbage collection.

Figure 9-11: Handler life cycle

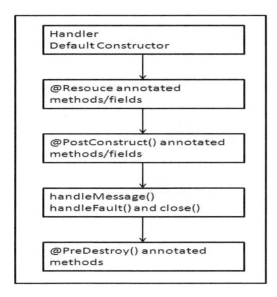

The order of execution of the handler life cycle methods are shown in Figure 9-11.

Let us now take the following example to demonstrate the above-specified steps.

```
public class ValidationHandler implements
SOAPHandler<SOAPMessageContext> {
    @Resource
    private WebServiceContext context;
```

```java
    // Default constructor.
    public ValidationHandler() {
        System.out.println("--- Default Constructor ---");
    }

    // callback method - invoked by the container.
    @PostConstruct
    private void init() {
        System.out.println("--- PostConstruct - Perform required
        initialization ---");
    }

    // process outbound and inbound messages
    public boolean handleMessage(SOAPMessageContext context) {
        return true;
    }

    // handle faults
    public boolean handleFault(SOAPMessageContext context) {
        return true;
    }

    // close
    public void close(MessageContext context) {
        System.out.println("--- ValidationHandler : close() ---");
    }

    @PreDestroy
    private void doCleanUp() {
        System.out.println("-- ValidationHandler - PreDestroy -
        doCleanUp() ---");
    }

    @Override
    public Set<QName> getHeaders() {
        return null;
    }
}
```

The first step is to create a handler class by implementing "SOAPHandler" interface.

```java
public class ValidationHandler implements
SOAPHandler<SOAPMessageContext> {
}
```

The following code injects any context specific resources using "javax.annotation.Resource" annotation.

```java
@Resource
private WebServiceContext context;
```

The following code create a default public constructor of the handler class

```java
public ValidationHandler() {
    System.out.println("--- Default Constructor ---");
}
```

The below provided "init()" method is annotated with "@PostConstruct" annotation. This method performs the required initializations if any.

```
@PostConstruct
private void init() {
    System.out.println("---- PostConstruct - Perform required
                initialization ----");
}
```

Implementing "handleMessage()" Method: This method is called for the normal processing of outbound-and-inbound messages. The entire soap message is available in this method to perform any application specific processing like validations, logging, encrypting data, decrypting the data, etc. After processing, this method can return any of the following:

- Return "true" indicates continue the processing with next available handler in a handler chain.
- Return "false" indicates stop further processing of available handlers in handler chain, so message not passed to the service endpoint.
- Throws a "RuntimeException"; indicates terminates the further processing of handler chain; start executing the "handleFault()" method of the current handler.

The method signature of the "handleMessage" is provided below:

```
public boolean handleMessage(SOAPMessageContext context) {
    return true;
}
```

Implementing "handleFault()" Method: This method is called for the fault message processing of outbound-and-inbound messages. The entire soap message is available in this method to capture the faults. After processing of the message this method can return any of the following:

- Return "true" indicates continue the processing with next available handler in a handler chain.
- Return "false" indicates stop further processing of available handler faults in a handler chain.
- Throws a "RuntimeException"; indicates terminates the further processing fault message in chain; and "close()" method of the each previously invoked handler in the chain is called.

The method signature of the "handleFault" is provided below:

```
public boolean handleFault(SOAPMessageContext context) {
    return true;
}
```

Implementing "close()" Method: This method concludes the message exchange between client and service endpoint. This method is called just before dispatching the final message to the service endpoint.

The method signature of the "close()" is provided below:

```
public void close(MessageContext context) {
    System.out.println("--- ValidationHandler : close() ---");
}
```

The below provided "doCleanUp()" method is used to perform cleanup activities if any. This callback method is invoked by the JAX-WS runtime.

```
@PreDestroy
private void doCleanUp() {
    System.out.println("---- ValidationHandler - PreDestroy -
                                doCleanUp() ----");
}
```

Example 5: SOAP Handler Example

The example handler provided below intercepts the inbound message; and validates the value of the employee id; if client sends any invalid input value of the employee id (example zero); handler class replaces the zero with default value before dispatching the message to the service endpoint. It validates only inbound messages to the web service endpoint; and outbound message are delivered to the client without any validations.

The "ValidationHandler" handler class implements "SOAPHandler" which intern extends "javax.xml.ws.handler.Handler" class. The "handleMessage()" method of the handler class receives the outbound-and-inbound messages; the SAAJ API is used for message processing.

The Web Service client sends the below provided inbound message to the service endpoint.

```
<soap:Envelope xmlns:soap="http://schemas.xmlsoap.org/soap/envelope/">
    <soap:Header/>
    <soap:Body>
        <ns1:getEmployee xmlns:ns1="http://jaxws.ws.learning.com/">
            <employeeId>000000</employeeId>
        </ns1:getEmployee>
    </soap:Body>
</soap:Envelope>
```

The "ValidationHandler" class intercepts the above message; reads the value of "<employeeId/>" element; If it has any invalid value of employee id; it replaces the employee id with default value before passing the message to the service endpoint.

The outbound message from the service endpoint is provided below:

```
<soap:Envelope xmlns:soap="http://schemas.xmlsoap.org/soap/envelope/">
    <soap:Body>
    <ns1:getEmployeeResponse xmlns:ns1="http://jaxws.ws.learning.com/">
        <return>
            <employeeId>99999</employeeId>
            <firstName>XXXXX</firstName>
            <lastName>XXXXX</lastName>
        </return>
    </ns1:getEmployeeResponse>
    </soap:Body>
</soap:Envelope>
```

Let us now examine the code example of the "ValideationHandler" class to have better understanding.

The "MESSAGE_OUTBOUND_PROPERTY" of the message context is used to determine the direction of the message at service endpoint. Its value is "true" for outbound messages, "false" for inbound messages. This flag is used to process only inbound messages.

```
Boolean isRequest = (Boolean)
context.get(MessageContext.MESSAGE_OUTBOUND_PROPERTY);
```

The following code receives the complete soap message from "SOAPMessageContext"; prints the message on the console.

```
SOAPMessage message = context.getMessage();
ByteArrayOutputStream out = new ByteArrayOutputStream();
message.writeTo(out);
String responseMessage = new String(out.toByteArray());
System.out.println("--- ValidationHandler entire message ---" +
responseMessage);
```

The following code extracts the message payload; iterates over the elements of the soap message body to obtain the value of employee id.

```
SOAPBody requestBody = message.getSOAPBody();
Iterator iterator = requestBody.getChildElements();
SOAPBodyElement bodyElement = (SOAPBodyElement) iterator.next();
```

The complete soap message handler code is shown in Listing 9-10. After completing the message processing the "handleMessage()" method returns "true"; so the handler will continue the message processing in a handler chain or dispatches the message to service endpoint.

Listing 9-10: SOAP message handler class

```
// ValidationHandler.java
package com.learning.ws.jaxws;

import org.w3c.dom.Element;
import org.w3c.dom.NodeList;
import javax.xml.ws.handler.soap.SOAPMessageContext;
import javax.xml.ws.handler.soap.SOAPHandler;
import javax.xml.ws.handler.MessageContext;
import javax.xml.soap.SOAPMessage;
import javax.xml.soap.SOAPBody;
import javax.xml.soap.SOAPBodyElement;
import javax.xml.soap.Node;
import javax.xml.namespace.QName;
import java.io.ByteArrayOutputStream;
import java.util.*;

public class ValidationHandler implements
                SOAPHandler<SOAPMessageContext> {

    public ValidationHandler() {}

    @Override
    public boolean handleMessage(SOAPMessageContext context) {
        /* message direction, true for outbound messages,
        false for inbound. */
        Boolean isRequest = (Boolean)
            context.get(MessageContext.MESSAGE_OUTBOUND_PROPERTY);

        if(!isRequest) {
            try {
```

```java
            SOAPMessage message =  context.getMessage();
            // Printing the message on the console.
            ByteArrayOutputStream out = new
                    ByteArrayOutputStream();
            message.writeTo(out);
            String inboundMessage = new String(out.toByteArray());
            System.out.println("-- complete inbound message --" +
            inboundMessage);

            // gets the SOAP body
            SOAPBody requestBody = message.getSOAPBody();
            Iterator iterator = requestBody.getChildElements();
            SOAPBodyElement bodyElement = (SOAPBodyElement)
                                        iterator.next();

            /* Iterates over the child elements to
            obtain the required value */
            String elementName = bodyElement.getNodeName();
            if(elementName != null &&
                elementName.contains("ns1:getEmployee")) {
                for(Element result : getElements(bodyElement.
                        getElementsByTagName("employeeId"))) {
                    //Obtain the employee id from inbound message
                    String employeeId =
                    getNamedElement(result,"employeeId").
                                        getTextContent();
                    Integer empId = new Integer(employeeId);

                    // Setting the default value
                    if(empId == 0) {
                        result.setTextContent("99999");
                    }
                }
            }
        } catch(Exception ex) {
            ex.printStackTrace();
        }
    }

// continue with handler chain
return true;
}

@Override
public boolean handleFault(SOAPMessageContext context) {
    return true;
}

@Override
public void close(MessageContext context) {
}

@Override
public Set<QName> getHeaders() {
    return null;
}
```

```
    // Utility method used for message processing
    private static List<Element> getElements(NodeList nodes) {
        List<Element> result = new
                ArrayList<Element>(nodes.getLength());
        for(int i = 0; i < nodes.getLength(); i++) {
            Node node = (Node) nodes.item(i);
            if(node instanceof Element) {
                result.add((Element)node);
            }
        }
        return result;
    }

    // Utility method used for message processing
    private static Element getNamedElement(Element element,String name){
    if(!element.getNodeName().equals(name))
        throw new IllegalArgumentException("Expected " + name +   ",but
        received " + element.getNodeName());
        return element;
    }
}
```

Example 6: SOAP Handler Chain Example

The Figure 9-12 shows the use of "LogHandler" and "ValidationHandler" in a handler chain. The configured handlers in a handler chain intercept the soap messages between the client and service endpoint.

Figure 9-12: Message Handler Chain

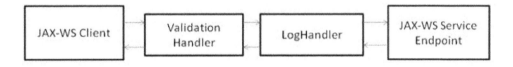

The steps required to develop a Web service using handlers are given below:

1. Create a "ValidationHandler.java" class
2. Create a "LogHandler.java" class
3. Create Web service endpoint interface and its implementation class
4. Configure handlers with Web Service endpoint
5. Create a Web Service client

The above-specified steps are described in the following sections:

Step 1: Create a ValidationHandler.java Class

Reuse the validation handler class created in our previous example. It pre-validates the input data.

Step 2: Create a LogHandler.java Class

The below-provided "LogHandler" class logs the incoming-and-outgoing messages. We can redirect the generated log messages to a log file using standard logging framework like Log4j.

The complete "LogHandler" class code is provided in Listing 9-11

Listing 9-11: SOAP message handler class used to log messages

```java
// LogHandler.java
package com.learning.ws.jaxws;

import java.util.Set;
import java.io.ByteArrayOutputStream;
import javax.xml.namespace.QName;
import javax.xml.ws.handler.MessageContext;
import javax.xml.ws.handler.soap.SOAPHandler;
import javax.xml.ws.handler.soap.SOAPMessageContext;
import javax.xml.soap.SOAPMessage;

public class LogHandler implements SOAPHandler<SOAPMessageContext> {
    public LogHandler() {}

    @Override
    public boolean handleMessage(SOAPMessageContext context) {
        try {
            SOAPMessage message = context.getMessage();
            // Printing the message on the console.
            ByteArrayOutputStream out = new ByteArrayOutputStream();
            message.writeTo(out);
            String responseMessage = new String(out.toByteArray());
            System.out.println("--- LogHandler entire message
                    --" + responseMessage);
        } catch(Exception ex) {
            ex.printStackTrace();
        }
        // continue other handler chain
        return true;
    }

    @Override
    public boolean handleFault(SOAPMessageContext context) {
            return true;
    }

    @Override
    public void close(MessageContext context) {}

    @Override
    public Set<QName> getHeaders() {
        System.out.println("--- LogHandler : getHeaders() ---");
        return null;
    }
}
```

Step 3: Create Web Service Endpoint Interface and its Implementation Class

The web service endpoint interface and its implementation are provided in Listing 9-12.

Listing 9-12: Service endpoint interface and its implementation

```java
// EmployeeService.java
```

```
package com.learning.ws.jaxws;

@WebService
public interface EmployeeService {
    @WebMethod(operationName="getEmployee")
    Employee getEmployee(@WebParam (name="employeeId") String
    employeeId) throws EmployeeFault;
}
```

The "getEmployee()" method of the web service endpoint receives the input from the client; and
sends the response back.

```
@WebService(name="EmployeeService",
        serviceName="employeeService",
        endpointInterface="com.learning.ws.jaxws.EmployeeService")
public class EmployeeServiceImpl implements EmployeeService {
    public Employee getEmployee(String employeeId) throws EmployeeFault{
        if(employeeId == null) {
            throw new EmployeeFault("Invalid input received");
        }
        Employee emp = new Employee();
        emp.setEmployeeId(employeeId);
        if("99999".equalsIgnoreCase(employeeId)) {
            emp.setFirstName("XXXXX");
            emp.setLastName("XXXXX");
        } else {
            /* Build your logic here to get the employee details. Using
            hard coded values */
            emp.setFirstName("John");
            emp.setLastNamc("Smith");
        }
        return emp;
    }
}
```

Step 4: Configure Handlers with Web Service Endpoint

There is no special server side configurations needed to attach message handlers to web service
endpoint. Apache-CXF framework provides "<jaxws:handlers/>" tag; which can used to configure
message handlers with any service endpoint. The complete handler configuration is provided
below:

```
<jaxws:endpoint id="employee"
    implementor="com.learning.ws.jaxws.EmployeeServiceImpl"
    address="/employee">
    <jaxws:handlers>
        <bean class="com.learning.ws.jaxws.ValidationHandler"/>
        <bean class="com.learning.ws.jaxws.LogHandler"/>
    </jaxws:handlers>
</jaxws:endpoint>
```

Step 5: Create a Web Service Client

The following Proxy client can be used to invoke the web service endpoint. It invokes the service
endpoint through configured intermediate message handlers. Listing 9-13 has a web service client
code used to invoke the web service endpoint.

Listing 9-13: Web service client code.

```java
// HandlerClient.java
package com.learning.ws.jaxws;

public class HandlerClient {

    public static void main(String args[]) throws Exception {
        try {
        HandlerClient client = new HandlerClient();
            client.invokeService();
        } catch(Exception ex) {
            ex.printStackTrace();
        }
    }

    private void invokeService() throws Exception {
        URL url = new
            URL("http://localhost:8080/wsbook/services/employee?wsdl");
        QName qname = new QName("http://jaxws.ws.learning.com/",
                "employeeService");
        Service service = Service.create(url, qname);
        EmployeeService employeeService =
            service.getPort(EmployeeService.class);
        Employee emp = employeeService.getEmployee("000000");
        System.out.println("Employee Id:" + emp.getEmployeeId() +
                    "-- First Name --" + emp.getFirstName() +
                    "-- Last Name --" + emp.getLastName());
    }
}
```

Server Side - Configuring SOAP Handler Chain Using Apache-CXF

There are two types of handler's client and server. It is possible to configure a handler chain to the client as well as server. There is no limit on the number handlers that can be used in a handler chain. The Figure 9-13 explains the use of handlers at client and server (service endpoint). The terminology outbound-and-inbound is used with respect to the client and service endpoint. The notation used for client side handlers is "CH1", "CH2" and server side handlers is "SH1" and "SH2". The client side handlers "CH1" and "CH2" intercept the outbound messages from the client; inbound messages it receives as a service response. Similarly server side handlers "SH1" and "SH2" intercept the inbound messages received from the client; sends the outbound response from service endpoint. The message path between client and service endpoint is shown Figure 9-13.

Figure 9-13: Using Handler Chain with client and service endpoint

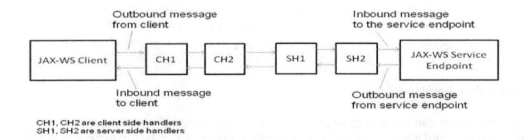

CH1, CH2 are client side handlers
SH1, SH2 are server side handlers

The below provided example demonstrates the use of server side handlers. Apache-CXF framework provided "<jaxws:handlers/>" tag can be used to configure message handlers to any service endpoint.

The complete configuration is provided below:

```xml
<?xml version="1.0" encoding="UTF-8"?>
<beans xmlns="http://www.springframework.org/schema/beans"
    xmlns:xsi="http://www.w3.org/2001/XMLSchema-instance"
    xmlns:jaxws="http://cxf.apache.org/jaxws"
    xmlns:cxf="http://cxf.apache.org/core"
    xsi:schemaLocation="http://www.springframework.org/schema/beans
    http://www.springframework.org/schema/beans/spring-beans.xsd
    http://cxf.apache.org/jaxws
    http://cxf.apache.org/schemas/jaxws.xsd
    http://cxf.apache.org/core
    http://cxf.apache.org/schemas/core.xsd ">

    <!-- Loads CXF modules from cxf.jar file -->
    <import resource="classpath:META-INF/cxf/cxf.xml"/>
    <import resource="classpath:META-INF/cxf/cxf-extension-soap.xml"/>
    <import resource="classpath:META-INF/cxf/cxf-servlet.xml"/>
    <import resource="classpath:META-INF/cxf/cxf-extension-jaxrs-
        binding.xml"/>

    <jaxws:endpoint id="employee"
            implementor="com.learning.ws.jaxws.EmployeeServiceImpl"
            address="/employee">
        <jaxws:handlers>
            <bean class="com.learning.ws.jaxws.ValidationHandler"/>
            <bean class="com.learning.ws.jaxws.LogHandler"/>
        </jaxws:handlers>
    </jaxws:endpoint>
</beans>
```

Client Side - Configuring SOAP Handler Chain Using Apache-CXF

Apache-CXF framework provides "<jaxws:handlers/>" tag; which can used to configure message handlers to any web service client. This is similar to the one used for service endpoint.

The complete configuration is provided below:

```xml
<?xml version="1.0" encoding="UTF-8"?>
<beans xmlns="http://www.springframework.org/schema/beans"
    xmlns:xsi="http://www.w3.org/2001/XMLSchema-instance"
    xmlns:jaxws="http://cxf.apache.org/jaxws"
    xmlns:cxf="http://cxf.apache.org/core"
    xsi:schemaLocation="http://www.springframework.org/schema/beans
    http://www.springframework.org/schema/beans/spring-beans.xsd
    http://cxf.apache.org/jaxws
    http://cxf.apache.org/schemas/jaxws.xsd
    http://cxf.apache.org/core
    http://cxf.apache.org/schemas/core.xsd ">

    <!-- Loads CXF modules from cxf.jar file -->
```

```xml
<import resource="classpath:META-INF/cxf/cxf.xml"/>
<import resource="classpath:META-INF/cxf/cxf-extension-soap.xml"/>
<import resource="classpath:META-INF/cxf/cxf-servlet.xml"/>
<import resource="classpath:META-INF/cxf/cxf-extension-jaxrs-
binding.xml"/>

<jaxws:client id="springHandlerClient"
     serviceClass="com.learning.ws.jaxws.EmployeeService"
     address="http://localhost:8080/wsbook/services/employee">
    <jaxws:handlers>
        <bean class="com.learning.ws.jaxws.ValidationHandler"/>
        <bean class="com.learning.ws.jaxws.LogHandler"/>
    </jaxws:handlers>
</jaxws:client>
</beans>
```

Listing 9-14 has a web service client program which is used to invoke the service endpoint. View the output on console to track the message path between web service client and endpoint.

Listing 9-14: Web service client code.

```java
public class CXFClientHandler {
    private CXFClientHandler() { }

    public static void main(String args[]) throws Exception {
        ClassPathXmlApplicationContext context
            = new ClassPathXmlApplicationContext(new String[]
                    {"applicationContext-client.xml"});

        EmployeeService employeeService = (EmployeeService)
                    context.getBean("springHandlerClient");

        Employee emp = employeeService.getEmployee("000000");
        System.out.println("Employee Id:" + emp.getEmployeeId() +
                "-- First Name --" + emp.getFirstName() +
                "-- Last Name --" + emp.getLastName());
        System.exit(0);
    }
}
```

Test Yourself - Objective Type Questions

1. How do you intercept a SOAP message between client and service endpoint?
    a) Using Handlers
    b) Using @WebServiceProvider annotation
    c) Using @WebService annotation
    d) Using @SOAPMessageHandlers annotation
    e) Using JAX-WS proxy

2. What are the valid message modes a *Dispatch* client can use for sending the messages?
    a) Envelope and Body
    b) Envelope, Header and Body
    c) MESSAGE and PAYLOAD

d) DOCUMENT and RPC

e) None are valid

3. Which of the below given statements are valid w.r.t. Dynamic client API using Dispatcher client and Provider-based service implementation.

a) When using the PAYLOAD mode, the dispatch client is only responsible for providing the contents of the <soap:Body/> and JAX-WS runtime adds the <soap:Envelope/> and <soap:Header/> elements.

b) The service endpoint implementation class is declared with @WebService annotation.

c) The service endpoint implementation class is declared with @WebServiceProvider annotation.

d) When using the PAYLOAD mode, the dispatch client is responsible for providing the entire soap envelope including <soap:Envelope/>, <soap:Header/> and <soap:Body/> elements.

e) All are valid statements

Answers to Test Yourself

1. The correct answer is A. The mechanism used to intercept soap messages is soap message Handlers.

2. The correct answer is C. The valid message modes are PAYLOAD and MESSAGE.

3. The correct answer is A and C. The answer D is invalid because it the definition of MESSAGE mode not PAYLOAD mode. In case of MESSAGE mode the JAX-WS runtime does not add any elements.

Chapter 10. Apache-Axis2

Apache-Axis2 is another popular open-source framework can be used for developing fully featured JAX-WS compatible Web Services. Axis2 is a WSDL/SOAP engine; it is the successor to its "Axis1" web services framework. Axis2 is completely rewritten and redesigned from its previous Axis1 Web Services framework. Axis2 implementation is available for "Java" and "C". This chapter will address the Java-based web services development using Apache-Axis2 framework.

In this chapter will discuss the following topics:

- Web services development using Apache-Axis2 framework.
- Setting-up the Axis2 environment
- The Build and Deployment instructions for Axis2
- The tools and utilities used for Axis2 code generation.
- Writing custom modules using Axis2
- How to use SOAP message handlers using Axis2
- The Axis2 supported client and service endpoint design scenarios.
- Comparison between Axis2 and CXF web service frameworks
- Comparison between SOAP and Restful web services

Axis2 Advantages

- It provides support for both SOAP and REST-based web service endpoints.
- It provides support for multiple languages, Java and C.
- It provides support for static and dynamic clients.
- It provides support for various data bindings such as *adb*, *xmlbeans*, *jibx*, and *jaxbri* so forth.
- It provides support for JAX-WS annotations.
- It provides in-built support for XML based service endpoints.
- Axis2 provides various command line utilities, Ant and Maven-based tools for code generation.
- It provides support for building custom modules. These modules can easily integrate with service endpoints.
- The new Axis2 architecture is modular-based; some extent it eliminates the class loading conflicts that occurred due to the incompatibility between the different versions of the jar files.

Axis2 Disadvantages

- Not backwardly compatible with their older versions.
- There is no standard approach defined for migrating from Axis1 to Axis2. Axis2 is completely redesigned, so it requires code rewrite.

Prerequisite and Setting-up the Axis2 Environment

Before attempting for Web service development make sure Axis2 environment is ready to deploy your Web services. Axis2 framework provides a web module (war file) which can be deployed in any web container. It is a web application which provides the admin functionality for developer to view, deploy and un-deploy the web services. The Axis2 environment setup instructions with Tomcat server are given below:

1. Download "axis2.war" file from apache site.
2. Deploy "axis2.war" into Tomcat container: Copy "axis.war" into "apache-tomcat/webapps" directory and start the server using "startup.bat".
3. Invoke the home page of the console using "http://localhost:8080/axis2/". The home page provides various links for navigation. The Axis2 environment is ready for deployment.

The primary concept used in Axis2 packaging is "aar" file. Axis2 expects service archive file to be packaged with ".aar" extension for deployment. The "aar" file contains service classes, deployment descriptors, and its dependent jar files. The structure of "aar" is shown in Figure 10-1.

Figure 10-1: AAR file structure

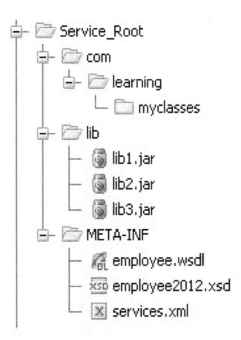

1. Package the "services.xml" file, service WSDL file; and other XSD files inside the "/META-INF" directory.
2. Package all dependent jar files inside "/lib" directory
3. The Web service endpoint classes follow the standard Java package notation as shown in the Figure 10-1.

Once the environment setup is ready, we can start web services development. The following sections illustrate the web service development methodologies in greater detail.

Prerequisite and Setting-up the Axis2 Environment

Development Methodologies

There are two different ways we can develop a Web service endpoint using Axis2.

- Develop Web service endpoints using plain Java classes (also called POJO's).
- Write a WSDL document first; generate Java classes using Axis2 framework provided tools.

The steps required to develop a web service using first approach is provided below.

Example 1: Java First Development (Also Called Code First)

In this approach, start the Web service development with Java classes. The development, debugging and deployment of this type of Web service is simple and easy. The steps required to develop a web service of this type are given below:

1. Create a service endpoint interface
2. Create a service implementation class
3. Create a "services.xml" configuration file
4. Create a service archive (aar) file and deploy it in Tomcat server
5. Verification of deployed service endpoint
6. Write a client to invoke the deployed service endpoint

The above-specified steps are described in the following sections:

Step 1: Create a Service Endpoint Interface

In this example, take a simple Java class as service endpoint without any annotations. The service endpoint interface "EmployeeService" has two methods. The endpoint interface is provided in Listing 10-1.

Listing 10-1: POJO-based web service endpoint interface

```java
// EmployeeService.java
package com.learning.ws.axis2;

public interface EmployeeService {
    Employee getEmployee(String employeeId) throws EmployeeFault;
    String getEmployeeAddress(String employeeId) throws EmployeeFault;
}
```

Use the below provided "Employee.java" bean class for data population:

```java
// Employee.java
package com.learning.ws.jaxws;

public class Employee {
    private static final long serialVersionUID = 1121313L;
    private String employeeId;
    private String lastName;
    private String firstName;

    // Generate getters and setters for the above
}
```

The below given exception class is used for exception handling:

```java
// EmployeeFault.java
package com.learning.ws.axis2;

public class EmployeeFault extends java.lang.Exception {
    public EmployeeFault() {
        super();
    }

    public EmployeeFault(String message) {
        super(message);
    }

    public EmployeeFault(String message, Throwable cause) {
        super(message, cause);
    }
}
```

Step 2: Create a Service Implementation class

The above defined interface methods are implemented in its implementation class. The endpoint implementation class code is provided in Listing 10-2.

Listing 10-2: Web service implementation class.

```java
// EmployeeServiceImpl.java
package com.learning.ws.axis2;

public class EmployeeServiceImpl implements EmployeeService {
    public Employee getEmployee(String employeeId) throws EmployeeFault{
        Employee emp = new Employee();
        emp.setEmployeeId(employeeId);
        if("99999".equalsIgnoreCase(employeeId)) {
            emp.setFirstName("XXXXX");
            emp.setLastName("XXXXX");
        } else {
            emp.setFirstName("John");
            emp.setLastName("Smith");
        }
        return emp;
    }

    public String getEmployeeAddress(String employeeId) throws
    EmployeeFault {
        return "3943 Roundabout CIR, Chandler, Arizona, 85226";
    }
}
```

Step 3: Create a services.xml Configuration File

The "services.xml" file is an axis framework specific configuration file used for declaring the service name, service endpoint class, operations, input/return type mappings, and message receivers of the web service endpoint.

Development Methodologies

The following tags are used for defining the "in-only" and "in-out" parameters of an operation. Use the following tag for "in-only" (Read only) operations:

```
<messageReceiver mep="http://www.w3.org/2004/08/wsdl/in-only"
    class="org.apache.axis2.rpc.receivers.RPCInOnlyMessageReceiver"/>
```

The following configuration is used for "in-out" (Read-Write) operations:

```
<messageReceiver mep="http://www.w3.org/2004/08/wsdl/in-out"
        class="org.apache.axis2.rpc.receivers.RPCMessageReceiver"/>
```

The below provided XML is used for service configuration.

```
<parameter name="ServiceClass"locked="false">
    com.learning.ws.axis2.EmployeeServiceImpl
</parameter>
```

The methods of a service endpoint class have both "in" and "out" parameters, so "RPCMessageReceiver" class is used for message exchange pattern.

The complete "services.xml" file is provided below:

```
<service name="employeeService">
    <description>The axis2 employee web service</description>
    <messageReceivers>
    <messageReceiver mep="http://www.w3.org/2004/08/wsdl/in-out"
        class="org.apache.axis2.rpc.receivers.RPCMessageReceiver"/>
    </messageReceivers>
    <parameter name="ServiceClass"locked="false">
        com.learning.ws.axis2.EmployeeServiceImpl
    </parameter>
</service>
```

Step 4: Create Service Archive (aar) File and Deploy it in Tomcat Server

The structure of the generated aar file is shown Figure 10-2.

Figure 10-2: AAR file structure

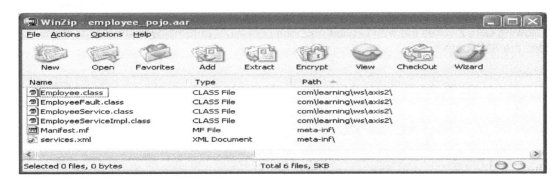

Follow the below-provided steps to deploy an "aar" file into the Tomcat container.

1. Package the Web Service endpoint and its dependent classes into an aar file. Make sure "services.xml" file is placed inside the "/META-INF" directory.
2. Make sure the "axis2.war" file is deployed in tomcat before going for aar deployment.
3. Copy the created aar file into tomcat "\apache-tomcat-6.0.28\webapps\axis2\WEB-INF\services" directory.
4. Start the tomcat using "startup.bat" file available in "apache-tomcat-6.0.28\bin" directory.
5. Verify the server console, server log files and make sure aar is deployed without any errors.

Step 5: Verification of the Deployed Service Endpoint.

After the aar file deployment, carryout the following tests to make sure the service is deployed without any errors.

The following URL provides the list of services:

```
http://localhost:8080/axis2/services/listServices
```

The following URL provides the WSDL of the deployed service:

```
http://localhost:8080/axis2/services/employeeService?wsdl
```

The following URL invokes the web service endpoint operation "getEmployee()" and provides the XML output:

```
http://localhost:8080/axis2/services/employeeService/getEmployee?employee
Id=823147
```

It provides the below given response XML:

```
<ns:getEmployeeResponse xmlns:ns="http://axis2.ws.learning.com">
    <ns:return xmlns:ax21=http://axis2.ws.learning.com/xsd
        xmlns:xsi="http://www.w3.org/2001/XMLSchema-instance"
            xsi:type="ax21:Employee">
        <ax21:employeeId>12133</ax21:employeeId>
        <ax21:firstName>John</ax21:firstName>
        <ax21:lastName>Smith</ax21:lastName>
    </ns:return>
</ns:getEmployeeResponse>
```

The following URL invokes the web service endpoint operation "getEmployeeAddress()" and provides the XML output:

```
http://localhost:8080/axis2/services/employeeService/getEmployeeAddress?e
mployeeId=823147
```

It provides the below given response XML:

```
<ns:getEmployeeAddressResponse xmlns:ns="http://axis2.ws.learning.com">
    <ns:return>
        3943 Roundabout CIR, Chandler, Arizona, 85226
    </ns:return>
</ns:getEmployeeAddressResponse>
```

Step 6: Write a Client to Invoke the Deployed Service Endpoint

Axis2-framework provided "RPCServiceClient" can be used to invoke the POJO based web service endpoint. Specify the endpoint URL of the running web service.

```
RPCServiceClient serviceClient = new RPCServiceClient();
Options options = serviceClient.getOptions();
EndpointReference targetEPR = new EndpointReference(
        "http://localhost:8080/axis2/services/employeeService");
options.setTo(targetEPR);
```

After setting the endpoint reference, use the "invokeBlocking()" method of the service client to obtain the response.

```
QName getEmployee = new QName("http://axis2.ws.learning.com",
"getEmployee");
Object[] inputParams = new Object[]{"123456"};
Class[] returnTypes = new Class[]{Employee.class};
Object[] response = serviceClient.invokeBlocking(getEmployee,
                        inputParams, returnTypes);
Employee employee = (Employee) response[0];
```

Run the below provided class to see the output. The web service client code is provided in Listing 10-3.

Listing 10-3: Web service client.

```
// Axis2Client.java
package com.learning.ws.axis2;

import javax.xml.namespace.QName;
import org.apache.axis2.addressing.EndpointReference;
import org.apache.axis2.client.Options;
import org.apache.axis2.rpc.client.RPCServiceClient;

public class Axis2Client {
    public static void main(String args[]) throws java.lang.Exception {
        try {
            Axis2Client client = new Axis2Client();
            client.invokeService();
        } catch (java.lang.Exception ex) {
            ex.printStackTrace();
        }
    }

    private void invokeService() throws java.lang.Exception {
        RPCServiceClient serviceClient = new RPCServiceClient();
        Options options = serviceClient.getOptions();
        EndpointReference targetEPR = new EndpointReference(
            "http://localhost:8080/axis2/services/employeeService");
        options.setTo(targetEPR);

        // Calling getEmployee() method of the service endpoint.
        QName getEmployee = new QName("http://axis2.ws.learning.com",
                        "getEmployee");
        Object[] inputParams = new Object[]{"823147"};
```

```
          Class[] returnTypes = new Class[]{Employee.class};
          Object[] response = serviceClient.invokeBlocking(getEmployee,
                              inputParams, returnTypes);
          Employee employee = (Employee) response[0];
          System.out.println("Employee Id: " + employee.getEmployeeId()+
                      " Last Name,  " + employee.getLastName() +
                      " First Name, " + employee.getFirstName());

          // Calling getEmployeeAddress() method of the service endpoint.
          QName getEmployeeAddress = new
              QName("http://axis2.ws.learning.com","getEmployeeAddress");
          inputParams = new Object[]{"123456"};
          returnTypes = new Class[]{String.class};
          response = serviceClient.invokeBlocking(getEmployeeAddress,
                    inputParams, returnTypes);
          String address = (String) response[0];
          System.out.println("--- address  --- " + address);
      }
}
```

NOTE: The above client code works with axiom-1.2.8 and axis-2-1.5.1 jars. Other combinations of axiom and axis-based jars are throwing runtime exceptions. This comment is valid only for web service client program.

Example 2: WSDL (Contract) First Development using XMLBeans

In this approach, developer first creates a WSDL document (also called contract). This WSDL is used for generating the Java service endpoint skeleton, stub, and its dependent classes.

The steps required to develop a web service of this type are given below.

1. Create a WSDL file
2. Create a XML schema definition document
3. Generate xml beans, skeletons, stubs, and other dependent Java classes using "WSDL2Java" utility.
4. Create a "services.xml" configuration file
5. Create a service archive (aar) file and deploy it in Tomcat server
6. Verification of deployed service endpoint
7. Write a client to invoke the deployed service endpoint

The above-specified steps are described in the following sections.

Step 1: Create a WSDL File

Axis2-provided utilities generate the Java classes from WSDL and vice versa. The following provided WSDL generates the Java classes using "org.apache.axis2.wsdl.WSDL2Java" utility available with Axis2 framework.

The below provided WSDL is using external XSD. This XSD is imported in "<wsdl:types/>" section of the WSDL document.

```
<xs:schema xmlns:xs="http://www.w3.org/2001/XMLSchema">
    <xs:import namespace="http://axis2.ws.learning.com/
```

```
                    provider/employeeDemographicService/demographic/
                    getDemographicInformation/2012/"
            schemaLocation="demographics2012.xsd"/>
</xs:schema>
```

The request message definition is given below. The "msg1:getDemographicInformation" *type* is defined in XSD.

```
<wsdl:message name="GetEmployeeDemographicRequestMessage">
    <wsdl:part name="getDemographicInformation"
            element="msg1:getDemographicInformation"/>
</wsdl:message>
```

The response message definition is given below.

The "msg1:getDemographicInformationResponse" type is defined in XSD file.

```
<wsdl:message name="GetEmployeeDemographicResponseMessage">
    <wsdl:part name="getDemographicInformationResponse"
            element="msg1:getDemographicInformationResponse"/>
</wsdl:message>
```

The "port type" definition maps to Java endpoint interface. This endpoint interface has one operation, this is "getDemographicInformation()"

```
<wsdl:portType name="EmployeeDemographicPortType">
    <wsdl:operation name="getDemographicInformation">
        <wsdl:input message="GetEmployeeDemographicRequestMessage"/>
        <wsdl:output message=
                "GetEmployeeDemographicResponseMessage"/>
    </wsdl:operation>
</wsdl:portType>
```

The complete WSDL file is given below. This WSDL is used for code generation, is named "employee_demographics.wsdl".

```
<wsdl:definitions name="EmployeeDemographicService"
        targetNamespace="http://axis2.ws.learning.com/provider/
                    employeeDemographicService/demographic/2012/"
        xmlns="http://axis2.ws.learning.com/provider/
                    employeeDemographicService/demographic/2012/"
        xmlns:soapbind="http://schemas.xmlsoap.org/wsdl/soap/"
        xmlns:wsdl="http://schemas.xmlsoap.org/wsdl/"
        xmlns:xs="http://www.w3.org/2001/XMLSchema"
        xmlns:msg1="http://axis2.ws.learning.com/provider/
                    employeeDemographicService/demographic/
                    getDemographicInformation/2012/">

    <wsdl:types>
        <xs:schema xmlns:xs="http://www.w3.org/2001/XMLSchema">
            <xs:import namespace=
                "http://axis2.ws.learning.com/provider/
                employeeDemographicService/demographic/
                getDemographicInformation/2012/"
                schemaLocation="demographics2012.xsd"/>
```

```
        </xs:schema>

    </wsdl:types>

    <wsdl:message name="GetEmployeeDemographicRequestMessage">
        <wsdl:part name="getDemographicInformation"
                element="msg1:getDemographicInformation"/>
    </wsdl:message>

    <wsdl:message name="GetEmployeeDemographicResponseMessage">
        <wsdl:part name="getDemographicInformationResponse"
                element="msg1:getDemographicInformationResponse"/>
    </wsdl:message>

    <wsdl:portType name="EmployeeDemographicPortType">
        <wsdl:operation name="getDemographicInformation">
            <wsdl:input message=
                "GetEmployeeDemographicRequestMessage"/>
            <wsdl:output message=
                "GetEmployeeDemographicResponseMessage"/>
        </wsdl:operation>
    </wsdl:portType>

    <wsdl:binding name="EmployeeDemographicSoapBinding"
                type="EmployeeDemographicPortType">
        <soapbind:binding style="document"
                transport="http://schemas.xmlsoap.org/soap/http"/>
            <wsdl:operation name="getDemographicInformation">
                <soapbind:operation soapAction=
                        "http://axis2.ws.learning.com/provider/
                        employeeDemographicService/demographic/
                        getDemographicInformation/2012/"
                        style="document"/>
                <wsdl:input>
                    <soapbind:body parts="getDemographicInformation"
                            use="literal"/>
                </wsdl:input>
                <wsdl:output>
                    <soapbind:body parts=
                            "getDemographicInformationResponse"
                            use="literal"/>
                </wsdl:output>
            </wsdl:operation>
    </wsdl:binding>

    <wsdl:service name="employeeDemographicService">
        <wsdl:port name="EmployeeDemographicService"
                binding="EmployeeDemographicSoapBinding">
        <soapbind:address location=
                "http://localhost:8080/axis2/services/
                    employeeDemographicService"/>
        </wsdl:port>
    </wsdl:service>

</wsdl:definitions>
```

Step 2: Create a XML Schema Definition Document

The following external schema document is used to define the structure of the endpoint operations. The input-and-output parameters of a service endpoint operation are wrapped inside request-and-response elements.

Let us examine how the element names of XSD are mapped to the generated Java classes of a request object. The request data elements of the service endpoint are provided below.

```
<xs:complexType name="EmployeeDemographicsRequest_Type">
    <xs:sequence>
    <xs:element name="inputData" type="xs:string"/>
    </xs:sequence>
</xs:complexType>
<xs:element name="getDemographicInformation"
            type="EmployeeDemographicsRequest_Type">
    <xs:annotation>
        <xs:documentation>
            Request of the Demographics info Service
        </xs:documentation>
    </xs:annotation>
</xs:element>
```

The Axis2-provided "WSDL2Java" utility generates the Java classes using the above provided XML definition. The element name "getDemographicInformation" maps to the "getGetDemographicInformation()" method, and element name "inputData" maps to the "getInputData()" method of the generated request Java object.

The corresponding equivalent Java code used in service endpoint, for getting the input data from client is provided below:

```
String inputData = request.getGetDemographicInformation().getInputData();
```

Similarly, let us examine how the elements names of the XSD are mapped to generated Java classes of a response object. The response data elements of the service endpoint are provided below.

```
<xs:complexType name="EmployeeDemographicOutput_Type">
    <xs:sequence>
        <xs:element name="ouputData" type="xs:string"/>
    </xs:sequence>
</xs:complexType>

<xs:complexType name="EmployeeDemographicResponse_Type">
    <xs:sequence>
        <xs:element name="info"
                type="EmployeeDemographicOutput_Type" minOccurs="0">
            <xs:annotation>
                <xs:documentation>
                    The information returned within the response
                </xs:documentation>
            </xs:annotation>
        </xs:element>
    </xs:sequence>
</xs:complexType>
```

```
<xs:element name="getDemographicInformationResponse"
        type="EmployeeDemographicResponse_Type">
    <xs:annotation>
        <xs:documentation>
            Results of the Employee Demographics service
        </xs:documentation>
    </xs:annotation>
</xs:element>
```

- The element name "getDemographicInformationResponse" maps to the getGetDemographicInformationResponse() method of a generated Java class.
- The element name "info" maps to getInfo() method of a generated Java class.
- The element name "ouputData" maps to getOuputData() method of the generated response Java object.

The corresponding equivalent Java code used in the Web Service client for getting the response from service endpoint is provided below:

```
String outputData =
response.getGetDemographicInformationResponse().getInfo().getOuputData();
```

The below provided XSD is used for code generation. The highlighted element names are used in client and service endpoint for accessing the data from request-and-response elements.

```
<?xml version="1.0" encoding="UTF-8"?>
<xs:schema xmlns =
"http://axis2.ws.learning.com/provider/employeeDemographicService/demogra
phic/getDemographicInformation/2012/"
xmlns:xs="http://www.w3.org/2001/XMLSchema"
targetNamespace="http://axis2.ws.learning.com/provider/employeeDemographi
cService/demographic/getDemographicInformation/2012/"
    elementFormDefault="unqualified"
    attributeFormDefault="unqualified" version="1.0">

<xs:complexType name="EmployeeDemographicsRequest_Type">
    <xs:sequence>
        <xs:element name="inputData" type="xs:string"/>
    </xs:sequence>
</xs:complexType>

<xs:element name="getDemographicInformation"
            type="EmployeeDemographicsRequest_Type">
    <xs:annotation>
        <xs:documentation>
            Request of the Demographics info service
        </xs:documentation>
    </xs:annotation>
</xs:element>

<xs:complexType name="EmployeeDemographicOutput_Type">
    <xs:sequence>
        <xs:element name="ouputData" type="xs:string"/>
    </xs:sequence>
</xs:complexType>
```

```
<xs:complexType name="EmployeeDemographicResponse_Type">
    <xs:sequence>
        <xs:element name="info" type="EmployeeDemographicOutput_Type"
                    minOccurs="0">
            <xs:annotation>
                <xs:documentation>
                    The information returned within the response
                </xs:documentation>
            </xs:annotation>
        </xs:element>
    </xs:sequence>
</xs:complexType>

<xs:element name="getDemographicInformationResponse"
        type="EmployeeDemographicResponse_Type">
    <xs:annotation>
        <xs:documentation>
            Results of the Employee Demographics service
        </xs:documentation>
    </xs:annotation>
</xs:element>
</xs:schema>
```

Step 3: Generate XML Beans, Skeletons, Stubs and Other Dependent Java Classes using "WSDL2Java" utility.

The "WSDL2Java" utility requires WSDL input for code generation. This utility generates the xml beans, skeletons, stubs, and other dependent classes to implement the Web service. Add the below provided Ant target to your application build script. This ant target generates, and compiles the xml bean classes. Refer to Chapter12 for complete Ant script.

```
<target name="wsdl2java_Axis2">
    <echo message="Generating code using axis2 wsdlfile"/>
    <java classname="org.apache.axis2.wsdl.WSDL2Java" fork="true">
    <classpath refid="build.classpath"/>

    <!-- -d parameter sets the output root directory. This is where
         generated files are copied -->
    <arg value="-d"/>
    <arg value="xmlbeans"/>

    <!-- location of wsdl file-->
    <arg value="-uri"/>
    <arg file="C:/ book_ws/conf/META-INF/employee_demographics.wsdl"/>

    <!-- Generates server side code -->
    <arg value="-ss"/>

    <!-- Generates all the classes skeletons and stubs-->
    <arg value="-g"/>
    </java>
</target>
```

The above Ant target generates the following list of Java files in the specified location. Make sure the generated Java files use the correct package name before going for service endpoint implementation.

```
EmployeeDemographicServiceCallbackHandler.java
EmployeeDemographicServiceMessageReceiverInOut.java
EmployeeDemographicServiceSkeleton.java
EmployeeDemographicServiceStub.java
EmployeeDemographicOutputType.java
EmployeeDemographicResponseType.java
EmployeeDemographicsRequestType.java
GetDemographicInformationDocument.java
GetDemographicInformationResponseDocument.java
EmployeeDemographicOutputTypeImpl.java
EmployeeDemographicResponseTypeImpl.java
EmployeeDemographicsRequestTypeImpl.java
GetDemographicInformationDocumentImpl.java
GetDemographicInformationResponseDocumentImpl.java
```

The generated skeleton class has empty methods without any business logic. Now use "EmployeeDemographicServiceSkeleton.java" class to implement application specific business functionality. Let us review the generated skeleton class code snippet and see how it is mapped to WSDL and XSD.

The suffix "Skeleton" was added to the name of the service implementation class which is derived from the name as specified in WSDL. The target namespace specified in WSDL maps to the package name of the generated skeleton class.

The complete skeleton class used for endpoint implementation is provided below. The generated empty operation is filled with business logic. Let us review the snippets of this skeleton class and see what this endpoint is doing.

The following code receives the data from client:

```
String inputData =
getDemographicInformation.getGetDemographicInformation().getInputData();
```

The following private method is used to parse the input XML to obtain the required input data.

```
String employeeId = getEmployeeIdFromInputXML(inputData);
```

The complete method code used for parsing the XML is provided below. The Dom4j XPath expression is used to obtain the employee id value from the input XML.

```
private String getEmployeeIdFromInputXML(String inputXML) {
    try {
        SAXReader reader = new SAXReader();
        Document document = reader.read(new
                    ByteArrayInputStream(inputXML.getBytes()));
        Node node = document.selectSingleNode("//employee/employeeId");
        System.out.println("--- employeeId ---" + node.getText());
        return node.getText();
    } catch(Exception ex) {
        ex.printStackTrace();
    }
```

```
        return "99999";
}
```

The following code snippet is used for building the response.

```
GetDemographicInformationResponseDocument response =
    GetDemographicInformationResponseDocument.Factory.newInstance();
```

This private method "getDemographicData()" is used to build the response XML. This method aggregates the entire output into single response XML document.

```
String outputXML = getDemographicData(employeeId);
response.addNewGetDemographicInformationResponse().addNewInfo().setOuputD
ata(outputXML);
```

The complete skeleton class with business logic implementation is provided in Listing 10-4.

Listing 10-4: Web service implementation class.

```
/**
 * EmployeeDemographicServiceSkeleton.java
 *
 * This file was auto-generated from WSDL
 * by the Apache Axis2 version: 1.5.1
 */
package
com.learning.ws.axis2.provider.employeedemographicservice.demographic._20
12;

import
com.learning.ws.axis2.provider.employeedemographicservice.demographic.
getdemographicinformation._2012.
GetDemographicInformationResponseDocument;
import
com.learning.ws.axis2.provider.employeedemographicservice.demographic.
getdemographicinformation._2012.GetDemographicInformationDocument;
import org.dom4j.*;
import org.dom4j.io.SAXReader;
import java.io.ByteArrayInputStream;

/**
 * EmployeeDemographicServiceSkeleton java skeleton for the axisService
 */
public class EmployeeDemographicServiceSkeleton {

/**
 * Auto generated method signature
 *
 * @param getDemographicInformation
 */
Public GetDemographicInformationResponseDocument
getDemographicInformation(
    GetDemographicInformationDocument getDemographicInformation) {

    /* Receives the input data from client. This is an entry point to
    the service endpoint  */
```

```
            String inputData = getDemographicInformation.
                        getGetDemographicInformation().getInputData();

            // Obtains the required data from input XML
            String employeeId = getEmployeeIdFromInputXML(inputData);
            System.out.println("-----  employeeId -----" + employeeId);

            // Build the response XML
            GetDemographicInformationResponseDocument response =
                        GetDemographicInformationResponseDocument.
                        Factory.newInstance();
            String outputXML = getDemographicData(employeeId);
            response.addNewGetDemographicInformationResponse().
                    addNewInfo().setOuputData(outputXML);
            return response;
    }

    private String getDemographicData(String employeeId) {
        /* Implement your business logic here. Get the data from various
        sources, build response XML. */
        return createResponseXML(employeeId);
    }

    // A private method used to build the response XML
    private String createResponseXML(String employeeId) {
            Document document = DocumentHelper.createDocument();
            Element rootElement = document.addElement("employee");
            Element nameElement = rootElement.addElement("nameinfo");
            nameElement.addElement("id").addText(employeeId);
            nameElement.addElement("firstName").addText("John");
            nameElement.addElement("lastName").addText("Smith");

            Element homeAddressElement =
                rootElement.addElement("homeAddress");
            homeAddressElement.addElement("aptNumber").addText("2340");
            homeAddressElement.addElement("streetName").
                        addText("W.Roundabout Cir");
            homeAddressElement.addElement("city").addText("Chandler");
            homeAddressElement.addElement("zipcode").addText("85226");
            homeAddressElement.addElement("state").addText("AZ");
            homeAddressElement.addElement("country").addText("UAS");

            Element emailElement = rootElement.addElement("emailAddress");
            emailElement.addElement("personal").
                            addText("wsbook@mymail.com");
            emailElement.addElement("office").addText("srinivas@abc.com");

            Element phoneElement = rootElement.addElement("phones");
            phoneElement.addElement("personal").addText("480-645-6753");
            phoneElement.addElement("office").addText("602-667-6782");

            // Convert document to String
            String outputXML = document.asXML();
            System.out.println("--- outputXML ---" + outputXML);
            return outputXML;
    }
```

```
    // private method used to obtain the data from request XML
    private String getEmployeeIdFromInputXML(String inputXML) {
        try {
            SAXReader reader = new SAXReader();
            Document document = reader.read(new
                ByteArrayInputStream(inputXML.getBytes()));
            Node node =
                document.selectSingleNode("//employee/employeeId");
            System.out.println("--- employeeId ---" + node.getText());
            return node.getText();
        } catch(Exception ex) {
            ex.printStackTrace();
        }
        return "99999";
    }
}
```

Step 4: Create a "services.xml" Configuration File

The "services.xml" file is an Axis framework specific configuration file used for specifying the service name, service endpoint class, operations, input/return type mappings, and message receivers of the web service endpoint.

The "WSDL2Java" tool generates "**EmployeeDemographicServiceMessageReceiverInOut.java**" message receiver class. This class is used for message exchange pattern for *in-out* operation.

```
<messageReceiver mep="http://www.w3.org/ns/wsdl/in-out"
    class="com.learning.ws.axis2.provider.employeedemographicservice.
    demographic._2012.EmployeeDemographicServiceMessageReceiverInOut"/>
```

The below provided xml is used for configuring the service class.

```
<parameter name="ServiceClass" locked="false">
    com.learning.ws.axis2.provider.employeedemographicservice.
    demographic._2012.EmployeeDemographicServiceSkeleton
</parameter>
```

The complete "**services.xml**" file is given below:

```
<service name="employeeDmographicService">
    <description>
        The axis2 WSDL2Java Demographic web service
    </description>
    <messageReceivers>
        <messageReceiver mep=http://www.w3.org/ns/wsdl/in-out
                class="com.learning.ws.axis2.provider.
                employeedemographicservice.demographic._2012.
                EmployeeDemographicServiceMessageReceiverInOut"/>
    </messageReceivers>
    <parameter name="ServiceClass" locked="false">
            com.learning.ws.axis2.provider.employeedemographicservice.
            demographic._2012.EmployeeDemographicServiceSkeleton
    </parameter>
        <operation name="getDemographicInformation"
            mep="http://www.w3.org/2004/08/wsdl/in-out"namespace=
            "http://axis2.ws.learning.com/provider/
```

```
       employeeDemographicService/demographic/2012/">
       <actionMapping>
             http://axis2.ws.learning.com/provider/
             employeeDemographicService/demographic/
             getDemographicInformation/2012/
       </actionMapping>
       <outputActionMapping>
             http://axis2.ws.learning.com/provider/
             employeeDemographicService/demographic/2012/
             EmployeeDemographicPortType/getDemographicInformation
       </outputActionMapping>
    </operation>
</service>
```

Step 5: Create a Service Archive (aar) File and Deploy it in Tomcat Server

The following steps are followed to create/deploy an "aar" file into the Tomcat container.

1. Package the generated service skeleton and its dependent Java classes into an "aar" file. Make sure "services.xml", "employee_demographics.wsdl", "demographics2012.xsd" files are placed inside the "META-INF/" directory.
2. In this example, the axis2 generated xml bean classes and binary code is packaged into "allxmltypes.jar" file. The "WSDL2Java" utility generates resources (inside _apache_xmlbeans package) and binary code (inside org package). Make sure it is packaged into "lib/" directory of "aar" file. Axis2 runtime uses these generated files. The structure of the "allxmltypes.jar" file is shown in Figure 10-3.
3. Make sure the "axis2.war" file is deployed in tomcat before going for service "aar" deployment.
4. Copy the created "aar" file into tomcat "\apache-tomcat-6.0.28\webapps\axis2\WEB-INF\services" directory.
5. Start the Tomcat server using "startup.bat" file available in "apache-tomcat-6.0.28\bin" directory.
6. Verify the server console, server log files and make sure aar is deployed without any errors.

Figure 10-3: Axis2 generated resources and binary code

The structure of the generated "aar" file is shown Figure 10-4.

Figure 10-4: AAR file structure

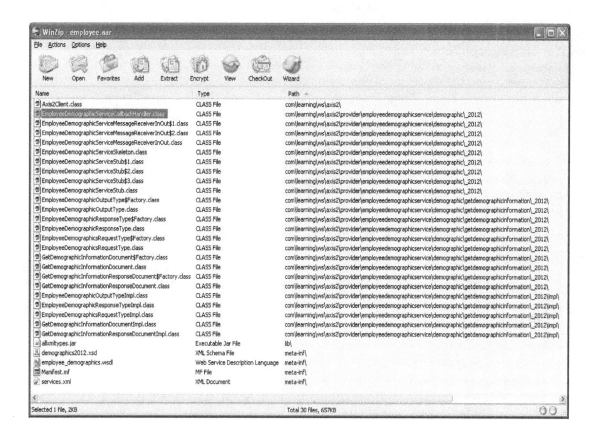

Step 6: Verification of the deployed service endpoint

After "aar" file deployment; carryout the following tests to make sure the service is deployed without any errors.

The following URL provides the list of services:

```
http://localhost:8080/axis2/services/listServices
```

The following URL provides the WSDL of the deployed service:

```
http://localhost:8080/axis2/services/employeeDmographicService?wsdl
```

The following URL provides the XSD of the deployed service:

```
http://localhost:8080/axis2/services/employeeDmographicService?xsd
```

Step 7: Write a Client to Invoke the Deployed Service Endpoint

We are ready to test the deployed web service. The "WSDL2Java" generated stub class is used to invoke the service endpoint.

This below provided client uses a private method "createInputXML()", to prepare the required input XML. It sends the complete request as a single XML string to service endpoint.

```
String inputData = createInputXML("123456");
EmployeeDemographicServiceStub stub = new
EmployeeDemographicServiceStub("http://localhost:8080/axis2/services/
employeeDmographicService");
GetDemographicInformationDocument input =
    GetDemographicInformationDocument.Factory.newInstance();
input.addNewGetDemographicInformation().setInputData(inputData);
```

The below provided code sends the input and obtains the output data as XML from service endpoint.

```
GetDemographicInformationResponseDocument response =
stub.getDemographicInformation(input);
String ouputData =
response.getGetDemographicInformationResponse().getInfo().getOuputData();
```

Run the below provided client to view the output.

```
private void invokeService() throws java.lang.Exception {
    // Sending the input data as XML to service endpoint
    String inputData = createInputXML("123456");
    EmployeeDemographicServiceStub stub = new
    EmployeeDemographicServiceStub
    ("http://localhost:8080/axis2/services/employeeDmographicService");
    GetDemographicInformationDocument input =
        GetDemographicInformationDocument.Factory.newInstance();
    input.addNewGetDemographicInformation().setInputData(inputData);

    // Get the output data as XML from service endpoint
    GetDemographicInformationResponseDocument response =
                        stub.getDemographicInformation(input);
    String outputData = response.getGetDemographicInformationResponse().
    getInfo().getOuputData();

    // Parse the outputData xml to obtain the required values.
}
```

The below given private method is used for creating the input XML. It converts the XML document to a Java String object.

```
private String createInputXML(String employeeId) throws Exception {
    Document document = DocumentHelper.createDocument();
    Element rootElement = document.addElement("inputData");
    Element employeeElement = rootElement.addElement("employee");
    employeeElement.addElement("employeeId").addText(employeeId);
    // converting input XML document to a String
    return document.asXML();
}
```

The complete web service client code is provided in Listing 10-5.

Listing 10-5: Web service client class.

```java
// Axis2Client.java
package com.learning.ws.axis2;

import org.dom4j.Document;
import org.dom4j.DocumentHelper;
import org.dom4j.Element;
import
com.learning.ws.axis2.provider.employeedemographicservice.demographic._20
12.EmployeeDemographicServiceStub;
import
com.learning.ws.axis2.provider.employeedemographicservice.demographic.get
demographicinformation._2012.GetDemographicInformationDocument;
import
com.learning.ws.axis2.provider.employeedemographicservice.demographic.get
demographicinformation._2012.GetDemographicInformationResponseDocument;

public class Axis2Client {

    public static void main(String args[]) throws java.lang.Exception {
        try {
            Axis2Client client = new Axis2Client();
            client.invokeService();
        } catch (java.lang.Exception ex) {
            ex.printStackTrace();
        }
    }

    private void invokeService() throws java.lang.Exception {
        // Sending the input data as XML to service endpoint
        String inputData = createInputXML("123456");
        EmployeeDemographicServiceStub stub = new
         EmployeeDemographicServiceStub("http://localhost:8080/flexweb/
            services/employeeDmographicService");
        GetDemographicInformationDocument input =
            GetDemographicInformationDocument.Factory.newInstance();
        input.addNewGetDemographicInformation().
                        setInputData(inputData);

        // Get the output data as XML from service end point
        GetDemographicInformationResponseDocument response =
        stub.getDemographicInformation(input);
        System.out.println("--- response ---" + response);
        String outputData = response.
                    getGetDemographicInformationResponse().
                    getInfo().getOuputData();
        System.out.println("--- outputData ---" + outputData);
    }

    private String createInputXML(String employeeId) throws Exception {
        Document document = DocumentHelper.createDocument();
        Element rootElement = document.addElement("inputData");
        Element employeeElement = rootElement.addElement("employee");
        employeeElement.addElement("employeeId").addText(employeeId);

        // converting input XML to a String
```

```
        System.out.println("--- String  --- " + document.asXML());
        return document.asXML();
    }

}
```

Example 3: Developing JAX-WS Complaint Web Services using Axis2

Apache-Axis2 framework can be used for developing fully featured Web Services compatible with JAX-WS standards. It supports JSR-181 annotations for web services development. The steps required to develop a Web service of this type are given below:

1. Create a service endpoint interface
2. Create a service implementation class
3. Create a "services.xml" configuration file
4. Create a service archive (aar) file and deploy it in Tomcat server
5. Verification of deployed service endpoint
6. Write a client to invoke the deployed service endpoint

The above-specified steps are described in the following sections:

Step 1: Create a Service Endpoint Interface

The only required annotation for service endpoint interface is "@WebService". The service endpoint interface "StockQuoteService" has one method: getScripsList(). It takes String input, and returns the list of stock scrips. Listing 10-6 provides the JAX-WS based service endpoint interface.

Listing 10-6: JAX-WS based web service endpoint interface.

```
// StockQuoteService.java
package com.learning.ws.axis2.jaxws;

import javax.jws.WebService;
import java.util.List;
@WebService
public interface StockQuoteService {
    List getScripsList(String type) throws Exception;
}
```

Step 2: Create a Service Implementation Class

The above interface defined method is implemented in its implementation class. The complete implementation class code is provided in Listing 10-7.

Listing 10-7: Web service implementation class code.

```
// StockQuoteServiceImpl.java
package com.learning.ws.axis2.jaxws;

import javax.jws.WebService;
import java.util.List;
import java.util.ArrayList;

@WebService(name="StockQuoteService",
            serviceName="StockQuoteService",endpointInterface=
```

```
              "com.learning.ws.axis2.jaxws.StockQuoteService")
public class StockQuoteServiceImpl implements StockQuoteService {
     public List getScripsList(String type) throws Exception {
          System.out.println("---- type ----" + type);
          List scripsList = new ArrayList();
          if("Dividend".equalsIgnoreCase(type)) {
               scripsList.add("WFC");
               scripsList.add("SLV");
               scripsList.add("GLD");
               scripsList.add("PALL");
          }
          return scripsList;
     }
}
```

Step 3: Create the services.xml Configuration File

The methods of the service endpoint class have both "in" and "out" parameters, so "RPCMessageReceiver" class is used for message exchange pattern.

The complete "services.xml" file is provided below:

```
<service name="stockQuoteService">
     <description>The axis2 JAX-WS web service</description>
     <messageReceivers>
     <messageReceiver mep="http://www.w3.org/2004/08/wsdl/in-out"
               class="org.apache.axis2.rpc.receivers.RPCMessageReceiver"/>
     </messageReceivers>
     <parameter name="ServiceClass" locked="false">
          com.learning.ws.axis2.jaxws.StockQuoteServiceImpl
     </parameter>
</service>
```

Step 4: Create a Service Archive (aar) File and Deploy it in Tomcat Server

The following steps are followed to deploy an "aar" file into the Tomcat container.

1. Package the Web service endpoint and its dependent classes into an "aar" file. Make sure "services.xml" file is placed inside the "META-INF/" directory.
2. Copy the created "aar" file into tomcat "\apache-tomcat\webapps\axis2\WEB-INF\services" directory.
3. Start the tomcat using "startup.bat" file available in "apache-tomcat\bin" directory.
4. Verify the server console, server log files and make sure "aar" is deployed without any errors.

Figure 10-5: aar file structure

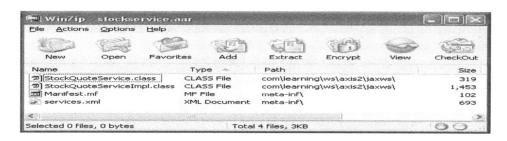

The structure of the generated "aar" file is shown in Figure 10-5.

Step 5: Verification of deployed service endpoint

After aar file deployment; carryout the following tests to make sure the service is deployed correctly without any errors.

The following URL provides the list of services:

```
http://localhost:8080/axis2/services/listServices
```

The following URL provides the WSDL of the deployed service:

```
http://localhost:8080/axis2/services/StockQuoteService?wsdl
```

The following URL provides the XSD of the deployed service:

```
http://localhost:8080/axis2/services/StockQuoteService?xsd
```

The following URL invokes the web service endpoint operation "getScripsList()" and it provides the XML output:

```
http://localhost:8080/axis2/services/StockQuoteService/getScripsList?type
=Dividend
```

The response XML is provided below:

```
<ns:getScripsListResponse xmlns:ns="http://jaxws.axis2.ws.learning.com">
    <ns:return>WFC</ns:return>
    <ns:return>SLV</ns:return>
    <ns:return>GLD</ns:return>
    <ns:return>RIM</ns:return>
</ns:getScripsListResponse>
```

Step 6: Write a Client to Invoke the Deployed Service Endpoint

Axis2 provides several client API's to invoke the deployed Web service endpoint. This particular example uses Axis Object Model (also called AXIOM) client. AXIOM is an XML-based object model developed for Apache Axis2; and it is similar to DOM.

The below provided private method is used for creating the request payload.

```
private static OMElement getOMElement() {
    OMFactory fac = OMAbstractFactory.getOMFactory();
    OMNamespace omNs = fac.
    createOMNamespace("http://jaxws.axis2.ws.learning.com", "ns");
    OMElement method = fac.createOMElement("getScripsList", omNs);
    // wraps the input parameters into <input/> element
    OMElement value = fac.createOMElement("input", omNs);

    // Sending input value as "Dividend"
    value.addChild(fac.createOMText(value, "Dividend"));
    method.addChild(value);
    return method;
```

```
}
```

The following client invokes the service endpoint using the above-created input.

```
OMElement result = serviceClient.sendReceive(payload);
```

Run the below provided client code to see the request-and-response. The web service client code is provided in Listing 10-8.

Listing 10-8: Web service client code.

```java
// StockQuoteClient.java
package com.learning.ws.axis2.jaxws;

import org.apache.axis2.client.Options;
import org.apache.axis2.client.ServiceClient;
import org.apache.axis2.addressing.EndpointReference;
import org.apache.axiom.om.OMElement;
import org.apache.axiom.om.OMFactory;
import org.apache.axiom.om.OMNamespace;
import org.apache.axiom.om.OMAbstractFactory;

public class StockQuoteClient {
    public static void main(String args[]) throws java.lang.Exception {
        try {
            StockQuoteClient client = new StockQuoteClient();
            client.invokeService();
        } catch (java.lang.Exception ex) {
            ex.printStackTrace();
        }
    }

    private void invokeService() throws java.lang.Exception {
        EndpointReference targetEPR = new EndpointReference
        ("http://localhost:8080/axis2/services/StockQuoteService");

        ServiceClient serviceClient = new ServiceClient();
        OMElement payload = getOMElement();
        Options options = new Options();
        options.setTo(targetEPR);
        serviceClient.setOptions(options);
        OMElement result = serviceClient.sendReceive(payload);

        // Parse the result to obtain the required data.
        System.out.println("--- result ---" + result);
    }

    // A private method used for creating the request payload
    private static OMElement getOMElement() {
        OMFactory fac = OMAbstractFactory.getOMFactory();
        OMNamespace omNs = fac.
        createOMNamespace("http://jaxws.axis2.ws.learning.com", "ns");
        OMElement method = fac.createOMElement("getScripsList", omNs);
        // wraps the input parameters into <input/> element
        OMElement value = fac.createOMElement("input", omNs);
```

```
        // Sending input value as "Dividend"
        value.addChild(fac.createOMText(value, "Dividend"));
        method.addChild(value);
        return method;
    }
}
```

Example 4: Developing "AXIOM" Based Endpoints Using Axis2

AXIOM stands for Axis Object Model. This is an XML-based object model similar to DOM and Dom4j. It uses pull based parsing technique while parsing the XML documents. This model was initially developed for Apache Axis2. The input parameter type for this kind of web service endpoint operation is "OMElement".

The steps required to develop a Web Service of this type are given below:

1. Create a service endpoint interface
2. Create a service implementation class
3. Create a "services.xml" configuration file
4. Create a service archive (aar) file and deploy it in Tomcat server
5. Verification of deployed service endpoint
6. Write a client to invoke the deployed service endpoint

The above-specified steps are described in the following sections:

Step 1: Create a Service Endpoint Interface

The only mandatory requirement for this type of service endpoint operation is input parameter type as "OMElement". The service endpoint interface "GradeManagerService" has one method: getSubjects(). It takes "OMElement" as input; and returns list subjects in a single "OMElement". The AXIOM-based web service endpoint interface is provided in Listing 10-9.

Listing 10-9: AXIOM-based endpoint interface.

```
// GradeManagerService.java
package com.learning.ws.axis2.axiom;

import org.apache.axiom.om.OMElement;

public interface GradeManagerService {
    OMElement getSubjects(OMElement gradeElement) throws Exception;
}
```

Step 2: Create a Service Implementation Class

The above defined method is implemented in its implementation class. The "getSubjects()" method of the service endpoint receives the input from the client; it parses the input XML to obtain the "grade" value. It returns the list of subjects based on grade received. The code provided below obtains the grade from input xml.

```
OMElement element = gradeElement.getFirstElement();
Integer grade = new Integer(element.getText()).intValue();
```

A private method "getOMElement()" is used to create the output response. The complete service endpoint implementation class code is provided in Listing 10-10.

Listing 10-10: Service endpoint implementation class.

```java
// GradeManagerServiceImpl.java
package com.learning.ws.axis2.axiom;

import org.apache.axiom.om.OMElement;
import org.apache.axiom.om.OMFactory;
import org.apache.axiom.om.OMAbstractFactory;
import org.apache.axiom.om.OMNamespace;

public class GradeManagerServiceImpl implements GradeManagerService {
    public OMElement getSubjects(OMElement gradeElement)
    throws Exception {
        // Obtain the input value from client.
        OMElement element = gradeElement.getFirstElement();
        Integer grade = new Integer(element.getText()).intValue();

        switch(grade) {
            case 9:
                return getOMElement();
            case 8:
                return getOMElement();
            default:
                return getOMElement();
        }
    }

    // private method used to build the output response.
    private OMElement getOMElement() {
        OMFactory fac = OMAbstractFactory.getOMFactory();
        OMNamespace omNs = fac.
        createOMNamespace("http://jaxws.axis2.ws.learning.com", "ns");
        OMElement method = fac.createOMElement("getSubjectsResponse",
                                               omNs);

        // wraps the output parameter into <subject1/> element
        OMElement value1 = fac.createOMElement("subject1", omNs);
        // Setting the value as "Mathematics" for subject1
        value1.addChild(fac.createOMText(value1, "Mathematics"));

        OMElement value2 = fac.createOMElement("subject2", omNs);
        value2.addChild(fac.createOMText(value2, "Reading"));

        OMElement value3 = fac.createOMElement("subject3", omNs);
        value3.addChild(fac.createOMText(value3, "Music and ART"));

        OMElement value4 = fac.createOMElement("subject4", omNs);
        value4.addChild(fac.createOMText(value4, "Computer Basics"));

        method.addChild(value1);
        method.addChild(value2);
        method.addChild(value3);
        method.addChild(value4);

        return method;
    }
}
```

Step 3: Create a "services.xml" Configuration File

The methods of the service endpoint class have both "in", "out" parameters and request-response is raw xml, so "RawXMLINOutMessageReceiver" class is used as a message receiver. The complete "services.xml" file is provided below:

```
<service name="GradeManagerService">
    <description>The axis2 AXIOM web service</description>
    <messageReceivers>
        <messageReceiver mep="http://www.w3.org/2004/08/wsdl/in-out"
            class=
            "org.apache.axis2.receivers.RawXMLINOutMessageReceiver"/>
    </messageReceivers>
    <parameter name="ServiceClass" locked="false">
        com.learning.ws.axis2.axiom.GradeManagerServiceImpl
    </parameter>
</service>
```

Step 4: Create a Service Archive (aar) File and Deploy it in Tomcat Server

The following steps are followed to deploy an "aar" file into the Tomcat container.

1. Package the web service endpoint and its dependent classes into an "aar" file. Make sure "services.xml" file is placed inside the "/META-INF" directory.
2. Copy the created "aar" file into "\apache-tomcat\webapps\axis2\WEB-INF\services" directory.
3. Start the tomcat using "startup.bat" file available in "apache-tomcat\bin" directory.
4. Verify the server console, server log files and make sure "aar" is deployed without any errors.

The structure of the generated "aar" file is shown in Figure 10-6.

Figure 10-6: AAR file structure

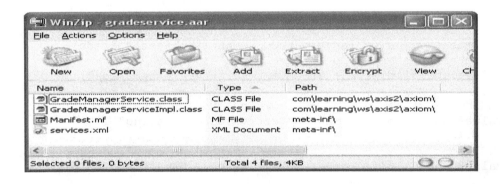

Step 5: Verification of Deployed Service Endpoint

After "aar" file deployment, carryout the following tests to make sure the service is deployed correctly without any problems.

The following URL provides the list of deployed services:

```
http://localhost:8080/axis2/services/listServices
```

The following URL provides the WSDL of the deployed service:

Development Methodologies

```
http://localhost:8080/axis2/services/GradeManagerService?wsdl
```

The following URL provides the XSD of the deployed service:

```
http://localhost:8080/axis2/services/GradeManagerService?xsd
```

The following URL invokes the web service endpoint operation "getSubjects()"; and it provides the XML output:

```
http://localhost:8080/acis2/services/GradeManagerService/getSubjects?grad
eElement=9
```

Step 6: Write a Client to Invoke the Deployed Service Endpoint

The Axis2 framework provides an XML-based client API to invoke the service endpoint. This web service uses AXIOM API to parse and to create request-response payload messages. The code snippet below creates the request payload using AXIOM API to pass it to the service endpoint.

```
OMFactory fac = OMAbstractFactory.getOMFactory();
OMNamespace omNs =
fac.createOMNamespace("http://jaxws.axis2.ws.learning.com", "ns");
OMElement payload = fac.createOMElement("getSubjects", omNs);
// wraps the input parameters into <grade/> element
OMElement value = fac.createOMElement("grade", omNs);

// Sending input value of grade as "9"
value.addChild(fac.createOMText(value, "9"));
payload.addChild(value);
```

The Axis2 provided "ServiceClient" class is used to invoke the web service endpoint. The "sendReceive()" method takes the request payload as input parameter to obtain the response from the service endpoint.

```
ServiceClient serviceClient = new ServiceClient();
Options options = new Options();
options.setTo(targetEPR);
serviceClient.setOptions(options);
OMElement response = serviceClient.sendReceive(payload);
```

Run the below client to view the request-and-response. The web service client code is provided in Listing 10-11.

Listing 10-11: Web service client code.

```
// GradeManagerClient.java
package com.learning.ws.axis2.axiom;

import org.apache.axis2.addressing.EndpointReference;
import org.apache.axis2.client.ServiceClient;
import org.apache.axis2.client.Options;
import org.apache.axiom.om.OMElement;
import org.apache.axiom.om.OMFactory;
import org.apache.axiom.om.OMAbstractFactory;
import org.apache.axiom.om.OMNamespace;
```

```
public class GradeManagerClient {
    public static void main(String args[]) {
        try {
            GradeManagerClient client = new GradeManagerClient();
            client.invokeService();
        } catch (java.lang.Exception ex) {
            ex.printStackTrace();
        }
    }

    private void invokeService() throws java.lang.Exception {
        EndpointReference targetEPR = new EndpointReference
        ("http://localhost:8080/axis2/services/GradeManagerService");

        // creating the request payload
        OMFactory fac = OMAbstractFactory.getOMFactory();
        OMNamespace omNs = fac.createOMNamespace
            ("http://jaxws.axis2.ws.learning.com", "ns");
        OMElement payload = fac.createOMElement("getSubjects", omNs);

        // wraps the input parameters into <grade/> element
        OMElement value = fac.createOMElement("grade", omNs);

            // Sending input value of grade as "9"
            value.addChild(fac.createOMText(value, "9"));
            payload.addChild(value);

            ServiceClient serviceClient = new ServiceClient();
            Options options = new Options();
            options.setTo(targetEPR);
            serviceClient.setOptions(options);

            // invokes the service endpoint.
            OMElement response = serviceClient.sendReceive(payload);

            // Parse the response to obtain the required data.
            System.out.println("--- response ---" + response);
    }
}
```

Writing Custom Modules Using Axis2

Axis2 framework provides support for writing custom modules. Axis2 uses module archive files to build-and-deploy custom modules; these modules are represented with ".mar" suffix and generated using jar command. These modules are used to implement application specific custom features such as security, logging of inbound-outbound soap messages, and message handler's configuration with client, service endpoint, and so forth.

Listing 10-5: Developing AXIS2-based custom modules

The steps required to configure Axis2 custom module are given below:

1. Create a module implementation class
2. Create a handler class

---

3. Create a "module.xml" configuration file
4. Create a module archive file (.mar file)
5. Modify "axis2.xml" file
6. Modify "services.xml" file to configure the module
7. Deploy the module archive file
8. Write a client to test the configured module.

The above-specified steps are described in the following sections:

Step 1: Create a Module Implementation Class

The module implementation class must implement "org.apache.axis2.modules.Module" interface. This is used to customize the module specific functionality. This example does not have any custom implementation so it is having empty method implementations. The module class implantation code is provided in Listing 10-12.

Listing 10-12: AXIS-specific module class implementation

```
// LogModule.java
package com.learning.ws.axis2;

import org.apache.axis2.AxisFault;
import org.apache.axis2.context.ConfigurationContext;
import org.apache.axis2.description.AxisModule;
import org.apache.axis2.description.AxisDescription;
import org.apache.neethi.Assertion;
import org.apache.neethi.Policy;

public class LogModule implements org.apache.axis2.modules.Module {
    public void init(ConfigurationContext configContext, AxisModule
    module) throws AxisFault {
        // Initialize the module
    }

    public void shutdown(ConfigurationContext configurationContext)
    throws AxisFault {
        // End of module processing
    }

    public void engageNotify(AxisDescription axisDescription) throws
    AxisFault {
    }

    public void applyPolicy(Policy policy, AxisDescription
    axisDescription) throws AxisFault {
    }

    public boolean canSupportAssertion(Assertion assertion) {
        return true;
    }
}
```

Step 2: Create a Handler Class

The handler class used for logging the soap messages is provided in Listing 10-13. The Axis2 handler class must implement "org.apache.axis2.engine.Handler" interface. The Axis2 provides

"AbstractHandler" an adapter for class for convenience; it has an empty implementation of the Handler interface methods. The "invoke()" method is the only required method the developer should focus to implement the handler related functionality. The complete message context is available in "invoke()" method which can be processed using SAAJ API.

Listing 10-13: SOAP handler used to log messages

```java
// LogHandler.java
package com.learning.ws.axis2;

import org.apache.axis2.handlers.AbstractHandler;
import org.apache.axis2.AxisFault;
import org.apache.axis2.engine.Handler;
import org.apache.axis2.context.MessageContext;

public class LogHandler extends AbstractHandler implements Handler {

    public InvocationResponse invoke(MessageContext msgContext)
        throws AxisFault {
        // Printing the entire soap envelope
        System.out.println(msgContext.getEnvelope().toString());
        return InvocationResponse.CONTINUE;
    }

    public void revoke(MessageContext msgContext) {
        System.out.println(msgContext.getEnvelope().toString());
    }
}
```

Step 3: Create a "modle.xml" Configuration File

The deployment configurations of the module are declared in "module.xml" file. It has the details of module implementation class; handler class; and various phases that explain when to execute module implementation functionality. Axis2 uses the concept of phases; each phase defines when to execute the handler functionality. The handler has four phases.

- InFlow — handler chain which runs for inbound messages.
- OutFlow — handler chain which runs for outbound messages.
- OutFaultFlow — handler chain which runs for outbound fault messages.
- InFaultFlow — handler chain which runs for inbound fault messages.

The "module.xml" configuration file is given below:

```xml
<module name="logging" class="com.learning.ws.axis2.LogModule">
    <InFlow>
        <handler name="InFlowLogHandler"
                class="com.learning.ws.axis2.LogHandler">
            <order phase="loggingPhase" />
        </handler>
    </InFlow>

    <OutFlow>
        <handler name="OutFlowLogHandler"
                class="com.learning.ws.axis2.LogHandler">
            <order phase="loggingPhase"/>
```

```
            </handler>
        </OutFlow>

        <OutFaultFlow>
            <handler name="FaultOutFlowLogHandler"
                    class="com.learning.ws.axis2.LogHandler">
                <order phase="loggingPhase"/>
            </handler>
        </OutFaultFlow>

        <InFaultFlow>
            <handler name="FaultInFlowLogHandler"
                class="com.learning.ws.axis2.LogHandler">
                <order phase="loggingPhase"/>
            </handler>
        </InFaultFlow>
    </module>
```

Step 4: Create a Module Archive File (.mar file)

Create a module archive file using jar command. The Ant target used for creating the ".mar" file is provided below.

```
<target name="make_logging_module">
    <jar jarfile="${output.dir}/loggingmodule.mar" update="false">
        <fileset dir="${class.dir}"
            includes="**/axis2/LogModule.class,
                **/axis2/LogHandler.class "/>
        <fileset dir="${basedir}/conf/axis2"
                includes="**/module.xml"/>
    </jar>
</target>
```

The structure of the generated module archive file is shown in Figure 10-7.

Figure 10-7: AAR file structure

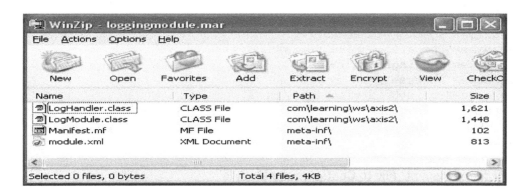

Step 5: Modify "axis2.xml" File

The module writer now has to integrate the logging module with Aixs2 runtime. Add the "loggingPhase" defined in "module.xml" to "Axis2.xml" configuration file. The "axis2.xml" file comes with "axis.war" distribution and it is available in "webapps\axis2\WEB-INF\conf" location.

The modified section of the "axis2.xml" file is given below:

```xml
<!-- ====================================================== -->
<!-- Phases    -->
<!-- ====================================================== -->
<phaseOrder type="InFlow">
    <!--   System predefined phases        -->
    <!--   System predefined phases        -->
    <!--    After Postdispatch phase module author or
           service author can add any phase he want      -->
    <phase name="OperationInPhase">
        <handler name="MustUnderstandChecker" class=
             "org.apache.axis2.jaxws.dispatchers.MustUnderstandChecker">
             <order phase="OperationInPhase"/>
        </handler>
    </phase>
    <phase name="soapmonitorPhase"/>
    <phase name="loggingPhase"/>
</phaseOrder>
<phaseOrder type="OutFlow">
    <!-- user can add his own phases to this area  -->
    <phase name="soapmonitorPhase"/>
    <phase name="OperationOutPhase"/>
    <!--system predefined phase-->
    <!--these phase will run irrespective of the service-->
    <phase name="RMPhase"/>
    <phase name="PolicyDetermination"/>
    <phase name="MessageOut"/>
    <phase name="Security"/>
    <phase name="loggingPhase"/>
</phaseOrder>
<phaseOrder type="InFaultFlow">
    <!--  user can add his own phases to this area  -->
    <phase name="OperationInFaultPhase"/>
    <phase name="soapmonitorPhase"/>
    <phase name="loggingPhase"/>
</phaseOrder>
<phaseOrder type="OutFaultFlow">
    <!--  user can add his own phases to this area  -->
    <phase name="soapmonitorPhase"/>
    <phase name="OperationOutFaultPhase"/>
    <phase name="loggingPhase"/>
    <phase name="RMPhase"/>
    <phase name="PolicyDetermination"/>
    <phase name="MessageOut"/>
    <phase name="Security"/>
</phaseOrder>
```

Step 6: Modify "services.xml" File to Configure the Module

The next step is to integrate the custom module with your Web Service. Take the "services.xml" created in our previous examples; include "<module/>" tag which refers to the "name" defined in "module.xml" file. The complete "services.xml" file is provided below:

```xml
<service name="employeeService">
    <description>The axis2 employee web service</description>
```

```
<module ref="logging"/>
<messageReceivers>
<messageReceiver mep="http://www.w3.org/2004/08/wsdl/in-out"
        class="org.apache.axis2.rpc.receivers.RPCMessageReceiver"/>
</messageReceivers>
<parameter name="ServiceClass" locked="false">
        com.learning.ws.axis2.EmployeeServiceImpl</parameter>
</service>
```

Step 7: Deploy Module Archive (.mar) File in Axis2

Deploy the previously created module archive file "loggingmodule.mar" into Axis2 runtime environment. Copy the "loggingmodule.mar" file in "webapps\axis2\WEB-INF\modules" directory. If modules directory is not available we can create one.

Step 8: Write a Client to Test the Configured Module.

Re-use the client created in Example1. Run the client and see the log messages on the server console. The complete client code is provided below:

```
private void invokeService() throws Exception {
    RPCServiceClient serviceClient = new RPCServiceClient();
    Options options = serviceClient.getOptions();
    EndpointReference targetEPR = new EndpointReference
            ("http://localhost:8080/axis2/services/employeeService");
    options.setTo(targetEPR);

    // getting the employee details
    QName getEmployee = new QName("http://axis2.ws.learning.com",
        "getEmployee");
    Object[] inputParams = new Object[]{"823147"};
    Class[] returnTypes = new Class[]{Employee.class};
    Object[] response = serviceClient.invokeBlocking(getEmployee,
                        inputParams, returnTypes);
    Employee employee = (Employee) response[0];
    System.out.println("Employee Id: " + employee.getEmployeeId() +
            "Last Name, " + employee.getLastName() +
            "First Name, " + employee.getFirstName());
}
```

The logging handler class prints the following request-and-response soap messages on the server console.

The request soap message is provided below:

```
<?xml version="1.0" encoding="utf-8"?>
<soapenv:Envelope xmlns:soapenv =
            "http://schemas.xmlsoap.org/soap/envelope/">
    <soapenv:Body>
        <getEmployee xmlns="http://axis2.ws.learning.com">
            <arg0 xmlns="">123456</arg0>
        </getEmployee>
    </soapenv:Body>
</soapenv:Envelope>
```

The response soap message is provided below:

```xml
<?xml version="1.0" encoding="utf-8"?>
<soapenv:Envelope xmlns:soapenv=
      "http://schemas.xmlsoap.org/soap/envelope/">
      <soapenv:Body>
      <ns:getEmployeeResponse xmlns:ns="http://axis2.ws.learning.com">
            <ns:return xmlns:ax21="http://axis2.ws.learning.com/xsd"
                  xmlns:xsi="http://www.w3.org/2001/XMLSchema-instance"
                  xsi:type="ax21:Employee">
                  <ax21:employeeId>823147</ax21:employeeId>
                  <ax21:firstName>John</ax21:firstName>
                  <ax21:lastName>Smith</ax21:lastName>
            </ns:return>
      </ns:getEmployeeResponse>
      </soapenv:Body>
</soapenv:Envelope>
```

Web Service Endpoint Design Scenarios

This section explain the various types of Web Service endpoint design options available for implementing web services using Axis2 framework. The commonly used service endpoint designs are listed below:

1. Creating a service endpoint using POJO
2. Creating a service endpoint using JAX-WS annotations
3. Generating a service endpoint using XMLBeans
4. Creating a service endpoint using AXIOM (Axis Object Model)

Creating a Service Endpoint Using POJO

The development, debugging and deployment of this type of web service are simple and easy. The plain Java classes (POJO) are used to develop the service endpoints. They are simple, easy to maintain and manage. An example web service endpoint code is given below:

```java
// EmployeeService.java
package com.learning.ws.axis2;

public interface EmployeeService {
    Employee getEmployee(String employeeId) throws EmployeeFault;
    String getEmployeeAddress(String employeeId) throws EmployeeFault;
}
```

Above defined methods are implemented in its implementation class.

```java
// EmployeeServiceImpl.java
package com.learning.ws.axis2;

public class EmployeeServiceImpl implements EmployeeService {
    public Employee getEmployee(String employeeId) throws EmployeeFault{
        // Fill this with the necessary business logic
    }
```

```
      public String getEmployeeAddress(String employeeId)
      throws EmployeeFault {
          // Fill this with the necessary business logic
          return "3943 Roundabout CIR, Chandler, Arizona, 85226";
      }
}
```

Generating a Service Endpoint Using JAX-WS Annotations

Apache-Axis2 framework can be used for developing fully featured web services compatible with JAX-WS standards. It uses JAX-WS provided annotations to mark the Java class as a service endpoint. The benefit of this service endpoint is, the development is conformant with JAX-WS standards.

```
// StockQuoteService.java
package com.learning.ws.axis2.jaxws;

import javax.jws.WebService;
import java.util.List;

@WebService
public interface StockQuoteService {
    List getScripsList(String symbol) throws Exception;
}
```

Above defined method is implemented in its implementation class.

```
// StockQuoteServiceImpl.java
package com.learning.ws.axis2.jaxws;

import javax.jws.WebService;
import java.util.*;

@WebService(name="StockQuoteService",
serviceName="StockQuoteService",
endpointInterface="com.learning.ws.axis2.jaxws.StockQuoteService")
public class StockQuoteServiceImpl implements StockQuoteService {
    public List getScripsList(String type) throws Exception {
        // Fill this with the necessary business logic
    }
}
```

Creating a Service Endpoint Using XMLBeans

In this approach developer first creates a WSDL document; this WSDL is used as an input for generating the Java service endpoint skeleton and its dependent classes. The Axis2-provided "WDSL2Java" utility is used to generate this service endpoint. An example Web Service endpoint code is given below:

```
// EmployeeDemographicServiceSkeleton.java
package com.learning.ws.axis2.provider.employeedemographicservice.
demographic._2012;

public class EmployeeDemographicServiceSkeleton {
```

```
/**
 * Auto generated method signature
 */
public GetDemographicInformationResponseDocument
    getDemographicInformation (GetDemographicInformationDocument
    getDemographicInformation) {
        // fill this with the necessary business logic
    }
}
```

Creating a Service Endpoint Using AXIOM (Axis Object Model)

The only mandatory requirement for this type of service endpoint operation is input parameter type of "OMElement". The service endpoint and client work with raw XML as request-and-response. The benefit of this service endpoint is; the client and server can aggregate the data from various sources into single xml element. Developer can use the appropriate parsing technique to obtain the data from request and response XML.

```
// GradeManagerService.java
package com.learning.ws.axis2.axiom;

import org.apache.axiom.om.OMElement;
public interface GradeManagerService {
    OMElement getSubjects(OMElement gradeElement) throws Exception;
}
```

Above defined method is implemented in its implementation class.

```
// GradeManagerServiceImpl.java
package com.learning.ws.axis2.axiom;

import org.apache.axiom.om.OMElement;
public class GradeManagerServiceImpl implements GradeManagerService {
    public OMElement getSubjects(OMElement gradeElement) throws
    Exception {
    // fill this with the necessary business logic
    }
}
```

Web Service Client Design Scenarios

There are several ways a client can invoke the deployed web service endpoint. The main focus of this section is to discuss the various client design scenarios used to invoke a deployed web service endpoint and their benefits of each. Let us review, how the various types of Axis2-provided client API's are used to invoke a deployed Web Service endpoint. The following Web Service client types are covered in detail.

- Creating client using "RPCServiceClient"
- Creating XML based client using AXIOM
- Creating client using Axis2 generated XMLBeans

Creating a Client Using RPCServiceClient

Axis2 framework provided "RPCServiceClient" class can be used to invoke the POJO-based web service endpoint. The client code used to invoke the web service endpoint is provided below:

```
private void invokeService() throws java.lang.Exception {
    RPCServiceClient serviceClient = new RPCServiceClient();
    Options options = serviceClient.getOptions();
    EndpointReference targetEPR = new EndpointReference
            ("http://localhost:8080/axis2/services/employeeService");
    options.setTo(targetEPR);

    // Calling getEmployee() method of the service endpoint.
    QName getEmployee =
        new QName("http://axis2.ws.learning.com", "getEmployee");
    Object[] inputParams = new Object[]{"123456"};
    Class[] returnTypes = new Class[]{Employee.class};
    Object[] response = serviceClient.invokeBlocking(getEmployee,
                            inputParams, returnTypes);
    Employee employee = (Employee) response[0];
    System.out.println(" Employee Id:  " + employee.getEmployeeId() +
                " Last Name,  " + employee.getLastName() +
                " First Name, " + employee.getFirstName());
}
```

Creating a XML-based Client Using AXIOM

The Axis2 framework provides an XML based client API to invoke the service endpoint. The web service client uses AXIOM API to parse; and to create request payload messages. The client code used to invoke the Web Service endpoint is given below:

```
private void invokeService() throws java.lang.Exception {
    EndpointReference targetEPR = new EndpointReference
            ("http://localhost:8080/axis2/services/GradeManagerService");

    // creating the request payload
    OMFactory fac = OMAbstractFactory.getOMFactory();
    OMNamespace omNs = fac.createOMNamespace(
                "http://jaxws.axis2.ws.learning.com", "ns");
    OMElement payload = fac.createOMElement("getSubjects", omNs);

    // wraps the input parameters into <grade/> element
    OMElement value = fac.createOMElement("grade", omNs);

    // Sending input value as "9"
    value.addChild(fac.createOMText(value, "9"));
    payload.addChild(value);

    ServiceClient serviceClient = new ServiceClient();
    Options options = new Options();
    options.setTo(targetEPR);
    serviceClient.setOptions(options);
    OMElement response = serviceClient.sendReceive(payload);

    // Parse the response XML to obtain the required data.
```

```
        System.out.println("--- response ---" + response);
}
```

Creating a Client Using Generated XMLBeans

In general, this type of client is used for "contract first" type of web services. The client can use Axis2-provided "WSDL2Java" utility to generate the stub and service endpoints from WSDL. The generated stub class can be used to invoke the service endpoint. The client code used to invoke the web service endpoint is provided below:

```
private void invokeService() throws java.lang.Exception {
    // Sending the input data as XML to service endpoint
    String inputData = createInputXML("123456");
    EmployeeDemographicServiceStub stub = new
            EmployeeDemographicServiceStub("http://localhost:8080/
            axis2/services/employeeDmographicService");
    GetDemographicInformationDocument input =
            GetDemographicInformationDocument.Factory.newInstance();
    input.addNewGetDemographicInformation().setInputData(inputData);

    // Get the output data as XML from service endpoint
    GetDemographicInformationResponseDocument response =
                        stub.getDemographicInformation(input);
    String outputData =
            response.getGetDemographicInformationResponse().
            getInfo().getOuputData();

    // Parse the outputData xml to obtain the required values.
}
```

Comparison between Apache-CXF and Apache-Axis2

This section compares the technical features of the open-source web service frameworks Apache-CXF and Apache-Axis2. Both of these projects are evolved from their existing frameworks; Axis2 is from its old popular "Axis1"; and CXF is from "Celtix" and "XFire" combination. Now CXF and Axis2 are available under Apache license. Sometimes it is essential to know which framework to be used in Web Services development, but there is no hard and fast rule to choose which one to use. The following table summarizes the pros and cons of each framework.

Feature	Apache-CXF	Axis2
Background and framework evolution	Celtix + XFire combination	From existing Axis1 series.
Spring integration	Clean integration with spring framework. Written with keeping spring framework in mind.	Axis is not, but supports
JAX-WS support	Is the number one priority	Is not the priority but supports. Some cases moved away from JAX-WS standard.
JAX-RS support	Provides more API level support and support for JSR-311.	Can develop Restful services but less API support
Support for Annotations	Superior annotations support at	Less compared with CXF

	various levels.	
Framework maturity	Well matured	Well matured
Migration from older versions	Not well defined. Requires code re-write	Not well defined. Requires code re-write
Support for multiple languages	Supports Java and JSON	C, C++ version is also available
Development style	Both - Java to WSDL and WSDL to Java	Both - Java to WSDL and WSDL to Java
Interoperability	Good	Good
Corporate back-up	IONA	WSO2
Life	CXF is catching up very quickly, very popular these days	Comparable with CXF
JDK versions support	Good for JDK 1.5 and higher	Good for JDK 1.5 and higher
Support for data binding frameworks	Supports JAXB	It supports various data binding frameworks such as adb, xmlbeans, jibx, jaxbri, and so forth.
Admin console for web services deployment and monitoring	Not available	Available. Axis2 provides admin console for "aar" file deployment.
Embedding the code into existing Java/Spring based applications	Very easy and CXF is recommended for this	Requires some effort to create "aar" files.
Ease of use	Quite simple	Same level
Framework set-up and development complexity	Quite simple, use framework provided jar files	Requires "axis2.war" deployment before going for development.
Community support and examples documentation	Very active	Very active.
Use of message handlers	Provides interceptors and annotations, it is very easy to configure handlers at client and server side.	Achieved using custom modules and it requires ".mar" deployment.
Support for logging SOAP messages at client and server side	Provides interceptors at client and server side.	It uses custom modules.
Want to expose existing Spring beans as Web Service endpoints	CXF is recommended	Possible but not preferred.
Want to deploy code as many independent services	It is part of existing application code.	Axis2 is recommended. Package each service into one "aar" file.
Embedding web services into your existing application code	CXF is recommended. No special environment set-up required.	It requires "axis.war" deployment before going for service archive (.aar) deployment.
Simple, easy to use and more JAX-WS support	CXF is recommended	Possible but not preferred.
Tight integration with Spring tags	CXF is recommended. CXF tags can be combined easily with Spring tags; both look similar.	Not recommended.

Comparison between SOAP and Restful Web Services

This section compares the SOAP-based Web Services with REST-based Web Services.

REST	SOAP
Java API for Restful Web Services (JAX-RS) is a Java specification (JSR-311) used for implementing Restful web services.	Java API for XML Web Services (JAX-WS) is a Java specification (JSR-224) used for implementing SOAP based web services.
The REST Web Services are Resource oriented. The Resources are further mapped to sub-resources	SOAP Web Services are activity oriented. Each operation of a service performs some functionality.
It uses XML over HTTP for communication. It provides support for all standard MIME types.	The message structure used to exchange information is SOAP.
It follows the core HTTP specification. The operations performed against the resources are GET, POST, DELETE and PUT.	The service operations are used for implementing the business logic.
REST is very often used with HTTP	SOAP is protocol independent.
It follows "contract-less" type of development methodology.	It follows either "code first" or "contact first" type of service development methodology.
The REST services are quite often used for request-response kind of message exchange pattern.	It supports several message exchange patterns like one-way, asynchronous, etc.
It can use "plain text" or "Web Application Description Language (WADL)" for describing the structure of the Web Service. It is not mandatory to use any standard, because the rules and priorities are elevated at URL level.	The specification used to document the details of the Web Service endpoint structure is "WSDL".
REST gives human readable results; by looking into the URL you can tell what it is.	The functionality is built inside the operations.
Simple, light weight and stateless in nature	Heavy weight due to excessive use of XML.
REST architecture is less complex. It uses HTTP.	Too many standards and specifications. Complex programming model.
Small learning curve.	Steep learning curve

Test Yourself - Objective Type Questions

1. What is the file extension used for developing Axis2 custom modules?
   a) .aar
   b) .war
   c) .ear
   d) .mar
   e) .rar

2. Which of the below given message receiver class can be used for sending and receiving raw XML data as request-and-response? Assuming the service uses in-out message exchange pattern.

---

a) RPCInOnlyMessageReceiver
b) RPCMessageReceiver
c) RawXMLINOutMessageReceiver
d) RPCServiceClient
e) Module

Answers to Test Yourself

1. The correct answer is D. The choice E is not correct because; the extension ".aar" is used for Axis service deployments.

2. The correct answer is C.

Chapter 11. Spring-WS

A decade old open-source Spring framework can be used for developing enterprise applications. The Spring framework provided IOC container is very popular since several years and it became the integral part of Java development for enterprise applications. In addition to the IOC container; Spring provides many extensions for various application layers for Java-based application development. The Spring provided MVC framework can be used for presentation layer framework, Spring JDBC API can be used for database layer framework; and similarly, Spring-based web service framework can be used for developing Java-based Web Services. The Spring Web Services (also called Spring-WS) is an open-source Web services framework used for developing SOAP-based Web services.

In general a Web Service can be developed in two different ways; the "contract-first" and "code-first". The Spring web services framework provide support for only "contract-first" type of web service development. The Spring-WS framework provides its own annotations and XML-based deployment descriptors for web services development. The Spring-WS can take the advantage of Spring IOC container; other core Spring framework provided features. The minimum requirement to develop Spring-based web services is JDK-1.5 and Spring-3.0.

In this chapter will discuss the following topics:

- The use of Spring-WS annotations and its deployment descriptors
- The advantages and disadvantages of Spring-WS.
- The Spring-WS supported web service development methodologies.
- Spring-WS service endpoint design scenarios
- Spring-WS client design scenarios
- How to configure SOAP message handlers using Spring-WS.

Prerequisite and Setting up the Environment

- The required jar files to develop Spring web services are provided along with the Spring web services distribution. Download the Spring web services from springsource.org website.
- Make sure the correct version of jar files is used for development to avoid the class loader jar file version mismatch exceptions. The complete distribution is available in the form of jar files; so no additional software needed for development.
- I tried Spring web services with several combinations, but only Spring-3.0.7 and Spring-WS-2.0.3 is working for complete end-to-end programs. I don't see any issues with other combinations while service deployment/development; but while invoking the service endpoints, the Spring provided web service template is throwing exceptions. So this comment is valid only for web service client programs.
- The below provided jar files are used for developing Spring-WS code examples. The Spring web services version-2.0.3 and Core Spring version-3.0.7 was used. The complete list of dependent jar files is provided in chapter12.

Spring-WS jar files	Core Spring jar files
spring-ws-2.0.3.RELEASE-all.jar	org.springframework.core-3.0.7.RELEASE.jar
spring-ws-2.0.3.RELEASE-sources.jar	org.springframework.core-sources-

	3.0.7.RELEASE.jar
spring-ws-core-2.0.3.RELEASE.jar	org.springframework.context-3.0.7.RELEASE.jar
spring-ws-security-2.0.3.RELEASE.jar	org.springframework.context.support-3.0.7.RELEASE.jar
spring-ws-support-2.0.3.RELEASE.jar	org.springframework.expression-3.0.7.RELEASE.jar
spring-xml-2.0.3.RELEASE.jar	org.springframework.beans-3.0.7.RELEASE.jar
	org.springframework.instrument-3.0.7.RELEASE.jar
	org.springframework.instrument.tomcat-3.0.7.RELEASE.jar
	org.springframework.oxm-3.0.7.RELEASE.jar
	org.springframework.oxm-sources-3.0.7.RELEASE.jar
	org.springframework.web-3.0.7.RELEASE.jar
	org.springframework.web.servlet-3.0.7.RELEASE.jar
	org.springframework.web-sources-3.0.7.RELEASE.jar
	org.springframework.test-3.0.7.RELEASE.jar
	org.springframework.context.support-sources-3.0.7.RELEASE.jar
	org.springframework.asm-3.0.7.RELEASE.jar
	org.springframework.asm-sources-3.0.7.RELEASE.jar

Spring-WS Architecture

Figure 11-1: Spring-WS Architecture using standard data types

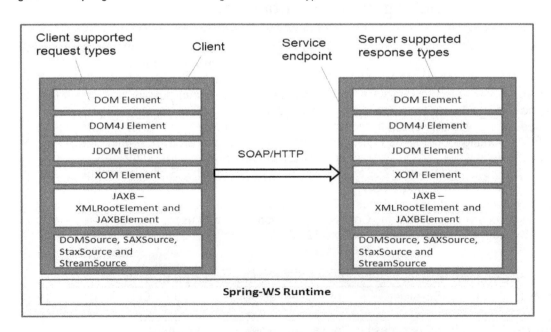

Spring Web Services architecture and its supported request-and-response types are shown in Figure 11-1. The client creates a request of the supported type to invoke the service endpoint. The service endpoint receives the client request; parse the xml to obtain the required input data. The service endpoint sends the response XML back to the client in the form of supported response types. We can use any suitable parsing technique to read/create the request-and-response xml. It provides XML-based and Java-based API support for configuring metadata related to client and service endpoint.

It is possible to use the custom data types for request-and-response messages, but it requires Spring adapters and some special configurations.

Spring-WS Advantages

- The Spring-WS can take advantage of the existing Spring IOC framework provided features.
- The Spring-WS provides support for various XML Java API's and marshalling techniques to handle request-and-response payloads. It supports Dom4j, JDOM, XOM, DOM, SAX, StAX, and JAXB annotated Java classes as parameters and return values.
- It is easy to expose an existing XSD of an application as a Web service.
- A single framework can be used for developing enterprise applications in all layers. The Spring framework can be used in MVC layer, Database layer, Web services layer and application can take advantage of Spring IOC container.

Spring-WS Disadvantages

- It provides support for only "contract-first" type of web services development.
- The development approach is not conforms to JAX-WS provided standards. It does not provide support for JSR-181 annotations.
- Less community support, poor documentation and availability of tutorials as compared with CXF and Axis-2 Web service frameworks.
- There are some issues reported, related to version mismatch of jar files used for Spring-WS, Spring-Core, Xalan, Xerces and SAAJ. The Spring Web services are working well with Spring-3.0.7 and Spring-WS-2.0.3 combination.

Spring-WS Annotations

Spring-WS provides annotations for developing Web Service endpoints. The list of annotations used to develop a Spring-based Web service is given below.

- @Endpoint
- @PayloadRoot
- @RequestPayload
- @ResponsePayload

@Endpoint

This annotation is used at class level to mark the class as a Web Service endpoint. The class annotated with @Endpoint annotation is used to receive the inbound XML requests from the clients. The annotated class can have one or more methods to receive the request payloads; and sends the response back to the invoking clients. The Web service endpoint operations processes the incoming XML; and prepare the response XML based on the input received from the service client. The class annotated with @Endpoint is a special kind of Spring component suitable to handle the XML requests-and-responses. The @Endpoint annotated classes are eligible for component scanning using Spring provided "<context: component-scan/>" xml tag. The details of the component scan are discussed later.

The use of the @Endpoint annotation is provided below.

```
@Endpoint
public class EmployeeEndPoint {
     // ...
}
```

@RequestPayload

This annotation is used with method parameters to receive the request XML messages. It maps the method parameter to the incoming message payload. The use of the @RequestPayload annotation is given below. The payload of the message is passed as a DOM element to the endpoint method.

```
public Element getEmployee(@RequestPayload Element employeeRequest)
throws Exception {
}
```

The entire input request "<getEmployeeRequest/>" is wrapped inside the "<soap:body/>" element of the soap message. A sample request payload is given below:

```
<getEmployeeRequest xmlns="http://springws.ws.learning.com/emp/schemas">
    <employee>
        <employeeId>6666666</employeeId>
    </employee>
</getEmployeeRequest>
```

@PayloadRoot

This annotation is used at method-level to route the incoming request XML messages. It routes the incoming messages to the appropriate method of the service endpoint class. Based on the incoming message "namespace" and its "local name" it decides which method to execute. This annotation is used to identify which method of the service endpoint to be executed based on the message payload.

An example input request message is provided below. The local name is "getEmployeeRequest" and its namespace is "http://springws.ws.learning.com/emp/schemas"; so it will invoke the "getEmployee()" method of the web service endpoint.

```
<getEmployeeRequest xmlns="http://springws.ws.learning.com/emp/schemas">
    <employee>
```

```
            <employeeId>6666666</employeeId>
      </employee>
</getEmployeeRequest>
```

The corresponding web service method signature for the above-specified request payload is provided below.

```
@PayloadRoot(namespace = "http://springws.ws.learning.com/emp/schemas",
            localPart="getEmployeeRequest")
public Element getEmployee(@RequestPayload Element employeeRequest)
throws Exception {
}
```

What happens if the "local name" or "namespace" of endpoint class does not match?

Let us now review the below provided request payload message. The local name of the below given payload is "<getEmployee>"; but the service endpoint expects "getEmployeeRequest" as local name; it does not know where to route the incoming request. The invoking client will throw an endpoint Not Found [404] exception.

Invalid request payload:

```
<getEmployee xmlns="http://springws.ws.learning.com/emp/schemas">
      <employee>
            <employeeId>6666666</employeeId>
      </employee>
</getEmployee>
```


@ResponsePayload

This annotation is used at method-level. It indicates the method return value should map to the response payload. The @ResponsePayload annotation is used only if the method has any return value; and it is not applicable if the method has void return type.

The use of the @ResponsePayload annotation is given below.

```
@PayloadRoot(namespace="http://springws.ws.learning.com/emp/schemas",
            localPart="getEmployeeRequest")
@ResponsePayload
public Element getEmployee(@RequestPayload Element employeeRequest)
throws Exception {
    // ...
    return response;
}
```

The supported method parameter, return types of a payload message request-and-response are listed below:

- W3C DOM Element
- Dom4j Element
- JDOM Element
- XOM Element
- JAXB Type - Any type that is annotated with XMLRootElement and JAXBElement

- DOMSource, SAXSource, StaxSource and StreamSource
- Any type supported by Spring OXM Marsheller.

Spring-WS supports above-specified list of standard types as parameters and return values. It is possible to use other data types; bit it requires Spring provided custom adapter classes.

Development Methodologies

The Spring-WS supports only "contact-first" kind of Web service development methodology. The contract-first development for Spring-WS starts with WSDL or XSD. The web service developer can create a WSDL for service endpoint or create an XSD with request-response types. The Spring-WS provided tools this take XSD as input; used to generate the WSDL dynamically.

Example 1: Spring-WS Endpoint with Dom4j API

This Web service endpoint is developed with Dom4j *Element* type as request-and-response payload. The steps required to develop a Spring-based Web service using Dom4j API is given below.

1. Create a XSD document
2. Create a service endpoint interface
3. Create a web.xml file
4. Create a springws-servlet.xml configuration file
5. Create a war file and deploy it in Tomcat server
6. Verify the generated WSDL document
7. Write a client to invoke the deployed service endpoint

The above-specified steps are described in the following sections:

This is an example of an employee web service; for a given employee id it provides the complete details about that employee. Let us now start with defining an XML schema for this service.

Step 1: Create a XSD Document

This is the first step to start with for developing a Spring-based web service.

- Convert the domain model to an XML type
- Create a XML request root element
- Create a XML response root element

The above defined XML types are used for request-and-response message payloads. The Spring runtime expects "Request" and "Response" suffix for data types.

The following XML element represents the request payload. This is the root element for the request payload message. The suffix "Request" is used to generate the WSDL message and part elements.

```
<xs:element name="getEmployeeRequest" type="emp:EmployeeRequest"/>
```

The following XML element represents the response payload. This is the root element for the response payload message. The suffix "Response" is used to generate the WSDL message and part elements

---

```
<xs:element name="getEmployeeResponse" type="emp:EmployeeResponse"/>
```

The following XML complex type represents the request payload type. It has only one input parameter employee id, of type string.

```
<xs:complexType name="EmployeeRequest">
    <xs:sequence>
    <xs:element minOccurs="0" name="employeeId" type="xs:string"/>
    </xs:sequence>
</xs:complexType>
```

The following XML complex type represents the response payload type. It wraps the complete employee details.

```
<xs:complexType name="EmployeeResponse">
    <xs:sequence>
        <xs:element minOccurs="0" name="return" type="emp:employee"/>
    </xs:sequence>
</xs:complexType>
```

The following XML complex type represents the details of an employee; it includes name, address, email and phone number.

```
<xs:complexType name="employee">
    <xs:sequence>
        <xs:element minOccurs="0" name="nameInfo" type="emp:nameInfo"/>
        <xs:element minOccurs="0" name="homeAddress"
                type="emp:homeAddress"/>
        <xs:element minOccurs="0" name="emailAddress"
                type="emp:emailAddress"/>
        <xs:element minOccurs="0" name="phones" type="emp:phones"/>
    </xs:sequence>
</xs:complexType>
```

The complete XML schema document is provided below, named as "employee.xsd".

```
<?xml version="1.0" encoding="UTF-8"?>
<xs:schema xmlns:xs="http://www.w3.org/2001/XMLSchema"
        xmlns:emp="http://springws.ws.learning.com/emp/schemas"
        elementFormDefault="unqualified"
        targetNamespace="http://springws.ws.learning.com/emp/schemas">

    <!-- Root element for request -->
    <xs:element name="getEmployeeRequest" type="emp:EmployeeRequest"/>

    <!-- Root element for response -->
    <xs:element name="getEmployeeResponse" type="emp:EmployeeResponse"/>

    <xs:complexType name="EmployeeRequest">
        <xs:sequence>
            <xs:element minOccurs="0" name="employeeId"
                    type="xs:string"/>
        </xs:sequence>
    </xs:complexType>
```

```xml
<xs:complexType name="EmployeeResponse">
    <xs:sequence>
        <xs:element minOccurs="0" name="return"
                type="emp:employee"/>
    </xs:sequence>
</xs:complexType>

<xs:complexType name="employee">
    <xs:sequence>
        <xs:element minOccurs="0" name="nameInfo"
                type="emp:nameInfo"/>
        <xs:element minOccurs="0" name="homeAddress"
                type="emp:homeAddress"/>
        <xs:element minOccurs="0" name="emailAddress"
                type="emp:emailAddress"/>
        <xs:element minOccurs="0" name="phones" type="emp:phones"/>
    </xs:sequence>
</xs:complexType>

<xs:complexType name="nameInfo">
    <xs:sequence>
        <xs:element minOccurs="0" name="id" type="xs:string"/>
        <xs:element minOccurs="0" name="firstName"
                    type="xs:string"/>
        <xs:element minOccurs="0" name="lastName"
                    type="xs:string"/>
    </xs:sequence>
</xs:complexType>

<xs:complexType name="homeAddress">
    <xs:sequence>
        <xs:element minOccurs="0" name="aptNumber"
                        type="xs:string"/>
        <xs:element minOccurs="0" name="streetName"
                        type="xs:string"/>
        <xs:element minOccurs="0" name="city" type="xs:string"/>
        <xs:element minOccurs="0" name="zipcode" type="xs:string"/>
        <xs:element minOccurs="0" name="state" type="xs:string"/>
        <xs:element minOccurs="0" name="country" type="xs:string"/>
    </xs:sequence>
</xs:complexType>

<xs:complexType name="emailAddress">
    <xs:sequence>
        <xs:element minOccurs="0" name="personal"
                    type="xs:string"/>
        <xs:element minOccurs="0" name="office" type="xs:string"/>
    </xs:sequence>
</xs:complexType>

<xs:complexType name="phones">
    <xs:sequence>
        <xs:element minOccurs="0" name="personal"
                    type="xs:string"/>
        <xs:element minOccurs="0" name="office" type="xs:string"/>
    </xs:sequence>
</xs:complexType>
```

```
</xs:schema>
```

Step 2: Create a Service Endpoint Interface

Create a service endpoint class to receive the request-and-response payloads. The Spring-WS provided annotations are used for endpoint class. This endpoint class is annotated using @Endpoint annotation; so it marks as a special kind of Spring component that can handle XML request-and-response messages.

```
@Endpoint
public class EmployeeEndPoint {
}
```

The following code checks the "localPart" and "namespace" of the incoming request-payload and routes to the appropriate method.

```
@PayloadRoot(namespace = "http://springws.ws.learning.com/emp/schemas",
             localPart = "getEmployeeRequest")
```

The following code represents the method signature of the service endpoint used to process the incoming request payloads, and sends the response back to the invoking client. This method uses Dom4j *Element* as a request parameter and return value.

```
@ResponsePayload
public Element getEmployee(@RequestPayload Element employeeRequest)
throws Exception {
}
```

The complete method code is provided below:

```
@PayloadRoot(namespace = "http://springws.ws.learning.com/emp/schemas",
             localPart = "getEmployeeRequest")
@ResponsePayload
public Element getEmployee(@RequestPayload  Element  employeeRequest)
throws Exception {
    // private method used for parsing the request payload
    String employeeId =
    getEmployeeIdFromInputXML(employeeRequest.asXML());
    if (employeeId == null || employeeId == "") {
        employeeId = "99999999";
    }

    // private method used for creating the response payload
    Element response = createResponseXML(employeeId);
    System.out.println("-- response Message --" + response.asXML());
    return response;
}
```

The below provided private method is used for parsing the request payload. This method obtains the data from incoming XML to apply the business logic. The Dom4j API is used for creating the request-and-response payloads.

```
String employeeId = getEmployeeIdFromInputXML(employeeRequest.asXML());
```

The below provided private method is used for creating the response payload. It creates the response payload. In real world we obtain the data from persistent store.

```
Element response = createResponseXML(employeeId);
```

The complete web service endpoint class code is provided in Listing 11-1.

Listing 11-1: Developing Spring-based endpoint using Dom4j

```java
// EmployeeEndPoint.java
package com.learning.springws;

import org.springframework.ws.server.endpoint.annotation.*;
import org.dom4j.*;
import org.dom4j.io.SAXReader;
import java.io.ByteArrayInputStream;
import java.util.Iterator;

@Endpoint
public class EmployeeEndPoint {

    @PayloadRoot(namespace=
            "http://springws.ws.learning.com/emp/schemas",
            localPart = "getEmployeeRequest")
    @ResponsePayload
    public Element getEmployee(@RequestPayload Element employeeRequest)
    throws Exception {
        // private method used for parsing the request payload
        String employeeId =
            getEmployeeIdFromInputXML(employeeRequest.asXML());
        if(employeeId == null || employeeId == "") {
            employeeId = "99999999";
        }

        // private method used for creating the response payload
        Element response = createResponseXML(employeeId);
        System.out.println("--response Message --" + response.asXML());
        return response;
    }

    // private method used for creating the response payload.
    private Element createResponseXML(String employeeId) {
        Document document = DocumentHelper.createDocument();
        Element responseElement =
                document.addElement("getEmployeeResponse");
        Element rootElement = responseElement.addElement("employee");
        Element nameElement = rootElement.addElement("nameinfo");
        nameElement.addElement("id").addText(employeeId);
        nameElement.addElement("firstName").addText("John");
        nameElement.addElement("lastName").addText("Smith");

        Element homeAddressElement =
                rootElement.addElement("homeAddress");
        homeAddressElement.addElement("aptNumber").addText("2340");
        homeAddressElement.addElement("streetName").
                            addText("W.Roundabout Cir");
        homeAddressElement.addElement("city").addText("Chandler");
```

```java
        homeAddressElement.addElement("zipcode").addText("85225");
        homeAddressElement.addElement("state").addText("AZ");
        homeAddressElement.addElement("country").addText("USA");

        Element emailElement = rootElement.addElement("emailAddress");
        emailElement.addElement("personal").
                        addText("wsbook@mymail.com");
        emailElement.addElement("office").addText("srinivas@abc.com");

        Element phoneElement = rootElement.addElement("phones");
        phoneElement.addElement("personal").addText("480-645-6753");
        phoneElement.addElement("office").addText("602-667-6782");
        return rootElement;
    }

    /* private method used for parsing the request payload to get the
    data*/
    public String getEmployeeIdFromInputXML(String inputXML) throws
    Exception {
        SAXReader reader = new SAXReader();
        Document document = reader.read(new
                        ByteArrayInputStream(inputXML.getBytes()));
        Element root = document.getRootElement();
        String employeeId = null;
        for (Iterator i = root.elementIterator(); i.hasNext();) {
            Element element = (Element) i.next();
            for (int j = 0,size = element.nodeCount(); j < size; j++) {
                Node node = (Node) element.node(j);
                    if (node instanceof Element) {
                        if ("employeeId".
                            equalsIgnoreCase(node.getName())) {
                        employeeId = node.getText();
                        }
                    }
            }
        }
        System.out.println("--- employeeId: ---" + employeeId);
        return employeeId;
    }
}
```

Step 3: Create a web.xml File

This is a standard Java EE container specific configuration which requires for any web services framework. The Spring provided servlet "MessageDispatcherServlet" class is used for HTTP transport. This servlet has to be configured in web applications web.xml file. The servlet name and its mapping are given below.

```xml
<servlet>
    <servlet-name>springws</servlet-name>
    <servlet-class>
        org.springframework.ws.transport.http.MessageDispatcherServlet
    </servlet-class>
    <init-param>
        <param-name>transformWsdlLocations</param-name>
        <param-value>true</param-value>
```

```
        </init-param>
</servlet>

<servlet-mapping>
    <servlet-name>springws</servlet-name>
    <url-pattern>/services/*</url-pattern>
</servlet-mapping>
```

The endpoint URL which contains **"/services/"** URL pattern is routed through the Spring-WS configured message dispatcher servlet.

The following configuration is used for location transformation. So it allows us to access the WSDL without specifying the absolute path.

```
<init-param>
    <param-name>transformWsdlLocations</param-name>
    <param-value>true</param-value>
</init-param>
```

So we can specify locationUri="/services/employeeService/" where ever we use it in Spring configurations, instead of locationUri="http://localhost:8080/springws/services/employeeService/". This is further discussed in next section.

Step 4: Create a springws-servlet.xml Configuration File

This file contains the Spring Web services related information such as endpoints, interceptors, etc. It loads all the defined Spring beans into the Spring IOC container. The name of the xml file follows the standard Spring syntax. The suffix should be "servlet"; and the prefix of the xml file should match the value of the "<servlet-name/>" tag specified in web.xml. The name used in web.xml is "springws"; so the file name "springws-servlet.xml" is used in this example. The prefix and suffix should be separated with a hyphen.

The file name syntax is: {prefix}-{suffix}.xml which is springws-servlet.xml.

The complete XML file is given below. Let us now examine each element and its significance. The configurations specified in this XML are used for Spring IOC container.

```
<?xml version="1.0" encoding="UTF-8"?>
<beans xmlns="http://www.springframework.org/schema/beans"
        xmlns:xsi="http://www.w3.org/2001/XMLSchema-instance"
        xmlns:context="http://www.springframework.org/schema/context"
        xmlns:sws="http://www.springframework.org/schema/web-services"
        xsi:schemaLocation="http://www.springframework.org/schema/beans
        http://www.springframework.org/schema/beans/spring-beans-
        3.0.xsd
        http://www.springframework.org/schema/web-services
        http://www.springframework.org/schema/web-services/web-
        services-2.0.xsd
        http://www.springframework.org/schema/context
        http://www.springframework.org/schema/context/spring-context-
        3.0.xsd">

    <context:component-scan base-package="com.learning.springws"/>

    <sws:annotation-driven/>
```

```
    <sws:dynamic-wsdl id="employee"
        portTypeName="EmployeePortType"
        locationUri="/services/employeeService/"
        targetNamespace="http://springws.learning.com/emp/definitions">
        <sws:xsd location="/WEB-INF/employee.xsd"/>
    </sws:dynamic-wsdl>

</beans>
```

The following code will detect the beans defined in the base package and loads them into the Spring IOC container without any overhead. So we can auto wire the required bean classes in our application code.

```
<context:component-scan base-package="com.learning.springws"/>
```

The following code is used to intimate the beans of Spring IOC container are annotation supported. So the service endpoint class can use Spring-WS provided annotations such as @Endpoint, @PayloadRoot, etc. This XML tag enables the use of annotations in web service endpoint classes.

```
<sws:annotation-driven/>
```

The Spring Web services can generate a WSDL from XSD schema. The elements of the schema which has suffix "Request" and "Response" is used for generating the WSDL *messages* and *part* elements. Spring runtime generates WSDL operations for all request-and-response elements.

```
<sws:dynamic-wsdl id="employee"
    portTypeName="EmployeePortType"
    locationUri="/services/employeeService/"
    targetNamespace="http://springws.learning.com/emp/definitions">
    <sws:xsd location="/WEB-INF/employee.xsd"/>
</sws:dynamic-wsdl>
```

The below given XML tag is used to generate the WSDL for a given XML schema. The attribute "Id" is used to access the WSDL document.

```
<sws:dynamic-wsdl id="employee"
```

This attribute name "portTypeName" maps to the <wsdl:portType/> of the generated WSDL. The *port name* and generated WSDL is given below:

The port name is given below:

```
portTypeName="EmployeePortType"
```

The generated WSDL is given below:

```
<wsdl:portType name="EmployeePortType">
    <wsdl:operation name="getEmployee">
        <wsdl:input message="tns:getEmployeeRequest"
            name="getEmployeeRequest"/>
        <wsdl:output message="tns:getEmployeeResponse"
            name="getEmployeeResponse"/>
    </wsdl:operation>
</wsdl:portType>
```

The following attribute name "locationUri" represents the location of the Web service endpoint. The transform "transformWsdlLocations" enabled in web.xml so no need to specify the absolute URL.

```
locationUri="/services/employeeService/"
```

The following attribute name "targetNamespace" represents the target namespace used for generating the WSDL document.

```
targetNamespace="http://springws.learning.com/emp/definitions
```

The following XML element represents the location of the xml schema document used for generating the WSDL dynamically.

```
<sws:xsd location="/WEB-INF/employee.xsd"/>
```

Step 5: Create a war File, and Deploy it in Tomcat Server

1. Build a war file using Ant or any other build tool. Make sure the following files are packaged correctly in war file.
   a. Service endpoint implementation class
   b. Any utility classes used for data access.
   c. The web.xml file should be packaged into "WEB-INF/" directory.
   d. The springws-servlet.xml configuration file should be packaged into "WEB-INF/" directory.
   e. All dependent jar files should be packaged into "WEB-INF/lib" directory.

2. Deploy the war file in any servlet container.
   a. Copy the packed war into "apache-tomcat/webapps" directory
   b. Start the tomcat sever by running the "startup.bat" batch file available in "apache-tomcat/bin" directory
   c. View the server console output/logs; make sure war file is deployed without any errors.

The structure of the generated war file is shown in Figure 11-2:

Figure 11-2: war file structure

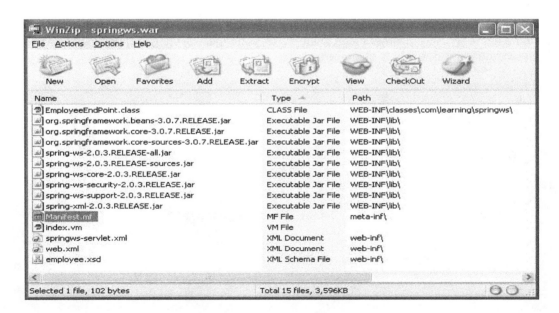

Development Methodologies

NOTE: Refer to Chapter12 for the complete list of jar files required to develop these code examples.

Step 6: Verify the Generated WSDL Document

Access the WSDL file from web browser to make sure the service is deployed properly without any errors. Use the below given URL to view the complete WSDL.

```
http://localhost:8080/springws/services/employeeService/employee.wsdl
```

- The server name and port used = **localhost:8080**
- The web application context (default name is war file name) = **springws**
- The URL pattern defined in web.xml file is = **services**
- The name specified in location URI = **employeeService**
- The "id" attribute value of the "<sws:dynamic-wsdl>" tag = **employee**

Spring-WS framework uses "dot" notation to access the generated WSDL document. All other frameworks like CXF and Axis2 uses question mark (?) notation to access the generated WSDL documents.

Spring web service framework notation to access the WSDL is given below:

```
http://localhost:8080/springws/services/employeeService/employee.wsdl
```

Other web service frameworks notation to access the WSDL is given below:

```
http://localhost:8080/bookws/services/employeeService/employee?wsdl
```

Step 7: Write a Client to Invoke the Deployed Service Endpoint

Spring web services framework provided "WebServiceTemplate" class can be used for accessing the deployed web service endpoint. There are two different ways a client can set the values of the metadata.

- Using Spring provided Java API
- Using XML-based configuration.

The XML-based configuration is used for the below provided client.

This following XML element is used for setting the message factory. This is the default setting used for Spring; so its use is optional.

```
<bean id="messageFactory"
    class="org.springframework.ws.soap.saaj.SaajSoapMessageFactory"/>
```

This following XML element is used for setting the protocol used for message transfer. By default Spring uses HTTP as a transfer protocol; so its use is optional.

```
<bean id="messageSender" class=
    "org.springframework.ws.transport.http.CommonsHttpMessageSender"/>
```

The "WebServiceTemplate" is the core template used for accessing the web service endpoint. The only mandatory required property for the web service template is "defaultUri"; it specifies the location of the deployed web service endpoint.

```
<bean id="webServiceTemplate"
    class="org.springframework.ws.client.core.WebServiceTemplate">
    <property name="defaultUri"
    value="http://localhost:8080/springws/services/employeeService/"/>
</bean>
```

The below provided "applicationContext-client.xml" file is used for client specific configurations.

```
<?xml version="1.0" encoding="UTF-8"?>
<beans xmlns="http://www.springframework.org/schema/beans"
    xmlns:xsi="http://www.w3.org/2001/XMLSchema-instance"
    xmlns:context="http://www.springframework.org/schema/context"
    xmlns:sws="http://www.springframework.org/schema/web-services"
    xsi:schemaLocation="http://www.springframework.org/schema/beans
    http://www.springframework.org/schema/beans/spring-beans-3.0.xsd
    http://www.springframework.org/schema/web-services
    http://www.springframework.org/schema/web-services/web-services-
    2.0.xsd
    http://www.springframework.org/schema/context
    http://www.springframework.org/schema/context/spring-context-
        3.0.xsd">

    <bean id="messageFactory" class=
        "org.springframework.ws.soap.saaj.SaajSoapMessageFactory"/>

    <bean id="messageSender" class=
    "org.springframework.ws.transport.http.CommonsHttpMessageSender"/>

    <bean id="webServiceTemplate"
        class="org.springframework.ws.client.core.WebServiceTemplate">
        <constructor-arg ref="messageFactory"/>
        <property name="messageSender" ref="messageSender"/>
        <property name="defaultUri" value=
        "http://localhost:8080/springws/services/employeeService/"/>
    </bean>
</beans>
```

Now let us review the client code to invoke the endpoint. The code given below is used for getting the handle of the web service template which is configured in "applicationContext-client.xml" file.

```
ClassPathXmlApplicationContext context
    = new ClassPathXmlApplicationContext(new
            String[]{"applicationContext-client.xml"});
WebServiceTemplate webServiceTemplate = (WebServiceTemplate)
                        context.getBean("webServiceTemplate");
```

This below provided private method is used for creating the input request payload. The Dom4j API is used for creating the request XML payload.

```
String requestXML = createInputXML(employeeId);
```

The created input request payload is provided below. The request payload must use the same local part name (getEmployeeRequest) and namespace (http://springws.ws.learning.com/emp/schemas) as we specified in the web service endpoint using @PayloadRoot annotation. It matches these values to route the incoming request to an endpoint method. The Spring runtime constructs the SOAP envelope using this request payload.

The input request-message is provided below:

```
<getEmployeeRequest  xmlns="http://springws.ws.learning.com/emp/schemas">
    <employee>
        <employeeId>6666666</employeeId>
    </employee>
</getEmployeeRequest>
```

The Spring runtime generated SOAP request for this case is provided below:

```
<soapenv:Envelope
        xmlns:soapenv="http://schemas.xmlsoap.org/soap/envelope/">
    <soapenv:Body>
        <getEmployeeRequest
            xmlns="http://springws.ws.learning.com/emp/schemas">
            <employee>
                <employeeId>6666666</employeeId>
            </employee>
        </getEmployeeRequest>
    </soapenv:Body>
</soapenv:Envelope>
```

The "sendSourceAndReceiveToResult" method of the Spring web service template can be used for accessing the web service endpoint.

```
Source source = new StringSource(requestXML);
Result result = new StringResult();
webServiceTemplate.sendSourceAndReceiveToResult(source, result);
```

The service client can use any parsing technique to obtain the required data from response payload. The complete client code used to access the web service endpoint is Listed in 11-2.

Listing 11-2: Client for accessing Spring-based endpoint.

```java
// SpringWSClient.java
package com.learning.springws;

import org.springframework.ws.client.core.WebServiceTemplate;
import
org.springframework.context.support.ClassPathXmlApplicationContext;
import org.springframework.xml.transform.StringSource;
import org.springframework.xml.transform.StringResult;
import org.dom4j.*;
import javax.xml.transform.Source;
import javax.xml.transform.Result;

public class SpringWSClient {

    public static void main(String args[]) {
        try {
```

```
            SpringWSClient client = new SpringWSClient();
            client.invokeService("6666666");
        } catch (Exception ex) {
            ex.printStackTrace();
        }
    }

    private void invokeService(String employeeId) throws Exception {
        ClassPathXmlApplicationContext context
            = new ClassPathXmlApplicationContext(new
                String[]{"applicationContext-client.xml"});
        WebServiceTemplate webServiceTemplate = (WebServiceTemplate)
                        context.getBean("webServiceTemplate");

        String requestXML = createInputXML(employeeId);
        Source source = new StringSource(requestXML);
        Result result = new StringResult();
        webServiceTemplate.sendSourceAndReceiveToResult(source,result);

        // Parse the result using some parsing technique.
        System.out.println("-- result --" + result.toString());
    }

    // private method used for creating the request payload.
    private String createInputXML(String employeeId) throws Exception {
        Document document = DocumentHelper.createDocument();
        Element requestElement =
            document.addElement("getEmployeeRequest",
                "http://springws.ws.learning.com/emp/schemas");
        Element employeeElement=requestElement.addElement("employee");
        employeeElement.addElement("employeeId").addText(employeeId);
        // converting input XML to a String
        return document.asXML();
    }
}
```

The result of the web service endpoint is provided below. Use suitable parsing technique to obtain the employee information.

```
<?xml version="1.0" encoding="UTF-8"?>
<getEmployeeResponse>
    <employee>
        <nameinfo>
            <id>6666666</id>
            <firstName>John</firstName>
            <lastName>Smith</lastName>
        </nameinfo>

        <homeAddress>
            <aptNumber>2340</aptNumber>
            <streetName>W.Roundabout Cir</streetName>
            <city>Chandler</city>
            <zipcode>85225</zipcode>
            <state>AZ</state>
            <country>USA</country>
        </homeAddress>
```

```
                <emailAddress>
                     <personal>wsbook@mymail.com</personal>
                     <office>srinivas@abc.com</office>
                </emailAddress>

                <phones>
                     <personal>480-645-6753</personal>
                     <office>602-667-6782</office>
                </phones>
          </employee>
</getEmployeeResponse>
```

Example 2: Spring-WS SOAP Message Handler Framework

The very common requirement while developing Web Services is to use the message handlers to intercept request-and-response soap messages. Spring-based Web services provide a good support to configure the message interceptors with client and service endpoint to manipulate the request-and-response soap messages. This section illustrates the use of Spring interceptors with client and service endpoint.

Service Endpoint Side — Configuring SOAP Handler using Spring-WS

The endpoint handler class must implement the "org.springframework.ws.server.EndpointInterceptor" interface to configure the interceptor with service endpoint. This interface has four methods defined; the endpoint interceptor class must implement these four methods to process the request-and-response payloads. The four methods of this interface are listed below.

- boolean handleRequest() throws java.lang.Exception;
- boolean handleResponse() throws java.lang.Exception;
- boolean handleFault() throws java.lang.Exception;
- void afterCompletion() throws java.lang.Exception;

Now lets us write our own interceptor class to log the request-and-response payloads. Listing 11-3 has the complete class code can be used to log the soap messages with service endpoint.

Listing 11-3: Developing Spring-based SOAP message handlers

```java
// LogMessageHandler.java
package com.learning.springws;

import org.springframework.ws.server.EndpointInterceptor;
import org.springframework.ws.context.MessageContext;
import org.springframework.ws.WebServiceMessage;
import java.io.ByteArrayOutputStream;

public class LogMessageHandler implements EndpointInterceptor {

     public boolean handleRequest(MessageContext messageContext,Object o)
     throws Exception {
          WebServiceMessage requestMessage = messageContext.getRequest();
          if (requestMessage != null) {
               // Printing the request message on the console.
```

```
            ByteArrayOutputStream out = new ByteArrayOutputStream();
            requestMessage.writeTo(out);
            String request = new String(out.toByteArray());
            System.out.println("--- Endpoint request ---" + request);
        }
        return true;
    }

    public boolean handleResponse(MessageContext messageContext,
                    Object o) throws Exception {
        WebServiceMessage responseMessage =
                    messageContext.getResponse();
        if (responseMessage != null) {
            // Printing the response message on the console.
            ByteArrayOutputStream out = new ByteArrayOutputStream();
            responseMessage.writeTo(out);
            String response = new String(out.toByteArray());
            System.out.println("-- Endpoint response --" + response);
        }
        return true;
    }

    public boolean handleFault(MessageContext messageContext, Object o)
    throws Exception {
        return true;
    }

    public void afterCompletion(MessageContext messageContext, Object o,
    Exception e) throws Exception {
    }
}
```

The above class simply logs the request-and-response payload messages on the server console. Let us now examine code snippets and its significance.

The following endpoint class must implement Spring framework provided "EndpointInterceptor" interface.

```
public class LogMessageHandler implements EndpointInterceptor {
}
```

The following method is used to receive the complete request message.

```
public boolean handleRequest(MessageContext messageContext, Object o)
throws Exception
```

The following method is used to receive the complete response message.

```
public boolean handleResponse(MessageContext messageContext, Object o)
throws Exception
```

The following method is used to handle faults related soap messages.

```
public boolean handleFault(MessageContext messageContext, Object o)
throws Exception
```

The following method is used to perform required clean-up activities.

```
public void afterCompletion(MessageContext messageContext, Object o,
Exception e) throws Exception
```

The "hasResponse()" method of the "MessageContext" object can be used to know the direction of message; which is request or response. It returns "false" for the request messages, "true" for response messages.

```
Boolean hasResponse = messageContext.hasResponse();
```

How to integrate the above provided interceptor class with service endpoint.

The Spring framework provided "<sws:interceptors/>" tag can be used to integrate the interceptors with service endpoint.

```
<sws:interceptors>
    <sws:payloadRoot
        namespaceUri="http://springws.ws.learning.com/emp/schemas">
        <bean class="com.learning.springws.LogMessageHandler"/>
    </sws:payloadRoot>
</sws:interceptors>
```

Add the above provided XML to "springws-servlet.xml" file to log the request-and-response soap messages with service endpoint. The complete "springws-servlet.xml" file is given below:

```
<?xml version="1.0" encoding="UTF-8"?>
<beans xmlns="http://www.springframework.org/schema/beans"
    xmlns:xsi="http://www.w3.org/2001/XMLSchema-instance"
    xmlns:context="http://www.springframework.org/schema/context"
    xmlns:sws="http://www.springframework.org/schema/web-services"
    xsi:schemaLocation="http://www.springframework.org/schema/beans
    http://www.springframework.org/schema/beans/spring-beans-3.0.xsd
    http://www.springframework.org/schema/web-services
    http://www.springframework.org/schema/web-services/web-services-
    2.0.xsd
    http://www.springframework.org/schema/context
    http://www.springframework.org/schema/context/spring-context-
    3.0.xsd">

    <context:component-scan base-package="com.learning.springws"/>

    <sws:annotation-driven/>

    <sws:dynamic-wsdl id="employee"
        portTypeName="EmployeePortType"
        locationUri="/services/employeeService/"
        targetNamespace="http://springws.learning.com/emp/definitions">
        <sws:xsd location="/WEB-INF/employee.xsd"/>
    </sws:dynamic-wsdl>

    <sws:interceptors>
        <sws:payloadRoot namespaceUri=
            "http://springws.ws.learning.com/emp/schemas">
            <bean class="com.learning.springws.LogMessageHandler"/>
        </sws:payloadRoot>
```

```
    </sws:interceptors>

</beans>
```

Client Side — Configuring SOAP Handler using Spring-WS

The client side handler class must implement the Spring framework provided interface
"org.springframework.ws.client.support.interceptor.ClientInterceptor" to configure the interceptor
with Web service client. This interface has three methods defined; the client side interceptor class
must implement these three methods to process the request-and-response payloads. The three
methods of this interface are listed below.

- boolean handleRequest() throws java.lang.Exception;
- boolean handleResponse() throws java.lang.Exception;
- boolean handleFault() throws java.lang.Exception;

Now lets us write our own interceptor class to log the request-and-response payloads. Listing 11-4
has the complete Java code that can be used to log the soap messages with web service client.

Listing 11-4: Using Spring-based SOAP message handlers

```java
// ClientLogMessageHandler.java
package com.learning.springws;

import
org.springframework.ws.client.support.interceptor.ClientInterceptor;
import org.springframework.ws.client.WebServiceClientException;
import org.springframework.ws.context.MessageContext;
import org.springframework.ws.WebServiceMessage;
import java.io.ByteArrayOutputStream;
import java.io.IOException;

public class ClientLogMessageHandler implements ClientInterceptor {

    public boolean handleRequest(MessageContext messageContext) throws
        WebServiceClientException {
    WebServiceMessage requestMessage = messageContext.getRequest();
        try {
                if (requestMessage != null) {
                // Printing the request message on console.
                ByteArrayOutputStream out = new
                    ByteArrayOutputStream();
                requestMessage.writeTo(out);
                String request = new String(out.toByteArray());
                System.out.println("--  Client Request --" + request);
                }
        } catch (IOException ex) {
            ex.printStackTrace();
        }
        return true;
    }

    public boolean handleResponse(MessageContext messageContext) throws
    WebServiceClientException {
        WebServiceMessage responseMessage=messageContext.getResponse();
        try {
```

```
            if (responseMessage != null) {
                // Printing the response message on console.
                ByteArrayOutputStream out = new
                            ByteArrayOutputStream();
                responseMessage.writeTo(out);
                String response = new String(out.toByteArray());
                System.out.println("--Service Response--" +response);
            }
        } catch (IOException ex) {
            ex.printStackTrace();
        }
        return true;
    }

    public boolean handleFault(MessageContext messageContext) throws
    WebServiceClientException {
        return true;
    }
}
```

How to configure the above provided interceptor class with web service client.

The "setInterceptors()" method of the "WebServiceTemplate" object can be used to configure the array of interceptors with web service client to process the request-and-response messages. The Spring-based interceptors can be added in two different ways.

- Non XML-based using Spring Java API
- Using XML-based configurations

CASE 1: Non XML-based Using Spring Java API

In this approach Spring-based Java API can be used to configure the interceptors with web service client. An example code is provided below.

```
ClientLogMessageHandler[] handler = new ClientLogMessageHandler[1];
handler[0] = new ClientLogMessageHandler();
WebServiceTemplate webServiceTemplate = new WebServiceTemplate();
webServiceTemplate.setDefaultUri("http://localhost:8080/springws/services
/employeeService/");
webServiceTemplate.setInterceptors(handler);
```

The below provided code can be used to configure the interceptors with web service client.

```
private void invokeService(String employeeId) throws Exception {
    ClientLogMessageHandler[] handler = new ClientLogMessageHandler[1];
    handler[0] = new ClientLogMessageHandler();
    WebServiceTemplate webServiceTemplate = new WebServiceTemplate();
    webServiceTemplate.setDefaultUri("http://localhost:8080/
                    springws/services/employeeService/");
    webServiceTemplate.setInterceptors(handler);

    // private method used to create a request payload.
    String requestXML = createInputXML(employeeId);
    Source source = new StringSource(requestXML);
    Result result = new StringResult();
```

```
webServiceTemplate.sendSourceAndReceiveToResult(source, result);
System.out.println("--- result ---" + result.toString());
}
```

CASE 2: XML-based Configurations

The Spring also supports XML-based configuration to configure the interceptors with Web service client. The XML used to configure the interceptor bean with web service template is provided below:

```xml
<bean id="webServiceTemplate"
      class="org.springframework.ws.client.core.WebServiceTemplate">
    <constructor-arg ref="messageFactory"/>
<property name="defaultUri" value=
    "http://localhost:8080/springws/services/employeeService/"/>
    <property name="interceptors" ref="logMessages"/>
</bean>

<bean id="logMessages"
      class="com.learning.springws.ClientLogMessageHandler"/>
```

The below provided code can be used with web service client.

```java
private void invokeService(String employeeId) throws Exception {
    ClassPathXmlApplicationContext context
        = new ClassPathXmlApplicationContext(new
                     String[]{"applicationContext-client.xml"});
    WebServiceTemplate webServiceTemplate = (WebServiceTemplate)
                             context.getBean("webServiceTemplate");

    String requestXML = createInputXML(employeeId);
    Source source = new StringSource(requestXML);
    Result result = new StringResult();
    webServiceTemplate.sendSourceAndReceiveToResult(source, result);
    System.out.println("--- result ---" + result.toString());
}
```

It is possible to configure any number of interceptors between client and service endpoint. Also Spring provides support to write log messages to Log4j configured log file.

Example 3: Spring-WS Endpoint with JDOM API

This type Web service endpoint is developed with JDOM Element type as request-and-response payload. JDOM is an open source XML parsing framework can be used for reading/writing XML documents. JDOM is an alternative to SAX and DOM. JDOM provides higher level API for parsing XML documents. The steps required to develop a Spring-based Web service using JDOM API is given below.

1. Create a XSD document
2. Create a service endpoint interface
3. Create the springws-servlet.xml configuration file
4. Create a web.xml file
5. Create a war file and deploy it in Tomcat server
6. Verify the generated WSDL document
7. Write a client to invoke the deployed service endpoint

Development Methodologies

The above-specified steps are described in the following sections:

This example demonstrates the use of holiday Web service; for a given year it provides the list of federal holidays. Let us now start defining the xml schema of the service.

Step 1: Create a XSD Document

The first step is to prepare a XSD of the web service endpoint. Convert the domain model to an XML types; and create a XML root element for request-response payloads. The complete XML schema document is provided below. Spring run time uses this XSD for generating the WSDL.

```xml
<?xml version="1.0" encoding="UTF-8"?>
<xs:schema xmlns:xs="http://www.w3.org/2001/XMLSchema"
    xmlns:hol="http://springws.ws.learning.com/holidays/schemas"
    elementFormDefault="unqualified"
    targetNamespace="http://springws.ws.learning.com/holidays/schemas">

    <!-- Root element for request -->
    <xs:element name="getHolidayRequest" type="hol:HolidayRequest"/>

    <!-- Root element for response -->
    <xs:element name="getHolidayResponse" type="hol:HolidayResponse"/>

    <xs:complexType name="HolidayRequest">
        <xs:sequence>
            <xs:element minOccurs="0" name="year" type="xs:string"/>
        </xs:sequence>
    </xs:complexType>

    <xs:complexType name="HolidayResponse">
        <xs:sequence>
            <xs:element minOccurs="0" name="holidays"
                                    type="hol:holidays"/>
        </xs:sequence>
    </xs:complexType>

    <xs:complexType name="holidays">
        <xs:sequence>
            <xs:element minOccurs="0" name="holiday" type="xs:string"/>
        </xs:sequence>
    </xs:complexType>
</xs:schema>
```

Step 2: Create a Service Endpoint Interface

Create a service endpoint class to receive the request-and-response payloads. The Spring-WS provided annotations are used for service endpoint class.

The complete service endpoint code is provided in Listing 11-5.

Listing 11-5: Developing Spring-based web service using JDOM API

```java
// HolidayServiceEndpoint.java
package com.learning.springws;

import org.springframework.ws.server.endpoint.annotation.Endpoint;
```

```java
import org.springframework.ws.server.endpoint.annotation.PayloadRoot;
import org.springframework.ws.server.endpoint.annotation.ResponsePayload;
import org.springframework.ws.server.endpoint.annotation.RequestPayload;
import org.jdom.Element;
import org.jdom.Document;
import org.jdom.input.SAXBuilder;
import org.jdom.output.XMLOutputter;
import java.io.InputStream;
import java.io.ByteArrayInputStream;
import java.util.List;
import java.util.Iterator;

@Endpoint
public class HolidayServiceEndpoint {
    @PayloadRoot(namespace =
            "http://springws.ws.learning.com/holidays/schemas",
            localPart = "getHolidayRequest")
    @ResponsePayload
    public Element getEmployee(@RequestPayload Element holidayRequest)
    throws Exception {
        // Converting the JDOM element to a Java String
        XMLOutputter outputter = new XMLOutputter();
        String inputRequest = outputter.outputString(holidayRequest);
        System.out.println("--- inputRequest ---- " + inputRequest);

        // Private method used to parse the XML to obtain the year
        String year = getYear(inputRequest);

        // Private method used to build the response XML
        Element holidayResponse = buildHolidaysResponse(year);

        return holidayResponse;
    }

    private String getYear(String inputRequest) throws Exception {
        InputStream is = new
            ByteArrayInputStream(inputRequest.getBytes("UTF-8"));
        SAXBuilder builder = new SAXBuilder();
        Document document = builder.build(is);
        Element root = document.getRootElement();
        List children = root.getChildren();
        Iterator iterator = children.iterator();
        String year = "";
        while (iterator.hasNext()) {
            Element child = (Element) iterator.next();
            year = child.getValue();
        }

        System.out.println("--- year --- " + year);
        return year;
    }

    private Element buildHolidaysResponse(String year) throws Exception{
        Element responseElement = new Element("getHolidayResponse",
            "http://springws.ws.learning.com/holidays/schemas");
        Document myDocument = new Document(responseElement);
        Element holidaysElement = new
```

```
         Element("holidays").setAttribute("year", year);
responseElement.addContent(holidaysElement);

Element janElement1 = new Element("January").
                    setText("02-jan-2012");
holidaysElement.addContent(janElement1);

Element janElement2 = new Element("January").
                    setText("16-jan-2012");
holidaysElement.addContent(janElement2);

Element febElement = new Element("February").
                    setText("20-feb-2012");
holidaysElement.addContent(febElement);

Element mayElement = new Element("May").
                    setText("28-may-2012");
holidaysElement.addContent(mayElement);

Element julyElement = new Element("July").
                    setText("04-july-2012");
holidaysElement.addContent(julyElement);

Element septElement = new Element("September").
                    setText("03-sept-2012");
holidaysElement.addContent(septElement);

Element octElement = new Element("October").
                    setText("08-oct-2012");
holidaysElement.addContent(octElement);

Element novElement1 = new Element("November").
                    setText("12-nov-2012");
holidaysElement.addContent(novElement1);

Element novElement2 = new Element("November").
                    setText("22-nov-2012");
holidaysElement.addContent(novElement2);

Element decElement = new Element("December").
                    setText("25-dec-2012");
holidaysElement.addContent(decElement);

XMLOutputter outputter = new XMLOutputter();
outputter.output(myDocument, System.out);

return responseElement;
    }
}
```

The below provided private method is used to parse the XML to obtain the value of the year.

```
String year = getYear(inputRequest);
```

The blow provided private method is used to prepare the response XML. It contains the list of federal holidays for year 2012.

```
Element holidayResponse = buildHolidaysResponse(year);
```

Step 3: Create a springws-servlet.xml Configuration File

This file contains the Spring web services related information such as endpoints, interceptors, and so forth. It loads the defined Spring beans into the Spring container. The WSDL is generated dynamically using Spring provided XML tag "<sws:dynamic-wsdl/>".

```xml
<?xml version="1.0" encoding="UTF-8"?>
<beans xmlns="http://www.springframework.org/schema/beans"
    xmlns:xsi="http://www.w3.org/2001/XMLSchema-instance"
    xmlns:context="http://www.springframework.org/schema/context"
    xmlns:sws="http://www.springframework.org/schema/web-services"
    xsi:schemaLocation="http://www.springframework.org/schema/beans
    http://www.springframework.org/schema/beans/spring-beans-3.0.xsd
    http://www.springframework.org/schema/web-services
    http://www.springframework.org/schema/web-services/web-services-
    2.0.xsd
    http://www.springframework.org/schema/context
    http://www.springframework.org/schema/context/spring-context-
    3.0.xsd">

    <context:component-scan base-package="com.learning.springws"/>

    <sws:annotation-driven/>

    <sws:dynamic-wsdl id="holidays"
                portTypeName="HolidayPortType"
                locationUri="/services/holidayService/"
                targetNamespace=
                "http://springws.learning.com/holidays/definitions">
        <sws:xsd location="/WEB-INF/holidays.xsd"/>
    </sws:dynamic-wsdl>
</beans>
```

Step 4: Create a web.xml File

Re-use the web.xml we created in Example1

Step 5: Create a war file; and Deploy it in Tomcat Server

- Build a war file using Ant or any other build tool. Make sure files are packaged correctly in a war file.
- Deploy the war file in any servlet container.

The structure of the generated war file is shown in Figure 11-3:

Step 6: Verify the Generated WSDL Document

Access the WSDL file from web browser to make sure service is deployed without any errors. Use the below provided URL to view the complete WSDL.

```
http://localhost:8080/springws/services/employeeService/holidays.wsdl
```

Figure 11-3: war file structure

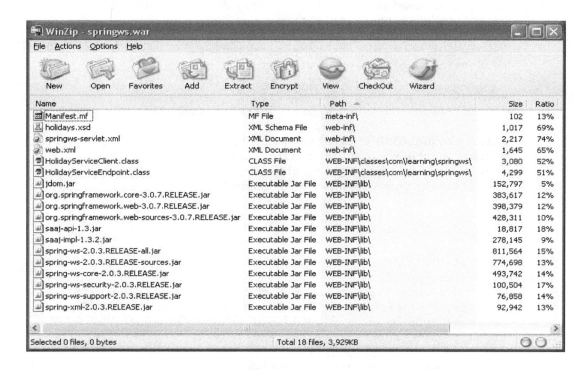

Step 7: Write a Client to Invoke the Deployed Service Endpoint

The Spring Web services framework provided "WebServiceTemplate" class can be used for accessing the deployed web service endpoint. This web service client can set the endpoint related metadata using Spring-based Java API or it can use XML-based configuration. The below provided web service client is using Spring-based Java API. The complete Web service client code is provided in Listing 11-6.

Listing 11-6: Spring-based web service client

```java
// HolidayServiceClient.java
package com.learning.springws;

import org.springframework.ws.client.core.WebServiceTemplate;
import org.springframework.xml.transform.StringSource;
import org.springframework.xml.transform.StringResult;
import org.jdom.Element;
import org.jdom.Document;
import org.jdom.output.XMLOutputter;
import javax.xml.transform.Source;
import javax.xml.transform.Result;

public class HolidayServiceClient {
    public static void main(String[] args) throws Exception {
        try {
            HolidayServiceClient client = new HolidayServiceClient();
            client.invokeService("2012");
        } catch (Exception ex) {
            ex.printStackTrace();
        }
    }
```

```
private void invokeService(String year) throws Exception {
    ClientLogMessageHandler[] handler = new
                        ClientLogMessageHandler[1];
    handler[0] = new ClientLogMessageHandler();
    WebServiceTemplate webServiceTemplate = new
                        WebServiceTemplate();
    webServiceTemplate.setDefaultUri
    ("http://localhost:8080/springws/services/holidayService/");

    String requestXML = createRequestXML(year);
    Source source = new StringSource(requestXML);
    Result result = new StringResult();
    webServiceTemplate.sendSourceAndReceiveToResult(source,result);

    System.out.println("--- result ---" + result.toString());
}

private static String createRequestXML(String year)
throws Exception {
    Element requestElement = new Element("getHolidayRequest",
        "http://springws.ws.learning.com/holidays/schemas");
    Document myDocument = new Document(requestElement);
    Element yearElement = new Element("year");
    yearElement.setText(year);
    requestElement.addContent(yearElement);

    XMLOutputter outputter = new XMLOutputter();
    String input = outputter.outputString(myDocument);
    System.out.println("--- input  --- " + input);

    return input;
}
}
```

The below provided method is used for creating the input request XML.

```
private static String createRequestXML(String year) throws Exception {
    // ...
}
```

The created request XML is provided below:

```
<?xml version="1.0" encoding="UTF-8"?>
<getHolidayRequest xmlns=
            "http://springws.ws.learning.com/holidays/schemas">
    <year xmlns="">2000</year>
</getHolidayRequest>
```

The below provided code is used for invoking the service endpoint. The output is printed on the console; use suitable parsing technique to obtain the data.

```
webServiceTemplate.sendSourceAndReceiveToResult(source, result);
```

This Web service response XML is provided below:

```xml
<?xml version="1.0" encoding="UTF-8"?>
<getHolidayResponse
        xmlns="http://springws.ws.learning.com/holidays/schemas">
    <holidays xmlns="" year="2000">
        <January>02-jan-2012</January>
        <January>16-jan-2012</January>
        <February>20-feb-2012</February>
        <May>28-may-2012</May>
        <July>04-july-2012</July>
        <September>03-sept-2012</September>
        <October>08-oct-2012</October>
        <November>12-nov-2012</November>
        <November>22-nov-2012</November>
        <December>25-dec-2012</December>
    </holidays>
</getHolidayResponse>
```

Example 4: Spring-WS Endpoint with JAXB API

This Web service endpoint is developed with JAXB Object type as request-and-response payload. The request-response objects are annotated with JAXB annotations. The steps required to develop a Web service of this type are given below.

1. Create a XSD document
2. Create a service endpoint interface
3. Create a Request object using JAXB API
4. Create a Response object using JAXB API
5. Create a springws-servlet.xml configuration file
6. Create a web.xml file
7. Create a war file and deploy it in Tomcat server
8. Verify the generated WSDL document
9. Write a client to invoke the deployed service endpoint

The above-specified steps are described in the following sections:

This example demonstrates the use of stock change web service; for a given stock symbol it provides the current price and its price change. Let us now start defining the xml schema of the service.

Step 1: Create a XSD Document

The first step is to prepare a XSD of the Web Service endpoint. Convert the domain model to an XML types; and create a XML root element for request-response payloads. The complete XML schema document is provided below. Spring runtime use this schema document to generate the WSDL.

```xml
<?xml version="1.0" encoding="UTF-8"?>
<xs:schema xmlns:xs="http://www.w3.org/2001/XMLSchema"
        xmlns:stock="http://springws.ws.learning.com/stock/schemas"
        elementFormDefault="unqualified"
        targetNamespace=
            "http://springws.ws.learning.com/stock/schemas">

    <!-- Root element for request -->
```

```
<xs:element name="getStockRequest" type="stock:StockRequest"/>

<!-- Root element for response -->
<xs:element name="getStockResponse" type="stock:StockResponse"/>

<xs:complexType name="StockRequest">
    <xs:sequence>
        <xs:element minOccurs="0" name="symbol" type="xs:string"/>
    </xs:sequence>
</xs:complexType>

<xs:complexType name="StockResponse">
    <xs:sequence>
        <xs:element minOccurs="0" name="return"
                        type="stock:stockdata"/>
    </xs:sequence>
</xs:complexType>

<xs:complexType name="stockdata">
    <xs:sequence>
        <xs:element minOccurs="0" name="todayPrice"
                    type="xs:string"/>
        <xs:element minOccurs="0" name="change" type="xs:string"/>
    </xs:sequence>
</xs:complexType>

</xs:schema>
```

Step 2: Create a Service Endpoint Class

Create a service endpoint class to receive the request-response payloads. This Web service endpoint is developed with JAXB annotated classes as request-response types. The Web service endpoint is expecting "StockRequest" as request type; and returning "StockResponse" as response type.

The complete service endpoint class code is provided in Listing 11-7.

Listing 11-7: Developing Spring-based web service using JAXB API

```
// StockServiceEndpoint.java
package com.learning.springws;

import org.springframework.ws.server.endpoint.annotation.Endpoint;
import org.springframework.ws.server.endpoint.annotation.PayloadRoot;
import org.springframework.ws.server.endpoint.annotation.ResponsePayload;
import org.springframework.ws.server.endpoint.annotation.RequestPayload;
import javax.xml.bind.JAXBContext;
import javax.xml.bind.Marshaller;
import java.io.StringWriter;

@Endpoint
public class StockServiceEndpoint {

    @PayloadRoot(namespace =
            "http://springws.ws.learning.com/stock/schemas",
            localPart = "getStockRequest")
    @ResponsePayload
```

```
public StockResponse getStockInformaton(@RequestPayload
            StockRequest stockRequest) throws Exception {

    // Getting the input data from client request
    String symbol = stockRequest.getSymbol();

    // JAXB annotated response object
    StockResponse response = new StockResponse();

    // Apply the business logic based on input received.
    if (symbol != null && symbol.equalsIgnoreCase("GLD")) {
        response.setTodayPrice("32.15");
        response.setChange("1.13");
    } else {
        response.setTodayPrice("XXXX");
        response.setChange("XXXX");
    }

    // marshalling the Java object to a XML; to print the XML
    StringWriter writer = new StringWriter();
    JAXBContext context = JAXBContext.newInstance(
                            StockResponse.class);
    Marshaller m = context.createMarshaller();
    m.marshal(response, writer);
    System.out.println("-- Response --" + writer.toString());

    return response;
    }
}
```

Step 3: Create a Request Object Using JAXB API

The request object must conform to the following rules.

- The request-response types must be annotated with "@XmlRootElement" element
- The "@XmlRootElement" annotation member values "name", "namespace" must match the "localPart", "namespace" specified with "@PayloadRoot" annotation of the service endpoint

The complete Request object code is provided in Listing 11-8.

Listing 11-8: Request object used for the service endpoint

```
// StockRequest.java
package com.learning.springws;

import javax.xml.bind.annotation.XmlRootElement;
import javax.xml.bind.annotation.XmlElement;
import javax.xml.bind.annotation.XmlType;

@XmlRootElement(name="getStockRequest",
            namespace="http://springws.ws.learning.com/stock/schemas")
@XmlType(name="StockRequest")
public class StockRequest {

    private static final long serialVersionUID = 1L;
    private String symbol;
```

```
    @XmlElement(name="symbol")
    public String getSymbol() {
        return symbol;
    }

    public void setSymbol(String symbol) {
        this.symbol = symbol;
    }
}
```

Step 4: Create a Response Object Using JAXB API

The class provided below is used for service method response. This class must use "@XmlRootElement" annotation.

The complete Response object code is provided in Listing 11-9

Listing 11-9: Response object used for the service endpoint

```
// StockResponse.java
package com.learning.springws;

import javax.xml.bind.annotation.XmlRootElement;
import javax.xml.bind.annotation.XmlElement;
import javax.xml.bind.annotation.XmlType;

@XmlRootElement(name = "getStockResponse",
        namespace = "http://springws.ws.learning.com/stock/schemas")
@XmlType(name="StockResponse",
        propOrder = {"todayPrice", "change"})
public class StockResponse {

    private static final long serialVersionUID = 1L;
    private String todayPrice;
    private String change;

    @XmlElement(name = "todayprice")
    public String getTodayPrice() {
        return todayPrice;
    }

    public void setTodayPrice(String todayPrice) {
        this.todayPrice = todayPrice;
    }

    @XmlElement(name = "change")
    public String getChange() {
        return change;
    }

    public void setChange(String change) {
        this.change = change;
    }
}
```

Step 5: Create a springws-servlet.xml Configuration File

This file contains the Spring web services related information such as endpoints, interceptors, JAXB marshaller, and so forth. It loads the defined Spring beans into the Spring container. The WSDL is generated dynamically using Spring provided XML tag "<sws:dynamic-wsdl/>".

```xml
<?xml version="1.0" encoding="UTF-8"?>
<beans xmlns="http://www.springframework.org/schema/beans"
    xmlns:xsi="http://www.w3.org/2001/XMLSchema-instance"
    xmlns:context="http://www.springframework.org/schema/context"
    xmlns:sws="http://www.springframework.org/schema/web-services"
    xsi:schemaLocation="http://www.springframework.org/schema/beans
    http://www.springframework.org/schema/beans/spring-beans-3.0.xsd
    http://www.springframework.org/schema/web-services
    http://www.springframework.org/schema/web-services/
                        web-services-2.0.xsd
    http://www.springframework.org/schema/context
    http://www.springframework.org/schema/context/
                        spring-context-3.0.xsd">

    <context:annotation-config/>
    <context:component-scan base-package="com.learning.springws"/>
    <sws:annotation-driven/>

    <sws:dynamic-wsdl id="stockchange"
                    portTypeName="StockChangePortType"
                    locationUri="/services/stockService/"
                    targetNamespace=
                "http://springws.ws.learning.com/stock/definitions">
        <sws:xsd location="/WEB-INF/stockchange.xsd"/>
    </sws:dynamic-wsdl>

    <bean id="jaxb2Marshaller"
        class="org.springframework.oxm.jaxb.Jaxb2Marshaller">
        <property name="classesToBeBound">
            <list>
                <value>com.learning.springws.StockRequest</value>
                <value>com.learning.springws.StockResponse</value>
            </list>
        </property>
            <property name="schema" value="/WEB-INF/stockchange.xsd"/>
    </bean>

    <bean id="marshallingPayloadMethodProcessor" class=
            "org.springframework.ws.server.endpoint.adapter.method.
            MarshallingPayloadMethodProcessor">
        <constructor-arg ref="jaxb2Marshaller"/>
        <constructor-arg ref="jaxb2Marshaller"/>
    </bean>

    <bean id="defaultMethodEndpointAdapter" class=
                    "org.springframework.ws.server.endpoint.adapter.
                    DefaultMethodEndpointAdapter">
        <property name="methodArgumentResolvers">
            <list>
                <ref bean="marshallingPayloadMethodProcessor"/>
            </list>
```

```
            </property>
            <property name="methodReturnValueHandlers">
            <list>
                 <ref bean="marshallingPayloadMethodProcessor"/>
            </list>
            </property>
        </bean>
</beans>
```

Step 6: Create a web.xml Configuration File

Reuse the web.xml file we created in Example1.

Step 7: Create a war File and Deploy it in Tomcat Server

Figure 11-4: war file structure

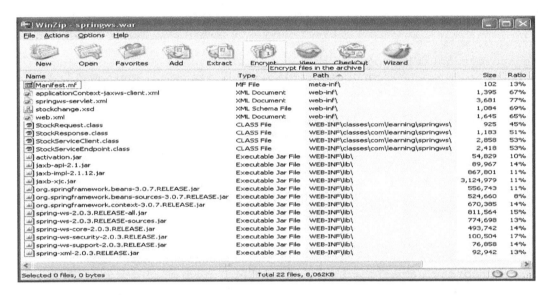

- Build a war file using Ant or any other build tool. Make sure files are packaged correctly in a war file.
- Deploy the war file in any servlet container.

The structure of the generated war file is shown in Figure 11-4:

Step 8: Verify the Generated WSDL Document

Invoke the deployed web service with below provided URL. You can view the complete WSDL.

```
http://localhost:8080/springws/services/stockService/stockchange.wsdl
```

Step 9: Write a Client to Invoke the Deployed Service Endpoint

Reuse the applicationContext-client.xml we created in Example1. Add the below provided XML to "applicationContext-client.xml" file.

```
<bean id="webServiceTemplate"
```

```
                class="org.springframework.ws.client.core.WebServiceTemplate">
        <constructor-arg ref="messageFactory"/>
        <property name="defaultUri" value=
                "http://localhost:8080/springws/services/stockService/"/>
        <property name="messageSender" ref="messageSender"/>
</bean>
```

The client used to invoke the web service endpoint is provided in Listing 11-10. Run this client to view the output.

Listing 11-10: Client to invoke the web service endpoint

```java
// StockServiceClient.java
package com.learning.springws;

import org.springframework.context.support.
            ClassPathXmlApplicationContext;
import org.springframework.ws.client.core.WebServiceTemplate;
import org.springframework.xml.transform.StringSource;
import org.springframework.xml.transform.StringResult;
import javax.xml.bind.JAXBContext;
import javax.xml.bind.Marshaller;
import javax.xml.transform.Source;
import javax.xml.transform.Result;
import java.io.StringWriter;

public class StockServiceClient {

    public static void main(String[] args) throws Exception {
        try {
            StockServiceClient client = new StockServiceClient();
            client.invokeService("GLD");
        } catch (Exception ex) {
            ex.printStackTrace();
        }
    }

    // Invoking the web service endpoint
    private void invokeService(String stockSymbol) throws Exception {
        ClassPathXmlApplicationContext context = new
                ClassPathXmlApplicationContext
            (new String[]{"applicationContext-jaxws-client.xml"});
        WebServiceTemplate webServiceTemplate = (WebServiceTemplate)
                context.getBean("webServiceTemplate");

        String requestXML = createInputXML(stockSymbol);
        Source source = new StringSource(requestXML);
        Result result = new StringResult();
        webServiceTemplate.sendSourceAndReceiveToResult(source,result);

        // Printing the response XML on the console.
        System.out.println("-- Response XML is --" +result.toString());
    }

    // private method used to create an input request
    private String createInputXML(String stockSymbol) throws Exception {
        // JAXB annotated request object
```

```
        StockRequest request = new StockRequest();
        request.setSymbol(stockSymbol);

        // Converting the Java objects into XML to see the request
        StringWriter writer = new StringWriter();
        JAXBContext context=
                JAXBContext.newInstance(StockRequest.class);
        Marshaller m = context.createMarshaller();
        m.marshal(request, writer);
        System.out.println("-- Request XML is --" + writer.toString());

        return writer.toString();
    }
}
```

The "StockServiceClient" provides the below given request payload to the service endpoint. The "createInputXML()" method of the "StockServiceClient" class is used to create the below provided request payload.

```
<?xml version="1.0" encoding="UTF-8" standalone="yes"?>
<ns2:getStockRequest
        xmlns:ns2 = "http://springws.ws.learning.com/stock/schemas">
    <symbol>GLD</symbol>
</ns2:getStockRequest>
```

The Web service response is provided below. Use suitable parsing technique to obtain the values from XML.

```
<?xml version="1.0" encoding="UTF-8"?>
<ns3:getStockResponse
        xmlns:ns3="http://springws.ws.learning.com/stock/schemas">
    <todayprice>32.15</todayprice>
    <change>1.13</change>
</ns3:getStockResponse>
```

Web Service Endpoint Design Scenarios

The Spring-based Web services supports only "contract-first" kind of web services. The web service provider starts the service development with XSD or WSDL. In general, the service endpoint method has one input parameter and one return value. Input parameters maps to the request-payload; and return value maps to the response-payload. The Web service endpoint supported request-and-response types are listed below:

- W3C DOM Element
- DOM4j Element (Refer to Example1)
- JDOM Element (Refer to Example3)
- XOM Element
- JAXB Type - Any type that is annotated with "XMLRootElement" and "JAXBElement" (Refer to Example4)
- DOMSource, SAXSource, StaxSource and StreamSource
- Any type supported by Spring OXM Marsheller

The below provided Web service endpoints are using "Dom4j", "JDOM" and "JAXB" data types. Similarly, other supported types can be used for designing the service endpoints.

The below provided endpoint is using Dom4j's "org.dom4j.Element" type for mapping the request-and-response payloads.

```
public org.dom4j.Element getEmployee(@RequestPayload org.dom4j.Element
employeeRequest) throws Exception {
}
```

The below provided endpoint is using JDOM's "org.jdom.Element" type for mapping the request-and-response payloads.

```
public org.jdom.Element getEmployee(@RequestPayload org.jdom.Element
employeeRequest) throws Exception {
}
```

The below provided endpoint is using JAXB annotated classes for mapping the request-and-response payloads.

```
public StockResponse getStockInformaton(@RequestPayload StockRequest
stockRequest) throws Exception {
}
```

Web Service Client Design Scenarios

The main class used for accessing the Spring-based Web service endpoint is "WebServiceTemplate". This class contains methods to send "Source" as request-payload, and receives response-payload as "Source" or "Result". The Web service client can also marshal request objects to XML and un-marshal the response XML to objects. The commonly used client methods of the Spring web service template class are listed below.

The following method sends the "Source" as input and receives "Result" as output.

```
webServiceTemplate.sendSourceAndReceiveToResult(source, result);
```

The following method sends the "Source" as input and receives "Object" as output.

```
Object result = webServiceTemplate.marshalSendAndReceive(source);
```

The Spring-WS can re-use your existing Spring expertise while developing Web services. This book has covered the three open-source web service frameworks for developing enterprise applications. All these frameworks provide similar features; none is superior to the others. Which framework will you choose in your application? It is totally depends on the application requirement, developers comfort and their prior experience with it .The primary objective is to illustrate each Web service framework to explore the technical capabilities, so make your own judgment based on the requirement.

Test Yourself - Objective Type Questions

1. Which of the following statements correctly explains the use of @PayloadRoot annotation?
   a) The annotation @PayloadRoot is used at class level to mark the class as web service endpoint.
   b) It routes the incoming messages to the appropriate method of the service endpoint class.
   c) This annotation is used at method level and it indicates how the method return value should map to the response payload.
   d) This annotation is used for configuring SOAP message interceptors
   e) Spring-WS does not support this annotation.

2. The XML schema definition for the request-payload is given below. Select the correct request payload message which conforms to the below provided XSD.

```
<?xml version="1.0" encoding="UTF-8"?>
<xs:schema xmlns:xs="http://www.w3.org/2001/XMLSchema"
        xmlns:emp="http://springws.ws.learning.com/emp/schemas"
        elementFormDefault="unqualified"
        targetNamespace=
            "http://springws.ws.learning.com/emp/schemas">
  <xs:element name="getEmployeeRequest" type="emp:EmployeeRequest"/>
  <xs:complexType name="EmployeeRequest">
        <xs:sequence>
            <xs:element minOccurs="0" name="employeeId"
                            type="xs:string"/>
        </xs:sequence>
  </xs:complexType>
</xs:schema>
```

a)
```
<employess xmlns="http://springws.ws.learning.com/emp/schemas">
  <employee>
        <employeeId>6666666</employeeId>
  </employee>
</getEmployeeRequest>
```

b)
```
<getEmployeeRequest xmlns="http://springws.ws.learning.com/emp/ ">
  <employee>
        <employeeId>6666666</employeeId>
  </employee>
</getEmployeeRequest>
```

c)
```
<getEmployeeRequest
        xmlns="http://springws.ws.learning.com/emp/schemas">
  <employee>
        <employeeId>6666666</employeeId>
  </employee>
</getEmployeeRequest>
```

d)
```
<employee>
        <employeeId>6666666</employeeId>
```

```
</employee>
```

e)
```
<employeeId>6666666</employeeId>
```

3. What is the purpose of "<sws:dynamic-wsdl/>" xml tag while developing the Spring-based web services.
    a) It is used for generating the Java classes from WSDL document
    b) It is used for accessing the user defined static WSDL from web browser
    c) It is used for JAXB for marshalling XML to Java objects
    d) The spring web services provided <sws:dynamic-wsdl/> tag is used to generate the WSDL dynamically for a given XSD input.
    e) All the above statements are correct.

4. Which of the below provided Spring class can be used with service client for accessing the web service endpoint?
    a) JdbcTemplate
    b) MessageDispatcherServlet
    c) WebServiceTemplate
    d) ClientInterceptor
    e) EndpointInterceptor

5. Which of the below provided methods of "EndpointInterceptor" interface can be used for processing of soap messages at service endpoint. Select the correct answer.
    a) handleRequest(), handleResponse(), handleFault() and afterCompletion()
    b) handleRequest(), handleResponse() and handleFault()
    c) handleMessage(), handleFault(), close() and getHeaders()
    d) handleRequest(), handleMessage(), init() and getHeaders()
    e) handleRequest(), handleResponse(), handleMessage() and handleFault()

Answers to Test Yourself

1. The correct answer is "B". The choice "A" is referring to the @Endpoint annotation and choice "C" is referring to the @ResponsePayload annotation. The choices "D" and "E" are invalid.

2. The correct answer is "C". The request-payload message must use the local part and namespace that is defined in the XML schema document. The local part used in this case is "getEmployeeRequest" and namespace used for the request-payload is "http://springws.ws.learning.com/emp/schemas". If you don't use the specified local part and namespace URI; the client will throw the following exception.
    org.springframework.ws.client.WebServiceTransportException: Not Found [404]

3. The correct answer is "D". It is used for generating the WSDL from XSD. The choice "B" is valid for "<sws:static-wsdl/>" tag. All other choices are incorrect.

4. The correct answer is "C". The JdbcTemplate is used for accessing the relational databases; "ClientInterceptor" and "EndpointInterceptor" are used for soap message processing.

5. The correct answer is "A". It has four methods. The choice "B" is correct for Spring-WS provided "ClientInterceptor" interface.

Chapter 12. Tools, Ant Scripts and Deployment

We have seen various types of Web service development in previous chapters. How can these Web services be packaged for deployment into any servlet container? This chapter will address the packaging, building, and deploying instructions needed to deploy the Web services in any Java servlet container. The Web services artifacts are packaged into a WAR file for deployment. The generated WAR file can be deployed in any Java-compatible servlet container. The information provided in this chapter is useful for setting up the environment and deployment.

In this chapter will discuss the following topics:

- The structure of the WAR file
- The required build and deployment instructions for Web services
- The required JAR files to compile and run the Web service examples
- The complete Ant script used to package the Web service code examples
- Web service debugging and monitoring tools

Deployment Instructions

The Web service classes and configuration files are packaged into a WAR file that can be deployed in any Java servlet container. Build a WAR file using Ant or any other build tool, and make sure the files are packaged correctly. The physical structure of a WAR file is shown below in Figure 12-1.

Figure 12-1: WAR file structure

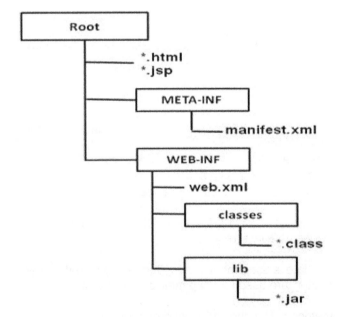

The rules to package the various artifacts are listed below.

- Package all HTML and JSP files inside the root directory.
- Package the "web.xml" file and the Spring application context XML files inside the "WEB-INF/" directory.
- Package all of the Java class files inside the "WEB-INF/classes" directory.
- Package all of the dependent JAR files inside the "WEB-INF/lib" directory.

Deploy the generated WAR file in any Java-compatible servlet container. The steps required to deploy a WAR file in Apache-Tomcat are given below.

- Copy the packaged WAR file into the "apache-tomcat/webapps" directory.
- Start the Tomcat server by running the "startup.bat" batch file, available in the "apache-tomcat/bin" directory.
- View the server console output and logs; make sure the WAR file is deployed without any errors.
- Clear the server cache for each deployment—Remove the generated files in the "apache-tomcat/temp" directory, and delete the expanded WAR file before attempting a new deployment.

The directory structure of the project created in IDE is shown below in Figure 12-2. This structure is provided only for reference; it is not mandatory that you copy this directory structure in your IDE. Create your own directory structure and refer to it in your build script.

Figure 12-2: Project directory structure

The expanded view of the "conf" directory and its subdirectories are shown in Figure 12-3. The "conf" directory contains the list of configuration files used for Web services development.

Figure 12-3: Configuration files

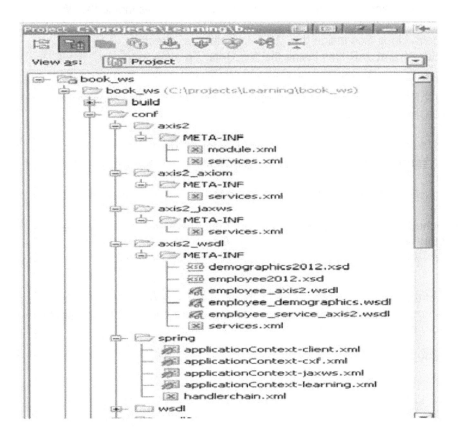

The directory structure is shown in above two diagrams, because the Ant scripts refer to them while generating the WAR files. The following topic will discuss the WAR file generation using the Ant tool.

Building Ant Scripts

The Ant script used for generating WAR and AAR files is given below. The Ant script provides ant targets for generating WAR and AAR files. These ant targets are used for building the tutorial examples. Refer to the corresponding code examples in the respective chapters, and follow the step-by-step instructions provided. This Ant script has the following list of ant targets.

- Ant target for generating a WAR file to demonstrate the Apache-CXF tutorial examples
- Ant target for generating Web service endpoints from WSDL for Apache-CXF and Axis2
- Ant target for generating the AAR file for the "code first" type of Web service endpoint
- Ant target for generating the AAR file for the Axis2 custom module demo
- Ant target for generating the AAR file for the JAX-WS example demo
- Ant target for generating the AAR file for the AXIOM example demo

The complete Ant script is given below. Follow the inline comments to identify the required Ant targets.

```
<project name="WS Book demo (WS)" basedir=".." default="compile">
```

```xml
<!-- Initializing the project directories -->
<property name="build.dir" value="${basedir}/build"/>
<property file="${build.dir}/build.properties"/>

<property name="war-name" value="wsbook.war"/>
<property name="aar-name" value="employee.aar"/>
<property name="aar-name-wsdl-java" value="employee.aar"/>

<property name="library.dir" value="${basedir}/lib"/>
<property name="target.dir" value="${basedir}/target"/>
<property name="source.dir" value="${basedir}/src"/>
<property name="class.dir" value="${basedir}/classes"/>
<property name="output.dir" value="${basedir}/output1"/>
<property name="resources.dir" value="${basedir}/resources"/>
<property name="axis2dir.dir"
        value="${basedir}/classes/com/learning/axis2"/>
<property name="web.dir" value="${basedir}/webcontent"/>
<property name="velocity.dir" value="${web.dir}/vm"/>
<property name="webinf.dir" value="${web.dir}/WEB-INF"/>
<property name="conf.spring.dir" value="${basedir}/conf/spring"/>

<property name="wsdl-name" value="employee.wsdl"/>
<property name="wsdl-path" value="${build.dir}/${wsdl-name}"/>
<property name="build-gen" location="${build.dir}/gen"/>
<property name="package-name"
        value="com.learning.ws.jaxws.wsdl2java"/>
<property name="package-path"
        value="com/learning/ws/jaxws/wsdl2java"/>

<!-- Setting the project classpath-referring to the lib directory-->
<path id="build.classpath">
    <fileset dir="${library.dir}">
        <include name="**/*.jar"/>
    </fileset>
</path>

<target name="init">
    <mkdir dir="${class.dir}"/>
    <mkdir dir="${output.dir}"/>
    <filter token="contextApp" value="${context.path}"/>
    <condition property="contextRoot" value="${context.path}">
        <not>
            <equals arg1="" arg2="${context.path}"/>
        </not>
    </condition>
    <condition property="contextRoot" value="/">
        <equals arg1="" arg2="${context.path}"/>
    </condition>
    <filter token="contextRoot" value="${contextRoot}"/>
</target>

<!-- Target used for compiling the source code -->
<target name="compile" depends="init">
<javac debug="on" nowarn="on" deprecation="true"
        destdir="${class.dir}" includes="**/*.java"
        srcdir="${source.dir}" source="1.6" target="1.6">
        <classpath>
```

```xml
                    <path refid="build.classpath"/>
                </classpath>
        </javac>
</target>

<!-- Target used for cleanup - It deletes the classes and generated
  war files -->
<target name="clean" description="delete all compiled objects">
<delete dir="${class.dir}"/>
        <delete dir="${output.dir}"/>
</target>

<!--Apache-CXF - Target used for generating the war file -->
<target name="war" depends="compile">
        <war warfile="${output.dir}/${war-name}" update="false"
            webxml="${webinf.dir}/web.xml">
                <webinf dir="${webinf.dir}" includes="*"
                                        excludes="web.xml"/>
                <webinf dir="${basedir}/conf/spring" includes="*"/>
                <webinf dir="${basedir}/conf" includes="**/*.wsdl"/>
                <classes dir="${class.dir}" includes="**/*.class, *.xml"/>
                <classes dir="${resources.dir}" includes="*.properties"/>
                <classes dir="${build.dir}" includes="version.properties"/>
                <lib dir="${library.dir}" includes="*.jar"
                                        excludes="log4j.jar"/>

                <fileset dir="${velocity.dir}"/>
                <fileset dir="${web.dir}" includes="images/**"/>
                <fileset dir="${web.dir}" includes="js/**"/>
                <fileset dir="${web.dir}" includes="css/**"/>
        </war>
</target>

<!-- Apache-CXF - Target used to generate and compile JAX-WS/JAXB
code from WSDL -->
<target name="wsdl2java_cxf">
        <echo message="Running WSDL2Java task"/>
        <delete quiet="true" dir="${build-gen}"/>
        <mkdir dir="${build-gen}"/>
        <java classpathref="build.classpath" fork="true"
                classname="org.apache.cxf.tools.wsdlto.WSDLToJava">
                <!-- -d parameter sets the output root directory -->
                <arg value="-d"/>
                <arg value="${source.dir}"/>
                <!-- -p parameter gives the package for CXF code
                generation-->
                <arg value="-p"/>
                <arg value="${package-name}"/>
                <!-- -validate parameter requests WSDL validation before
                 generation -->
                <arg value="-validate"/>
                <!-- actual input WSDL -->
                <arg value="${wsdl-path}"/>
        </java>
        <!-- Compile the generated code -->
        <mkdir dir="${build-gen}/bin"/>
        <javac srcdir="${source.dir}" destdir="${build-gen}/bin"
```

```xml
                debug="true">
                <classpath>
                    <path refid="build.classpath"/>
                </classpath>
            </javac>
    </target>

    <!-- Axis2 - Target used for Generating the "aar" file for code
    first approach -->
    <target name="aar_javatowsdl" depends="compile">
        <jar jarfile="${output.dir}/${aar-name}" update="false">
            <fileset dir="${class.dir}"
                    includes="**/axis2/Employee.class,
                    **/axis2/EmployeeFault.class,
                    **/axis2/EmployeeService.class,
                    **/axis2/EmployeeServiceImpl.class"/>
            <fileset dir="${basedir}/conf/axis2"
                includes="**/services.xml"/>
            <!--<fileset dir="${basedir}" includes="lib/*.jar"/>-->
        </jar>
    </target>

    <!-- Axis2 - Target used to generate and compile JAX-WS/JAXB code
    from WSDL -->
    <target name="wsdl2java_Axis2">
        <echo message="Generating code using axis2 wsdlfile"/>
        <java classname="org.apache.axis2.wsdl.WSDL2Java" fork="true">
            <classpath refid="build.classpath"/>
            <!-- -d parameter specifies the databinding type -->
            <arg value="-d"/>
            <arg value="xmlbeans"/>
            <!-- location of wsdl file-->
            <arg value="-uri"/>
            <arg file="C:/projects/Learning/book_ws/conf/axis2_wsdl/
                    META-INF/employee_demographics.wsdl"/>
            <!-- Generates server side code -->
            <arg value="-ss"/>
            <!-- Generates all the classes skeletons and stubs-->
            <arg value="-g"/>
        </java>
    </target>

    <!-- Axis2 - Target used for generating the "aar" file for WSDL
    first approach -->
    <target name="aar_axis2_for_deploy_wsdl2java" depends="compile">
        <jar jarfile="${output.dir}/${aar-name-wsdl-java}"
                    update="false">
            <fileset dir="${class.dir}" includes="**/axis2/**"/>
            <fileset dir="${basedir}/conf/axis2_wsdl"
                    includes="**/*.xml,
                    **/*.wsdl, **/*.xsd"/>
            <fileset dir="${basedir}" includes="lib/allxmltypes.jar"/>
        </jar>
    </target>

    <!-- Target used for creating a jar file which contains all Axis2
    dependent classes -->
```

```
<target name="make_jar_for_axis2_generated" depends="compile">
    <jar jarfile="${output.dir}/allxmltypes.jar" update="false">
        <fileset dir="${basedir}/resources" includes="**/**"/>
        <fileset dir="${class.dir}" includes="org/**"/>
    </jar>
</target>

<!-- Axis2 - Target used for generating the "aar" file
for Axis2 custom module demo -->
<target name="make_logging_module">
    <jar jarfile="${output.dir}/loggingmodule.mar" update="false">
        <fileset dir="${class.dir}"
            includes="**/axis2/LogModule.class,
                      **/axis2/LogHandler.class "/>
        <fileset dir="${basedir}/conf/axis2"
            includes="**/module.xml"/>
    </jar>
</target>

<!-- Axis2 - Target used for generating the "aar" file for Axis2
jax-ws demo -->
<target name="aar_axis2_jaxws" depends="compile">
    <jar jarfile="${output.dir}/stockservice.aar" update="false">
        <fileset dir="${class.dir}"
            includes="**/axis2/jaxws/StockQuoteService.class,
                      **/axis2/jaxws/StockQuoteServiceImpl.class "/>
        <fileset dir="${basedir}/conf/axis2_jaxws"
            includes="**/services.xml"/>
    </jar>
</target>

<!-- Axis2 - Target used for generating the "aar" file for Axis2
AXIOM demo -->
<target name="aar_axis2_axiom" depends="compile">
    <jar jarfile="${output.dir}/gradeservice.aar" update="false">
        <fileset dir="${class.dir}"
            includes="**/axis2/axiom/GradeManagerService.class,
                      **/axis2/axiom/GradeManagerServiceImpl.class "/>
        <fileset dir="${basedir}/conf/axis2_axiom"
            includes="**/services.xml"/>
    </jar>
</target>
</project>
```

The following Ant target is used for building the Spring-WS war file.

```
<target name="war" depends="compile">
    <war warfile="${output.dir}/${war-name}" update="false"
                    webxml="${webinf.dir}/web.xml">
        <webinf dir="${webinf.dir}" includes="*" excludes="web.xml"/>
        <webinf dir="${basedir}/conf/spring" includes="*"/>
        <webinf dir="${basedir}/conf/springws" includes="**/*.xsd"/>
        <webinf dir="${basedir}/conf" includes="**/*.wsdl"/>
        <classes dir="${class.dir}" includes="**/*.class, *.xml"/>
        <classes dir="${resources.dir}" includes="*.properties"/>
        <classes dir="${build.dir}" includes="version.properties"/>
```

```
        <lib dir="${library.dir}" includes="*.jar"
                            excludes="log4j.jar"/>

        <fileset dir="${velocity.dir}"/>
        <fileset dir="${web.dir}" includes="images/**"/>
        <fileset dir="${web.dir}" includes="js/**"/>
        <fileset dir="${web.dir}" includes="css/**"/>
    </war>
</target>
```

List of Jar files

The JAR files used for developing the Web service code examples are given below. These JAR files are used to develop demo code examples. Make sure you use the correct version of JAR files to avoid class loader version-mismatch-related exceptions.

axiom-api-1.2.8.jar	jdom.jar
axiom-dom-1.2.8.jar	jetty-6.1.21.jar
axiom-impl-1.2.8.jar	jetty-util-6.1.21.jar
axis2-adb-1.5.1.jar	jsr173_1.0_api.jar
axis2-adb-codegen-1.5.1.jar	jsr250-api-1.0.jar
axis2-codegen-1.5.1.jar	jsr311-api-1.0.jar
axis2-corba-1.5.1.jar	neethi-2.0.4.jar
axis2-fastinfoset-1.5.1.jar	neethi-5.1.0-cxf-2.2.jar
axis2-java2wsdl-1.5.1.jar	ojdbc14.jar
axis2-jaxbri-1.5.1.jar	org.springframework.aop-3.0.3.jar
axis2-jaxws-1.5.1.jar	org.springframework.asm-3.0.3.jar
axis2-jibx-1.5.1.jar	org.springframework.aspects-3.0.3.jar
axis2-json-1.5.1.jar	org.springframework.beans-3.0.3.jar
axis2-kernel-1.5.1.jar	org.springframework.context-3.0.3.jar
axis2-metadata-1.5.1.jar	org.springframework.context.support-3.0.3.jar
axis2-mtompolicy-1.5.1.jar	org.springframework.core-3.0.3.jar
axis2-saaj-1.5.1.jar	org.springframework.expression-3.0.3.jar
axis2-spring-1.5.1.jar	org.springframework.instrument-3.0.3.jar
axis2-transport-http-1.5.1.jar	org.springframework.instrument.tomcat-3.0.3.jar
axis2-transport-local-1.5.1.jar	org.springframework.jdbc-3.0.3.jar
axis2-xmlbeans-1.5.1.jar	org.springframework.jms-3.0.3.jar
commons-beanutils.jar	org.springframework.orm-3.0.3.jar
commons-codec-1.4.jar	org.springframework.oxm-3.0.3.jar
commons-collections.jar	org.springframework.instrument-3.0.3.jar
commons-digester.jar	org.springframework.instrument.tomcat-3.0.3.jar
commons-discovery.jar	org.springframework.jdbc-3.0.3.jar
commons-fileupload-1.1.jar	org.springframework.jms-3.0.3.jar
commons-fileupload.jar	org.springframework.orm-3.0.3.jar
commons-httpclient-3.1.jar	org.springframework.oxm-3.0.3.jar
commons-io-1.2.jar	org.springframework.test-3.0.3.jar
commons-lang.jar	org.springframework.transaction-3.0.3.jar

commons-logging.jar	org.springframework.web-3.0.3.jar
commons-validator.jar	org.springframework.web.portlet-3.0.3.jar
cxf-2.2.5.jar	org.springframework.web.servlet-3.0.3.jar
cxf-api-2.2.5.jar	org.springframework.web.struts-3.0.3.jar
cxf-tools-wsdlto-core-2.0.10.jar	saaj-api-1.3.jar
dom4j.jar	saaj-impl-1.3.2.jar
framework-adapter-1.0.jar	spring-maven-ant-tasks-2.0.7.jar
geronimo-activation_1.1_spec-1.0.2.jar	spring-xml-2.0.3.RELEASE.jar
geronimo-annotation_1.0_spec-1.1.1.jar	tcpmon.jar
geronimo-javamail_1.4_spec-1.6.jar	velocity-1.4.jar
geronimo-servlet_2.5_spec-1.2.jar	velocity-tools-1.2.jar
geronimo-ws-metadata_2.0_spec-1.1.2.jar	woden-api-1.0M8.jar
httpcore-4.0.1.jar	wsdl4j-1.6.2.jar
javax.servlet.jar	wstx-asl-3.2.9.jar
jaxb-api-2.1.jar	xmlbeans-2.3.0.jar
jaxb-impl-2.1.12.jar	xml-resolver-1.2.jar
jaxb-xjc.jar	XmlSchema-1.4.5.jar
jaxen-1.1-beta-6.jar	

The list of JAR files specified above is available with any Spring, Apache-CXF, and Apache-Axis2 distribution. These JAR files can also be downloaded from the "http://findjar.com/" Web site. The software and its corresponding version number is given below.

Software/Framework used	Version
Apache-Tomcat	6.0.28
JDK	1.6.0_14
Apache-CXF	2.2.5
Apache-Axis2	1.5.1

Web Services Testing and Monitoring Tools

The Web services monitoring tools are used to monitor outbound-and-inbound messages. This information is used for debugging and testing purposes. The monitoring tools are placed between the client and the service endpoint to intercept the request-and-response messages. The monitoring tools commonly used for Web services debugging and testing are given below.

- TCP Monitor
- SOAP UI

TCP Monitor

The steps to configure a TCP monitor utility to log the outbound-and-inbound messages are given below.

1. The TCP monitor utility is an open-source tool available as an executable JAR file. Download the "tcpmon.jar" file.

2. Execute the JAR (select the JAR and press enter); this will open the following window.

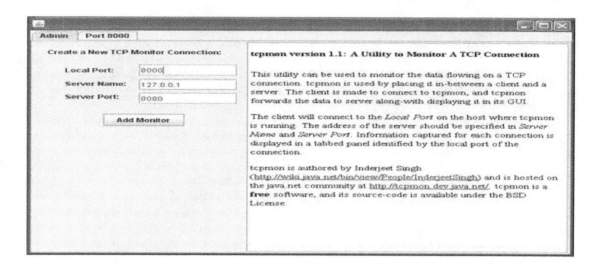

3. Enter the following details on the left-hand side of the window; then click the "Add Monitor" button.
   - Local Port: The port where the TCP monitor is running.
   - Server Name: The server name where the Web service is running
   - Server Port: The port that the Web service is using

4. After you complete these steps, you will see a new tab in the window. Click the "Submit to Server" button; then run the Web service client to see the request-and-response messages on the newly added tab as shown below.

Figure 12-1: TCP Monitor

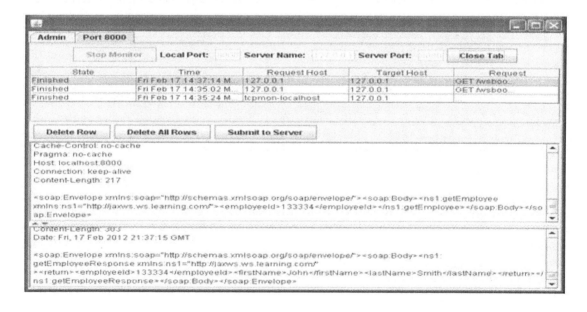

5. Make sure the Web service client submits the request to the TCP monitor's local port. The Web service client submits the request to the TCP monitor, and the TCP monitor forwards it to the

service endpoint. The provided below Web service client code is using port 8000 instead of 8080.

```
private void testJAXWSClient() throws Exception {
        URL url = new
                URL("http://localhost:8000/wsbook/services/employee?wsdl");
        QName qname = new QName("http://jaxws.ws.learning.com/",
                                "employeeService");
        Service service = Service.create(url, qname);
        EmployeeService employeeService =
                service.getPort(EmployeeService.class);

        String address =
                employeeService.getEmployeeAddressInfo("823147");
        Employee emp = employeeService.getEmployee("133334");
}
```

6. Click on Stop Monitor button to stop logging the messages.

SOAP UI

The steps to configure a "SOAP UI" tool to log the outbound-and-inbound messages are given below.

1. Install the SOAP UI software.

2. Open the SOAP UI tool; then click on File -> New SOAP UI Project ->. Enter the project's name and WSDL location ->. Click on OK.

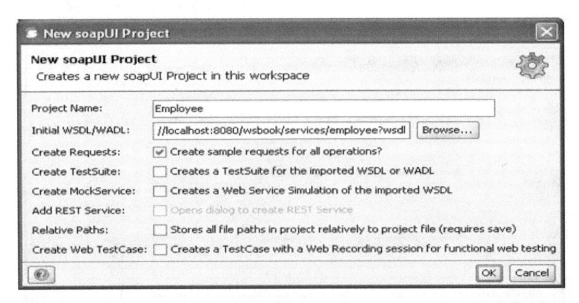

3. You will now see a new screen that is divided into three parts. The left side displays the Web service operations, the middle displays the input request, and the right side displays the Web service response.

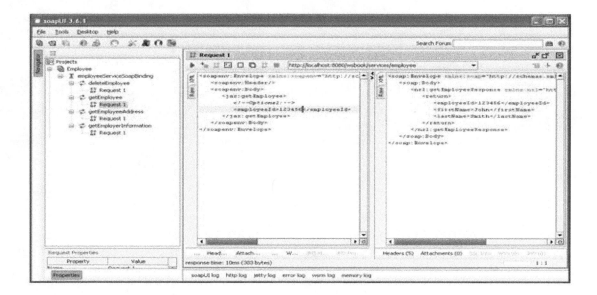

4. Enter the input data in the middle panel, and then click on "Submit" (green arrow). The response message will be displayed in the right window panel.

References

The below given documents and web links are referenced in this book.

Architectural Styles and the Design of Network-based Software Architectures
http://www.ics.uci.edu/~fielding/pubs/dissertation/top.htm

Making Right Architecture Decision – Restful Services vs. "BIG" Services
http://www.jopera.org/files/www2008-restws-pautasso-zimmermann-leymann.pdf

JAX-RS Specifications - http://download.oracle.com/otndocs/jcp/jaxrs-1.0-fr-eval-oth-JSpec/

Java API for XML Processing (JAXP) Tutorial
http://java.sun.com/webservices/reference/tutorials/jaxp/html/intro.html

Java API for XML Processing (JAXP) Tutorial
http://java.sun.com/webservices/reference/tutorials/jaxp/html/dom.html

SAX API Specification - http://www.saxproject.org/apidoc/overview-summary.html

Dom4j framework for XML Processing - http://dom4j.sourceforge.net/dom4j-1.6.1/guide.html

Processing XML with Java - http://www.jdom.org/downloads/docs.html

Universal Resource Identifiers - Axioms of Web Architecture
http://www.w3.org/DesignIssues/Axioms.html

Apache Axis2 - http://cxf.apache.org/

Basic Profile Version 1.1 - http://www.ws-i.org/profiles/basicprofile-1.1-2004-08-24.html

SOAP Version 1.2 - http://www.w3.org/TR/soap/

SOAP Version 1.2 Primer - http://www.w3.org/TR/2007/REC-soap12-part0-20070427/

SOAP with Attachments API for Java (SAAJ) Specification 1.1
http://download.oracle.com/otndocs/jcp/7752-saaj-1.1-spec-oth-JSpec/

The SOAP with Attachments API for Java (SAAJ) Specification 1.1
http://java.sun.com/webservices/saaj/downloads/saajarchive.html

Basic Profile Version 1.1 - http://www.ws-i.org/Profiles/BasicProfile-1.1.html

Java API for XML Web Services Annotations
http://jax-ws.java.net/jax-ws-ea3/docs/annotations.html

Java Platform, Standard Edition 6 API Specification
http://docs.oracle.com/javase/6/docs/api/javax/xml/bind/annotation/XmlType.html

Creating and Using SOAP Message Handlers
http://docs.oracle.com/cd/E12840_01/wls/docs103/webserv_adv/handlers.html

WSDL Specification - http://www.w3.org/TR/wsdl

WSDL Version 2.0 Adjuncts - http://www.w3.org/TR/wsdl20-adjuncts/wsdl20-adjuncts.pdf

WSDL Version 2.0 Primer - http://www.w3.org/TR/wsdl20-primer/wsdl20-primer.pdf

WSDL Version 2.0 Part 2: Predefined Extensions - http://www.w3.org/TR/2004/WD-wsdl20-extensions-20040803/

WSDL SOAP Binding Styles - http://www.ibm.com/developerworks/webservices/library/ws-whichwsdl/

Apache Axis2 - http://axis.apache.org/axis2/java/core/

Spring Web Services - http://www.springsource.org/spring-web-services#documentation

TOGAF Open Group Standard - http://pubs.opengroup.org/architecture/togaf9-doc/arch/

A Tool to Monitor Traffic on TCP Connections - http://java.net/projects/tcpmon

Getting Started SoapUI - http://www.soapui.org/Getting-Started/installing-on-windows.html

Index

---

www.ingramcontent.com/pod-product-compliance
Lightning Source LLC
Chambersburg PA
CBHW061923080326
R17960100001B/R179601PG40689CBX00003B/1